D1276791

"A must for every home, school, and parish library, this volume is a ready-reference book. Much more than just a dictionary."

The Message

"Entries are well chosen. Language is clear. Theology is current and credible. This book is worth having on your resource shelf."

National Catholic Reporter

"...compact but comprehensive reference book of basic information on Catholic teachings, beliefs, values, practices....It should be very helpful and serviceable to many homes and teachers."

Liguorian

"A comprehensive and compact reference book of basic information on the Catholic church. Excellent!"

Rev. Charles Dollen
The Priest

"This compendium offers to interested non-Catholics a better understanding of the religion of many of their friends and neighbors."

Mabel C. Simmons
New Orleans

The NEW CONCISE CATHOLIC DICTIONARY

REYNOLDS R. EKSTROM

TWENTY-THIRD PUBLICATIONS
Mystic, Connecticut 06355

and

the columba press
Dublin, Ireland

Second printing of Revised Edition 1995

This edition published simultaneously by

The Columba Press
93 The Rise
Mount Merrion, Blackrock
Co Dublin, Ireland
ISBN 1-85607-118-9

and

Twenty-Third Publications
185 Willow Street
P.O. Box 180
Mystic, CT 06355
(203) 536-2611
800-321-0411

ISBN 0-89622-622-0
Library of Congress Catalog Card Number 94-60980
Printed in the U.S.A.

Contents

LIST OF ARTICLES

See Index starting on page 271 for a very complete listing of terms of interest incorporated within these major articles.

Introduction

The idea for this book was first formed almost twenty years ago. Over the years, many of my friends, family members, students, and co-workers have questioned what it means to be Catholic today. They have asked (and many times I have too) what is so unique, important, and distinctive about being a Catholic Christian. They have wondered if Catholic beliefs, values, and practices really differ all that much from those of other Christian religions. They have frequently appeared unsure which beliefs, attitudes, and practices to hand on to the next generations. Many seem to have been worried about how to discuss Catholic tradition confidently—especially with children, adolescents, and members of other church congregations—in a way that truly emphasizes a Catholic identity that is both Christian and unique.

This purpose of this dictionary is to introduce or re-introduce you to a wide variety of teachings, historical facts, convictions, values, emerging theological and pastoral insights, and spiritual practices that remain special and basic to the worldwide Catholic community. Of course, this book will not cover everything about the Catholic tradition past and present. What handbook could? Yet it does include hundreds of topics because the scope of the overall topic here—Catholic teachings, values, and practices—is vast and all-encompassing. In all, I hope to offer Catholics and those inquiring about the Catholic way a book that will help answer questions, clear up some uncertainties, and build up confidence in one's ability to know and explain Catholic beliefs, customs, and concepts in a convenient manner.

Three features are included in this book to maximize its usefulness.

The list of major articles starting on page vii has two kinds of entries. Some are listed with a page number indicating where the article begins. Other entries are followed by a cross reference—e.g., Seder (see Passover). Words and phrases listed this way will help guide you to major terms that appear under a different title.

A second kind of cross reference is used in the body of

the book. At the end of each article, you are referred to other articles for more information on the same subject. For example, at the end of Confirmation, it is suggested: "See also Anointing, Baptism, Catechumenate and the RCIA, Godparents, and Sacraments."

Finally, there is a very complete (28 pages) index at the back of this volume, directing you to hundreds of terms that may wish to find in these pages.

To achieve brevity and clarity, but also to avoid over-simplification, the following four-step process has been used to explain most of the topics addressed in major articles:

Step 1: A clear and concise definition of the topic under consideration will be provided.

Step 2: Historical considerations about the topic will be developed briefly to show how the Catholic community's understanding and appreciation of the beliefs, values, and spiritual practices have developed over the centuries.

Step 3: Some recent theological thinking about the topic at hand will be provided whenever it is available.

Step 4: Current official teachings and positions of the church on the subject of the article will be emphasized.

Because treatments of the topics in this handbook are necessarily brief, it is hoped that readers will want to do some follow-up, in-depth study of the Catholic tradition. To facilitate this further investigation, a select bibliography of contemporary resources has been included in the back section of this volume.

A marvelous, living tradition has been handed on to Catholics over the centuries. Many contemporary Catholics—as well as many, many who wish to become members of the Catholic Christian community—yearn to fully investigate, understand, and be able to confidently discuss this ongoing religious story. Many likewise seek to hand on the Catholic tradition faithfully and carefully to children in their households, to spiritually-alienated family members, to non-Catholic inquirers with whom they come in contact, and to students in their classes. If this dictionary helps them to do any of these things in some way then it will have served its purpose.

A

ABORTION is any procedure by which a fetus is deliberately removed from its mother's womb before it becomes capable of independent life. The church community teaches that an embryo or fetus is actually a living human being. Therefore no other human being has the right to terminate this life. In the United States and in many other countries, abortions are allowed by law. Nevertheless the church teaches that abortion is wrong because it takes away a defenseless human being's right to life. Many Catholics today belong to the national "Right to Life" campaign, a pro-life, anti-abortion movement. The term "abortion" comes from Latin roots (*abortio*) that refer to "miscarry."

Abortions were performed often during the 1st century after Jesus. Members of early Christian communities were taught that they must never seek abortions. At least one very early church document called abortion an act of murder. Several church leaders—including Clement of Alexandria, Saint Jerome, and Saint Augustine—taught that abortion is an immoral practice. During the 4th century, the church of Spain decreed that persons who seek an abortion of a fetus could never receive the Eucharist again. Many Catholic popes and great teachers over the centuries have likewise condemned abortion. In more recent times, Pope John XXIII and Vatican Council II have noted the evil effects of legalized abortions on the whole of society. Numerous church leaders affirm that human life does indeed begin at the very moment of conception. Therefore, direct abortion causes the unnecessary death of a fully human individual.

According to Catholic teaching, abortion violates the fifth commandment. The bishops of the United States have declared that abortion is a sin against the weak and the helpless and that all Catholics should work hard to end the modern practice of abortion. The bishops have also noted that women, men, and families involved in abortions today need and deserve the constant help of all Catholics as they try to find real solutions to their problems.

Canon 1398 of the Code of Canon *Law* states that a "person who procures a successful abortion incurs an automatic excommunication" from the Catholic community. In 1988, the Holy See noted that abortion, in this sense, includes the "ejection of an immature fetus" from the womb, but "also the killing of the same fetus in whatever way at whatever time from the moment of conception...."

Accidental ejection of the fetus (e.g., in the case of miscarriage) is not morally wrong. Yet any form of direct abortion, whether therapeutic, psychological, or preventative, cannot be justified under church law. Indirect abortion (e.g., in surgery necessary to save the life of the mother) is not considered morally wrong when situations honestly warrant it.

In 1991, in his encyclical *Centesimus annus*, John Paul II noted that at times "human ingenuity seems to be more directed [today] toward limiting, suppressing, or destroying the sources of life—including recourse to abortion which is so widespread in the world—than toward defending and opening up the possibilities of life."

(See also Commandments of God, Excommunication, Morality, and Sin.)

ABRAHAM   was the first of the great ancestors and founders of the Hebrew people. Christians and Jews alike honor Abraham for his great faith and complete trust in God. The Bible reports that Abraham was the husband of Sarah and the father of Isaac. He lived about 1800 years before Jesus of Nazareth and was the leader of a tribe (or clan) of people. Abraham answered a special call from God and faithfully moved his family, his clan members, and his possessions from the city of Haran to the land called Canaan, as he believed God wanted.

Such nomadic migrations by clans were common at the time. Yet there are several reasons why Abraham's story is unique and of enduring importance to all Christians: 1) God chose to reveal Godself personally to Abraham; 2) Abraham was the first person to wholly trust and believe in the one, true God; 3) Abraham trusted in a personal friendship between the one God and humankind; and 4) God loved Abraham so much that God made a covenant with him, promising Abraham—and his people, the ancestors of the Israelites—a beautiful new homeland and countless descendants and blessings if they would just respond to God in faith and try to fulfill God's commands.

Catholics revere Abraham as one of the great fathers of the Hebrew people—the nation of Israel and the chosen people of God. From this nation came Jesus of Nazareth, the messiah, God's living Word, who proclaimed the establishment of a new covenant and a "new people of God." Catholics look upon Abraham as a model of faith and trust for all humankind but especially for all the baptized.

(See also Bible, Covenant, Hebrews, and Old Testament.)

ABSTINENCE   is a spiritual-growth practice by which one stays away from eating certain foods. The term comes from the Latin *abstinere*, "to keep away from." Current church law calls Catholics to avoid eating meat and meat-related products on certain days of the year in order to do penance for wrongdoing and to develop a sense of self-denial and Christian self-discipline.

Abstinence from meat and other foods has long been a popular way to do penance. At one point, church law demanded that Catholics abstain from meat on all Fridays. This tradition was rooted in the belief that

Jesus Christ died (gave up his life for all humanity) on a Friday. Catholics have honored Friday as a special penitential day of the week.

During 1966, the church rule regarding every-Friday abstinence was relaxed by Pope Paul VI. Since then, only Ash Wednesday, Good Friday, and the Fridays of the season of Lent have been days of complete abstinence from meat and meat-products. All church members 14 years of age and older are expected to refrain from consumption of meat on these days. Ash Wednesday and Good Friday are likewise days of fasting for Catholics.

While easing the abstinence rules, the church community has re-issued a general challenge to all its members to do penance freely and to voluntarily practice personal self-denial for the sake of Christian spiritual health. Abstinence is seen as a sign by which one freely shows a desire to become less self-centered, to overcome sinful inclinations, and to become united, in some small way, to the sacrifice and death of Jesus of Nazareth. Some people stress the worth of other types of self-giving, self-disciplinary Christian behaviors as forms of abstinence. These include retreats, prayer, works of mercy, and daily Christian witness through kindness, patience toward others, and concern for the needs of the poor.

(See also Ash Wednesday, Church Laws, Fasting, and Lent.)

ACTS OF THE APOSTLES is that book in the Christian Scriptures that immediately follows the four gospels. The author of the gospel of Luke wrote Acts, about the year 80 c.e., in order to tell about some of the outstanding events and pastoral happenings in the earliest days of the Christian community. The Acts of the Apostles was never intended to be a complete history of the early followers of Jesus of Nazareth. The early Greek name of this book was *Praxeis Apostolon*—"acts of apostles." Thus the current title of the book is not quite accurate, since the book does indeed tell of much more than simply the personal endeavors of the original apostles of Jesus.

The first major portion of the book centers on Saint Peter, the first pope of the Christian community. The second portion centers on the missionary and evangelizing works of Saint Paul and his companions. The real "turning point" in the Acts of the Apostles is its report on what has come to be known as the first Council of Jerusalem. After that meeting of post-resurrection community leaders, members of the Christian way turned their focus away from Jerusalem and the strict laws of the Jewish faith and began to reach out to the non-Jews (gentiles) in the city of Rome and to many peoples and cultures around the world.

Some Bible scholars today believe that Luke was a preacher who traveled with Saint Paul. Catholic Christians view Acts of the Apostles as an inspired work that shows how the "good news" of Jesus was spread throughout the whole world, and that it is the Spirit of God—the same Spirit sent by the risen Jesus to his followers—who guides the life of the people of God today.

(See also Apostles, Bible, Luke, and New Testament.)

ACTUAL SIN   is any willful thought, action, or failure-to-act that either weakens or causes a total disruption in our loving relationship with God. The sin that weakens the relationship between an individual and God has traditionally been called venial sin. Serious sin that causes a complete break in the relationship between an individual and the Creator has been traditionally referred to as mortal sin or deadly sin.

According to church tradition, actual sin differs from original sin in that human beings are personally and "actually" responsible for it; in the case of original sin, human beings are born into a human race and world deeply affected by an inclination toward sinfulness overall and toward personal evil in particular. Actual sin, whether serious or not-so-serious, can be forgiven by God whenever anyone who has sinned is truly sorry and desires to sin no more.

People often seek to renew their loving relationships with God after they have actually chosen to sin. Thus the people of God are offered the opportunity to confess their wrongdoing and to seek pastoral guidance and support and absolution from personal sinfulness in the sacrament of reconciliation. Certain seasons (such as Advent and Lent) and special, prayerful devotions (such as days of prayer and parish missions) have evolved to help Catholics repent and make reparation for their sins.

(See also Confessional, Original Sin, Reconciliation, and Sin.)

ADAM AND EVE   are the symbolic names given in the book of Genesis to the first man and woman of the human race. The word "Adam" has Hebrew origins that mean simply "the man." It is also a play on the Hebrew word for "dust" or "ground." " Eve," which means "the living one," also has Hebrew roots. The Bible says that Adam and Eve were the parents of three sons: Cain, Abel, and Seth.

There are two distinct accounts of creation in Genesis (1:26–2:3, and 2:4–25). Using highly poetic and symbolic imagery, Genesis says that God created Adam and Eve. The two enjoyed life in a paradise, sharing an intimate and grace-filled friendship with God and many other gifts, until they chose to sin and were expelled from their state of happiness.

At the beginning of the Christian era, Saint Paul compared Jesus with Adam, saying that Jesus of Nazareth was and is a "new Adam" through whom comes eternal life and the salvation of all humankind from the sin and evil introduced into the human experience by the first members of the human community. A number of great church figures (e.g., Saints Augustine, Irenaeus, and Thomas Aquinas) compared Eve with Mary, the mother of Jesus. The church teaches that through the personal disobedience of Adam and Eve—however that may have occurred and by whomever in the primitive days of the human race—the evils of sin entered the world.

Major statements and Catholic teachings about the creation of humankind were produced by the Fourth Lateran Council (1215), by Vatican I (1870), and by Pope Pius XII in his encyclical *Humani generis* (1950). During the 20th century there has been some debate among

Christians as to whether there was only one set of parents for the entire human race (monogenism), or more than one original set of human ancestors (polygenism). The Catholic community has consistently taught that all human beings come from a single pair of human parents. Paul VI declared in 1966 that the theory of polygenism has not yet been proved by modern science and must be avoided if it will lead to the denial of the church's doctrine on original sin. Therefore, in the church's view, there may have been more than one original set of human parents, but this does not necessarily conflict with traditional doctrinal statements on original sin. It is believed that further scientific studies will likely establish firmly whether polygenist or monogenist ideas are more correct.

The church today continues to emphasize that the one, good God freely and lovingly created the human race and the entire universe—giving human beings the gifts of grace and friendship. The Creator chose to make human beings in God's own image and has placed them at the highest level of the material universe. Humanity was meant by God to be happy and was given a lasting mission by the Creator to care for the world. Through sin, however, the first persons of the human race— Adam and Eve—jeopardized humanity's great relationship with God and the life of paradise God had made for all of the human community. The effects of this sin of Adam and Eve (called original sin) are inherited by all humans at the time of birth. While Adam is the original human parent of all human beings, Jesus Christ has become the "new Adam," providing the whole human community with the promise of salvation from sin and the eternal happiness rejected by Adam and Eve in their choice of sin.

(See also Creation, Grace, Original Sin, Salvation, and Sin.)

ADVENT   is the pre-Christmas season of the church's liturgical year which begins on the Sunday nearest to the feast of Saint Andrew on November 30. "Advent" comes from the term *adventus*, which means "coming." During this season members of the Catholic community anticipate, with a sense of joyfulness, the coming of the Word of God to Earth and the continuing presence of this Word in the worldwide church community. The bible readings shared in the Catholic liturgies of the Advent period are chosen to help church members understand the enduring meaning of the life of Jesus of Nazareth as well as the meaning of the prophetic presence of his Spirit in the Christian community to this day.

The Advent season was celebrated by Christians in some parts of Europe before the year 500, but not by the entire church until the 6th century. By the 8th century the first Sunday of Advent marked the beginning of the official church year. During the 9th century, Pope Gregory I shortened the Advent season from six weeks to the four weeks that precede Christmas. Pope Gregory also wrote many prayers and chose Bible readings for the liturgies of the season.

Catholics celebrate Advent in order to become more aware of Jesus' continuing presence in the church and to remember joyfully that the Word of God became human in order to offer hope and salvation from sinfulness to all of humanity. The readings from the Hebrew and Christian Scriptures in the liturgies of the first two weeks of the season focus on Jesus' coming at the world's end to judge all men and women. The readings for the following weeks of Advent focus on the special joy and hope of the Christmas event. The liturgical colors of the season—purple, rose, and white—signify Christian *metanoia* (change of heart and lifestyle) and the promise of Christian hope in Jesus. Advent is a special time for all believers to open their hearts more fully to the love of God and to the eternal salvation offered to all by the Savior of humanity, whose birth is celebrated on Christmas day.

(See also Advent Wreath, Christmas, Hope, and Liturgical Year.)

ADVENT WREATH   is a band of evergreen-style foliage curled or twisted into a circle, and decorated with four candles and other festive materials. The advent wreath is a symbol of hope in Jesus Christ, the Light of the world. During Advent, the four candles are lighted (one the first week, two the second, and so on) to indicate that light and human hope increase as the birth of the Word of life gets closer.

Wreaths have long been used in the Western world as signs of glorious victory. The advent wreath custom was begun by German Protestants in the mid-1500s. (Germans had observed for many centuries before a practice of holding festivals, in November, at which bright fires were lighted to ward off the cold and darkness of wintertime.) The advent wreath quickly spread among Catholics in Europe and eventually to church members in the United States. This spiritual custom became quite popular among U.S. Catholics in the early 1900s.

An advent wreath can be large or small. Wreaths are placed on tables or suspended from ceiling fixtures. They are found typically in family households, churches, and elsewhere. By custom, a wreath has three purple candles and one pink or white candle. The purple symbolizes penance and sorrow for sin. Pink (or white) represents a sense of hope and Advent's joyful expectation in the Light of the world.

Today, the church stresses the value of voluntary Christian self-denial during the Advent season. Yet it also views Advent as a time infused with hope and happiness as humankind awaits anew the coming of God's promised one, the messiah. The advent wreath should be used to remind Catholics and other Christians about the spiritual "cold and darkness" experienced by humanity as it awaited the birth of God's Word on Earth. In this sense, the light given off by the candles is the key symbol in the advent wreath. Spiritual practices often linked with the use of advent wreaths include reflection on the Bible, personal prayer, and Christian self-denial (e.g., abstinence or works of mercy)—all of which also help church members become more open to the re-birth of Christ in their families and the Christian community as a whole.

(See also Advent, Christmas, and Hope.)

AGAPE   This Greek term basically refers to love or, more particularly, to a sacred love feast. Among the earliest followers of Jesus, the agape was a holy meal held as a memorial of the Last Supper (a Passover meal) Jesus shared with his closest disciples. Therefore, from early Christian times, "agape" has referred to a special meal eaten together by members of the Christian community.

Tradition indicates that the Mass, the celebration of the Eucharist, was at first a very simple ritual (a "breaking of the bread" as at the Lord's Supper) within the larger context of a communal meal, an agape-style gathering, usually held in a house church—that is, in a Christian family household (Acts 2:46, 20:7). Abuses in this practice, however, caused the ritual of the Eucharist to be separated from the overall meal (1 Corinthians 11:17ff.). The agape-feast custom was not practiced by all church communities after that. It seems to have largely vanished from organized church traditions by the 600s or so.

In recent decades, the custom of sharing agape-style meals has been revived in some Christian settings. Linked to the festive spirit of the seder or Passover meal in general, the agape stresses a sense of Christian community, especially in ecumenical groups, and the joy to be experienced in the company of the Lord. Today, as in the past, there is no direct connection between the agape meal and the sacrament of the Eucharist. The agape is not an official liturgical expression of the church body. It is merely a social and festive experience, but one nevertheless focused on the "good news" of Christian life and on prayerful celebration in the name of Jesus.

(See also Church, as Home; Eucharist; Liturgy of the Word/Eucharist; and Passover.)

ALL SAINTS DAY   is a Catholic holy day of obligation celebrated annually on November 1. This is the solemnity on which the Catholic community honors all saints who are enjoying life with God in heaven—especially those saints who do not have feast days on the official church calendar. (The word "saint" has Latin roots meaning "holy" or "consecrated" to God.) All Saints Day is a solemnity, the highest rank of feast day in the liturgical year.

Christians were setting aside May 13 to honor all martyrs as early as the 4th century. In the year 609, Pope Boniface IV made a former pagan temple in Rome—the Pantheon—into a Christian church. He chose to do this on May 13 and thus dedicated this happy day and the new shrine to Mary and to all Christian martyrs. Pope Gregory III changed the date of this memorial celebration of all the martyrs and saints to November 1 in 732. By the 12th century all church members were recognizing November 1 as the official date for All Saints Day. An all saints vigil (a night of prayerful waiting for a feast) and an all saints octave (a joyful eight-day period of prayer following a feast) were once observed for All Saints Day, but these have not been observed by Catholics in the U.S. since 1955.

The church teaches that all men and women who have died and journeyed into the spiritual experience of heaven are saints. The solemnity of All Saints thus affords members of the church community an excellent, annual opportunity to venerate all the saints, to pray to them in a special way for assistance with human questions and troubles, and to learn about how to live an authentic Christian life of witness, prayer, and worship by following the saints' dynamic example. In 1977, Paul VI noted that all people of God should regularly honor those who have left humanity a permanent heritage of examples, a true school of human and Christian virtue. While the solemnity of All Saints officially remains a Catholic holy day in the U.S., the obligation to participate in the Eucharist (attend Mass) has been waived whenever November 1 occurs on either a Saturday or a Monday. This became a church rule in the U.S. with a decision rendered by the national bishops conference in December 1991.

(See also Canonization; Heaven; Martyr; Saints, Communion of; and Veneration.)

ALL SOULS DAY　　is a day set aside by the church annually, on November 2, to recall and pray for the dead who are in purgatory. The feast of All Souls was established by Saint Odilo in the 10th century so that monks in his abbey could offer special prayers and songs for the dead on the day after All Saints Day, November 1. The practice of recalling and praying for the dead soon became popular and eventually spread to many church communities in Europe and Latin America.

During the 15th century, some priests began offering three Masses on All Souls Day. This custom was made a formal church practice in the early 1920s, when Pope Benedict XV allowed priests to say three Masses on November 2—one to be offered for a special intention, one for the dead in purgatory, and one for the pope's intentions. Some historians now believe that the prayers and Masses on All Souls Day multiplied because of human fears and superstitions. The highly unusual custom of offering three Masses is still practiced by some priests to this day.

Catholic tradition regarding the feast of All Souls centers on the belief that even though some people have died and gone into the painful spiritual condition (or state) called purgatory, they nevertheless experience basic happiness in that they know they will at some point be fully united with God in glory and happiness. The souls in purgatory benefit from and need the prayers and works of charity of all Christian believers as spiritual helps in overcoming their spiritual separation from God.

All Souls Day annually provides Catholics a chance to pray and do Christian works in memory of the dead, but in reality every day presents a fine opportunity to do so.

(See also Heaven; Purgatory; Saints, Communion of; and Sin.)

ALMSGIVING　　is a gift or a compassionate service offered to someone, which is rooted in love for God and human beings. The word has Greek origins meaning "pity" or "human compassion." Depending on a Christian's motivation, almsgiving can be essentially a work of charity and mercy or a work of penance. In either case, it involves freely giving one's time, presence, money, or material goods (e.g., clothing) in a spirit of Christian self-discipline and love.

The church tradition of almsgiving traces back to the earliest followers of Jesus who believed they should share what they had with the poor and other needy persons. Later, as self-denial practices such as lenten prayer, fasting, and abstinence from certain foods (e.g., meats, sweets) took hold in the church community, Catholics realized that the money and food they saved ought to be freely given to others. Catholic teachings stress that penances and various works of mercy, like almsgiving, are signs of real self-giving love and are essential to building Christian community and the full realization of the reign of God.

Today, the church once again underscores the Christian obligation to give as much as one can to meet the needs of others as fully as possible. True spiritual almsgiving is love and kindness toward one's enemies or toward strangers—those on the margins of or excluded from the community of the baptized—whatever their races, beliefs, personal histories, or social status. Almsgiving, in all, can involve free sharing of one's personal presence, materials, or time in order to serve human needs. Though it should be done freely and compassionately, voluntary almsgiving is nevertheless a basic responsibility or duty of every baptized person.

(See also Charity, Works of Mercy.)

ALTAR is a centrally located, table-like structure in a church at which the liturgy of the Eucharist—also known as the sacrifice of the Mass—is celebrated. The word "altar" in Hebrew means "place for slaughtering" or "place of sacrifice." The altar is sometimes referred to as "the table of the Lord" by Catholics. In-church altars tend to be made of stone and are permanently fixed to a central place on the floor. Movable altars for the Eucharist can be used outside of church buildings and often are made of wood.

The Bible gives us over 400 references to altars. Ritual sacrifices to God took place on altars. Altars were seen by the Hebrews as the place at which the divine and the human came into touch in a special way.

The earliest Christian altars were probably ordinary wooden family dinner tables in Christian households. On these, the original agape feasts and eucharistic meals were shared. From the early times of the church, altars have been covered with decorative cloth (a banquet symbol) and highlighted by candles nearby (a symbol of the Spirit's presence). Eventually altars became ornate marble constructions pushed to the back (east wall) of the church sanctuary and thus far removed from the midst of the worshiping assembly. Tabernacles, crucifixes, candles, icons, and artwork were usually placed on church altars.

Recent Christian thought and reforms have stressed anew that the Eucharist is a sacrificial meal to be shared by all believers. Thus, contemporary Catholic altars have once again begun to look like real tables and are being re-situated in central places in the church building so that presiders at Mass can face the worshiping assembly and all can move freely and easily around the altar table. Also, although there is a traditional church association between the martyrs/saints and Catholic altars (for years, church altars held relics of the saints in a special altar stone), today Catholics recognize that altars are dedicated to God only. Altar stones and saintly relics in altars are not now required.

Altars should be located in church spaces so that they naturally draw the focus of the Christian gathering at prayer. Artwork, candles, and the tabernacle are generally kept off the altar surface. In fact, tabernacles and "side altars" are often found in small chapels off to the sides of the main space in a Catholic church.

Altars of sacrifice are consecrated (blessed) for official church worship in a special blessing rite. The altar is the center of a worshiping assembly's prayer of thanksgiving and glory to God. When used within or outside of a church, the eucharistic altar should be a sturdy table, skillfully built, made of very becoming and solid materials.

(See also Agape; Church, as Home; Eucharist; and Tabernacle.)

ANGELS in Christian thought and tradition are spiritual but personal beings, created prior to the universe by God, who possess intuitive knowledge, have free will, and are naturally superior to human beings. Angels worship God, act as God's messengers to humanity, and prayerfully watch over human beings. The word has Hebrew and Greek origins meaning "messenger" or "announcer."

The ancient Hebrews saw God ruling over the cosmos with the assistance of divine but subordinate helpers ("hosts of heaven," "morning stars" in the Hebrew Scriptures). In the Christian Scriptures, angels were pictured as God's messengers who assisted Jesus of Nazareth and some of his close followers. Over the centuries Christians developed a tradition that said God made many angels, all of them happy, but some angels (led by the devil or Satan, also known later as Lucifer) failed to love the Creator. They wanted God's power and position. They chose to rebel, but the all-powerful, all-good God banished them, sending them eternally into the alienation and punishment of hell. Since the 3rd century, Christians have believed that church members and others personally have an angel to support them and watch out for their physical and spiritual welfare. By the 1500s, a feast honoring the Guardian Angels had appeared in southern Europe. In 1608, Pope Paul V made this a liturgical feast for the whole church community. In 1670, Clement X set October 2 as the date for the feast of all holy guardian angels.

A branch of Christian theology called angelology identifies categories or "choirs" of angels in heaven (in order of importance): seraphim, cherubim, thrones, dominations, principalities, powers, virtues, archangels, and angels. Some thinkers speak of belief in angels as a traditional spiritual help by which humanity has tried to feel more in touch with an unseen but good God and by which Christians are reminded inspirationally of spiritual truths that sin and evil will never overcome. Others see angels as comforting and consoling or even spiritually challenging presences that urge people to be morally upright—the direct opposite of the tempting, evil devil. This goes along with traditional Catholic thought about angels' ongoing mission "to light and guard" and guide human beings through this existence.

Catholic tradition views angels as immortal, spiritual beings made by God (and called by God) to personally minister to human needs, worship the divine, and follow God's will. Angels can pray to God on behalf of human causes, just as evil angels (devils) can try to cause humans to sin. Three archangels—messengers to human beings—have been given names in Christian thought: Michael, Raphael, and Gabriel.

The notion of guardian angels is deeply embedded in long-standing Catholic tradition but it is not an essential doctrine of the faith. A few of the Bible passages to which Catholics look for spiritual insight about angels as guardians and messengers include Psalm 91:11–12, Matthew 4:1–11, Matthew 18:10, Luke 1:26–38, Luke 24:1–8, Acts 1:6–11, and Acts 12:6–11.

(See also Annunciation, Devil, Free Will, Heaven.)

ANNULMENT is an official decision on the part of the church that a marriage was invalid from its very beginning and, therefore, never really existed. This decision is usually made by a diocesan marriage tribunal or by some other church authority, such as a local bishop or the Roman Rota (marriage court of appeal) at the Vatican. A more accurate church term for the annulment decision is a decree of nullity. The word is rooted in the Latin *annullare*, "to bring to nothing."

There are a number of bases and grounds (diriment impediments) on which marriages traditionally have been considered invalid and, therefore, on which annulments have been granted to church members in the past and present. For instance, if marriage partners never intended to have children or if they did not intend to make their relationship permanent, an annulment can be granted. If a Catholic is married to another by a non-Catholic minister without special permission, if a man and woman have married but have never had sexual intercourse, or if one of them had not been baptized by the time of the marriage, the church often grants an annulment. Often petitions for annulment are somehow related to psychological factors such as gross immaturity on the part of one or more spouses in a marriage or the inability of one or more in a marital relationship to truly love another.

In order to be validly married, couples must enter their marital covenant freely and with full understanding of what they are committing themselves to. However many pastorally-minded individuals today and many helping professionals (e.g., psychologists and social workers) recognize that pressures and stresses placed on men, women, and families—and on everyday household life—make true and lasting commitments more and more difficult today. Some members of the Catholic community have strongly emphasized the church's continual need to show pastoral care and sensitivity to those who have experienced serious marital life disruptions, family separations, and other marriage-related troubles due to unfortunate circumstances. They have urged diocesan marriage tribunals and other Catholic authorities to recognize pastorally that in some cases—for a number of understandable reasons—couples have never been able to live a sacramental, covenant relationship. Ministry to the separated, divorced, and remarried has been an emerging field of ministry among Catholics in recent decades.

All church members are bound to observe Catholic marriage laws. Church rules relating to Christian marriage, as well as to separations of spouses, can be found in the Code of Canon Law. Officially, diocesan marriage tribunals are the local agencies responsible for researching and settling matters regarding the validity or invalidity of marriages. When a church authority grants a decree of nullity (annulment), the man and woman involved are then free to enter valid marriages with other partners and yet remain in union with the Catholic community.

The granting of annulments, church leaders say, should not be seen as a change in the church's teaching on the permanence of Christian marriage. Rather they point out that some persons who have married were never really capable of doing so in a spirit of covenant love.

Note of Interest: In 1991, the marriage tribunals in U.S. dioceses reported 63,933 ordinary-case annulments granted. Reasons for these, according to canonical norms, included 42,617 for invalid consent to the marriage, 195 cases of impotence, 2442 for other impediments, and 18,679 cases of "defect of form." In the Catholic community around the globe, there were 80,711 decrees of nullity issued in the year 1991.

(See also Covenant, Matrimony.)

ANNUNCIATION   is a solemn church feast (a solemnity), celebrated on March 25, which honors the deep mystery of the incarnation of the Word of God on Earth. Through the annunciation experience, the archangel Gabriel told a young, unmarried virgin Mary that she would give birth to a child named *Jeshua*, meaning "Yahweh saves" (Luke 1:26–38). The Latin roots of "annunciation" roughly mean "proclamation."

Tradition indicates that Mary must have been very young at the time she said yes to God and conceived Jesus. At the time, women became engaged to be married when they were about 14 years old. She was probably living in Nazareth when she learned about the impending birth of her child. The earliest Christian communities cherished the ideas that Mary received this miraculous revelation from God in full and complete faith and that the pregnancy was a powerful result of the grace of God's Spirit. The doctrine of virgin birth has been officially proclaimed by Christian writers and teachers since the early 3rd century. The feast of the Annunciation has been celebrated by the church in some fashion since the year 430.

The heart of belief in the Annunciation is that Jesus, the incarnate Word of the Most High, is unique in history and God's greatest revelation. Christian faith looks to the young virgin Mary's total trust in her God, even though she was unmarried and vulnerable to harsh social criticism, as a sign of what Israel could be and how the Christian church, a new Israel, should respond always to the Creator.

It is now recognized that the date of the Annunciation feast—March 25—reveals the feast's particular connection to the mysteries of the incarnation and Christmas. March 25 comes exactly nine months before December 25. Some early Christian communities seem to have viewed March 25 as a date also related to Jesus of Nazareth's passover to new life through his death and resurrection. Thus, the moment of the new Creation and new Israel—Jesus' death and resurrection—could be associated ritually with the miraculous conception of Jesus in the virgin Mary.

Through the celebration of the Annunciation of the Lord on March 25 each year, Catholics remember Mary's faith, her thorough acceptance of and true love for God's Word, and especially the great divine revelation to all humanity that was made possible through Jesus of Nazareth. Church members also continue to honor her physical purity and openhearted, guileless commitment to the reign of God. Catholics are cautioned not to confuse teachings on the Annunciation with the dogma on the Immaculate Conception of Mary.

(See also Christmas, Immaculate Conception, Jesus of Nazareth, Joseph, and Mary.)

ANOINTING   involves the process of pouring or rubbing special oil on a person or thing in order to make the "anointed" sacred and consecrated to God. "Anoint" comes from the Middle English *anoynten*—"to smear."

The ancient Israelites used olive oil for medical purposes, for fuel, for bathing, and for anointing persons and things in sacred ceremonies. Anointing was done ritually to freshen and strengthen a person and to fortify him or her with the Spirit of God when an important mission was to be undertaken. Prophets and priests were the ones who did this ritual anointing. Israelite kings—for example, Saul, David, and Solomon—were all anointed.

According to Christian tradition, the Word of God became human in order to offer a universal salvation and God's enduring friendship to the entire human community. This Word was known as Jesus of Nazareth, and then later as Jesus the Christ. "Christ" is derived from the Greek term *christos*, or "the anointed." Christians believe that Jesus of Nazareth healed many people who were suffering through sicknesses and other ills. The gospels and the Acts of the Apostles indicate that some of the earliest followers of Jesus also healed many sick people and, in some cases, anointed them. The epistle of James (5:14–15) notes that anointing the sick and infirm with oil, in the name of the risen Jesus Christ, will help strengthen and heal them. The church continues to anoint individuals with sacred oils in the sacraments of baptism, confirmation, order, and anointing of the sick.

Holy chrism—the oil used in Catholic anointing ceremonies—is blessed and made ready for church community rituals by Catholic bishops every year on Holy Thursday.

(See also Anointing of the Sick, Baptism, Confirmation, and Order.)

ANOINTING OF THE SICK   is one of the seven sacraments recognized by the Catholic community. Persons who get very sick or become much weakened by long-term illness, and persons who are in immediate danger of death, are the usual recipients of this sacrament. A presbyter anoints individuals by placing holy oil on their foreheads and hands while saying, "Through this holy anointing, may the Lord in his love and mercy help you with the grace of the Holy Spirit.... May the Lord who frees you from sin save you and raise you up."

The term "anointing" comes from the Middle English *anoynten,* which means "to smear." In the 9th century a European church custom involved the anointing of the sick and dying in a "sacrament of the sick." By the 12th century this ritual was viewed as a last anointing before one's death and passage over to eternal life. By the 16th century, the time of the Council of Trent, Catholics had begun to speak of a sacrament called extreme unction. Church leaders have ordered, in more recent times, that this be known as anointing of the sick. The Catholic community has witnessed, therefore, some significant revisions in the rituals involved in providing this sacrament to church members.

Several official changes in the community's anointing rituals were made by the Holy See in January 1973. Anointing of the sick can now be celebrated within the celebration of the Eucharist (the Mass) in order that the prayers, good will, and witness of the entire assembly can be offered to the sick and dying members of the Christian body. When the sacrament is celebrated outside of Mass, the persons anointed first hear and respond to the Word of God (in a liturgy of the Word), confess their sinfulness to a priest, are then anointed with oil, and receive the Eucharist. In the course of this ritual, the minister who anoints represents the entire community of the baptized, which hopes and prays that all those who suffer any infirmities of body, mind, or soul will be made stronger and regain health in the name of the risen Jesus. Through this sacrament the whole church prays that Jesus' Spirit will grant "relief and salvation" to those who are anointed.

The church teaches that anointing of the sick and dying makes persons stronger in body and spirit and forgives sin. Catholics see this sacrament as a sign of God's great love and enduring concern for the bodily and spiritual health of the people of God. Anointing also is meant to remind Christians in a powerful, symbolic way that Jesus of Nazareth suffered much for the sake of humanity. James 5:14–15 is the biblical passage most often cited in the Catholic community to show that even the earliest followers of Jesus spiritually strengthened the sick and suffering members of the Christian way.

The church states that the following can and should receive this sacrament of the sick: 1) Those dangerously ill due to sickness or old age, 2) Older persons, if they are in a weakened condition, even though no dangerous illness is present, 3) Sick children, youth, and adults if they have sufficient use of reason to be comforted by this sacrament, 4) Individuals who have recovered from an illness after being anointed, 5) Individuals who have been anointed during an illness may receive this sacrament again if their danger becomes more serious, 6) A sick person should be anointed before surgery whenever a dangerous illness is involved, and 7) Persons who lose consciousness or the use of reason may be anointed if as faithful Christians they would have sought the sacrament if they were still in control of their faculties. Church presbyters are not permitted to anoint the bodies of individuals who have already died, but if there is any doubt whether a person has or has not died, the sacrament may be administered conditionally.

The *Catechism of the Catholic Church* notes that a most proper time for anointing has certainly arrived once a believer begins to be in danger of death due to illness, old age, or another cause. The Catechism goes on to say that the main effects of this sacrament include the gift of Spirit, union with the redemptive passion of Jesus, the strengthening of the faith of the church community as a whole, and preparation for one's final journey toward God and the happiness of heaven.

(See also Anointing, Death/Dying, Presbyters, Sacraments, and Sin.)

ANTI-SEMITISM   is the phrase commonly used to describe attitudes and actions of any sort that reveal prejudice, hatred, harassment, or racial discrimination toward Jewish people. Anti-Semitism can take many forms. It can be expressed in cruel and hostile behavior, or it can take shape within psychological or social antagonisms. It is often directed at Jewish organizations and businesses, not just Jewish individuals.

Anti-Semitism has both ancient and modern roots. Since the earliest days of the Christian community, there have been many misunderstandings between Jews and followers of Jesus. Primitive Christianity, in fact, first blossomed within a Jewish culture and this led to many unfortunate and long-lasting conflicts with traditional Judaism. More recently, in the 1870s, Wilhelm Marr led a movement in Germany that sought to wipe out all Jewish influences in German life and culture. The emergence of Nazi power in Europe, in the 1930s and 1940s, led to vicious persecutions and the attempt to eliminate the Jewish race from Earth. About six million Jews were killed in the Nazi-driven holocaust of the time.

Christianity sprang from a Jewish reform movement. Christians often claim that the Christian religion is a fulfillment of the hopes and prophecies of ancient Israel as found in the Hebrew Scriptures. This, however, does not justify cruel or racist attitudes toward Jews in any way. Such things are directly opposed to the Christian ideals of charity and compassionate service toward all. Some commentators refer to all forms of Christian anti-Semitism as a lasting heresy in Christian thought and practice.

In 1937, Pius XI taught (*Divini redemptoris*) that all anti-Semitism is incompatible with Christian truth. Given the Jewish roots of Christianity, he added that all Christian people "are spiritually Semites." In 1986, Pope John Paul II visited Rome's chief synagogue to express the church's solidarity with Jewish concerns and later visited and wept at the site of a Nazi extermination camp.

Today, it is recognized that the Jewish people still remain God's original chosen ones. Therefore, Catholics are discouraged from actively trying to convert Jews away from Judaism to the Christian faith. Church members recognize the mutual gains to be made through contemporary, ongoing Jewish-Catholic dialogues. In the U.S. in the early 1990s, key issues for such inter-religious discussions were the contemporary revival of anti-Semitism and how to combat it, the treatment of Jewish and Catholic matters in American educational institutions, and the need for Catholic-Jewish cooperation on social justice and peacemaking projects.

(See also Catholic-Jewish Relations, Hebrews, Zionism.)

Note of Interest: Discrimination refers to treating people in divisive ways or selecting some individuals or races for unfair, unjust treatment. Since the 1960s, the church has re-emphasized its teaching that any persecution or discrimination against any man, woman, or child is morally wrong. The Vatican II statement, Declaration on the Relationship of the Church to Non-Christian Religions, said that Catholics must reject, as completely foreign to Christian life, discrimination against and harassment directed at human beings of any race, color, religion, or way of life. With regard to anti-Semitism in particular, the document clearly stated that Christians, motivated by a gospel spirit of love, must avoid and speak out against all hatred, discrimination, and other negative treatment against Jewish people at all times, in all places.

APOCALYPSE is known today to many as the book of Revelation, the last book in the Christian Scriptures (New Testament). "Apocalypse" derived from the Greek *apokalypsis*, means roughly "an uncovering" or "revealing." The Apocalypse centers on the visions of a man named John of Patmos. These visions revolved around events to come, and they included dire warnings about moral troubles in the world faced by very early Christians.

The book of Revelation was probably completed about the year 95 c.e. and seems to be the work of several authors and editors. Some church leaders at first rejected the authenticity of the Apocalypse for the enduring Christian community, but later church authorities agreed that it should, indeed, be part of sacred Scripture. Bible scholars now believe that the text of the Apocalypse, using the Hebrew Scriptures (Old Testament) as a basic resource, tells of a crisis-time during the earliest days of Christianity and how the forces of goodness and the Spirit must continually struggle with the forces of evil and sin.

The literary form of the book of Revelation must be considered in order to accurately interpret and understand it today. This book is now thought to be a narrative (and allegory) in which a prophet named John receives revelations (the "visions" of John) from the risen Jesus. The book describes these visions using rich imagery. The revelations in the Apocalypse often seem to focus on a situation of conflict and persecution suffered by John's contemporaries in the persecuted Christian community. The Roman Emperor of the time is described as an oppressor and as the Antichrist.

Modern biblical scholars generally hold that the original hearers of the book of Revelation understood that the sinful, corrupted world must be transformed by the Spirit of Jesus before the reign of God, promised by Jesus of Nazareth, could truly become a reality for all persons. Therefore, in the Apocalypse, reality is described as a continuing struggle between the powers of goodness and grace and the powers of evil and sin. Physical death in the Apocalypse is not a finality, not just a pointless and bitter end. Just as Jesus endured powerlessness, pain, and death, so must his followers, especially during periods of persecution. Just as Jesus has been raised from the dead, so will all his faithful followers enjoy eternal light and life and happiness, like the risen Jesus, in the reign of God. In other words, in this life all followers of the life-changing gospel of Jesus must be prepared to endure hardships and suffering as they strive for justice, peace, true Christian holiness, and the perfection of the world to come.

The authors of the Apocalypse are not precisely known. The apostle and evangelist John was probably not the author, nor were the writers/editors of the Johannine epistles and the gospel of John. Catholics now tend to see that the book of Revelation is not to be used as a tool for predicting or revealing the end of the world. Much more research is needed in order for the Catholic community and others to fully grasp the meanings and purposes of the book of Revelation for early Christian communities as well as for present-day church members.

(See also Bible, Fundamentalism, New Testament, and Revelation.)

APOLOGETICS   is a skillful presentation of the reasonableness, truth, and ultimate value of Christian faith. The origins of the term are found in the Greek language, meaning "speak in defense" of someone or something. A Christian "apology," therefore, is a reasonable verbal or written defense of a Christian belief, in particular, or Christian tradition as a whole.

In early church days, apologetics emerged as carefully drafted written defenses of the Christian religion. In church history, a number of early Christian preachers and writers who explained the teachings, values, and traditions of the Christian community came to be known as the great church apologists. A more recent great Christian apologist and convert to Catholicism was Cardinal John Henry Newman, who wrote the masterpiece *Apologia pro Vita Sua*.

Apologetics today is considered a function of Catholic fundamental theology. A contemporary apologist, in that sense, is one skilled and wise in clarifying matters that pertain to foundational Christian doctrines and those things that God has revealed through Christian faith and tradition. The church acknowledges today that methods of presentation and persuasive arguments on the value of Catholic Christianity must be adapted effectively to the needs, languages, and customs of peoples and cultures in order to be intelligible to modern audiences. It also recognizes that contemporary Christian apologists must draw upon the writings and resources from various fields of human study in their efforts to fully present ideas about the validity of Christian faith for the world today.

(See also Evangelization, Theology, and Tradition.)

APOSTASY refers to the knowing and complete refusal by a baptized person to remain faithful to Christian faith and traditions. One who commits apostasy is known as an apostate. The word has Greek roots, which refer to a deserter, runaway, or one who "stands away from" someone or something.

In the early Christian experience, apostasy meant that a person baptized and initiated into Christian community had gone over completely and forever to a pagan religion, thus standing apart from the gospel of Jesus and the way of Christian life. Today, as in recent centuries, apostasy means that a baptized person completely rejects the Christian vision and the church community (Hebrews 6:1–8).

At times, even now, traditional phrases like "apostasy from order" and "apostasy from religious community" are occasionally used. The first refers to a situation in which one who is ordained rejects fully the obligations of and the way of life of the ordained without official permission. The latter refers to members of religious communities who have taken perpetual vows yet fully leave that way of life behind in an unauthorized fashion.

Apostasy and heresy are not synonymous. Apostasy involves a full and free refusal of Christian faith and a thorough departure from church life. Heresy involves a knowing and personal, hard-hearted denial of a particular and essential (dogmatic) Catholic teaching. Both lead, however, to excommunication (i.e., exclusion from the Catholic Christian community).

In a sense, both personal apostasy and heresy, while they disrupt the fundamental unity shared by Christians, can lead toward positive effects. The life-witness of those who become alienated and leave church life, and the unorthodox teachings of others, can lead ultimately to doctrinal clarifications and stronger communal bonds much needed by the Christian community in today's individualistic, choice-oriented world.

Today, the church urges all its members to understand why persons sometimes reject the gospel or become alienated from the institutional church in such a way as to walk away from active Catholic life. It also urges outreach to and dialogue with such alienated individuals in a spirit of Christian reconciliation. Catholic thought stresses that faith in God is a gift that does not prevent human and intense doubt, struggles, alienation, or doctrinal dissent. In such times, however, one should on one's own—or at the strong encouragement of others—remain faithful to God and the Catholic tradition through prayer, lifestyle, and personal spiritual choices.

(See also Baptism, Excommunication, and Faith.)

Note of Interest: Dissent essentially means a fundamental disagreement or a difference of opinion. It is possible to experience a radical sense of dissent with Catholic teachings, values, and practices—the Catholic way—overall. More limited forms of dissent, though, are more typical today. In the Catholic view, one must accept all essential church teachings and may not dissent over a dogma, even if one's disagreement is expressed sincerely or with positive intentions. However, one may in certain cases express dissent over (not completely assent to) a church teaching that is non-dogmatic. In fact, in some ways, such Christian dissent is basically inevitable today. Theological opinion seems to emphasize that doctrinal dissent, in light of one's Christian conscience, can result when a baptized person a) cannot make basic sense of a church teaching, b) sees conflict between a teaching and related Christian doctrines/insights, c) sees conflict between his or her Christian life experience and the proposed teaching, or d) knows there is significant dissent by highly reasonable, experienced, and knowledgeable members of the church community over the teaching.

(See also Doctrine, Dogma, and Theology.)

APOSTLES according to Christian tradition, were the twelve persons chosen by Jesus of Nazareth to hear and believe in his proclamations of the good news of salvation, to follow him in a special way, and to reach out—after becoming personal witnesses to Jesus' resurrection and new life in God—to share his life-changing message and values with peoples and cultures (all of humanity) throughout the world. Lists of the original apostles were constructed for the gospels of Mark, Matthew, and Luke, and for the Acts of the Apostles. The names of the twelve apostles were Simon Peter, Matthew, James the Greater, James the Less, John, Judas, Andrew, Philip, Bartholomew (also called Nathaniel), Thomas, Thaddeus (also known as Jude), and Simon the Zealot. After the death of Judas, the apostle who betrayed Jesus, a man named Matthias was chosen to replace him. Saint Paul is often referred to as an apostle but he was not one of the original twelve.

In the Hebrew Scriptures, the nation of Israel (the original chosen people of God) was made up of twelve tribes led by the twelve sons of Jacob. In the Christian Scriptures, Jesus of Nazareth gives his twelve apostles responsibility to lead the community of believers (the new Israel and the new people of God), proclaim the reign of God in Jesus' name, and guide all who are baptized and who have faith in the gospel. Tradition teaches that the twelve apostles and others preached the gospel message, worshiped God in the risen One's name, healed the sick with the help of his Spirit, and evangelized many individuals and communities in accord with the mission they had received from Jesus after his resurrection from death (Mark 16:15).

Regarding the Catholic community's belief in apostolic succession, the apostle Peter—the leader of the twelve apostles—has often been called the first pope. (All popes who have come after him have been Peter's direct successors.) All twelve apostles have been considered the first bishops. (A Catholic bishop therefore is known as an authentic successor of the original twelve.)

(See also Acts of the Apostles, Apostolic Succession, Bishop, and Discipleship.)

Note of Interest: Numerous biblical scholars have looked into the New Testament-era evidence regarding women and presbyteral ministries. Some have concluded in a convincing way that the circle of twelve—known traditionally as the apostles—is the only exclusively male group associated with Jesus of Nazareth. These men in all likelihood came from a wider circle of disciples (those who heard Jesus' call and freely chose to follow him), which was not restricted to males (see Mark 15:40–41 and Luke 8:1–3). While the heralded small group of twelve were apostles, the actual circle of apostles was probably much wider—including, among others, Paul and Barnabas. Some knowledgeable thinkers and writers have suggested that there were women apostles—for example, Mary of Magdala, a woman named Junia mentioned in Romans 16:7, and Phoebe, who appears in Romans 16:1. Thus, in all, New Testament evidence indicates that both men and women were apostles—close followers of Jesus of Nazareth and personal witnesses to his resurrection from the dead—in the primitive community of Christian believers.

APOSTOLIC SUCCESSION   is a phrase expressing a traditional Catholic belief that the bishops of the church community are the authentic successors as a whole to the original apostles selected by Jesus of Nazareth. Thus, the notion of apostolic succession implies that all bishops share in the authority and power of the apostles and have responsibility for the pastoral guidance and governance of the worldwide Catholic community.

Both the Christian Scriptures and long-held church traditions provide sources for the Catholic doctrine on apostolic succession. The original apostles were empowered by the Spirit of the risen Jesus at Pentecost to be effective gospel witnesses to the whole world (Acts 1:8, 2:1–47). By the late 1st century, Clement I wrote to Christians in the city of Corinth about the concept of apostolic empowerment and succession. Over time, church members came to see each pope (the bishop of Rome) as a true successor to the apostle Peter, head of the apostles and first vicar of Christ in Rome, and all other bishops as equally entrusted with the enduring Christian mission to spread the gospel worldwide, pastorally care for the people of God, and authoritatively guide, preserve, and defend the community of faith.

Recent Catholic thought about this matter has noted that the Creator is often revealed to human beings through others, especially when they show genuine loving support, assistance, and Christian concern for humanity. It is believed that the risen Jesus of Nazareth left behind a body of apostolic-era witnesses to carry on his timeless mission to share good news about the reign of God and to serve the real needs of all the world. The apostolic roots of the church's present organization and structures came into focus only after Easter and in the light and inspiration of Pentecost.

The Christian community today has its one dynamic mission, but it needs many human beings and their spiritual gifts, skills, and challenges for its wide diversity of ministries. The Catholic bishops share uniquely in the particular ministries of teaching the gospel to all, administering the church's affairs, and calling all persons to Christian holiness. In a way, however, all church members participate in the reality of apostolic succession whenever they teach or serve others, in the spirit of the gospel, in concert with the faith of the global Catholic community.

Vatican II re-emphasized that the church community is "apostolic"— a living body that has been and always will be headed by a permanent college or assembly of leaders—the bishops and the pope. In 1991, a Vatican statement noted that the Catholic faith recognizes "an unbroken line of episcopal ordination from Christ down through the centuries to the bishops of today and an uninterrupted continuity in Christian doctrine from Christ to those today who teach in union with the college of bishops and its head, the successor of Peter." The church today acknowledges that these Catholic beliefs, along with a few essential others, often lie at the heart of ecumenical disagreements and dialogues.

Apostolic succession is conferred upon each bishop in the process of ordination—the gift of the Spirit through the laying on of hands. The *Catechism of the Catholic Church* notes, therefore, that the whole church is apostolic in that it 1) was built on "the foundation of the Apostles," 2) guards and teaches the doctrinal treasures learned from the Lord's followers, and 3) will continue the faith tradition nurtured by the apostles, particularly through the work of the apostles' true successors, until the time of Jesus Christ's second coming.

(See also Apostles, Bishops, Collegiality, and Pope.)

APPARITIONS   is a term rooted in the Latin *apparere*, which means "to attend or appear." An apparition is an extraordinary, visible appearance—a supernatural vision or private revelation—seen by one or more persons.

There are a number of extraordinary, supernatural visions recorded in the Bible (e.g., Genesis 26:24, 1 Samuel 3:1–14, Daniel 8:15–18, Luke 1:26–38, Acts 8:26, Acts 9:10). Since the beginning of the Common Era (since the time of Jesus of Nazareth), visions and private revelations of Jesus, Mary, and others have been claimed by devout Christians. Through its history, the church community has honored and approved certain apparitions—that is, it has recognized the reality of certain extraordinary sacred appearances. In recent times some church-accepted apparition sites have become much loved places to which Christian pilgrims and spiritual searchers frequently journey. These include (the dates of the apparitions are noted): Guadalupe (Mexico), 1531; Rue de Bac (France), 1830; LaSallette (France), 1846; Lourdes (France), 1858; Fatima (Portugal), 1917; Beauraing (Belgium), 1933; and Banneau (Belgium), 1933.

Although the church community has approved officially a number of apparitions and spiritual shrines, it does not view the messages communicated to human beings in supernatural visions as part of official Catholic doctrine. The reality of any divine apparition does not have to be accepted by church members as an essential truth of Catholicism. Many theological themes today stress that God can "speak" to (communicate with)—and thus reveal Godself to—human beings and human groups in countless natural and non-extraordinary ways. It is perhaps wise for thinking Christians to respect the possibility of supernatural private revelations from the Creator, yet they need not feel that the church community is trying to force anyone toward belief in religious apparitions or spiritual devotions now linked with such visions.

Some apparitions have been completely rejected, and some have not had official church comment made about them. In this case, approval means the church decides—by using certain set criteria—that nothing in association with the appearance is counter to Catholic doctrine or the spiritual health and holiness of the people of God. Since many people can wrongly be convinced that God is breaking into their lives or communities in an extraordinary manner, and because overall it is nearly impossible to fully assess the reality of mystical and miraculous episodes, the church does not require anyone to believe in reported apparitions as a condition of Catholic faith.

(See also Devotion, Doctrine, Medal, and Revelation.)

ASCENSION THURSDAY is a special, annual solemnity on the church's liturgical calendar that celebrates the glorified and victorious return of the Word of God—the risen Jesus—to heaven. The observance of the Ascension occurs on a Thursday, 40 days after Easter. Ascension is a holy day in the Catholic community of the United States. The word "ascension" is rooted in the Latin *scandere*, which basically means "to mount" or "to climb." The Ascension honors the moment when the risen Jesus entered the place of eternal life (heaven) in order to send his comforting but challenging Spirit, the Paraclete, to his followers.

Early Christians considered the Ascension one of the greatest feasts. They saw it as a wonderful sign that all human beings are meant to be united with their Creator in happiness in heaven forever. The gospels of Luke and John seem to indicate that Jesus' ascension experience happened on Easter night. The Acts of the Apostles, however, places it some forty days after Easter Sunday. The reason for the Ascension, however, is much more crucial than questions about when it occurred. The core meaning of the Ascension of Jesus is that the Word of God returned (or rose) to heaven in full glory and now, as in all Christian eras, sends forth his Spirit to guide the church community and all of God's creation.

The Solemnity of the Ascension is meant to be a powerful, ritual reminder that Jesus—who lived, died, was raised by God from the dead—will come again in glory at the end of time to fully establish the reign of God which he so compellingly proclaimed. The Ascension likewise begins the prayerful nine-day wait for Pentecost. Catholic tradition maintains that the risen Jesus is not removed or absent from the world. Rather he is present among his followers—and potentially to all human beings and all cultures—through his life-giving Spirit. The Ascension, Catholics believe, is a powerful sign of coming happiness with God in heaven and the coming reign of God that Jesus promised to all of humanity. Accounts of the Ascension of the risen Jesus in the Christian Scriptures include Mark 16:19, Luke 24:51, and Acts 1:2.

(See also Easter, Heaven, Paraclete, and Resurrection.)

ASH WEDNESDAY   is a movable-date church celebration that occurs each year about six and and one-half weeks before Easter. Ash Wednesday is the first day of Lent. On this date annually, through a simple ritual, ashes from burned palms, a symbol of the human need for repentance, are placed in the sign of the cross on the forehead of church members.

In the world of Hebrew symbolism, ashes represented sadness, troubles, grief, or unworthiness (see Job 2:8, 30:19; Psalm 102:10). Some harsh Israelite penances included the public wearing of "sackcloth and ashes" (Jeremiah 6:26, Matthew 11:21). Many early Christians carried on this tradition of public penances for sinful wrongdoing. About the year 600, Gregory the Great set Ash Wednesday as the first day of Lent. He likewise extended this Christian season of penance to its present length of over six weeks. By the 800s, some local churches were celebrating a public Ash Wednesday ritual, for publicly-recognized sinners, much like the one we know today. During the 11th century, the church shifted the focus to all members of the body of Christ, not just publicly-known sinners.

Today the palm branches from the previous Passion (Palm) Sunday are burned and the resulting ashes are blessed. Various dry leaves or other natural materials are used whenever palms are not available. A traditional saying has long been used as a priest or pastoral associate crosses an individual's forehead with ashes: "Remember, you are dust and unto dust you shall return." The Lenten themes of humility, sorrow for sin, and need for God's forgiveness are brought to mind also in alternate sayings now used in the Ash Wednesday ritual: e.g., "Turn away from sin and be faithful to the gospel."

Catholic tradition holds that ashes are a church sacramental that remind the faithful to do lenten penances. Ashes also show that human existence can perish—but life with God in heaven, a result of Christian faith, can last forever. Catholic priests bless the ashes and distribute them to others. In cases of pastoral need, however, others may be designated to help the presiding priest distribute ashes or actually substitute for a priest if the ashes to be used have been blessed at a previous time. Ash Wednesday remains a day of fasting and abstinence for Catholics worldwide, according to a decree by Pope Paul VI.

(See also Fasting, Holy Week, Lent, and Sacramentals.)

ASSUMPTION OF MARY   is a solemn feast celebrated each year by the church community on August 15. It is a holy day in the United States. On this day Catholics remember and honor the Virgin Mary, the mother of Jesus of Nazareth, and her entry into heaven.

The feast of the Assumption was a popular celebration among Christians in Middle Eastern lands by the 5th century. Its celebration was widespread in Europe some 200 years later. In 1568 Pope Pius V made the feast of the Assumption a holy day for the entire church. The fact of Mary's assumption into the glory of heaven was later proclaimed a Catholic dogma by Pope Pius XII on November 1, 1950 with the statement *Munificentissimus deus.*

Officially the Catholic community teaches that Mary, the mother of Jesus, was assumed into heaven—with her body and soul united—but Catholic doctrine does not specify whether or not she died before her assumption. Since the early days of the Christian church, many have thought that Mary was taken by God into heaven prior to death because she was sinless and because her life was a statement of total faith in the will of the Creator.

While the Assumption of Mary a remains solemnity and holy day for Catholics in the United States, the obligation for church members to attend Mass (participate in the Eucharist) has been waived whenever August 15 occurs on a Saturday or Monday. This became a U.S. church practice as a result of a decision made by the national bishops conference in December 1991.

(See also Dogma, Heaven, Mary, and Veneration.)

ATHEISM   is a manner of thinking and acting through which a human being denies the reality of God. A contemporary word that describes the typical attitude of an atheist is unbelief. In recent years the church community has noted that atheism is one of the major problems plaguing humankind in the present age. The term is derived from the Greek *atheos*, which means "without a god."

Some say that the obvious increase in the number of persons who profess atheism in modern societies (making it truly one of the more obvious "signs of the times" to be read and responded to by Christians) can be attributed to increased cynicisms, stresses, social pressures, and overt criticisms of religious systems, beliefs, and institutional leaders in our postmodern era. Many of these attitudes can be traced directly to the 19th-century philosophical works of Hegel, Marx, Engels, Comte, Schopenhauer, Nietzsche, and others.

Recent church leaders and teachers have consistently spoken out against the evils of atheism. In the 20th century, five popes have spoken about how to deal with this problem, including Pope John Paul II. During the mid-1960s, Vatican Council II addressed matters pertaining to contemporary atheistic behaviors in the Pastoral Constitution on the Church in the Modern World. The Council speculated on some common causes of atheism today, including: 1) failure to believe in God because God is a great mystery, 2) over-reliance on scientific rationales for one's beliefs, 3) a humanism that extols the place of human beings in creation to the exclusion of the divine, 4) mistaken ideas about God or religion or both, 5) protest against the very existence of evil, 6) lives focused upon gaining pleasures or consumption of material goods, and 7) the immoral or unworthy example of those who profess belief in God.

Two particular notions seem to fuel atheistic attitudes and lifestyles. The first notion is that faith and dependence on a Creator is somehow in contradiction to true human freedom and independence. The second notion is that religious beliefs and religious systems are like drugs (opiates) that confuse people and cause them to blindly hope in an unreal future, in a nebulous eternity, rather than deal with social problems (e.g., poverty and injustices) in our day. Church leaders at Vatican II suggested two "remedies" for contemporary atheism: Christians should 1) show the world clearly that Christian faith does not deny human freedom or in any way belittle authentic human rights and dignity, and 2) urge church members to witness daily to the gospel message, proclaim Christian teachings, and encourage all people of God to participate in works of justice, mercy, and forgiveness.

Today many Catholics also believe that "sincere and prudent dialogue" on the gospel, on social and economic problems that thwart modern human development, and on modern personal pressures will help address issues raised by the proponents of atheism. Vatican II reminded the human community that the people of God as a whole bear some responsibility for the increase of atheism in various cultures in the 20th century. It noted that when church members willfully neglect their Christian formation, teach doctrines incorrectly, or remain deficient in their religious, moral, or social lives they are covering over the "authentic face of God and religion."

The Vatican has established an official Pontifical Council for Dialogue with Non-Believers. Founded by Paul VI in 1965, as the Secretariat for Non-Believers, and renamed by John Paul II in 1988, this council is dedicated to the study of atheistic systems of thought and undertakes various dialogues with groups of non-believers around the world.

(See also Faith, Free Will, God, Humanism, and Trinity.)

Note of Interest: An agnostic is different from an atheist. While the latter freely denies the reality of God's existence, an agnostic person holds to the theory that humans cannot scientifically know or discover the spiritual and immaterial. Thus they cannot know—with certainty—that the spiritual, immaterial, unseen God really exists. "Agnostic" and "agnosticism" come from the Greek *agnostos*, which means "unknowable."

B

BALTIMORE CATECHISM is a book containing basic doctrines and practices of the Catholic faith that has been used in the United States (more so in previous generations than at the present) to instruct young people and adults through a catechetical question-and-answer method.

In November 1884, the American bishops met for the Third Plenary Council of Baltimore, a meeting convened by Archbishop James Gibbons. During the final days of this two-month meeting, the U.S. bishops commissioned a priest, Fr. DeConcilio, to write a basic catechism that could be used for simple religious instructions. When this project was completed, a draft text of the catechism was forwarded to the bishops. They suggested numerous changes, and so a revision was undertaken in 1896. The text revisions continued until 1941.

The Baltimore Catechism, as it came to be known in Catholic communities throughout North America, was the most widely used basic religion text in Catholic schools and parish religious education programs until the 1960s. Most Catholic educators now consider it inadequate and outdated. Its theological expressions and ideas about Christian life and spirituality have not been revised to reflect developments in the Catholic community as a whole since Vatican II (1960s). Also, the Baltimore Catechism's view of mainstream, popular culture and modern Western lifestyles is not in total harmony with the church's more recent teachings about God's revelation, the world, contemporary technologies, scientific advancements, and the proper development of human communities.

In 1992, a contemporary catechism for the worldwide Christian community—the *Catechism of the Catholic Church*—was published by the Holy See in Rome. This new universal catechism has been designed to be a reference text for Catholic pastors, parents, and catechists. Its primary purpose is to provide a foundational text from which local bishops or national bishops conferences can develop culturally-adapted, theologically accurate, local-level catechetical resources, as the Baltimore Catechism was originally meant to be.

(See also Catechesis, Catechism of the Catholic Church, Confraternity of Christian Doctrine, and Parish.)

BAPTISM is the first sacrament received by all Catholic Christians. It is one of the three sacraments of Christian initiation. Through this sacrament, those baptized become members of the body of Christ and the new people of God, the worldwide Christian community. Baptism may be received only once. It can be administered by infusion (water poured over one's head) or by immersion (one's entire body plunged into water). The words of Christian baptism are: "I baptize you in the name of the Father, and of the Son, and of the Holy Spirit." The English term "baptize" is derived from a Greek verb that means "dipping in water."

Through the water, prayers, and rituals of Christian baptism, persons participate in the dying and rising to new life of Jesus of Nazareth. This spiritual reality has been symbolized dramatically in baptisms done by immersion. Up to the middle of the 5th century most baptism candidates were adults. After long and prayerful preparations—"catechumenate" periods—candidates were immersed in water, confirmed by the local bishop, and then received Eucharist—all in one ceremony (usually celebrated at the annual Easter Vigil).

From the end of the 5th century until now, the church community has stressed the need for infant baptism and, for various reasons, has often delayed confirmation until preteen or teenage years. Likewise the Catholic community often has not emphasized the ancient practice of lengthy and intense spiritual preparations for full Christian initiation as it did in early centuries of church life.

The ritual of baptism is a special welcome for persons of various ages and backgrounds into the Christian family of God. Baptism is a gift, but it is also a call to engage in the great mission of all Christians. It challenges all Christians, as reborn sons and daughters of the Creator, to confess before all men and women the faith they have received from God, from their parents and family, and from the Christian body as a whole.

The church community calls all believers to view baptism as the first step in one's initiation into the fullness of Christian life. There are two separate baptismal rites—one for adults and children of catechetical age, and one for infants and younger children. Adults, adolescents, and catechetical age children are expected to undergo a rather long stage-by-stage catechumenate and formation process—in the Rite of Christian Initiation of Adults—before their reception of the sacrament of baptism. (For more information on this, read the church document Rite of Christian Initiation of Adults and see the article on the Catechumenate and the RCIA in this book.)

Baptisms now often take place within the celebration of the Eucharist to pastorally emphasize the close relationship between the sacraments of initiation. A very special time for all baptisms is the Easter Vigil, and the Sundays of the Easter season.

Official church guidelines on the sacrament of baptism—the spiritual gateway to all the sacraments—can be found in canons 849-878 in the Code of Canon Law. The Catechism of the Catholic Church cites the ancient call to baptism first spoken by the apostle Peter and issued since apostolic times by the Christian community to all of humanity—"Repent, and be baptized every one of you in the name of Jesus so that your sins may be forgiven, and you will receive the gift of the Holy Spirit" (Acts 2:38). The Catechism indicates that in this sacrament of initiation everyone baptized experiences forgiveness of sins, spiritual rebirth as "a new creation" in Christ, and incorporation into the living body of Jesus on Earth. Through the water and the seal of baptism, one becomes pledged to serve God as a Christian through active participation in church worship, active Christian witness, and a lifestyle imbued by Christian discipleship and charity.

(See also Baptistry, Catechumenate and the RCIA, and Sacrament.)

BAPTISTRY   is the separate room or place in a Catholic church where baptisms take place. Baptistry also refers to the basin or bowl-like container in a church over which baptisms are performed.

From the 4th century until about the year 1000, baptistries were usually shallow pools large enough for the entire body to be drenched by the waters of the sacrament poured over the head. When infant baptisms became a norm in Catholic life, baptistries were then made smaller to allow pouring just a little water over the foreheads of the little children brought into the Christian community. Over the centuries, and even to this day, many baptistries have included images of John the Baptist baptizing Jesus. Since the baptism of infusion—pouring water over the head—is still a popular way to baptize infants and adults, many church baptistries are small fonts or basins, several feet tall, located in the front of a church or some place closer to the main altar.

In modern Catholic churches, baptistries are frequently located very close to the sanctuary and main altar because baptisms are now frequently celebrated during Mass. The church thus wishes to emphasize the close union between baptism and Eucharist, two of the sacraments of initiation. Baptisms within Sunday Mass are meant to remind worshipers that every Sunday is a time for spiritual rebirth and renewal in Jesus, a little Easter, for all Christians.

(See also Altar, Baptism, and Sacristy.)

BEATITUDES   are spiritual guidelines, or ways of life, by which one develops the basic attitudes necessary to live an authentic Christian life. The Beatitudes can be found in Matthew 5 and in Luke 6. They introduce the Sermon on the Mount passage spoken by Jesus in the gospel of Matthew. The beatitudes indicate how human beings should deal with troubles such as poverty, hunger, sorrow, and oppression in order to become blessed—worthy of life in the reign of God. "Beatitude" traces to Latin and French roots that refer to "blessed" and "happiness."

The beatitude is a literary device found in both the Hebrew and the Christian Scriptures. Beatitudes are referred to over 25 times in the book of Psalms and other Old Testament volumes. The best known biblical beatitudes however can be located in Matthew 5:3–11 and Luke 6:20–22. The New Testament beatitudes identify how to work toward Christian perfection and eternal happiness in the kingdom of the Creator.

The church teaches that Christians who live according to the beatitudes of Jesus are persons guided by his loving Spirit. Those who would live the beatitudes must be willing to serve the sick, the poor, and the unfortunate, as Jesus did. See pages 267-268 for Matthew's list of beatitudes. Luke's are as follows: Blessed are you when they insult you and persecute you and utter every kind of slander against you because of me. Be glad and rejoice, for your reward is great in heaven; they persecuted the prophets before you in the very same way.

(See also Humility, Morality, Option for the Poor, Reign of God, and Works of Mercy.)

BENEDICTION OF THE BLESSED SACRAMENT is a short ceremony in which the Eucharist (in the form of a large consecrated host) is venerated by Catholic church members. During the benediction ceremony, the host is usually placed in a gold container called a monstrance and placed in a location on or near the main church altar for all gathered to see. The assembly generally sings hymns and says special prayers during the benediction. The presbyter who presides at Catholic benediction then blesses the whole assembly with the monstrance.

This devotional practice dates back to the 1400s. It was rooted, originally, in a spiritual desire felt by Catholics to have the Eucharist (the blessed sacrament) displayed to them on important Catholic feasts, such as the feast of Corpus Christi. Despite its long history, benediction was not recognized as an official liturgical activity in the church until 1958.

Benediction developed to enrich the spiritual lives of church members in a time different from the present era. It is not to be regarded today in any way as a substitute for the eucharistic liturgy or for reception of the Eucharist during Mass. Since the early 1960s the practice of celebrating benediction in local Catholic parishes and elsewhere has declined to a great degree. In 1973, the Vatican noted that an extended period of exposition of the Eucharist—to enhance the devotional and prayer lives of parishioners—should be provided in local faith communities once a year. "Shorter expositions of the Eucharist (benediction) are to be arranged in such a way that. . . readings of the word of God, songs, prayers, and a period of silent prayer" regularly can be incorporated easily into the devotional ceremony.

(See also Eucharist, Devotion, Forty Hours Devotion, and Worship.)

BIBLE is a collection of 73 books that were written by numerous authors who were inspired by God. The word is derived from the Greek *biblia*, meaning "books." The Bible is often referred to as the Word of God or sacred Scripture. More copies of the Bible have been printed, purchased, and read than of any other book in history.

The first and longest part of the Bible is called the Hebrew Scriptures, commonly called the Old Testament by Christians. The Hebrew Scriptures reveal how humanity came to know the one true God. It was composed over many hundreds of years while the Hebrews, the chosen people of Yahweh, awaited the coming of a messiah and savior promised by God. There are 46 books in the Old Testament.

The second major portion of the Bible is called the Christian Scriptures, or the New Testament. The New Testament is composed of 27 books that were written between the year 55 and the early 100s c.e. The Christian Scriptures were written in Greek (whereas the Hebrew Scriptures were written mostly in Hebrew), and center on the life, death, and resurrection of Jesus of Nazareth and on the early community of his followers whose mission was to preach and spread Jesus' good news of salvation to all humanity.

Catholics believe the Bible is God's sacred and inspired word. God guided human writers to communicate important truths about Godself and about the destiny of the entire human community through biblical texts. Many of the teachings of the Catholic Christian community are directly based upon the content of the Bible. Two encyclicals key to understanding the church's position on the reading, use, and interpretation of the Scriptures are *Providentissiumus deus*, by Pope Leo XIII, and *Divino afflante spiritu*, by Pius XII. In 1993, while marking the anniversaries of the publication of these documents, Pope John Paul II noted that the entire church community must encourage the continuing study of the Bible. He added, "Biblical thought must be constantly translated into contemporary language so that it can be expressed in a way suited to its listeners." Catholics, said John Paul II, should be urged to read and reflect on God's Word in the Bible every day.

(See also Bible, Books of; Exegesis; Inspiration; and Revelation.)

BIBLE, BOOKS OF   There are 73 books in the Bible—46 in the Hebrew Scriptures (Old Testament) and 27 in the Christian Scriptures (New Testament). In the 16th century, during the Council of Trent, church leaders made the critical decision about which books should be included in the official Catholic canon of the Bible. The following books are those included in the Old and New Testaments. (The common abbreviation of each book is in parentheses.)

Hebrew Scriptures

The Pentateuch: Genesis (Gn), Exodus (Ex), Leviticus (Lv), Numbers (Nm), Deuteronomy (Dt).

Historical Books: Joshua (Jos), Judges (Jgs), 1 Samuel (1 Sm), 2 Samuel (2 Sm), 1 Kings (1 Kgs), 2 Kings (2 Kgs), 1 Chronicles (1 Chr), 2 Chronicles (2 Chr), Ruth (Ru), Ezra (Ezr), Nehemiah (Neh), Tobit (Tb), Judith (Jdt), Esther (Est), 1 Maccabees (1 Mc), and 2 Maccabees (2 Mc).

The Prophets: Isaiah (Is), Jeremiah (Jer), Ezekiel (Ez), Lamentations (Lam), Baruch (Bar), Daniel (Dn), Hosea (Hos), Joel (Jl), Amos (Am), Obadiah (Ob), Jonah (Jon), Micah (Mi), Nahum (Na), Habakkuk (Hb), Zephaniah (Zep), Haggai (Hg), Zechariah (Zec), Malachi (Mal).

Wisdom Books: Job (Jb), Psalms (Ps), Proverbs (Prv), Ecclesiastes (Eccl), Song of Songs (Sg), Wisdom (Wis), Sirach (Sir).

Matthew (Mt), Mark (Mk), Luke (Lk), John (Jn), Acts of the Apostles (Acts), Romans (Rom), 1 Corinthians (1 Cor), 2 Corinthians (2 Cor), Galatians (Gal), Ephesians (Eph), Philippians (Phil), Colossians (Col), 1 Thessalonians (1 Thes), 2 Thessalonians (2 Thes), 1 Timothy (1 Tim), 2 Timothy (2 Tim), Titus (Ti), Philemon (Phlm), Hebrews (Heb), James (Jas), 1 Peter (1 Pt), 2 Peter (2 Pt), 1 John (1 Jn), 2 John (2 Jn), 3 John (3 Jn), Jude (Jude), Revelation (Rv).

(See also Exegesis, Inspiration, New Testament, and Old Testament.)

BIRTH CONTROL/CONTRACEPTION is any method used to prevent women from conceiving or from bearing children. Common types of birth control are artificial contraceptives, abortion, the rhythm method, and not having sexual intercourse at all. Official Catholic teaching has long seen the latter two methods as the chief acceptable forms of birth control. However, the use of contraceptives such as "the pill," is permitted for a number of special medical reasons.

Birth control is practiced today by couples and individuals for economic, social, population control, medical, and religious reasons. Early church community leaders believed that the prime purpose of sex in marriage was procreation (i.e., having children). The church has long held that using illicit means of birth control is a serious moral error. Many popes, such as Gregory IX, Pius XI, and Pius XII, have noted the evils of disapproved forms of birth control and contraception.

Current theological thought about marriage, which has developed much over recent decades, accepts two prime reasons for sex in marriage: 1) the sharing of one's whole self in love with one's marriage partner, and 2) procreation. Sexual acts, according to recent thinking, have special value for humans, which go far beyond procreation issues. Some Catholics have argued in recent years that various uses of the rhythm method of birth regulation, and abstinence from sex altogether for sound moral reasons, can show signs of mature, thoughtful parenting in today's world.

In 1964 Paul VI began a study of contraception issues with respect to Catholic tradition. This church-sponsored study culminated with the publication of the document *Humanae vitae* in July 1968. Through this document, the pope held that all sexual acts must be open to conception. *Humanae vitae* added that Catholics could only use the rhythm method or abstinence methods for birth control purposes. The church has urged every Catholic to study and assent to this teaching. Over the years, however, many Catholics have not been able to accept and follow the teachings of the church on birth control and contraceptive issues.

Since the 1960s, the church has called members of the global Catholic body to remember that each has a serious duty to reflect and pray in good conscience before deciding to make use of birth control methods that are counter to official positions of the church's leadership. In June 1993, Pope John Paul II acknowledged that church teaching on birth control is very difficult for many Catholics to follow. He claimed that one key reason for this is "inadequate and insufficient explanation" of Catholic doctrine on the matter by church leaders. John Paul has recently urged all bishops to promote teaching on contraception issues in catechetical and pastoral programs before and after marriage. Such efforts, he has said, will help the church defend and preserve the "sacred reality" of the family in today's world.

(See also Abortion; Church, as Home; Family Ministry; and Morality.)

Note of Interest: Regarding natural family planning, Catholic family life programs have, for several decades, advocated the use of natural family planning methods. The Vatican has recently held that both church and governments throughout the world should increase efforts to promote natural family planning because its approaches are basically reliable, safe, and morally correct when it comes to both avoiding and achieving actual pregnancies. In 1993, the Pontifical Council for the Family noted that the Catholic community as a whole should be thanked because it has consistently and strongly encouraged couples all over the world to strive for responsible parenthood through the use of "natural methods of regulating fertility."

BISHOP   is the usual ordained leader of a local church community and territory called a diocese. The bishop serves as the chief spiritual leader and head presbyter of a diocese. The word is derived from the Greek *episkopos*, which means "one who is an overseer." The church community holds that all bishops are the true successors of the apostles of Jesus. The college of bishops (i.e., all bishops in union with the pope, the bishop of Rome) works in unity (collegially) to teach, guide, serve, and pastorally care for the church worldwide.

In the early church, various persons with various gifts for ministry were recognized as leaders and vicars in their local communities because (at first) they had actually been appointed by the original apostles or (later) because their local communities had carefully chosen them to act as pastoral overseers. Soon, however, local churches were led by one male overseer only—what we today call a bishop. Whenever issues and concerns arose that affected a number of churches in different parts of the Christian world, bishops gathered for meetings, now known as synods and councils, which were designed to guide and direct church members.

For a long time, local bishops were selected by people in their individual communities. In succeeding centuries, however, it became the pope's task (which is how it remains today) to select and appoint bishops to dioceses around the globe. The pope alone calls others to the episcopate because, according to long-held Catholic tradition, he is the "supreme visible bond of communion (worldwide) among the particular churches" in the one global church community. The *Catechism of the Catholic Church* refers to bishops as having achieved "the fullness of the sacrament of order." Vatican II maintained that a priest who becomes a bishop receives a "fullness of power which in both the liturgical practice of the church and the language of the (church's) fathers is called the high priesthood, the summit of sacred ministry."

The bishop usually is the proper, ordinary, and immediate pastor of a diocese. A bishop, therefore, is sometimes referred to by Catholics as the "ordinary" of a diocese. When other bishops are appointed to help an ordinary lead and serve a diocese, these other bishops are given the title of auxiliary bishop. Catholic bishops are expected to care for their individual dioceses, yet each is also called to work as a partner with other bishops to guide and care for the church on regional, national, and global levels. Each bishop becomes a part of the worldwide college of bishops which—in union with the pope—leads and serves the church universal. Catholics trust that bishops are the authentic successors of the apostles. Thus they are to be seen by Catholics as true teachers, leaders, guides, and shepherds who oversee the flock of the faith community.

Church tradition stresses that bishops should exercise their power as people of service among the people of God. Therefore, some of the chief duties of Catholic bishops today—in addition to watching out for the overall welfare of their dioceses—include preaching the gospel, instructing the faithful, presiding at liturgies, helping those who are needy, ordaining priests, and participating in the ordinations of other bishops.

(See also Apostles, Apostolic Succession, Collegiality, Diocese, and Order.)

Note of Interest: The Catholic bishops in the United States belong to the National Conference of Catholic Bishops (NCCB). This conference or body of bishops was established in 1966 and soon after received the approval of the Vatican. The roots of the NCCB lie in annual meetings of U.S. bishops begun by Benedict XV in 1919. The entire body of bishop-members of the NCCB today gathers twice a year for meetings and discussions. All bishops who serve in the United States and its territories have voting rights and membership in the NCCB. Vatican II's document on the pastoral office of bishops envisioned conferences such as the NCCB when it called for "a council in which the bishops of a given nation or territory jointly exercise their pastoral office to promote the greater good of the church...especially through the forms and methods of the apostolate adapted fittingly to the circumstances of the age." The NCCB is the parent organization of the United States Catholic Conference, which is headquartered in Washington, D.C.

C

CANDLES are used during celebrations of the Eucharist and other church rituals as signs of the presence of the Spirit of Jesus. They are also meant to remind Catholics of the life of grace shared by humanity. Candles lend a sense of dignity and holiness to the activities taking place during church worship. Candles are never used by the Catholic community simply as a substitute for other kinds of light. "Candle" comes from Latin and Middle English roots referring to "light, torch, and shine."

The earliest members of gospel-based communities often burned candles during funeral services and at the graves of martyrs. St. Jerome believed that candles were signs of the joy in Christ shared by all church members. By the 7th century, Christians were using lighted candles in processions during the Eucharist. During the 11th century, burning candles were placed on altars for Mass on a regular basis. In the 1600s the church decreed that some candles must be burning near the altar during every celebration of the Eucharist. Officially speaking, candles are considered sacramentals of the Catholic community.

(See also Altar, Paschal Candle, Sacramentals, and Vigil Lights.)

CANONIZATION is the process by which the church declares officially that a person who has died is in heaven and should be honored as a saint. Thus, the church declares that the person canonized either died a martyr for the faith or lived a life of heroic Christian witness worthy of imitation by all. Before a Catholic canonization can take place, the church must conduct a thorough study of the potential saint's life and personal faith history. A potential canonization is first declared blessed, then beatified, and finally canonized.

Honoring martyrs at the sites of their graves during joyous ceremonies was a common practice among early followers of Jesus of Nazareth. Non-martyrs and other heroic Christian witnesses who had died, such as Martin of Tours, were being venerated as saints by the late 300s. Since many people were thought to be worthy of sainthood by the 10th century, the church initiated an official recognition (canonization) process for them. The first person officially canonized by the Catholic community was Saint Ulrich, named a saint by Pope John XV in 993.

In 1588 Sixtus V asked a special commission to study the lives of holy men and women who had died and to advise him as to which of them should be officially named saints of the church. A form of this study group still exists in the church and still advises the pope on matters related to beatifications and canonizations. It is now called the Congregation for the Causes of Saints and is headquartered in Rome at the offices of the Holy See. Since the time of Leo XIII (the late 1800s), hundreds of individuals have been beatified and officially canonized by the church. The complete listing of "blessed" persons and saints is maintained and kept current by the Vatican in the book of Roman Martyrology. Some persons who lived and died in or near the United States and who have been canonized in recent years include Elizabeth Ann Seton, Frances Cabrini, and John Neumann, and some Jesuits martyred in North America.

The church holds that all persons who have died and have then entered the happiness of heaven are saints—not just those who have been officially canonized by the Catholic community. During the period 1982–1994, Pope John Paul II canonized dozens of saints and declared many other deceased persons as beatified. The proper veneration of saints honored through the canonization process and other saints in heaven is formally discussed in the Code of Canon Law, canons 1186–1187.

(See also Heaven; Martyr; Saints, Communion of; Witness; and Veneration.)

CANON LAW   is a body of rules or norms drawn up for the correct administration and government of all Catholic church matters. The term "canon" is based on an Egyptian word that refers to a measuring tool. The official volume of canon law is called the Code of Canon Law. The current Code contains 1752 canons (official rules) by which the church community is to be guided. This volume is divided into seven books: 1) general norms, 2) the people of God, 3) the teaching office of the church, 4) the office of sanctifying in the church, 5) temporal goods of the church, 6) sanctions in the church, and 7) processes related to marriage tribunals and annulment procedures.

During the early Middle Ages, church rules were called the canonical order. By the 12th century such rules were known as sacred canons. The first person to fully study the complete history of canon law was Ludovicus Thomassinus, a 17th-century priest. In all, therefore, the Catholic community's ability to do a thorough, scholarly study of canon law is a fairly recent development. In the year 1904 Pius X indicated his opinion that the church needed an official and new codification of all its rules. A group of cardinals, bishops, special consultants, and university professors worked on this huge project. By 1914 they had finished most of their work. The new Code was later presented to Catholics worldwide by Benedict XV. This Code of Canon Law went into effect on Pentecost Sunday, 1918.

In 1963 Pope John XXIII appointed a group of 29 cardinals to study ways to revise the church's canon law. The resulting revised Code of Canon Law became effective twenty years later on November 27, 1983. (This Code is for church members under the Roman rite only. A separate code of canons for Eastern Catholics has been in effect since 1991.) The revised Code serves as the official guidebook for the orderly, pastoral administration of all church affairs. An office of the Holy See—known as the Pontifical Commission for the Interpretation of Legislative Texts—is officially responsible for helping bishops, presbyters, and other church members interpret and understand the universal laws of the Catholic community found in the Code.

Current thinking maintains that canon law helps the church overall operate smoothly as a spiritual entity and earthly organization by providing a guide that spells out various rights and duties of church members around the globe. Rules and guidelines are necessary, but guidelines are not always perfect. Thus canon law, in a sense, should be regarded today as a work in progress—something that continually needs to be refined, redefined, and more fully explained and developed.

In 1993, ten years after the most recent official revision of the church's canon laws, a Vatican official noted a church crisis in contemporary times in that so many people do not seem to feel bound to observe the church rules that the Code spells out. He claimed that this makes it difficult for church norms to truly guide the conduct of various Christian individuals and communities. He added that a growing need for democracy in all areas of life and a current spirit of moral relativism in pop culture have sometimes weakened the sense among Catholics and other Christians that canon law should be adhered to faithfully.

(See also Church, Laws of; Holy See; and Magisterium.)

CAPITAL SINS are also known as the seven deadly sins or the seven capital vices. Fundamentally, these are moral weaknesses that can lead to many other situations of sin and significant personal problems if they become habits.

In church history, the capital or deadly sins have been identified as pride, covetousness, lust, anger, gluttony, envy, and sloth. In truth, these human (self-centered) vices are the sources of many types of personal sin; and they give testimony to one's choice(s) not to fully, radically live the Christian ideal of charity, holiness, and virtuous service to humanity.

The Catholic church claims these vices are "deadly" because they can lead to very serious sin and conditions of estrangement from God and others. Pride is the central capital vice, the root of the other deadly vices. It is found to some degree in all forms of personal sinfulness. Catholic tradition also maintains that the seven capital sins are countered by Christian virtues such as humility, simplicity, chastity, meekness, temperance, unselfish love, and diligence.

(See also Holiness, Sin, and Virtue.)

CARDINAL is a member of that select group of bishops who make up the church's college of cardinals. Cardinals act as primary advisers and assistants to the pope. A main duty of the college of cardinals is to elect a new pope whenever necessary. The word comes from the Latin term *cardo*, which means "hinge." Eugene IV said that cardinals are like the hinges on which all church government turns.

The first cardinals were bishops, priests, and deacons in 6th-century Rome who helped elect the popes of that time. The college of cardinals was begun in 1150. During 1179, Pope Alexander III decreed that only a pope could choose men to become cardinals of the church. In 1586, Pope Sixtus V indicated that the church should have a total of 70 cardinals, perhaps a symbol recalling the 70 elders of the Hebrew people from Old Testament times. Paul VI raised this number to 145 in 1973, and John Paul II fixed it at 152 in 1985, but only 120 of these, it was declared, could take part in papal selections. Some present-day cardinals are bishops of large archdioceses around the globe; others are leaders of offices in the Vatican government, known as the Roman Curia or Holy See. The Code of Canon Law published in 1918 stated officially that all cardinals must be ordained presbyters. (Previous to this, there actually had been cardinals in the church who had not experienced the sacrament of order.) John XXIII later ordered that they must also be bishops. This norm is also noted in the current Code of Canon Law.

A three-step process is used for creating a cardinal. First, a bishop is named by the pope at a secret consistory. Then, this bishop is told about his appointment in an official biglietto (a notice) from the Vatican. Finally, during a special liturgy, the new cardinal celebrates the Eucharist with the college of cardinals in Rome. In 1971 it was decreed by Paul VI that all cardinals who reach the age of 80 must retire. They, therefore, can no longer participate in selections of popes, but they do remain members of the sacred college. Those who work in Curia departments in Rome must retire from office at the age of 75.

(See also Bishop, Holy See, Order, and Pope.)

Notes of Interest: 1) one deacon has been named a cardinal of the church. His name was Giacomo Antonelli, a Vatican secretary of state under Pius IX. Antonelli died in 1876. 2) Sometimes a cardinal is chosen by the pope in pectore (or in petto), which means the public is not informed of the choice for particular reasons. Some think that Pope John Paul II declared a Chinese bishop a cardinal in pectore late in 1979.

CATECHESIS   is a term derived from the Greek *katechein*, which means to "re-sound" or "re-echo." It also refers to an "oral teaching." Catechesis is a form of the church's ministry of the word and a key element in the Christian community's mission of evangelization.

True catechesis is much more than merely instruction about Catholic Christian beliefs, values, and practices. It is instruction of others plus a personal sharing of faith by committed Christians so that the entire people of God may be continually converted to a fully Christian life—that is, a life turned away from sinfulness, centered on the risen Jesus, and living in hope for the everlasting reign of God.

"Catechesis" (in its Greek form) appears in the Christian Scriptures six times. Its use indicates a type of oral witness about faith in Jesus of Nazareth and his gospel. In the very first communities of Jesus' followers, catechesis was used to prepare adults for initiation into the community of believers through baptism and the Eucharist. These adults made up the original "catechumenates" of Christianity. It is quite likely that catechesis continued once catechumens had become full church members. This post-baptismal, catechetical activity was called *mystagogia*—pondering the great mysteries of gospel faith.

When the catechumenate process basically disappeared in succeeding centuries, prior to the onset of the Middle Ages, the word catechesis was practically lost to Christian communities. At the time of the Protestant Reformation (16th century), a form of catechesis returned in the word catechism. Catechisms were books used by church leaders to educate children, youth, and adult inquirers (converts) about the teachings, rules, and practices of the church. For about four centuries (mid-1500s to mid-1900s), the Catholic catechism remained the primary tool for the religious instruction of the church community. Two famous catechisms produced by the official church were the Roman Catechism (first issued by Pope Pius V in 1566) and the later Baltimore Catechism, produced in the United States during the late 1800s. By the early 20th century a number of church leaders had begun to consider newer and better techniques for catechizing others. After Vatican II (1962–1965) and the 1977 international synod of bishops, the word catechesis once again became a familiar term for Catholics.

Vatican II called for fresh approaches, methods, materials, etc., for use in contemporary catechesis. It commissioned the writing of a General Catechetical Directory, which appeared in 1971, to help catechists around the world. In 1979 the Catholic bishops of the United States published a national catechetical directory, called Sharing the Light of Faith, which offered principles, guidelines, and ideas for catechists. More recently, the Vatican has produced a basic text designed to help local conferences of bishops to prepare culturally-appropriate, doctrinally-sound catechisms for modern believers and inquirers, in accord with canon 775 of the Code of Canon Law. This universal document is known today as the *Catechism of the Catholic Church*.

Authentic catechesis shares the whole message of Christianity—the basics of the Word plus the doctrines and values in church tradition—with others. Catechesis, therefore, must be centered on the message and values of Jesus. It is aimed at all members of the church—adults, youth, and children alike—to help deepen and mature their faith. Catechesis is the responsibility of every church member, and should be ongoing and lifelong.

In many places Catholics who serve as catechists receive special kinds of formation and updating in their teaching skills and theological knowledge to help prepare them for their ministry. Many parishes have persons who direct or coordinate the catechetical activities of their local communities. Today these ministers are often called directors of religious education (DREs), coordinators of religious education (CREs), and ministers of Christian formation.

The Code of Canon Law indicates that "parents above others are obliged to form their children in the faith," but it is the "serious duty, especially on the part of pastors of souls, to provide for the catechesis of the Christian people" so that the practice of the faith among the faithful "becomes living, explicit, and productive through formation in doctrine and the experience of Christian living." Church guidelines pertaining to catechetical formation for all inquirers and church members can be found in the Code, canons 773–780.

(See also Catechism of the Catholic Church; Church, Laws of; Confraternity of Christian Doctrine; Evangelization; Faith; and Witness.)

Note of Interest: Soon after the release of his landmark statement on Catholic catechesis, *Catechesi tradendae,* Pope John Paul II noted in 1981 that the "effectiveness of catechesis will depend largely on (our) capacity to give a Christian meaning to everything that makes up (human) life in this time." The pope has emphasized since then the significance of catechesis in families, parishes, schools, and through the use of mass media. He has added that the living Christian witness of modern catechists must match their proficiency and skills in teaching church doctrines and values.

CATECHISM OF THE CATHOLIC CHURCH is a recently published official church volume meant to be, in the words of Pope John Paul II, a foundational "sure and authentic reference text for teaching Catholic doctrine and preparing local [national-level] catechisms." In addition, the new universal Catholic catechism has been designed to show the full content and harmony of all the elements of Christian faith, to aid anyone who simply wishes to deepen his or her knowledge of Catholicism, to support ecumenical efforts, to explain the essential beliefs and hopes of Catholic tradition, and to assist national bodies of bishops in writing various catechisms adapted to cultural, socio-economic, and technological concerns in their own countries. The word "catechism" derives from Greek roots meaning "re-echo" and "to instruct."

The new Catechism is the first such universal text published since the Roman Catechism, produced under the direction of Pius V in 1566, soon after the Reformation and the church's Council of Trent. In 1985, an international synod of bishops celebrated the 20th anniversary of Vatican II, reflected on its teachings, and said "many have expressed the desire that a catechism or compendium of all Catholic doctrine regarding faith and morals be composed...[as] a point of reference," for Christians worldwide, "suited to the present life of Christians." In 1986, John Paul II commissioned 12 cardinals and bishops to prepare a draft of this new reference catechism. This Vatican commission was assisted by a larger, diverse-interest editorial committee, which actually wrote the nine subsequent drafts of the catechism text. By 1992, over 24,000 recommendations and critical observations from worldwide consultations had been incorporated into the final version of the new universal catechism. The official text was approved in June 1992. The English edition became available in June 1994.

Some commentators have expressed great concern about the catechism project as a whole. They ask how anyone could faithfully adapt a single, universal catechism (a uniform presentation of Catholic doctrines, values, and practices) to the diverse needs, cultural issues, languages, particular spiritual questions, and other signs of the times among the global people of God in a wide variety of human cultures, especially in the United States, given what some criticize as an emerging and influential U.S. "cultural Catholicism."

The official *Catechism of the Catholic Church*, six years in the making, is intended as a general use reference text. It is also a source book that bishops' groups can use to draft culturally-adapted local catechetical texts on Catholic doctrine. In 1993, John Paul II urged pastors, catechists, parents, and others to receive it as an aid to their mission to proclaim Christian teachings and gospel values.

(See also Baltimore Catechism, Catechesis, Deposit of Faith, Doctrine, and Magisterium.)

CATECHUMENATE AND THE RCIA   is a faith-formation process, implemented in a local parish over an extended period of time, that helps persons who wish to become members of the Catholic community to journey spiritually toward full initiation into the church. The Rite of Christian Initiation of Adults (RCIA) is focused on those who seek to become Christian through reception of the sacrament of baptism, confirmation, and Eucharist. These individuals are typically called "catechumens." Yet a similar multi-step, extended faith-formation process is often used to help those already baptized, but not catechized, to come into full communion with the Catholic community through confirmation and the Eucharist. Such persons are often referred to as "candidates."

The catechumenate process aims specifically at the Christian initiation of individuals and the ongoing faith growth of the local community that sponsors them. It seeks to guide all who wish to follow Jesus and the gospel today toward an active and prayerful participation in the church community overall and to challenge them, in a spiritually inviting way, to be faith-filled witnesses to the risen Lord. The term "catechumenate" has roots similar to the word catechesis. Both derive from the Greek *katechein*, which basically refers to "instruct orally."

A catechumenate process, similar to what we have today, seems to have evolved in the Christian community from the 2nd to the 5th centuries for the initiation of new members into the body of Christ. Soon after this, however, use of the process gradually declined. Through the centuries, for various reasons, the baptism of infants and the confirmation of children and young adolescents became prevailing practices in the Western church, and thus the significant conversion-centered process of Christian initiation for adults and older youth was not much emphasized.

Vatican II called for a full restoration and renewal of the catechumenate process. Given the spiritually challenging and changing circumstances in human cultures around the globe, said the council, individuals and communities could benefit much from a challenging, gospel-oriented call to conversion and the support available in Christian community life. In 1972 the Rite of Christian Initiation of Adults (RCIA) was published by the Vatican. An edition adapted and approved for use in the United States became mandatory in 1988.

The RCIA outlines four basic stages (or phases) that can lead maturing persons (e.g., adults and adolescents) toward full initiation into the community of the baptized. The rituals celebrated during the catechumenate period are designed to help the faith community (those already baptized) rediscover the gospel and the Spirit of God working in and through the catechumens and candidates and the Christian body as a whole. The RCIA, therefore, is aimed at helping all members of the community of Jesus to experience authentic spiritual renewal and deeper commitment to the gospel's call to ongoing Christian conversion and Christian values.

The spiritual-formation stages or steps in the RCIA are known as:

1) Inquiry. Individuals seek out a local faith community to learn about becoming a follower of the Catholic Christian way. They are welcomed by the community and begin a period of evangelization and basic catechetical instruction.

2) Catechumenate. Catechumens and candidates learn more about Christian life and values over an extended period of time. The catechumenate phase, therefore, centers on additional catechetical instruction, growth in knowledge about church laws and norms, progressive forms of spiritual formation, and the call to deepening Christian conversion. This period is marked particularly by the rite of election.

3) Enlightenment (Illumination). Catechumens and candidates engage in a spiritually-challenging period of faith growth designed to lead them to the sacraments of initiation. This period is characterized particularly by rituals known as "the scrutinies" and the final choice to enter full communion with the Catholic church. The enlightenment phase generally begins as the season of Lent begins and culminates with baptism, confirmation, and Eucharist at the Easter Vigil.

4) Mystagogy. This term often is roughly equated to post-baptismal catechesis. Yet the mystagogy phase of the overall catechumenal (RCIA) process is actually focused on helping the newly initiated to observe the Easter season and the other liturgical seasons of the church on an ongoing basis, on urging them to participate in Christian service and ministries, and on their ongoing catechetical formation.

Catholics believe that pastoral implementation of the catechumenate in local church communities can prove to be a prime time for catechesis and spiritual formation for all adults and families in the parish too. At the Easter Vigil, the presbyter who baptizes a catechumen should likewise administer the sacrament of confirmation. In some cases, for candidates for full reception into the church, a "conditional baptism" can be offered to them in cases in which there is reason to doubt the validity of their original baptism.

The Rite of Christian Initiation of Adults provides guidelines for the Christian formation and initiation of children of catechetical age into the church. This approach to the basic initiation process is sometimes referred to today as the RCIC—Rite of Christian Initiation of Children.

(See also Baptism, Catechesis, Confirmation, Conversion, Election, Godparents, and Inquiry.)

Note of Interest: The *Catechism of the Catholic Church* summarizes the basics of church doctrine on Christian initiation in articles 1229–1233. It says that from the time of the original apostles and disciples of Jesus, becoming a Christian has been accomplished by a journey through several stages of initiation. This journey, the Catechism concludes, can be accomplished quickly or more slowly, yet certain essential elements must always be integral parts of it: proclamation of God's Word, acceptance of the gospel and the call to Christian conversion, a profession of Christian faith, baptism in the Spirit, and access to the other sacraments of initiation (article 1229).

CATHOLIC   is a term with Greek roots meaning "universal" or "general." Usually it is employed today to describe a member of the Roman Catholic church or to describe the worldwide church community itself. Catholic Christian faith is an expression of the new people of God, the universal Christian church. Catholic peoples believe they share in God's love, mercy, forgiveness, and other gifts through the life, death, and resurrection of Jesus of Nazareth.

The earliest members of the Christian community, after much debate, realized that the followers of the risen Jesus on Earth must be inclusive and must reach out to all types of people, all cultures, and all levels of human society. Early church leaders eventually used "catholic" to describe the Christian community overall and the individual members of it. Church elders later used catholic as a term to separate the authentic (faithful) Christian community from heretical groups. In the 4th century, a Spanish bishop, St. Paciamus, claimed, "Christian is my name, Catholic is my surname."

The notion of a church that is catholic expresses the belief that the community of Jesus' followers is missionary at its heart. "Catholicism" acknowledges that the gospel of Jesus should be shared with all persons and cultures, in all times, and Christian love and service must be offered to the human community in all locales. Therefore, true catholicity in the world is a Christian goal or ideal still to be realized. The church community is a reality in progress, in the state of becoming.

Contemporary thinkers remind us that the Spirit of God is at work in the many efforts of the Catholic community and its ministers. Yet, this Spirit expresses itself dynamically through many other non-Catholic, even non-Christian individuals, cultures, and religions around the world. The church must learn how to better discern the insights, spiritual gifts, and talents that non-Catholic and Catholic individuals alike have to offer to the Catholic community to help in the enduring mission to proclaim the good news of Jesus to all and to seek perfect Christian (worldwide) holiness.

The Catholic church strives to be a universal spiritual family, a religious home for any and all who seek the wisdom and way of Christianity. It continues to reach out around the globe—to all peoples and nations—convinced that this urgent mission to be "good news" and reform the created order was entrusted to the apostles and the whole Christian body by Jesus himself (Mark 16:15, Matthew 28:19–20). Vatican II taught that the "one true religion subsists in the catholic and apostolic church," yet holiness and great wisdom from God's Spirit can be revealed—and must be heeded wherever it can be found—in individuals, cultures, other Christian communities, and non-Christian communities alike.

Catholics believe that there is a unique Catholic Christian identity. In the Catholic way, there are certain doctrines, traditions, moral codes, spiritual practices, and sacramental rituals not honored in other Christian congregations. The recent *Catechism of the Catholic Church* maintains that the term catholic genuinely applies to those united in their hearts to the universal Catholic church through the bonds of profession of the creed, celebration of the seven sacraments, and acceptance of the church's apostolic succession and means of governance.

(See also Apostolic Succession, Ecclesiology, Evangelization, and People of God.)

CATHOLIC-JEWISH RELATIONS   In the past thirty years or so, the Catholic community has officially produced a number of important statements about contemporary Catholic-Jewish relations and has participated in some key dialogues and projects with the world's Jewish community. The Second Vatican Council explored this topic in some detail with its 1965 document called Declaration on the Relationship of the Church to Non-Christian Religions. Vatican II noted that there are special spiritual bonds between the new people of God (the Christian community around the globe) and the chosen people of Yahweh, the descendants of Abraham (the worldwide Jewish community). The beginnings of Christian faithfulness to God can be traced to certain patriarchs and prophets of the Hebrew people. The Catholic community teaches that it awaits, in a spirit of hope, the day when all peoples, including the Jewish community, will address the Creator of all with a single voice and will seek to do God's will in concert.

The church urges all of its members to strictly avoid all forms of anti-Semitism (discrimination, hatred, persecution, harassment) directed at Jewish individuals and communities. The church has proclaimed that the Jewish people of today—and the Jews from centuries past—are in no way cursed by God nor are they to be blamed in any manner for the suffering and death of Jesus of Nazareth.

The Catholic bishops of the United States set up a secretariat for Catholic-Jewish relations, in Washington, D.C., in 1967. In 1985 its chief aims were updated to say, "The general purposes of all Catholic-Jewish meetings (and relationships) is to increase our understanding of both Judaism and the Catholic faith, to eliminate sources of tension and misunderstanding, to initiate dialogue or conversation on different levels, to multiply intergroup meetings between Catholics and Jews, and to promote cooperative social action." A Vatican commission, now called the Commission on Religious Relations with Jews, was begun in 1974 by Pope Paul VI. Also, about that time, the Catholic bishops of the United States seriously urged all local Catholic communities to study Paul's writings in Romans 9 and 11 in order to better understand the Jewish community's deep relationship with God, its spiritual bonds to the Christian community, and its love for its cherished homeland. In 1987 Pope John Paul II noted that the many historical "sufferings endured by the Jews are also for the Catholic church a motive for sincere sorrow, especially when one thinks of the indifference and sometimes resentment which...have divided Jews and Christians" through the centuries. Earlier, in 1986, John Paul had acknowledged and reaffirmed that God's great covenant relationship with the Jewish community is "irrevocable" in a way that shows clearly that the "Jewish religion is not extrinsic to (Christianity), but in a certain way is intrinsic to our own religion. With Judaism, therefore, we have a relationship which we do not have with any other religion."

(See Anti-Semitism, Hebrews, Judaism, and Zionism.)

C.E.   is a reference to the phrase "of the common era." It is often used today in place of a.d. *(anno domini)*—which means in the year of the Lord. The modern parallel to c.e. is b.c.e., or "before the common era." It replaces in many cases the more traditional b.c.—before Christ. The references c.e. and b.c.e. are now frequently found in educational, catechetical, and other contemporary texts. Essentially they sensitively acknowledge that the traditional b.c. and a.d. references are Christian in origin. Because Western society is a more multicultural and diverse religious environment today than ever before—with many non-Christian individuals and communities present, e.g., Muslims, Jews, Buddhists—the more common b.c.e. and c.e. are used.

CELIBACY   is the voluntary state of remaining unmarried and of abstaining from sexual intercourse. Church law demands that presbyters remain unmarried and celibate. Members of religious orders are also expected to be celibates. The term comes from the Latin *caelibatus*, that is, to live the single life.

Celibacy has been freely chosen and practiced by some Christians since the earliest days of church life. By the 4th century a number of priests were required by church rules in Europe to remain celibate. In 1139 the Second Lateran Council taught that marriage was forbidden for anyone who received the sacrament of order. During the 16th century, with the Council of Trent, definitive church teachings on the religious discipline of celibacy were formulated. These teachings are still basically followed by various members of the Catholic community worldwide.

In recent times, there has been much discussion, even some heated debates, over the church's official celibacy laws. These dialogues have frequently centered on the real purpose of and the debatable necessity of celibacy in the modern age. A number of church critics have argued that celibacy can and should be optional in some cases, for presbyters in particular. Vatican II stated that celibacy is a precious gift that should be held in high esteem by the entire people of God. It reminded church members that it takes great commitment plus personally chosen self-denial and self-sacrifice to faithfully live a healthy celibate existence. Some thinkers now hold that the church should offer greater spiritual supports and practical assistance to presbyters and also to all who choose to live as celibates in the world today.

The church teaches that celibacy is a sign of faith and hope in the reign of God and a sign of total Christian devotion to the Creator of all. Sometimes church teachers in our time speak of celibacy as a sign of holiness—that is, true commitment to the good news of salvation. Saint Paul identified celibacy as a great spiritual help to those Christians who want to focus their life energies on giving Christian life and hope to others. Though celibacy is a disciplinary requirement of canon law for priests, John Paul II noted in 1992 that it should be seen as more than a church law to be obeyed. He said a choice for celibate life signifies "unconditional acceptance" of presbyteral ministry in a society "no longer marked by Christian values" as a whole. In 1979, John Paul II wrote a letter to all Catholic priests claiming that prayer will help modern presbyters to remain faithful to their commitment to a celibate lifestyle.

The Code of Canon Law details the disciplines associated with the Catholic practice of celibacy among the ordained in canons 247, 277, 291, and 1037. The canon that speaks of celibate lifestyles for members of religious communities is canon 599.

(See also Holiness, Order, Religious Orders, and Vows.)

Note of Interest: On celibacy and the diaconate, church law indicates today that candidates for the sacrament of order may marry before they become permanent deacons—but marriage and remarriage after ordination are forbidden. This is in accord with a church discipline in place since the late 7th century.

CHANT   is a traditional style of music used in Roman Catholic prayer and worship. It is characterized by very elaborate and precise composition. The various sources of Christian chant include Hebrew, Greek, Latin, and Asian music and prayer.

The most primitive Christian chants probably took shape about the time that Roman church rites were established. Pope St. Gregory the Great published a book of chants (the Antiphonal) in the 6th century.

Pope Gregory showed much interest in church music overall, but his relationship to what eventually came to be known as Gregorian Chant seems unclear. The most ancient existing versions of original Gregorian Chant date back to the 800s. Members of the Benedictine religious community began a revival of chant for Christian worship and restored many early music chant texts in the 19th century. This contributed much to the contemporary movement toward renewal of the Christian liturgy.

Chant as it is known today is actually a blend of plainchant, Gregorian chant, and Ambrosian chant. Interestingly, there was a revival of interest in religious chant music in American pop culture in the mid-1990s, especially through the popularity of cassettes and CDs by the Benedictine monks of Spain and the rock-music group Enigma.

(See also Worship.)

CHARISMATICS   are those who live and act in sympathy with a movement known as the Catholic Charismatic Renewal begun in earnest in the U.S. and all over the globe several decades ago. Charismatics are sometimes called Catholic pentecostals—that is, members of a new Catholic pentecostal movement. "Charismatic" has Greek roots *(charis)* that mean "gifted."

The personal, intense experience that many charismatics share is called a "baptism of the Holy Spirit," through which God's Spirit recharges them and fills them with spiritual energy and enthusiasm. This enthusiasm, according to charismatics in the church community, gives some of them one or more special gifts—such as healing of the body or glossolalia (the ability to speak in tongues). Catholic charismatic communities—some small and some large—often meet weekly in groups to pray, sing, share community spirit, and testify about personal faith experiences.

The modern charismatic movement in the U.S. developed a special momentum through the efforts of the Chi-Rho Society of Duquesne University, established in 1967. It soon spread to universities in Michigan and Indiana, and then around the world to over 100 countries. In the late 1970s over 3000 groups were meeting in the U.S. There were about 6,000,000 charismatics throughout the world at that time.

The charismatic movement across the globe has frequently and enthusiastically encouraged renewal of church life through the work of the Holy Spirit. It remains an attempt by some to restore the lively, spirit-filled attitude of the post-Pentecost followers of Jesus to the Catholic community in our day. In 1976 the American bishops gave cautious support to the movement. Pope Paul VI also gave modern charismatics significant support. The enthusiasm, fellowship, love for Jesus and Scripture, sharing of personal gifts, and ecumenical sharing with Protestant Christians—all things characteristic of certain Catholic charismatic communities—can be very helpful to the spiritual lives of individuals. It is important to remember, however, that the church had not lost the Spirit in any way before the beginning of the contemporary charismatic renewal.

The church sees the charismatic renewal movement as an ongoing reminder of our need to rely on the Spirit of the risen Jesus—just as the first disciples did. In March 1992, Pope John Paul II cautioned that charismatic groups should remain in basic cooperation with their local bishops and the Vatican. He praised the movement for its ability to promote a spiritual way of life in the world today. However, John Paul added that "whatever shape the charismatic renewal (in the future) takes—in prayer groups, in covenant communities, in communities of life and service—the sign of its spiritual fruitfulness will always be a strengthening of [its] communion with the universal church and local churches" too.

(See also Pentecost, Trinity.)

CHARITY is one of the three theological virtues. The others are faith and hope. The word traces to the Latin *caritas*, meaning dearness or a high level of affection. In his epistles Paul proclaims that charity is the greatest of all the virtues. This particular virtue enables people to love God and others unselfishly and without condition, as they themselves would want to be loved and deeply cared for.

Over the centuries acts of charity have been performed by Christian individuals and communities in many, many ways. Sharing with the needy or helping those who have problems have been seen as basic ways of being charitable. True Christian charity also includes offering prayers and good deeds for those who have died and have entered purgatory. Christians believe that following Jesus by showing true love for one's "enemies" becomes genuinely possible through the virtue and gift of charity and is, in fact, a radical or counter-cultural sign of Christian charity.

Church members rely on the powerful meditation by Paul in 1 Corinthians 13:4ff. to spiritually grasp and explain the many dimensions and challenges inherent in the practice of Christian love and charity. Love for God, all others, and for oneself in unselfish ways mysteriously can help make the reign of God more present as a living, breathing reality on earth for all humanity. Through charitable acts Christians are called and challenged to make the world a better place for the entire human race and to give themselves freely, as living sacrifices in the image of Jesus of Nazareth, in order to love and help others toward God's reign. True charity is a gift from God received by all Christians at the time of baptism. Willingness to love and serve God and to love, serve, and respect others every day, in the here and now, is an ideal that must be lived by baptized persons in order to journey toward life with the Creator in heaven. Pope John Paul II has stated that acts of Christian charity help the church to meet the real needs of the human race, and especially help many overcome poverty and their physical hungers.

The *Catechism of the Catholic Church* reminds all church members of the timeless words of Jesus—"...abide in my love...[for] this is my commandment, that you love one another as I have loved you" (John 15:9, 12). It then notes that such charity is the source and goal of all Christian witness, words, and deeds. The Catechism also notes that charity's fruits can be seen wherever real joy, peace, and mercies are shared in human relationships and interactions.

(See also Almsgiving, Option for the Poor, Virtue, and Works of Mercy.)

CHRISTIAN UNITY WEEK   is an annual 8-day period, observed January 18–25, during which Christians of various denominations— Catholics and non-Catholics alike—come together in prayer for the restoration of full unity among all Christian peoples of the world.

This observance started with the "Chair of Unity Octave," which began officially in 1908 in the United States. Later, in 1935, Abbé Paul Couturier in France retitled the octave the Week of Prayer for Christian Unity. Couturier hoped that Christians united in prayer and ecumenical spirit would "cause hearts to grow into one another and finally unite minds in the eternal light of the one Christ." The observance of the octave retained a fairly heavy Catholic, "return to the Roman church" flavor prior to Couturier, a theme that alienated many non-Catholic Christians. In 1948, once the World Council of Churches (WCC) was founded, the WCC began to sponsor the Week of Prayer for Christian Unity. During the 1960s, with the publication of the Vatican II Decree on Ecumenism, all Catholics were encouraged to participate in this one, unified observance with other Christians of the world. Some of the barriers and prejudices between Catholics and "separated communities" of other Christians were lessened as a result. By 1966 a standard leaflet for the annual Week of Prayer was being published by the joint working group of the WCC and Catholic community leaders. In the United States, in recent years, the Atonement Friars, at the Graymoor Ecumenical Institute in New York, have prepared Week of Christian Unity annual materials for local Catholic communities.

Vatican II pointed out that separate Christian churches and ecclesial communions remain close to the Catholic church despite various doctrinal and traditional differences. Church leaders and theologians at the Council urged dialogue among church bodies and common prayer wherever and whenever possible. Also, Vatican II asked each individual Christian to strengthen his or her trust in Christ's will for unity among all the baptized and to then undertake the vigorous work of renewal and reform among all Christian individuals, communities, and churches around the globe. In January 1993, a leader of the U.S. bishops' Committee for Ecumenical and Interreligious Affairs said common prayer, joint reflection among all Christians, and the search for full unity in baptism and the Lord "is the quest central to the identity of all…who confess Jesus Christ" as God's Son and the redeemer of the world.

(See also Ecumenism, Prayer, and Reformation.)

CHRISTMAS   is that day of the church year on which the birth of Jesus of Nazareth is celebrated. The Christmas celebration occurs on

December 25, a Catholic solemnity and holy day of obligation. The word is based upon the old English *Christes maesse*, which roughly means the "Mass of Christ."

The Christmas feast has been celebrated by Christians since at least the year 354. Some scholars believe that Christmas was placed on December 25 to offset the pagan influences of a non-Christian winter solstice feast called "birthday of the sun." Other scholars have noted that the date may have a closer connection to the date of Christ's death. In the view of some ancient Christians, Jesus would have died on the same day of the year that he was conceived. March 25 was popularly held as the day of his death and, consequently, of his conception (see reference under Annunciation). In this way of thinking, therefore, exactly nine months from the day of Jesus' conception is December 25.

It is generally accepted today that Jesus the Christ was probably born several years (maybe as many as seven) earlier than our traditional dating process would indicate (see reference under c.e.). The mistake in identifying the actual birth year is probably due to Denis the Small, a 6th-century monk who began the practice of dating events in history "a.d."—*anno domini*—which means "in the year of the Lord."

Christmastide, or the Christmas season, begins for Catholics with a vigil, or evening Mass, on December 24, and it continues until the Sunday following January 6, Epiphany. The final day of Christmastide recalls and honors the baptism of the Lord and the beginning of his public ministry.

The solemnity of Christmas is second in importance only to Easter. Priests are permitted to celebrate three Masses on this day. The custom of having three eucharistic celebrations for Christmas, one for the vigil, one for dawn, and one for the daytime, dates back to Pope Gregory the Great in the 6th century.

(See also Annunciation, Christology, Jesus of Nazareth, and Liturgical Year.)

CHRISTOLOGY   is the study of Jesus Christ: who he was, who he is, his divine and human natures, his mission and ministry to humankind, and his own consciousness of who he was in relation to God the Father. Christology is distinguished from soteriology—which strictly speaking is the theological study of the saving works of the redeemer.

A number of church councils have reflected deeply on the mysteries of the incarnation, on Christology, and on formal declarations about Jesus the Christ. The Council of Nicaea (Nicaea I, 325 c.e.) attacked a heresy by Arius. Arius denied that Jesus was divine. The first Council of Constantinople, held in 381, also attacked Arianism. In 431 the Council of Ephesus upheld belief in the essential unity of the divine and human natures in Jesus. In 451 the Council of Chalcedon, under the leadership of Pope Leo I, condemned the monophysite heresy, which claimed that Jesus had a divine nature but no human nature. Later, Nicaea II (in 787) proclaimed that Jesus really was the Son of God because he had a divine nature rather than because he experienced some mystical form of "adoption" by God.

In recent decades, theologians have frequently referred to a Christology "from above" and a Christology "from below." Christological thinking "from above" first focuses, basically, on the eternal Word of God (the *logos*) in heaven who proceeds to Earth and offers salvation to an alienated, sinful humankind. The theologies of Saints John and Paul, for example, present a "from above" Christology. Christological thinking "from below" centers more on the historical Jesus of Nazareth who through his life and ministry proves that he was sent by the Creator God to reconcile God and humanity and to offer salvation to all persons, all communities, and all cultures in all times. The synoptic gospels largely employ a Christology "from below."

(See also Councils, Christological; Jesus of Nazareth; Jesus, Titles of; Messiah; and Redeemer.)

CHURCH, AS HOME   is a contemporary phrase acknowledging that the Christian family household is the primary cell of the overall church community, the people and "family" of God. A more time-honored Catholic Christian phrase used to express the same idea is that the family is an *ecclesia domestica* (a "domestic church").

The ancient Hebrews saw the family of origin as a force that helped shape the nation of Israel overall and the quality of its community life in particular. The heart of family life was imaged as a covenant-style love between persons. Family relationships thus were seen to be symbolic of the loving relationship between Yahweh (God) and the Hebrew people.

Early followers of Jesus emphasized that families were the key building blocks (or cells) of the spiritual family of God's chosen ones. In a sense, they saw the entire Christian community as the household of God's family. Most primitive Christian gatherings for prayer and "breaking of the bread" (celebration of the Eucharist) occurred in "house churches," with ordinary Christian householders hosting and presiding over the sacred rituals.

In recent decades, Catholic congregations have been actively reclaiming and re-emphasizing the traditional notion of the family household as a "church of the home" and a "church in miniature." In 1981, John Paul II, in his statement, "The Role of the Christian Family in the Modern World," challenged all Christian families—whatever their composition, racial background, or economic and social status—to witness authentically to the gospel of Jesus and to develop "in such a way that...the family is a living image and historical representation of the mystery of the church" itself. In 1987 the bishops of the United States stated that those contemporary families that live in authentic harmony with Catholic tradition reveal God to the wider world and experience a sense of Christian community—thus, they deserve to be called "the domestic church."

(See also Community, Covenant, Family, and People of God.)

CHURCH, IMAGES OF   Numerous images or symbols can be used to describe the reality Christians call church. Each image that is centrally recognized by Catholic communities today develops a particular aspect or element of the mystery of the church community as a whole. Taken together, the many images, symbols, and phrases that can be used to describe the church of Jesus Christ reveal a richness, depth, and diversity in the life shared by the baptized within the global community of Jesus' followers.

In all, Catholic tradition today tends to stress that the church is a mystery. In other words, it is a reality that cannot be fully captured by human thought and words. In a 1963 address to Vatican II attendees, Paul VI noted that the church is a mystery imbued with the hidden presence of the one God. Like Jesus of Nazareth, it is a historical, visible reality on Earth that mysteriously manifests the true presence of the divine. Vatican Council II used numerous images to illustrate things about the church Many of these can be found in the Dogmatic Constitution on the Church, but some are also located in other council documents. The more widely known images of the church include:

People of God. This image refers to the full, global community of church members with Jesus Christ at its head. This new and holy people is a lasting seed of unity, hope, and salvation for the whole human race, sent forth into the whole world as the light of the world and the salt of the earth. The people of God, in Catholic perspectives, is a "new Israel," a sign of the new covenant between God and humankind. (See 1 Peter 2:9–10; Acts 20:28; Matthew 5:13–16; 2 Corinthians 3:6.)

Community. The church is often referred to as a true community of Christ's followers, especially in the celebration of the sacraments and in other communal acts of worship and through living, virtuous witness to Christian values by members of the church.

Mystical Body and Body of Christ. Just as each human being is a part of the entire body of humanity, so each church member is a part, in a mystical manner, of the whole of Christ's body (the church). Since the head of this community, the risen Jesus, is present in the unity of believers, all the members of the church ought to be molded into Christ's image until he is fully formed in them. The Spirit of the risen Jesus vivifies, unifies, and moves the whole body toward greater peace and harmony in many ways. (See 1 Corinthians 12:12–13, 27–30; Colossians 3:15; Ephesians 4:4, 5:23.)

Sacrament. In its relationship with the risen Jesus, the church is a kind of sacrament of intimate union with God, and a sacrament of the unity of all humankind. That is, the church is a sign and instrument of such union and unity. As a universal sacrament of salvation the church unites God and human beings, yet it also unites human beings with one another.

Temple of God. The "house of God" was founded on Jesus of Nazareth and is the dwelling place of the one, good God amidst the human community. In picturing the church as the holy temple of the Creator, Vatican II compared individual Christians to living stones that grow and develop into a strong building which represents the new reign of God. (See 1 Corinthians 3:9, 2 Corinthians 6:16, Ephesians 2:19–22, Revelation 21:3, 1 Peter 2:5.)

Sheepfold. With Jesus as the good shepherd and prince of all shepherds, the church is said to be a sheepfold, guided by human shepherds but ceaselessly led and nourished by the good shepherd himself. (See John 10:11–15; Isaiah 40:11; Ezekiel 34:11ff.; 1 Peter 5:4.)

Field of God and Vineyard. Today the church is sometimes spoken of as a tract of land to be cultivated or a choice vineyard to be nurtured. The true vine in the vineyard of God on Earth is the risen Jesus who gives life and much spiritual fruitfulness to all diverse, living branches (individuals, communities, and human cultures) that are members of the one church body. (See 1 Corinthians 3:9, Romans 11:13–26; Matthew 21:33–43; John 15:1–5.)

Visible Structure. The visible structure of the church body interlocks in harmony with the spiritual community so that the church is comprised of divine and human elements, just like the one redeemer of humankind and head of the body, Jesus Christ. This image tends to remind contemporary Christians that the church is an institution with a hierarchical structure.

Bride of Christ. The church is depicted as Christ's one true spouse. The image suggests that the Risen Jesus loves the church community as his bride. As such, all church community members must seek a relationship with Jesus' Spirit so that they can grow in holiness, reach the fullness that God has envisioned for them, and work to become a dynamic force on Earth working to bring into being the eternal reign of God. (See Ephesians 5:22–29.)
(See also Community, Ecclesiology, and People of God.)

CHURCH, LAWS OF   are seven important church rules—among many norms in church life—with which all Catholics should be familiar and which all members of the Catholic community are bound to follow faithfully. In church language, these are sometimes also called precepts of the church. A precept is an order or a command given to someone or to a community.

An original listing of six special church commands for Catholics in the United States was issued by the Third Council of Baltimore in 1886. These laws were the same as six church precepts observed in Great Britain at that time and which had been printed in 19th-century English catechisms. Special rules included in the precepts of the church, such as fasting or the fulfillment of one's "Easter duty," date back to 9th-century prayer books. In 1439 Saint Antoninus discussed ten binding laws of the church in his writings. Later Saint Peter Canisius taught that there were five special church laws. An official number of precepts for the Catholic community worldwide was set at six by Saint Robert Bellarmine in 1589. A seventh rule, currently listed third below, was recently introduced by U.S. Catholic bishops and added to Bellarmine's listing from the 16th century. It urges all Catholics to take part in lifelong, continuing adult religious education (lifelong catechesis) in order to further their formation in faith and Christian values.

The seven current precepts or laws of the church for members of the American Catholic community are:

1) To keep holy the day of the Lord's resurrection; to worship God by participating in Mass every Sunday and holy day of obligation; and to avoid those activities that would hinder renewal of soul and body (e.g., needless work and business activities, unnecessary shopping, etc.).
2) To lead a sacramental life; to receive holy communion frequently—minimally, to receive holy communion at least once a year, between the first Sunday of Lent and Trinity Sunday; to receive the sacrament of penance regularly—minimally, to receive the sacrament of penance at least once a year (annual confession is obligatory only if serious sin is involved).
3) To study Catholic teaching in preparation for the sacrament of confirmation, to be confirmed, and then to continue to study and advance the cause of Christ.
4) To observe the marriage laws of the church; to give religious training (by example and word) to one's children; and to use parish schools and religious education programs.
5) To strengthen and support the church; to support one's own parish community and parish priests; and to support the worldwide church and the pope.
6) To do penance, including abstaining from meat and fasting from food on the appointed days.
7) To join in the missionary spirit and apostolate of the church.
(See also Canon Law, Easter Duty, Sabbath, and Sin.)

COLLEGIALITY   refers to the power held by the entire body of bishops of the church, in union with the pope, to teach and pastorally guide the global Christian community's mission of evangelization. Collegiality implies that just as Peter and the other apostles of Jesus worked together as a united group, or community, to share the good news of the gospel throughout the world, so their true successors—the pope (the bishop of Rome) and all other bishops—must work together in order to lead the church and to evangelize all cultures.

The term has its origins in the Latin *collegium*, which indicates a "society or fraternity." By the 5th century it was commonly used by Christian leadership to denote the unity of the bishops who governed all church community matters. Although the pope is the authentic head and primary leader for all Catholics around the world, it is the pope and the bishops together—collaborating as a unified community or society—who are charged with the duty to guide Catholic Christianity on a global scale as true shepherds, evangelizers, and concerned pastors. The term "collegiality" was given a special, renewed honor by the Second Vatican Council in the 1960s. Much more study must be done, and greater efforts made by Catholic leaders and others today, to find out how the modern community of Jesus' followers can best put collegiality into practice on a regular basis.

Collegiality can be lived out and put into practice on many levels of church life—for example, in local parish communities, in church-sponsored schools, and in diocesan pastoral offices. Collegial, pastoral service and ministry can be rendered to local communities and to individuals whenever faculties and pastoral (parish) teams draw together to collaborate for the common good of and for the sake of sharing the good news of the gospel with all whom they encounter in their local pastoral settings.

The Catholic community's current teachings on collegiality are detailed in the Vatican II document, the Dogmatic Constitution on the Church. Put simply, the foundational church belief regarding collegiality is that the pope (chief leader of all Christian churches worldwide and the bishop of Rome) and his chief collaborators (all other Catholic bishops) are charged with the responsibility of caring for their individual dioceses and for pastorally guiding the entire church community. This college of church authorities is expected to teach authentic doctrines, govern local communities regarding issues of faith and morals, and to help sanctify all Catholic Christians, especially by seeing that they are evangelized in a dynamic, ongoing manner and that they have ample opportunities to receive the sacraments. The Code of Canon Law points out that collegiality is most formally exercised by bishops in the church during ecumenical (global) synods. Yet it can be exercised in other ways too. In fact, canons 336–341 of the Code point out many aspects to the church's concept of collegial power as held by its ordained leaders. The *Catechism of the Catholic Church* speaks about the collegial character of the episcopal order, rooted in the "college" of Jesus' original apostles, and notes that each bishop must pastorally care for the particular (diocesan) church community in his trust while maintaining an active concern for all the churches of Earth.

(See also Apostolic Succession, Bishop, Diocese, Pope, and Synod of Bishops.)

Note of Interest: The term "collaboration" comes up frequently in dialogues about pastoral ministries. "Collaboration" has Latin roots meaning to "work together." In general, collaboration among members of pastoral ministry teams and staffs—from the grass-roots to the national and international levels—is an ideal for which those in church service should strive. Collaborative ministry efforts involve teams of ministers who spend time envisioning, planning, implementing, and evaluating ministry endeavors together. In some Hispanic communities, this "work together" for the sake of evangelization and the mission to serve others in the name of Jesus of Nazareth and his global community is known as the *pastoral de conjunto.*

COMMANDMENTS OF GOD   are ten precepts or commands found in the Hebrew Scriptures in Deuteronomy 5:6–21 and Exodus 20:1–17. The Ten Commandments are sometimes called the Decalogue. The term decalogue has both Greek and Latin roots which indicate ten words. The Hebrew Scriptures (Old Testament) indicate that God (Yahweh) revealed the decalogue (ten commands) to Moses, for the moral and religious welfare of God's chosen people.

The followers of Jesus have maintained that the Decalogue should be observed faithfully. They have also stressed, however, that the basic norm or guide to all of Christian existence is Jesus Christ himself and his ultimate revelation of God to the human community. Thus Jesus and his call to Christian life, morality, and love—issued to all persons past, present, and future—is the fulfillment of the covenant between God and human beings that first had the Decalogue as its basic set of moral guidelines. The *Catechism of the Catholic Church* points out that the Decalogue integrates human beings' relationship with God and relationships with other persons. It says that because the "ten words" of the Creator express humankind's fundamental duties toward God and neighbor, they reveal—in their basic content—serious, unchangeable obligations. The Catechism thus maintains that the duty to keep the commandments applies to all human beings—especially all Christian community members—always and everywhere.

The Catholic community recognizes that Jesus renewed the ten commandments of God and revealed the dynamic presence of God's Spirit in them, summing them up positively and dynamically with the timeless words, "You shall love your God and you shall love your neighbor as you love yourself" (Leviticus 19:18, Matthew 19:16–19). The "ten words" of God therefore, remain important guidelines to be followed by all faithful Christians and Jews.

The first three commandments of God center on humanity's relationship to God. The remaining seven commands center on person-to-person relationships.

The ten commandments are listed on page 267.

(See also God, Morality, Old Testament, Revelation, and Yahweh.)

COMMUNITY   is a unified group of individuals who share common beliefs, values, tasks, or responsibilities. Catholic Christians are members of a global community called church. They are also participants in local, particular communities of the baptized. These local communities are called parish churches, dioceses, and small Christian communities. Together the community of Christians around the world strives to follow the teachings and moral commands of God as revealed in Jesus of Nazareth, God's most perfect revelation to humanity. The contemporary term "community" has Latin origins *(communis)*, which refer to "common."

The Hebrews were the basic community, the original people of God, in ancient times, who shared a loving covenant relationship with their one God, Yahweh. The new community, or a new people of God, rooted in the fulfillment of the original covenant between the Creator and humanity, was established by Jesus of Nazareth and has spread—through the basic Christian mission of evangelization—to all parts of the world and into countless human cultures.

The meaning of community was very important to church leaders who attended Vatican Council II. They strongly urged all members of the one Christian church worldwide to see themselves as a community of persons dedicated to the greater unification (and re-unification) of the one body of Jesus Christ. In recent years, Catholics frequently have begun to refer to the church—at all levels, but especially at the grass-roots parish level—as a community of faith. Catholics speak of the Trinity— one God in three loving, divine expressions—as an ideal and as a model for what the communal people of God can actually become.

Vatican II stated that human beings were meant to live together and have a strong desire to live in harmony and peaceful co-existence with others. Through Vatican II documents, in the 1960s, the contemporary church has taught that the new People of God—from individual to individual, from culture to culture—should work hard to form a united and "single people" on Earth, a community of Christians sharing and living the gospel every day in thought, word, and deed.

(See also Church, Images of; Ecumenism; Koinonia; People of God; and Small Faith Communities.)

Note of Interest: Basic Christian Communities are being formed throughout the United States. Inspired by the Hispanic *comunidades ec- lesiales de base* models these communities are relatively small neighborhood churches or grass-roots groups that serve as important balances to larger, impersonal, highly traditional parish structures. Basic Christian communities are composed of individuals and families who value close personal relationships with other active Christians, the experience of authentic community, the opportunity to serve and minister to others, and the sharing of faith that is nourished by reflection on the gospels, social action, and prayerful celebration of the sacraments. Several factors have led to the development of basic Christian communities in this country, including dissatisfaction with the usual, often impersonal parish model of local church; the shortage of ordained ministers in some geographical areas; and the relative isolation of some rural Catholics.

The *comunidades eclesiales de base* are important to Catholic and Protestant churches around the globe, especially in Latin America, Africa, and Asia. In his apostolic exhortation, *Evangelii nuntiandi*, Paul VI showed interest and support for such basic communities, noting that they can indeed become authentic proclaimers of the gospel message. (For more information, see the article on Small Faith Communities.)

CONCELEBRATION is the joint or simultaneous celebration of the Mass by several priests or bishops. This group of celebrants is led by one chief presider yet they together say some of the prayers of the liturgy and consecrate the eucharistic gifts of bread and wine.

In the early Christian communities, concelebration occurred often, and has remained a common practice of Eastern Catholic churches. In the Roman Catholic church, however, it was restricted for a very long time and was only usually allowed during Masses at which priests and bishops were ordained. In trying to reclaim and update this Catholic tradition, the Second Vatican Council established basic guidelines for concelebration at Mass.

In the process of concelebration, the priests or bishops present pray some parts of the eucharistic prayer in unison. All concelebrants speak aloud and clearly the central words of consecration at the same time. At that time, they also extend their right hands and arms toward the altar of sacrifice.

General guidelines for ritual concelebration advocated by the documents of Vatican II say that the practice can be used: 1) at Masses on Holy Thursday (the day before Good Friday, and the day on which Jesus' last supper with his close followers and the first Eucharist celebration took place), 2) at Masses during church councils, synods, bishop conferences, and other such meetings, 3) at Masses in which priests and bishops are ordained, and 4) at Masses in local church communities where the needs of congregations do not require all priests available to preside at Mass individually, and 5) at Masses celebrated at any type of priests' meetings.

(See also Eucharist, Liturgy of the Word/Eucharist, and Presbyters.)

CONFESSIONAL is a small booth or compartment in which church members tell their sins to a priest and receive forgiveness—absolution—privately and anonymously. Usually the person who confesses to personal sin in a confessional in the church building kneels, separated from the presbyter by a thin curtain or screen. "Confess" and "confession" have Latin roots that mean "to acknowledge" or "to own."

During the earliest days of the Christian community, followers of Jesus often admitted their sinfulness and need for forgiveness to other individuals in the general church body. Private confessions to a presbyter and private penances became very popular only in later centuries. (For more insight on this, see the article in this book on Reconciliation.) The use of confessionals for private confessions became widespread after the Council of Trent in the 16th century. Saint Charles Borromeo, a cardinal in Milan, Italy (during the 16th century), was probably the first church leader to place a confessional booth within a Catholic church building. Confessionals are used by some Catholics even to this day to ensure that their sins will be heard and forgiven privately and anonymously.

Today many Catholic worship spaces include special side-rooms for the sacrament of penance. A reconciliation room, which is sometimes also referred to as a confession room, is an area set aside in a church building or in some other spiritually-appropriate environment for the celebration of reconciliation. The one who enters the room to confess his or her sinfulness and to receive sacramental absolution may choose to sit opposite the priest for face-to-face confession or may elect to sit or kneel with grillwork or a curtain separating him or her from the priest. The reconciliation room's inviting environment is meant to emphasize God's great mercy, comforting love, and ever-available forgiveness.

Presbyters (pastors and parochial vicars) who hear the private confessions of Catholic individuals are bound by church law to keep all sins confessed—whether within the confessional or outside of it (in cars or on long walks outdoors, for example)—completely secret for all time. This is referred to by the Catholic community as the seal of confession. Church law mandates that should a presbyter tell someone about a specific person's sin, heard during a private confession, he will be excommunicated from the church community (see canons 983 and 1388 of the Code of Canon Law.).

(See also Actual Sin, Excommunication, Reconciliation, and Sin.)

CONFIRMATION　　is a sacrament of initiation and one of the seven sacraments recognized by the Catholic Christian community. The sacrament of confirmation may be received only once in a lifetime. Catholic tradition teaches that the confirmation ritual strengthens baptized persons and, through its renewal of the gift of the Spirit of God first received in baptism, helps them to become more active, caring followers of Jesus. A Catholic bishop is the usual minister of confirmation; the bishop (or in some circumstances another presbyter) confers this sacrament by praying to the Spirit and by placing his hands over each person to be confirmed. The minister of confirmation then also anoints those confirmed with holy oil (chrism) by tracing the sign of the cross on their foreheads, saying, "_____(name of the person being confirmed), be sealed with the gift of the Holy Spirit."

In primitive Christian communities, when most newcomers and new members were adults, persons were usually baptized and confirmed during the same ceremony. As Christianity spread throughout the world and added many newly baptized members to its local communities, adult converts as well as infants and children were baptized by presbyters and later confirmed by bishops. According to Eastern Catholic traditions, persons in Eastern church communities are normally still baptized and confirmed in the same ceremony.

Several significant pastoral issues about the sacrament of confirmation have not yet been fully resolved by modern Catholic communities in the U.S. For instance, some ask if there is a best or most proper age for receiving confirmation. Others speculate on whether the original order for conferring the sacraments of initiation: baptism first, then confirmation, and then the Eucharist, should be restored by the church in dioceses as a whole—and they then call church members to reflect, if the sacramental sequence is to be restored, on whether there are, pastorally speaking, most proper age(s) for reception of the three sacraments and proper pastoral strategies by which the sacraments of initiation can be offered to those entering the church community. Study by people involved in local-level pastoral ministries (e.g., DREs, youth ministers, and pastors) and practical use of the Rite of Christian Initiation of Adults (RCIA) have helped many communities revivify approaches to sacramental confirmation for children, youth, and adults in recent decades.

An interesting line of thought that has emerged in youth ministry-related dialogues on confirmation centers on the whole notion of confirming one's faith. Because human life, human faith development, and God's grace are dynamic, evolving realities in the lives of human beings, some say that "confirmation" of one's faith must occur many times throughout one's lifetime. Therefore, to some thinkers, it makes sense to speak of a recurring confirmation-style ritual (a rite of maturing discipleship, for example) by which church members could elect to celebrate with the community—potentially numerous times in life—a confirmation of one's growth in faith and deepening relationship with Jesus and his community.

The *Catechism of the Catholic Church* notes that the sacrament of confirmation provides the baptized with a deepening of the gift of the Spirit received in the waters of baptism. It states, as has Catholic tradition through the ages, that confirmation completes one's baptism and marks the Christian with the seal of the Spirit to empower him or her for a full life of Christian witness. In canons 892 and 893 of the Code of Canon Law, the church community mandates that each candidate for confirmation must first be baptized and must have a sponsor, preferably a person who was a baptismal sponsor (or godparent) for the one being confirmed. In June 1993, the U.S. bishops decided that "in accord with canon 891 [of Canon Law]...[we] decree that the sacrament of confirmation in the Latin rite shall be conferred between the age of discretion, which is about the age of seven, and 18 years of age, within the limits determined by each diocesan bishop and with regard to the legitimate exceptions given in canon 891, namely, when there is danger of death or where, in the judgment of the minister, grave cause urges otherwise."

(See also Anointing, Baptism, Catechumenate and the RCIA, Godparents, and Sacraments.)

CONFRATERNITY OF CHRISTIAN DOCTRINE (CCD) was a catechetical system designed for local Catholic parish communities, providing a religious education for children and older youth not reached by Catholic schools, and for adult members of the local church.

The first local-level CCD programs were begun by Pope Pius IV in the city of Rome during the year 1560. Eleven years later Pius V decreed that this type of religious instruction was good for the entire church. He urged other Catholic bishops to initiate CCD programs in their dioceses. In 1905 Pius X stated that the CCD system was to be used to instruct all church members who did not know basic Catholic teachings. His successor, Pius XI, added that all Catholic parish communities should initiate CCD programs for the religious education of young people if they had not already done so. This teaching became part of church law officially in 1935. CCD headquarters in the United States were placed with the U.S. Catholic Conference in Washington, D.C. in 1933, which is where they remained until the early 1980s.

The phrase "Confraternity of Christian Doctrine" and its acronym, "CCD," are not much used today. It is not specifically referred to in the official revision of the Code of Canon Law. Though some parishes still speak of their child-centered and youth-centered models for religious education as "CCD classes," today many parish pastoral staff members, DREs, catechists, parents, and others refer more commonly to religious education programs, parish catechesis, and ministries of Christian education. Many local parishes and dioceses, however, still pursue the three primary and traditional goals of the original CCD vision: 1) provide sound, quality religious education programs for adults; 2) provide sound, Catholic religious education experiences for children, older youth, and their parents; and 3) provide a sound, introductory religious education for all individuals who are interested in or who inquire about joining the church community.

In recent years, while parishes and church-sponsored schools continue to devote much time, attention, money, and human resource hours to the Catholic religious education of young people (as was the case predominantly for decades in the use of the CCD model), the church is placing much more emphasis than in the past on the need for adult education, parent religious education, adult catechesis, and renewed efforts at foundational forms of evangelization in Catholic parish communities overall.

Vatican II (Decree on the Bishops' Pastoral Office in the Church) and the new Code of Canon Law indicate that every local faith community must have a properly organized, active system of catechesis in order to provide for the religious education needs of persons at all ages and all stages of faith development. Today the national effort at parish-based catechesis is guided by specialists in the field working at the Department of Education of the United States Catholic Conference (USCC) in Washington, D.C., and by the membership of the National Conference of Catechetical Leadership (NCCL), a body largely composed of diocesan religious education directors, their staff members, and parish-level associates.

(See also Catechesis, Inquiry, Laity, and Parish.)

Note of Interest: Three important, church-sponsored documents of interest on catechetical systems in the U.S. have been produced in recent years. These documents were designed for all persons actually involved in local-level catechetical programs and for those interested in how church parishes and dioceses have tried to evolve their catechetical models beyond the overall limitations of the traditional CCD approach to religious education. The documents are: Sharing the Light of Faith: National Catechetical Directory for Catholics in the United States; To Teach as Jesus Did; and Basic Teachings for Catholic Religious Education. All three were prepared and published by the National Conference of Catholic Bishops and can be obtained from the United States Catholic Conference in Washington, D.C. Another key document by another agency, the National Federation for Catholic Youth Ministry, is also available today, *The Challenge of Adolescent Catechesis,* published in 1986.

CONVERSION   is a dynamic and lifelong process by which a person changes his or her ways in order to become more devoted to the good news of Jesus of Nazareth, more involved in doing Christian charity, and more centered on a prayerful and growing relationship with the loving God revealed in the gospel. Conversion is often referred to as *metanoia.* *Metanoia,* when used in a Christian context, means a fundamental change of mind and heart by which one turns away from old and sinful ways in order to turn toward the lifestyle and moral values advocated by the Christian community. The word is rooted in the Latin *conversio,* which suggests a turning away or, rather, a turning around of one's way of life.

In the gospels and Acts of the Apostles, the fundamental call from Jesus and his apostles to others is one of repentance, conversion, and a challenge to accept Jesus' message of salvation for the sake of the already-present but not yet fully realized reign of God (Mark 1:15, Acts 2:38). By the 3rd century, and possibly earlier, persons who chose to convert to the Christian way of life were prepared for full membership (initiation into the Christian body) through a catechumenate period, first reception of the sacraments, and post-baptismal catechesis. Among believers in the early centuries of the Christian experience, a true follower of the gospel of the Lord was someone who experienced ongoing conversion and maturing faith in a dynamic and daily manner, one who wholly believed in Jesus' vision for the fulfillment of the human community and creation, and one whose complete lifestyle had been transformed by faith in the gospel.

In later centuries, as Christianity became a religion widely embraced throughout the Western world, a convert mentality crept into the church as a whole and into local-level church communities in particular. Thus adults and youth who wished to become Catholic were known as converts, but acknowledgment of their spiritual conversion and preparation for one's full initiation into the Catholic Christian church were largely centered on mere catechism-style classes with local pastors or parochial vicars (associate pastors) for the study of church doctrines and practices. The faith-formation concept of an in-depth, multi-dimensional, community-oriented preparation for baptism and for dynamic, lifelong conversion to the Christian way, through an extended catechumenate period, was largely lost to the church's story for a very long time.

Many Catholics today speak about life as if it were a journey through many phases of moral and faith development—phases or stages characterized by many faith-related questions, moral struggles, personal choices, acceptance points, and changes of mind and heart. The Christian challenge to all persons is to turn away from sinful ways, and all relationships and life-pursuits basically at odds with the gospel, in order to be free to turn wholeheartedly and daily toward the way of life and the moral values appropriate to the community of Jesus' followers. An authentic Christian way of life should give daily witness to the gospel. It involves a lifestyle by which a person (and the entire local Christian community), through the inspiration and guidance of the Spirit of God, struggles daily with faith-questions, chooses to do things in accord with the gospel, remains open in mind and heart to God's love, and attempts to grow (evolve) in the ability to serve humankind every day in a spirit of Christian charity. The church teaches that daily prayer—personal prayer and communal prayer, works of charity and mercy, and reception of the sacraments, especially the Eucharist and the sacrament of penance, are critical to the ongoing conversion of all the baptized.

Today the church offers a dynamic, multi-faceted faith formation process—a contemporary catechumenate—for those who wish to convert, to be baptized, and to enter (become fully initiated into the Catholic community): This process is outlined in the Rite of Christian Initiation of Adults (RCIA).

In speaking of ongoing Christian conversion, the *Catechism of the Catholic Church* calls members of the church community to challenge themselves and others to a permanent lifestyle of "inner conversion." Yet the Catechism also notes that personal conversion to the gospel imposes on all baptized persons a serious call and challenge: Each must work to bring family households, broader communities, human cultures, social institutions, and those responsible for the conditions of human life worldwide to an awareness that they should turn away from sin and daily follow the vision and values of Jesus of Nazareth.

(See also Catechumenate and the RCIA, Holiness, Inquiry, and Morality.)

COUNCILS, CHRISTOLOGICAL   are six ecumenical councils in church history that focused on important and lasting doctrines about Jesus Christ. Here are the names and dates of these six councils, as well as some details about each:

Nicaea I was held in 325, while Sylvester I was pope. About 300 bishops of the church attended. The First Council of Nicaea was actually called by Constantine (the Roman Emperor who had converted to the Christian way in the year 313) in order to deal with Arianism, i.e., the heresy (false teaching) of a man named Arius. Arius denied the true divinity of Jesus of Nazareth. Nicaea I condemned his teachings and declared him a heretic. The council then proclaimed that Jesus was wholly and truly both divine and human.

Constantinople I took place in 381, with about 150 bishops participating. Damasus I was pope at the time, yet he did not attend the council sessions. The Nicene Creed, which Catholics pray at the Sunday liturgy, took shape through the work of Constantinople I. New forms of Arianism and another heretical teaching, one that denied the divine nature of the Holy Spirit, were condemned by First Constantinople.

Ephesus was convened in 431. It was organized by the emperor Theodosius II. About 200 bishops participated in the five general sessions of this council. Saint Celestine I was pope at the time. Celestine was represented at the Council of Ephesus by some delegates. This council condemned the teachings of Nestorius. Nestorius denied the possibility of the unity of divine nature and human nature in Jesus Christ.

Chalcedon was held in 451. About 600 bishops attended its 17 general sessions. Saint Leo I (Leo the Great) was pope at that time. Chalcedon condemned a body of teachings known as monophysitism, which is also known to some persons still as Eutychianism (a reference to the teachings of a man named Eutyches). Monophysite doctrine essentially claimed that Jesus Christ had a divine nature but he did not genuinely have a human nature. In effect, then, monophysites denied the humanity of Jesus of Nazareth. This teaching was judged to be heretical and was condemned by church leaders at Chalcedon.

Constantinople III took place in 680, with about 170 bishops attending its 16 general sessions. Constantinople III declared heretical a teaching that maintained that Jesus Christ had a divine will but no human will. Agathonus and Leo II were the popes involved with this particular ecumenical council.

Nicaea II occurred in 787, when Adrian I was pope. About 300 bishops from various church communities participated in this council's eight sessions. Nicaea II cited and condemned the errors of a teaching that came to be known as adoptionism. In essence, adoptionism held that Jesus of Nazareth was the Son of God by adoption only—not through participation in the divine nature of the Creator.

(See also Apostasy; Christology; Councils, Ecumenical; Jesus of Nazareth; and Magisterium.)

COUNCILS, ECUMENICAL   are landmark meetings of Catholic bishops from around the world who come together in unity in order to teach, direct, and pastorally guide the universal Catholic community. Catholic tradition holds that whenever the bishops of the world meet in such a council they act in unity with the bishop of Rome, the pope, as a collegial body that has the full and highest power among Christians to teach and to govern all church members throughout the world. The term "council," used in this way, has Latin and Middle English origins that mean "assembly" and "call together."

Ecumenical councils have usually been convened by the pope, the ordinary of the diocese of Rome and traditionally the chief pastoral shepherd of the Christian flock throughout the globe. Popes also traditionally have identified the topics to be studied and discussed at such councils, have functioned as the leaders of all council sessions, and ultimately have confirmed the validity of ecumenical council teachings and declarations for all local and diocesan church communities around the world.

Catholic history recognizes the first church council as the meeting of the apostles in Jerusalem about the year 52 c.e. Other very important ecumenical church councils have included: 1) the Council of Nicaea (325), 2) the Fourth Lateran Council (1215), 3) the Council of Trent (1545–1563), 4) Vatican Council I (concluded in 1870), and 5) the Second Vatican Council (1962–1965), which was the most recent ecumenical council. Over the centuries there have been 21 councils that are recognized as ecumenical councils of the church community.

A council is truly "ecumenical" when the community of church leaders in attendance considers matters that concern the universal church (i.e., the spiritual welfare and governance of the global Christian community). The declarations and decrees of worldwide councils are binding for all Catholic individuals and all local, regional, and national Catholic communities.

The concept of collegiality is often discussed today in association with dialogues related to conciliar matters. The "college of bishops," in union with the pope, is empowered and therefore called to use its full authority to teach, pastorally guide, and otherwise lead the church body through the work of ecumenical council sessions. (There is still discussion and debate, however, about the many ways by which the pope, in his own right as bishop of Rome, and the worldwide body of Catholic bishops should collegially exercise power and authority in leading the church. For more details regarding this matter, see the articles on Apostolic Succession and Collegiality contained in this book.)

The church maintains that the solemn declarations, teachings, and decrees of ecumenical councils authentically, formally, and with highest authority express the beliefs and long-standing traditions of the whole Catholic community. It also holds that the pope, through the guidance of the Spirit of God, is the key figure who is to discern when it is an opportune moment to convene a general church council. Cardinals, archbishops, bishops, patriarchs, and other church leaders typically take part formally and cast official votes on important matters during the church's conciliar discussions. Other persons, including theologians and laypersons, attend and sometimes even speak at ecumenical councils, but they do not vote on official church matters and decrees at hand.

The most recent ecumenical council was Vatican Council II, convened by Pope John XXIII in 1962. It was concluded in 1965 by Pope Paul VI, John's successor. Approximately 2800 church leaders attended this council. Vatican II produced sixteen major church documents that outline important church teachings in contemporary terms and that focus on many other matters pertaining to the modern, worldwide Catholic community and the spiritual state of humankind.

(See also Apostolic Succession; Bishop; Collegiality; Councils, Christological; and Magisterium.)

Note of Interest: Sometimes a group of church leaders meets for regional, national, or provincial church councils. These are referred to as particular councils (rather than ecumenical councils) of bishops, since they are called in order to deal with issues concerning only one part or one segment of church life. The decisions reached during particular council meetings are not usually binding upon the universal Catholic community.)

COVENANT   is a sacred and loving relationship or agreement between God and human beings. The term has Latin roots *(convenire)* meaning "come together," "one mind," and "an agreement."

In ancient times covenants were agreements (something like business contracts) between two or more parties. Such covenants were finalized and confirmed through sacred rituals and ceremonies. The Hebrew Scriptures reveal that the ancient Hebrews agreed to a spiritual covenant friendship with God, which was much more than a mere business deal, and was to last forever. It was an agreement, offered by Yahweh, that would be rooted deeply in a mutual sense of relationship, love, and respect.

Actually, the Bible indicates that there was, in time, a series of loving and sacred covenants established between Yahweh and the Hebrew community. Some of the great figures associated with these covenant agreements are Abraham, Noah, and Moses. History shows that great misfortune and sorrow befell the people of Yahweh whenever they chose to jeopardize (through sinful choices and alliances) the original covenant relationship.

The church holds that Jesus of Nazareth, the Son of God and the Christ, is the one person who fulfilled and extended through his work of salvation the original covenant relationship between God and the human race. By his liberating death and resurrection to new life in God, Jesus began a new covenant between God and all of humanity. This new covenant relationship promises life and a holy friendship with God forever if human beings fundamentally accept Jesus' proclamations, follow him, and live their lives in accord with the values and the challenges of his gospel. The most sacred ritual activity by which Catholic communities express their belief in and celebrate this new and everlasting covenant with God is the Eucharist (the Mass).

Catholics believe that only God can initiate a sacred covenant relationship. Thus human beings individually and human groups, communities, and cultures as a whole are challenged to accept God's offer of covenant-style friendship in love and to respond to God wholeheartedly. The Catholic community also points out that all human relationships (e.g., personal friendships, family ties, professional contacts, and even business relationships) are rooted in the original God-human relationship and should be signs of that loving covenant. The love relationship between marriage partners, confirmed in the sacrament of matrimony, is often referred to as a covenant, a special symbolic witness to the lasting and loving friendship that has been established between the Creator and humankind.

(See also Hebrews, God, Monotheism, People of God, and Yahweh.)

CREATION   is the process of making something from nothing or causing something to exist where nothing existed before. The words "create" and "creation" have both Greek and Latin origins that refer to "make" and "accomplish." The Catholic community's doctrine on creation teaches that God is good, that the one God is the source of all that has being, and that this Creator has created the universe from nothingness. Catholic tradition likewise teaches that through creation God has freely chosen to reveal the divinity's great glory and love for all of creation.

The biblical accounts of creation can be found at the beginning of the Hebrew Scriptures in the book of Genesis (Genesis 1:1–2:4). Genesis indicates that God created the entire universe from nothing in six separate, symbolic acts or in a symbolic series of "six days" of creative activity. Humanity was placed at the highest level of created order (the "crown of creation") and human beings were lovingly made in God's own image and likeness.

The Catholic community has developed a number of significant teachings about the nature of God's creation and God's creative activity. Several general church councils spoke about creation, including the Fourth Lateran Council (1215), the Council of Florence (1438–45), the First Vatican Council (1870), and the Second Vatican Council (1962–1965, especially in its Constitution on the Church in the Modern World). In Christian art history, perhaps the most beautiful portrayal of God's creation of the universe was completed by the artist Michelangelo in the early 1500s. This artistic creation can be found today in the Sistine Chapel at Vatican City in Italy.

Contemporary theologians often emphasize that the creation of the physical universe should be seen as a first step in a wholistic process by which God's divine plan of salvation will be totally realized and by which God's full reign over all that is, and all that will be, will finally come to pass. Some point out that traces of false teachings that have cropped up periodically throughout Christian history—teachings claiming that physical matter, human life, or creation as a whole are evil or sinful in nature—continue to pop up in various ways even today and should be rejected, just as they have been rejected consistently throughout Catholic tradition.

Many modern scientists, Christian theologians, Catholic community leaders, and others today engage in studies and lively discussions about the nature of scientific evolution, the evolution of the human race in particular, and the Christian belief in God's creative power as it is described in the book of Genesis. The church maintains that there need be no essential conflict between scientific investigations into the origins of the universe and the evolutionary beginnings of the human race when these are held in dialogue with the church's official doctrine on God's creation. Creation is an enduring and unique sign of God's loving revelation to humanity and God's ongoing desire for human beings to want to be in relationship with the one, true God. Catholics are called to trust that God is all good and that all things God has created are good (Genesis 1:31).

The Catholic community holds that the human community—and the Christian community in particular—should recognize its serious responsibility to care for God's creation and to develop caring stewardship practices that help all people and cultures share in the abundance of God's great world. Current Catholic teaching strongly acknowledges the worth and dignity of human work and all other creative human activity as a reflection of God's own creative powers. Using the gifts one has received from God, every human being can participate in God's creation meaningfully and can act freely and responsibly as co-creators with the one, true Creator God.

(See also Creation Theology, God, Pantheism, Revelation, and Stewardship.)

CREATION THEOLOGY/CREATION SPIRITUALITY   each have a deep interest in exploring the proper relationships between the one Creator God, human beings, the global human community, and the created world/universe as a whole. Creation theology attempts to reflect in a Christian way on human beings' relationships to God's creation. It looks in particular at proper ecological care for (stewardship of) the physical world and at the redemption of the whole universe through the historical Christ-event which united God, all human beings, and the created order in a definite way in hope for the full reign of God. Put another way, creation theology reflects on the Christian search for holiness, human (personal) wholeness, and the well-being and spiritual wholeness of all peoples and all things.

In recent years, an off-shoot from creation theology—called creation spirituality—has been criticized frequently by the official church. As some see it, it is a modern form of pagan gnosticism, an ancient non-Christian philosophy and long-standing problem for Christianity. (Basically, gnostics follow an un-Christian system of thought that says one Deity [a Cosmos] permeates all life/creation and thus human knowledge or wisdom, not faith, leads one to this Cosmic God and salvation.) Others have viewed creation spirituality as an expression of a contemporary gnostic New Age Movement that mystically leads one to ideas such as 1) all reality shares one basic substance, 2) all is God (i.e., God is an all-permeating but impersonal energy force), 3) the inevitability of reincarnation, and 4) humankind's crying need for a lift in human knowledge and consciousness. Observers have noted that modern creation spirituality strives to blend personal spiritual growth with influences drawn from Christian mysticism, Native American and Eastern theologies, liberation theology, modern science, environmentalism, feminist ideas, and other traditions.

A center for the promotion of creation spirituality, called the Institute for Culture and Creation Spirituality, was begun in Oakland in the 1970s. Its leader was Rev. Matthew Fox, a theologian and writer. By the late 1980s, Fr. Fox had been criticized by the Vatican for promoting various spiritual practices and New Age-style expressions fundamentally in contrast to traditional Catholic teachings on the nature of human life, God's grace, God as Trinity, the sacraments, prayer and worship, and personal moral responsibility for life choices. He was dismissed from the Dominican order and, in early 1994, joined the Episcopal church.

Today, the church community looks at the New Age movement as basically anti-Christian, a blending of ideas from many non-Christian philosophies and religious cults. It continues to express great reservations about the overall thrust of the school of modern, cosmological creation spirituality. The Catholic church, however, holds the current purposes and hopes of creation theology in high regard. In recent decades, it has reaffirmed the need for changes advocated by today's creation theologians and Christian humanists, such as 1) greater care for the ecology of the world to "renew the face of Earth," 2) deeper relationship between a loving, personal Creator and human beings, 3) a better relationship overall between humankind and Earth, 4) better partnerships between men and women, 5) better understanding of how science, technology, and Christianity should relate, 6) greater appreciation of the value of human labor, 7) imaginative strides in social justice for all, 8) a deeper love for work, play, and worship of God, 9) enhanced dialogue between Christians and the thoughts/truths of great non-Christian religions and philosophies, and 10) a humble, ecological stewardship among all human cultures leading toward a global Christian consciousness on caring for God's creation. In these ways, according to creation theology proponents, human beings may strive to become co-creators with the one God and more mystical in their love for all persons and things created in God's image and likeness.

(See also Creation, Holiness, Humanism, and Theology.)

D

DAYS OF PRAYER are designated days in Catholic dioceses during which all Catholics of the diocese are called to pray for particular needs and concerns. In recent years, such periodic diocesan days of prayer have been scheduled at the discretion of local bishops. Typical themes for these days include prayer of thanksgiving to God, good harvests, forgiveness of human sinfulness, human rights, or justice and peace on Earth.

In some ways, the roots of such modern-era prayer can be found in the ancient Christian traditions of ember days and rogation days. During the early 200s, Pope Callistus I targeted certain days of the week (Wednesdays, Fridays, and Saturdays) as days of fasting several times per year (usually at the beginnings of nature's seasons). Seasonal days of prayer, penance, and thanksgiving (for healthy crops) four times a year came to be known as "ember days." (The German word *quatember* means "four seasons.") In France, during the 5th century, certain days were set aside by the church for doing penance and for prayer to God and the saints for protection against evil and damage to crops. These came to be called "rogation days." About the year 450, Pope Leo the Great noted that ember and rogation days should be observed by all Catholics with prayer, fasting, and works of Christian charity. By the year 1000, ember days and rogation day practices had spread throughout European countries. In 1078, Pope Gregory VII established fixed dates for the annual observation of ember days of prayer and penance in the Catholic community worldwide.

In our time, local bishops individually decide which days will be dedicated as days of prayer in Catholic dioceses. Current reflection on this matter emphasizes that regular personal prayer can be a powerful force for personal growth, social good, and Christian reconciliation—especially when it is linked in faith to the prayers of other members of the church community. Authentic prayer and spiritual reflection can make a person (and whole communities) more open to God's presence in the world and more genuinely devoted to providing Christian help to others.

Catholic tradition continues to value highly the practice of individual prayer and Christian communal prayer, especially when prayer gives thanks to God or seeks forgiveness for wrongdoings. In 1970, the Vatican directed national groups of bishops to identify annually either seasonal dates or periodic blocks of days for widespread prayer. In 1971, the U.S. bishops decided that individual days of prayer should be set annually in each Catholic diocese at times each local bishop would choose.

(See also Diocese, Prayer.)

DEACONS   are persons who receive the sacrament of order and are thus ordained, by their local bishop, to a rank in the hierarchy of the Catholic community just subordinate to that of presbyters (priests). The term comes from a Greek word *diakonia,* which basically refers to a "helper" or "one who serves."

The first deacons were chosen by the apostles to help with the day-to-day matters of their local faith communities. According to the Christian Scriptures, the very first deacons were named Stephen, Philip, Prochorus, Nicanor, Timon, Parmenas, and Nicholas (Acts 6:1–6). Saint Clement of Rome, a 1st-century bishop, noted that deacons were the very first fruits or harvest of the original apostles of Jesus of Nazareth.

Early deacons helped seat people prior to celebrations of the Eucharist, read biblical texts aloud during liturgies, preached on the Scriptures, led the general intercessions, helped distribute the Eucharist to various members of their Christian communities, and cared for the poor. In the early centuries of Christian life, especially in the East, there seems to have been a tradition of women serving as deacons. Research into this topic continues today. By the 4th or 5th century, Catholics of the Roman rite began to confer the order of the diaconate only on those men who were specifically preparing for the presbyterate (priesthood). In some ways, then, this served to limit the ministerial functions of deacons for many centuries in the Christian community and it caused the church to underemphasize the diaconate as a permanent and independent order in its own right. In recent years, developments in Catholic thinking and Catholic life have re-established the diaconate as a unique and important church ministry as well as a unique and important element in the overall hierarchy of the Catholic community.

A large number of Catholic men—some celibate, some married with families—have been ordained deacons in the United States in recent years. Married men who receive the sacrament of order are called permanent deacons. Seminarians who are studying for further ordination to the presbyterate are called transitional deacons. To be ordained a transitional deacon a man must be at least 25 years old and must promise never to marry after ordination. To be ordained a permanent deacon, an unmarried man must be at least 25 or, if married, must be at least 35 years of age. Married men must promise never to remarry should they become widowers after they are ordained. Preparations for ordination to the diaconate include several years of study and spiritual formation, often at the direction of the diocese in which deacon candidates will eventually serve. In 1968, Paul VI restored the permanent diaconate in the Roman church, following a call for such action by Catholic leaders at the Second Vatican Council.

Modern deacons assist presbyters at the altar during celebrations of the Eucharist, preach during liturgies, and distribute the sacrament to members of the church. Deacons, however, perform many other ministry services in local communities. For example, some do works of mercy and charity through social action committee assignments. Some catechize groups of individuals in the Rite of Christian Initiation of Adults and in parish religious education programs. In some cases, they also preside at funerals and officially witness marriage ceremonies on behalf of the church.

The *Catechism of the Catholic Church* speaks of the order of deacon as having a special relationship to the local bishop's own ministry. It notes that the sacrament of order empowers deacons to become servants of all and to engage, in particular, in the various ministries of Christian charity that the world today needs so badly.

In June 1993, twenty-five years after the church had taken official steps to restore the order of permanent deacon, there were about 10,000 permanent deacons serving in church communities in the United States and about 4000 candidates actively preparing for the diaconate.

(See also Bishop, Ministry, Order, and Presbyters.)

DEAD SEA SCROLLS or the Qumran scrolls, is the popular name given to writings found on scrolls in caves within the desert west of the Dead Sea, since 1947.

The Dead Sea Scrolls have been described by some as one of the greatest discoveries for the church community in the 20th century. They have been subjected to intensive scholarly examination. Specialists now recognize that these scroll manuscripts contain the complete text of the book of Isaiah, many pieces of other Hebrew Scripture books, and apocalyptic and messianic tracts, some of which speak about a messiah, one who was to come to save Israel during a troubled time called the apocalypse. Before these biblical-era materials were uncovered, the oldest known Hebrew manuscripts of biblical texts dated only to the 10th century of the common era.

Since 1947 literally hundreds of Hebrew scrolls have been excavated from the Qumran desert caves near the Dead Sea. In addition to the ancient biblical and apocalyptic manuscripts, some of the scrolls also describe the way people lived during the time of Jesus of Nazareth and give Jewish and Christian teachers great new insights into the Hebrew literature and Jewish history of the time of the shift from Old Testament to New Testament eras. A number of Catholic scholars have likewise noted that the ancient scrolls indicate that the canon (body) of the Hebrew Scriptures was formed and basically fixed before the start of the Christian period.

(See also Bible, Messiah, and Old Testament.)

DEATH/DYING is the climactic experience of human existence through which human beings die physically and then fully encounter the one true Creator of human life. The church community believes that death does not equal total extinction of the human spirit, for the human self lives on in some spiritual capacity after physical death. Catholic tradition emphasizes that all humans have been created by God to enjoy the happiness of life beyond this planet, and so all of human existence should be aimed at and summed up in the possibility of meeting God beyond natural time. The terms "death" and "dead" have Middle English origins meaning "cessation" or the "extinction of life."

It is clear from the book of Genesis, and from church traditions as well, that all the sufferings and pains now associated with the human passage through death were not part of God's original plan for humankind. Humanity's experience of death and dying is directly related to sin; all human suffering and death can be clearly traced to the effects of original sin. The Christian community, however, also maintains that God has conquered sin and death, once-and-for-all, by raising Jesus from death (Hebrews 2:14–18). Saints Athanasius and John Chrysostom, among other early church leaders, stressed that through his resurrection Jesus won a great victory for all of humanity over the power of sin and death. At the Council of Trent (16th century), church leaders taught that the sin of Adam (i.e., original sin) introduced the reality of physical death into human experience as a penalty for doing evil (Romans 5:12–14). The church's long-held, traditional belief in a particular judgment (each person is to be judged by God at the point of his or her physical death) has served for centuries to underscore that human death expresses a finality to one's life on Earth and that living a faith-filled, moral life is crucial for one's everlasting and spiritual happiness in the presence of the Creator.

Some theologians today argue that at the moment of death each person makes a decision for or against God, thus irreversibly shaping one's ultimate destiny. Other theologians argue that, since death is an inescapable part of human reality for all persons, the moral choices of a lifetime and one's whole way of life are the key factors that shape and determine one's ultimate end, and thus constitute elements of an ongoing, lifelong judgment of sorts that one creates for oneself.

The Second Vatican Council (1962–1965) taught that faith alone will help human beings to allay some of the natural fears associated with physical death and to center on hope in an eternal life with God (2 Corinthians 5:1). In its Pastoral Constitution on the Church in the Modern World, the Second Vatican Council declared that the human community naturally abhors the absolute ruin, the physical extinction and total disappearance of the human species on Earth. Yet, through the risen Jesus' victory over death, all human beings are called to unity with the risen One and to an endless sharing of a divine life of happiness of heaven, a spiritual existence beyond all the limitations of and all the corruptions of human life. In 1979 the Holy See addressed and reaffirmed longstanding church teachings on the individual's existence after death, the Christian doctrine on the resurrection of the dead at the end of natural time (Romans 8:11), and the purpose of prayer for those who have already died.

The Catholic community strives to offer genuine spiritual comfort, and especially the sacraments of baptism, reconciliation, Eucharist, and anointing of the sick (in appropriate situations) to persons who are sick and dying, in order to remind those preparing for physical death that through hope in the risen Jesus the riddles of sorrow and death grow less mysterious, less overwhelming, and truly meaningful to all of life. The *Catechism of the Catholic Church* indicates that although death marks the end of one's earthly existence and is truly a consequence of human sin and evil, all of death has been transformed by Jesus of Nazareth. Thus, because of Jesus' saving works, all persons can forever trust that in death the Creator is lovingly calling each of us to unity with God and that physical death is the final step in our pilgrimage toward our ultimate destiny in God's great plan for creation.

(See also Anointing of the Sick, Easter, Faith, Original Sin, and Sin.)

DEPOSIT OF FAITH   is the collective heritage of Christian doctrines, teachings, values, and practices entrusted by God, through Jesus of Nazareth, to the apostles and their legitimate successors. In other words, it is the sum total of Christian revelation and tradition handed over to the church by Jesus, particularly to the authoritative teaching office of the Catholic community (the magisterium).

The basic concept of a deposit of truth and wisdom lies in both Hebrew and Roman law. A deposit was an idea or item that a depositor entrusted another to preserve and watch over. The gospel of John and the letters of Paul to Timothy imply that the community of the risen Jesus has a duty to guard, preach, and interpret gospel truths for the sake of humanity. History shows that the apostles, and then succeeding Christian leaders, made the message and values of Christian faith relevant to the life questions and various needs of the individuals and cultures they encountered. Church teachers and leaders have extended this Christian tradition and, whenever necessary, have corrected mistakes and obvious errors in the non-authentic doctrines and practices of others. The terminology "deposit of faith" crept into Roman Catholic language in the latter part of the 16th century. It became more widely recognized and used as a result of the work of the First Vatican Council in 1869–1870.

Some recent theological discussions about this topic have stressed the image of church community and authority as servant to all humanity. Therefore, these discussions point out that church leadership—or the Catholic church as a whole—is not a dictatorship or the sole owner of a static "buried treasure" of Christian doctrines and values. It is a servant-guardian watching over many things entrusted to it, and to all the faithful. The servant church community must teach dynamically and interpret continually the lasting truths in the accumulated treasure of Christian faith in ways that prove meaningful and insightful to people today—from place to place and from culture to culture—and also in all eras to come.

The church teaches that the deposit of faith is good news that must be made relevant and inspirational to all church members and to all humanity at all times. In a sense, this is the most proper way for church leaders to preserve, protect, and safeguard it, as the apostles and their immediate successors did. Vatican I noted that the deposit of faith is God's revelation to the human race, which was communicated to the apostolic community and has been faithfully and authentically handed on by church teaching authorities through the ages. Vatican II also spoke of this divine trust *(depositum)* given to the church for safekeeping. It said the pope and bishops (the magisterium), in particular, must "strive painstakingly" to give apt expression to the unchangeable contexts of divine revelation.

The *Catechism of the Catholic Church* points out the role of the whole faith community regarding the faith that is handed on. It reminds all Christians of Jesus' words: "Whoever listens to you (apostles and their successors) listens to me." Thus, the members of the church should listen to and strive to live the directives of church pastors in accord with the different levels of their authority.

(See also Didache, Doctrine, Magisterium, Orthodoxy, Revelation, and Tradition.)

DEVIL is the supremely-evil spiritual being, also commonly known in the Christian tradition as Lucifer or Satan. Christians often think of "the devil" as the leader of the evil angels who were banished from heaven and into hell by God. "Devil" is actually Greek in origin. It refers to an "adversary" or "slanderer" (i.e., one who "speaks deceitfully" to others).

Hebrew Scriptures refer to an evil one and a devilish presence in the world called Beelzebub. The notion of a Satan (chief among the evil forces), an archenemy of Yahweh and humanity, emerged in Hebrew writings about the 2nd century b.c.e. The only time "devil" appears in Christian Scripture is in the gospel of John (6:70), in which Jesus calls the apostle Judas, under the complete sway of evil, a devil. The New Testament does speak forcefully about one dark figure, Satan, who is the evil prince of all demons, a tempter of human beings and true enemy of God. (A New Testament-era belief was that various demons—or devils—entered human lives to stir up evil thoughts and actions.) In 563, the Council of Braga developed many long-lasting Catholic concepts and views regarding Satan (the chief devil). The name Lucifer became popular among church members in the Middle Ages. Christian writers of the time mainstreamed many of the mythological traits of the devil that are still widely circulated in Christianity to this day.

Human sin is a powerfully disruptive and deceit-ridden force in human relationships and societies around the globe. Therefore, each person should take responsibility to avoid evil and to choose to act maturely in accord with the forces of goodness and the gospel of Jesus in all ways, at all times. The idea that some Satanic spirit or devil is to blame for human immorality ("the devil made me do it") is out of line with authentic Christian tradition. Just as Jesus of Nazareth freely chose to stand against the evil influences and sinful tendencies that had crept into all aspects of human existence in this era, Christians today must personally resist sinful inclinations and work hard to overcome the many effects of evil present in the social institutions and human cultures of our time.

Catholics believe firmly in God's graceful, ever-present love and forgiveness as effective forces that can overcome sinful human tendencies. In other words, Catholics trust that the powers of goodness, rooted in faith in a good Creator, are greater than any powers of human evil.

When the term devil is used in Catholic Christian discussions today it can refer legitimately to certain enduring Christian traditions about sin, to evil in the general sense, to the "leader" of evil spirits known as Satan, or to any of the fallen, evil angels spoken of in church history. In 1965, in the Vatican II document Pastoral Constitution on the Church in the Modern World, church leaders linked human evil and sin to the notion of the devil. They said human beings, though created without sin by God, abused their freedom via temptation by "personified Evil," thus seeking human and spiritual fulfillment apart from God. In essence, humanity thus chose to sinfully serve "the creature [the devil or human selfishness and sin] rather than the Creator."

(See also Angels, Exorcism, Heaven, Hell, and Sin.)

DEVOTION is a term drawn from the Latin *devotio*, for "vow" or "total dedication." It describes piety or spiritual focus in general or deep reverence for the holy in prayer. In the plural, the term "devotions" usually refers to prayers, rituals, spoken formulas, or physical gestures, used in private or with others, to worship God, to honor Mary and the saints, and, in some way, to request divine help.

There are ancient roots to the practice of Christian devotions. St. Clement of Rome, St. Ignatius, and other early church leaders spoke to Christians about prayer and ritual expressions handed down from the time of the apostles. Church devotions have often been referred to as "popular" because they were designed for and could be used by virtually any ordinary church member, whether in private or in communal settings. Devotions have often become very popular because they helped people meet spiritual needs largely untouched by rigid official church liturgical styles of their time.

For many years, the more popular Catholic communal devotions in the U.S. church were exposition of the Blessed Sacrament, Forty Hours, Benediction, and the Way of the Cross. Vatican II spoke highly about the use of popular religious devotions, as long as they genuinely respond to people's spiritual needs privately or communally and are in harmony with the church's guidelines and liturgical seasons.

Christian religious devotion is a free and voluntary focus on God and others in the spirit of the gospel. And, as Thomas Aquinas claimed, it is a virtue by which a person is inspired to worship the Creator and then dedicate everything in service to God and the world. The peaks of popularity of various devotions come and go. Some devotional practices are better known than others. In all, they can be helpful to one's faith life when they are genuine, even fervent Catholic expressions that turn Christians into involved (not passive) worshipers and persons who follow regular, rhythmic patterns of prayer.

It takes some time, generally, for the official church to approve and promote a spiritual, devotional practice. Local bishops are urged to observe the emergence and use of various devotional formats to see if they genuinely "foster spiritual closeness to God," as Pius XII put it, and to ensure that the practices are in harmony with Catholic doctrines and traditions so they can be accepted by the broader church community. In some places, many long-lasting public devotions (e.g, novenas, the Way of the Cross, candle-burning, litanies, and the Angelus prayer) no longer are as prominent as they once were. However, many individuals, small communities, and parishes throughout the world continue to use such devotions for spiritual growth.

(See also Prayer, Veneration, and Virtue.)

DIASPORA   is a Greek word essentially meaning "dispersion." It refers to the scattering, or dispersion, of Jewish people throughout Greek, Roman, and other world cultures for several centuries b.c.e. and after the beginning of the Christian era. Put another way, diaspora describes Jewish communities, in biblical times and afterward, located outside the Jewish homeland of Palestine.

The diaspora of the Israelites began in earnest with the fall of their northern kingdom to the Assyrians (734–721 b.c.e.). It was continued by the fall of their southern kingdom, Judah, to the Babylonians (598–587 b.c.e.). It was furthered in succeeding centuries as Jewish peoples migrated to other lands for personal and business purposes. Some think the most successful Jewish community of the diaspora was established in Alexandria, Egypt. Other significant, migratory Jewish settlements took root in Greece, Italy, Syria, and Asia Minor. Christian Scriptures speak of Jews from the diaspora in Acts 2:9–11.

The people of the diaspora began the Jewish network of synagogues that eventually stretched all the way back to their original homeland, Palestine. Those who lived in Greece are sometimes credited with the first Greek translation of the Old Testament, called the Septuagint. Unfortunately, the success enjoyed by some Jewish families in the diaspora fueled a rise in persecutions of Jews in some cultures, and this contributed heavily to enduring waves of anti-Semitism that have popped up around the world for many centuries.

(See also Anti-Semitism, Hebrews, and Zionism.)

DIDACHE   is an ancient and brief Christian document, drafted in Greek, which contains fascinating details about early Christian doctrines and rituals, plus glimpses of the community-management procedures of the first generations of Christians. The Greek word *didache* basically means "teaching." The title of the primitive document we call Didache could be called "Teaching of the Apostles."

Some evidence indicates that the Didache was written about 100–125 c.e, with some sections of the document perhaps being even older. It seems to have been greatly valued by the leaders of the early church because of its direct connections to apostolic-era teachings and communal traditions. The existence of the Didache, however, was virtually unknown from the early Patristic period until the later 19th century. In 1873, Philotheos Bryennios, a metropolitan in the Eastern Orthodox Church, discovered a copy of the Didache, dated 1056 c.e., in a church in Constantinople. It was published widely in 1883 and this instantly sparked much debate over the authenticity of the manuscript.

Over the decades since then, many scholars have come to agree that the currently-known text of the Didache is a genuine statement of apostolic-era (1st century) teachings, values, and practices in the community of Jesus' followers. It is not yet known exactly where or when the original Didache manuscript was composed. Some scholars speculate that it comes from a Christian community in Antioch, Syria. Some other scholars also believe that the Didache was as much valued by early Christian bodies as the first of the New Testament writings, such as the letters of Paul.

The Didache remains a foundational and crucial source of information about Christian existence in the decades immediately following the time of Jesus' apostles. It sheds fascinating and original light on a number of key Christian doctrines, communal traditions, and organizational roots that still greatly influence the faith of the Catholic community today.

(See also Apostles, Deposit of Faith.)

DIOCESE is a geographical area or territory under the leadership of a local bishop, who is also called the local ordinary. The term is Latin in origin. It refers to a "district." Another word for diocese, in church terminology, is "see."

By early 1991, there were 1851 dioceses in the Roman Catholic church worldwide. There were 320 dioceses and 82 archdioceses in all of North America. By mid-1992, in the U.S., there were 33 Roman Catholic archdioceses and 150 Roman Catholic dioceses. Historically, the principal components of a diocese have been the people of God gathered within the diocesan-church boundaries and the various institutions, properties, and other holdings of the church within the territory.

Every diocese is like a "church in miniature" or a family of God. The bishop is the spiritual and central unifying figure in a diocese. The many other members of the diocesan family—the laypersons, the religious community members, and the ordained—have many Christian graces, talents, and skills to offer the wider church and human community as a whole.

Vatican II indicated that the central purpose of every diocese is to serve the real needs of the people of God as perfectly as possible. The Council spoke of the Catholic diocese as a "particular church"—a grouping of local Christian communities or parish-church cells—"entrusted to a bishop (who is appointed by the Vatican) to be shepherded by him" with the cooperation and assistance of many types of Christian ministers.

A "diocesan curia" or government includes the administrative offices and personnel through which the bishop guides and directs the key pastoral matters of the diocesan church. Chief members of the diocesan curia include the vicar general, the chancellor, the members of the diocesan marriage tribunal, and the bishop's appointed consultors. Diocesan pastoral councils frequently give bishops today their expertise, support, and advice in the mission to share the gospel and form community within the diocese. Church leaders at Vatican II urged all members of each diocese to develop a special feeling for their own diocese so they will be always ready and willing to contribute time and talents to various church projects/services.

(See also Bishop, Holy See, and Parish.)

Note of Interest: A deanery is a particular section or district within a Catholic diocese. There are usually several deaneries in each Catholic diocese. The words "deanery" and "dean" have Latin roots that mean "one set in place over" others. A deanery is composed of at least several parish communities. A priest from one of these parishes is appointed by the local bishop to be the dean or episcopal vicar with supervisory responsibilities within the deanery. The dean or episcopal vicar should 1) actively help the clergy, pastoral associates, and ministry teams in area parishes to follow current liturgical guidelines and other church norms; 2) understand and follow the pastoral instructions of the bishop; 3) call deanery meetings and preside over them; and 4) complete annual deanery-level reports to diocesan agencies and officials. In some places, the role of dean or episcopal vicar has been replaced by local clergy representatives elected to serve on diocesan priest councils on behalf of deanery-style geographical districts.

DISCERNMENT is spiritual insight that leads an individual or group or community to decide whether or not something is in harmony with Christian life and values or inclined toward evil. The word "discern" means to "separate" or "distinguish between." Christian tradition notes that true discernment springs from the moral virtue known as prudence.

In ancient Jewish literature, the term discernment refers to deep reflection on the spiritual worthiness or unworthiness of certain individuals. In his letters, St. Paul wrote that each follower of Jesus must make prudent daily choices to be guided by the Spirit of Jesus (1 Corinthians 12–10; Romans 12:1–2, Ephesians 5:10–11). The need for daily discernment according to the Christian way is also mentioned in the first letter of John (1 John 4:1). Later, Thomas Aquinas spoke of a *discretio spirituum*—simple human wisdom (discernment), which is aided by the grace of prudence, which gifts people with insight on how to choose and behave faithfully when matters seem morally unclear. St. Ignatius of

Loyola, in the early 1500s, developed personal and intense spiritual exercises by which one can deal in a discerning Christian manner with various life questions through the aid of a spiritual director.

Christian prudence (discernment) is a virtue and life-skill by which one can realize God's will and act in harmony with gospel values. Thus it is a sign of maturing faith by which a person resolves interiorly, by means of personal conscience, to live by the power of grace rather than by the sinful messages and temptations that sometimes crop up in human relationships or the wider culture.

Catholic tradition emphasizes that authentic discernment is a conscientious, interior experience of the Spirit of God. This grace helps persons or communities decide what is or is not in accord with Christian charity. Its "fruits" (results) are deeper faith in Jesus, a sense of peaceful well-being, and greater ability to witness to the Christian way as a whole. As a spiritual-growth discipline, discernment through Christian spiritual direction helps individuals journey toward human wholeness (holiness) and develop an authentically-lived Christian spirituality. Genuine discernment helps one think and pray deeply about prudent choices, imprudent choices, past actions, relationships, and various motivations toward either goodness or evil. The aim of prudent judgment, and the discernment process as a whole, is not to search out the origins of one's inclinations to either Christian good or evil. It is to recognize, spiritually and practically, how one's life is fundamentally oriented in the here-and-now and how to better walk the path of Christian holiness.

(See also Grace, Holiness, Sin, and Virtue.)

Note of Interest: It is a fact of human life that limited individuals can experience God only through that which is either chosen, heard, seen, or otherwise experienced. To transcend imaginatively one's human limitations in order to "see" and co-create reality as God would see things is to experience Christian conversion. Spiritual direction, or spiritual guidance, is a psychologically deep faith-formation process by which someone seeks to keep his or her life on a proper Christian course and to realize more completely a holy way of life. A spiritual director is a male or female pastoral minister who guides others in this imaginative, deep discernment process. The process of direction is a corporate journey: Director and directed are united in faith. Decisions about that which is or is not prudent, in the Christian sense, however, must be made by those guided, not by the spiritual director. It is the Spirit of God, not just the professional and pastoral talents of the human spiritual guide, that leads persons to strive for a life directed by God's grace.

DISCIPLESHIP has its origin in the Latin *discipulus*, which means "follower" and "one who learns." Christian tradition claims there were at least 72 special disciples of Jesus of Nazareth, along with the 12 apostles, who received special training, instruction, and other formation from Jesus to be sent out by him on a mission to call others to repentance, preach the coming of God's reign, and heal the sick (Luke 10:1–9). The original disciples can also be seen as the hopeful student-followers of their rabbi, Jesus.

The equivalent of the term disciple appears only in the gospels and in the Acts of the Apostles. Acts 1:15 seems to speak of a group of 120 special disciples of the now-risen Jesus. In the history of the church, the 72 have been typically viewed as a body related faithfully—but not as intimately as the 12 apostles—to Jesus.

Discipleship is a way of life that must involve significant risk, hope, and a willingness to speak out in urgent, self-sacrificing, and countercultural ways to lift up the message and values of Jesus' good news. While this mission of evangelization was given to the original disciples, discipleship as a lifestyle and life-witness is the way that all baptized persons are called by the church to live in imitation of Jesus.

Catholic tradition stresses that discipleship never has and never will involve status-seeking positions or the ranks of power and authority in the world. Discipleship is an everyday way of life, hope, and ministry rooted in the gift of the Spirit instead. In baptism, one becomes a Christian disciple commissioned by the Spirit of Jesus to do outreach to various persons, groups, and cultures, to share his gospel message regarding the reign of God, heal human hurts, and serve the poor. Disciples today, as in the past, are those who truly 1) accept Jesus' challenge to sacrifice themselves in any ways necessary to share faith with others and reform the world, 2) put hope in God and God's reign over material values, 3) trust fully God's promise of salvation (rather than cling to self-interest, family of origin, or human life itself), and 4) free themselves entirely of mere worldly concerns to spend themselves completely in pursuit of God's love on Earth.

(See also Apostles, Baptism, Evangelization, Hope, and Reign of God.)

DIVORCE   is a legal judgment rendered by a civil court that the marriage between a man and woman no longer exists. Catholics hold that a true and valid marriage covenant can never be ended while both partners are still alive. Sometimes members of the Catholic community in fact do seek legal, civil divorces. According to church law, however, they must likewise obtain an official annulment (a decree of nullity) on their first legal marriage before they may remarry. The word has Latin roots meaning "to turn or go another way."

Jesus taught that any man or woman who is divorced and then remarries commits adultery (see Mark 10:6–12 and Luke 16:18). It has seemed likely to many Scripture scholars, past and present, that Jesus based this moral teaching, at least in part, on the book of Genesis and Jewish law. St. Paul was also instrumental in shaping and filling out early Christian doctrine on divorce (1 Corinthians 7:10–11). The Council of Trent, in the 16th century, restated the traditional Christian viewpoint that any person who remarries after previously entering into a valid marriage is guilty of the sin of adultery, an act that fundamentally contradicts the sixth commandment of the Creator.

There has been much pastoral interest, discussion, and ministerial initiative in the contemporary Catholic community on the issues of marital separation, divorce, and remarriage. At least one source in the early 1990s estimated that perhaps as many as six to eight million U.S. Catholics had experienced both civil divorce and remarriage. Theological thinking of our day continues, by and large, to express the traditional Christian concept that a valid marriage is a covenant agreement between a man and a woman. Thus a sacred covenant must continue (it truly survives) even if a couple were to separate or become divorced under civil law. From a pastoral point of view, church leaders and local pastoral staffs sensitively but strongly urge separated and divorced persons—and those seriously considering divorce or remarriage—to talk with a presbyter, a pastoral associate, or some other knowledgeable members of the Christian community about the conditions for a valid marriage according to church law and about the pastoral processes that the community uses to help persons in troubled and painful situations to obtain a Catholic annulment.

Though no valid marriage covenant can simply be terminated, pastorally sensitive ministers in the Catholic faith community often acknowledge that marital separation and legal divorce can serve, in some situations, to help individuals (and their children) find release from distressed relationships and can serve to protect their human rights, personal safety, and basic dignity. Local Catholic communities and dioceses today offer numerous, in-depth pastoral ministries to engaged couples (to help them better prepare for the ups and downs of modern married life and parenthood in general) and to those who have experienced the pains of separation, divorce, and remarriage, or abusive marital relationships.

According to Catholic tradition and teachings, any validly married person who has experienced marital separation or even civil divorce and who has not attempted to remarry, remains in full communion with the Catholic community and may participate fully in eucharistic celebrations and receive other sacraments. A person who has become divorced and has simply remarried in the civil sense—without seeking a decree of nullity (annulment) on his or her initial marital relationship—is to be always welcomed into the church's worshiping community but cannot validly receive the Eucharist. Church law prescribes that all Catholics and all those who will marry Catholics must always seek annulments of previous marriages in order that their current marriages can be validated by the faith community.

Today pastoral ministers and others gently but strongly encourage all divorced and remarried Catholics to seek special guidance and help from their local church communities and to participate actively in the many supportive ministry groups and personalized services that are provided. John Paul II has said that "men and women who live in situations considered irregular from the religious point of view need the spiritual assistance and the full help of the Church's affectionate concern....I encourage pastors to welcome people living in such situations, and to remain attentive to their needs so they can live their faith in baptism." He added that although divorced-and-remarried members of the Catholic tradition cannot presently receive the sacraments, they should not be made to feel alienated or separated from the faith community.

Church rules regarding separation of spouses and divorce can be found the Code of Canon Law, canons 1141–1155. The *Catechism of the Catholic Church* addresses matters concerning the marriage bond, separation, and divorce in articles 1639–40, 1644, and 2382–2386.

(See also Annulment, Covenant, Family Ministry, and Matrimony.)

DOCTRINE   refers to a particular, official Christian teaching. The word is also used to designate the entire body of Catholic community teachings—as in "Catholic doctrine." The term comes from the Latin root *docere*, which means "teaching" or "instruction." Christian doctrines are derived from Scripture, from the faith life, values, and practices of church communities, and from traditional Christian beliefs and moral guidelines. Church doctrines, according to Christian tradition, can only be developed and proclaimed, authentically and authoritatively, by the magisterium of the church.

Over the centuries, doctrines have focused attention on things revealed by God to the followers of Jesus of Nazareth. Catholic Christian teachings have been classified over the years as either doctrines or dogmas. While all doctrines center on great truths of faith and great mysteries revealed by God that should be accepted by all of the baptized, dogmas are doctrinal expressions that constitute infallible Catholic teachings and remain, therefore, more essential and authoritative than individual statements of other Christian beliefs. Thus in the entire body of church teachings, developed through the ages, all dogmas are true doctrines of Christian faith but not all Christian doctrines carry the weight and the great authority of dogmatic definitions.

Authentic church doctrines undergo a dynamic process of development. Though the fundamental revelations expressed to the human community in individual doctrines can never be altered or reshaped merely to suit human aims or purposes, the words used and the symbolic means by which a doctrine is proclaimed and explained may be developed and perhaps perfected over time in order that contemporary men and women can better grasp the essence of foundational Christian teachings. The Second Vatican Council (1962–1965) noted that doctrinal statements are a key part of the church's living tradition. Doctrine helps the members of the Christian community develop a deeper understanding of and a deeper appreciation for the Christian insights and practices that have been handed down faithfully to believers since the apostolic era.

Today the Roman Catholic community is called to trust that the ongoing process of defining and explaining church doctrine impels the people of God constantly forward toward complete apprehension of God's revelation. Doctrine will remain alive and significant for all peoples only if it is continually reflected upon, taught, dialogued about, faithfully formed anew, and reformed by and for church members in light of their chief spiritual questions and struggles. (Some church teachers today go so far as to suggest that the body of Christian doctrines should be thought out and rethought at all times in all communities, so that Catholic teachings can be more aptly and clearly stated in ways that respond to the spiritual needs of modern human beings, and so that doctrine as a whole will continue to help communities of the baptized uncover the great gospel-inspired truths to which traditional doctrinal teachings and practices point.)

In contemporary Catholic perspectives, church doctrine is a basis for the entire Christian way of life. Doctrines are not just teachings from a distant past, detached from the human spiritual quest for God and life's true meaning. Doctrine is handed on to local faith communities around the world by several means: 1) by the pope speaking on his own, 2) by the unified college of Catholic bishops including the pope, the bishop of Rome, and 3) by individual bishops or bishops conferences seeking to enlighten instruct the faithful. The Catholic church maintains that there is a hierarchy of truths within the large body of Christian doctrine, with dogmatic teachings, of course, taking spots of greatest honor in this hierarchy.

In 1978 Pope John Paul I noted that doctrinal formulas sometimes need updating. His comments echoed words by his predecessor, Paul VI, who wrote that the Roman church must continue to develop Christian doctrine in a dynamic way but also correct doctrinal errors as they crop up and set straight all teachers of false beliefs. Today the Congregation for the Doctrine of the Faith, headquartered at the Vatican, and an arm of the Roman Curia and the Holy See, is charged with the responsibility of promoting and conserving authentic Christian teachings. Its chief work is to examine various doctrinal and theological opinions from widespread church communities and cultures, to encourage study of emerging doctrinal questions and controversies, and to scrutinize theological writings from many sources.

(See also Deposit of Faith, Dogma, Orthodoxy, and Tradition.)

DOGMA is an infallible and solemnly recognized doctrine of the universal Catholic community. The church maintains that dogmatic beliefs have been revealed to humankind by the one God and therefore must be fully accepted by all baptized persons. Derived from the Greek language, the word means "that which one thinks to be true" and "to seem right." It also implies a public decree or an order rendered with great authority.

During the early centuries, the term "dogma" most probably was used to refer to either a particular religious belief among the followers of Jesus of Nazareth or to the sum total of all Christian beliefs and ritual practices. In later ages dogma was more widely understood by church members to describe, strictly speaking, the most authoritative of

Christian teachings, those traditional doctrines that center on certain truths divinely revealed to the followers of Jesus. Because dogmatic teachings are timeless and very essential to Catholic life and Roman Catholic identity, Pius XII strongly urged church members to fully accept the dogmatic teachings of the church community. In 1978 Pope Paul VI said Catholic Christians must assent to great, dogmatic Christian truths in order to be correct in one's Catholic faith.

A dogma is, in fact, a doctrine of the church, yet as an essential church statement of Christian faith a dogma bears greater weight in the Catholic community worldwide than any single Catholic doctrine. To fully comprehend a dogmatic statement, teachers and students of contemporary Catholicism are urged to find out what the formulators of the particular dogma originally intended to express, and to understand the precise meanings of the actual words and phrases used in defining a dogmatic teaching. Though the church officially maintains that each dogmatic teaching of the Catholic body expresses an infallible and divine truth (incapable of being in error), many theologians and others today remind us that, in the future, some Catholic dogmas may in fact be reworded—expressed more aptly, using terminologies and symbols that communicate well with certain peoples and cultures to whom dogmatic teachings seem strange or incomprehensible—or even reshaped somewhat in order that Catholic communities and others might better grasp significant religious truths and follow them more faithfully.

In official church terms, a dogma is a teaching pronounced in our day by the magisterium of the church. Catholic dogmas propose truths, revealed to humanity by a loving God, to which Catholics are challenged to give their complete belief and trust. Dogmatic teachings may be defined and taught by the pope in unity (one voice, as it were) with all the bishops of the church, or may be put forth by the pope alone whenever he speaks *ex cathedra* (i.e., infallibly or from the "chair of Peter"). All church dogmas are rooted in God's revelation as found in Scripture and the sacred tradition of the church community. Therefore, those who deliberately deny dogmatic teachings are considered to be guilty of the sin of heresy.

Typically, listings of the dogmas associated with Catholic Christian faith include beliefs on the Trinity, the incarnation of the Word of God, the real presence of Jesus in the Eucharist, the Immaculate Conception and the Assumption of Mary, the mother of Jesus, into heaven, and other key Catholic teachings.

(See also Collegiality, Deposit of Faith, Doctrine, Infallibility, Magisterium, and Orthodoxy.)

E

EASTER is the great annual Christian feast day and season celebrating Jesus of Nazareth's resurrection from death to new life in God. Belief in the definitive Easter event, God's raising of Jesus to life after death, is crucial to the entire Christian community, for in celebrating the Easter event Catholics and other baptized persons express their trust that the powers of human evil, sinfulness, and human death can truly be overcome and that all members of the human community can hope to be happy with God forever in heaven.

During the first centuries of the Christian experience, there was much debate among some leaders about a proper date for the annual Easter feast. In the year 190, Pope Victor I taught that Easter must be celebrated on a Sunday, since it was on this day that Jesus was raised from the dead. In 325 the Council of Nicaea declared that Easter must be held each year on the first Sunday after the first full moon of springtime. The entire Catholic community, though, did not accept this method of dating for Easter until the 7th century. Easter Sunday remains a solemn movable feast to this day. It is celebrated on a Sunday between March 22 and April 25.

The Easter season is meant to be a very happy, hope-filled time for all baptized persons and all others who believe in the message of Jesus because, through the Easter experience of Jesus, the loving and good Creator offers salvation and hope to all humanity. The church's observance of the Easter season lasts for 50 days, beginning with the Easter Vigil and concluding on Pentecost Sunday. The Catholic celebration of the Eucharist on Easter Sunday underscores the power of Christian hope and the ongoing need among Christians to celebrate Jesus' great resurrection in glory from the grip of death.

Through the joy of Easter, Catholics are called to unite with other Christians to acknowledge the abiding truth that all of humanity has been rescued from the grip of sin through the Jesus experience. Of course, every Sunday is meant to help all church members remember and celebrate the resurrection of the Lord. Thus, some Catholics refer to each Sunday as a "little Easter."

(See also Jesus of Nazareth, Holy Week, Resurrection, Sabbath/ Sunday, and Triduum.)

EASTER DUTY is the name given to a universal church rule requiring members of the Catholic community to receive the Eucharist at least once a year, sometime between the first Sunday of Lent and Trinity Sunday—i.e., one week after Pentecost. The Fourth Lateran Council, under Pope Innocent III, declared in 1215 that once-a-year reception of holy communion was necessary for all persons who had reached the "age of reason" (about seven). To underscore the significance of this church precept, some leaders of the church taught that a person could not enter a church building or receive a Christian burial if one's Easter duty had gone unfulfilled.

By the 16th century, for various reasons, it had become typical for Catholic church members in Europe to receive the Eucharist very infrequently, only about three times a year: at Christmas, at Easter, and on Pentecost Sunday. Since 1551 the church community has tried to reverse this widespread practice and has stressed that Catholic people ought to receive the Eucharist frequently. Saint Robert Bellarmine, a great church leader and teacher in the 1500s, urged this spiritual-growth practice. Later, in 1905, Pope Pius X expressed belief on behalf of the worldwide church that daily eucharistic reception was spiritually beneficial for all members of the Catholic faith community. The Code of Canon Law now indicates that all the "faithful are to hold the Eucharist in highest honor, taking part in the celebration of the [Mass often], receiving the sacrament devoutly and frequently…" (canon 898).

During the 1960s Vatican Council II declared that Catholic individuals should view every Mass as a holy meal or eucharistic banquet at which members of the church share the sacrament of the Eucharist as their special spiritual food and drink. Pope Paul VI, in March 1968, noted that the Easter duty is a spiritual and devotional practice that many Catholics fail to honor. He added that receiving communion regularly, particularly during the Easter season, is important to the Catholic community because it helps church members keep their lives centered on Jesus and on the various beliefs and hopes to which Christianity gives witness.

Church leaders today remind Catholics around the globe that completing one's Easter duty is a serious obligation of every person in every parish who has already received his or her first communion. In recent years the bishops of the United States have placed discussions about the Easter duty rule of the church in the context of the obligation placed on all the baptized to live daily in a sacramental way. The church precept (or church law) in the U.S. that relates directly to the Easter duty currently reads: "To lead a sacramental life: (one must) receive holy communion and the sacrament of penance regularly—minimally, to receive the sacrament of penance at least once a year (annual confession is obligatory only if serious sin is involved) and, minimally, to receive the Eucharist at least once a year between the first Sunday of Lent and Trinity Sunday."

The Code of Canon Law says (canon 920), "All the faithful, after they have been initiated into the [Eucharist], are bound by the obligation of receiving communion at least once a year. This precept must be fulfilled during the Easter season unless it is fulfilled for a just cause at some other time during the year."

(See also Church, Laws of; Easter; Eucharist; Pentecost; and Sacrament.)

ECCLESIOLOGY   is the study of the nature, meaning, mission, and structures of the Christian church community. The term ecclesiology can be traced to the Greek word *ekklesia*, which refers to a "gathering of believers," a "convocation," or an "assembly."

The first generations of those who chose to follow Jesus of Nazareth viewed the group of believers as a community of faith, and the body of Christ on Earth, with the risen Jesus at its head, and eventually as an *ekklesia*, an assembly or a Christian church. As the centuries passed, however, the church community began to be imaged and described by some as a visible structure or society, governed and taught authoritatively in the main by a hierarchy of ordained leaders (a clergy). This image of the church body dominated Catholic perceptions and teachings about ecclesiology during the 17th, 18th, and 19th centuries.

The long-term focus on the church as visible structure and institution reached something of a culmination with the First Vatican Council's dogmatic declaration on papal infallibility in July 1870. In 1943 Pope Pius XII officially stated that all members of the Catholic church worldwide ought to begin to re-emphasize the traditional Christian concepts that the global church of Jesus Christ is a mystical body and the community of the Lord on Earth, as well as a visible, earthly society. In the 1960s Vatican Council II emphasized that the Catholic Christian church should be imaged fundamentally as a mystery, as the people of God, and as a true and sacramental community of the baptized who should, in our later 20th-century time, begin to examine ways to re-establish and broaden relationships with the members of other Christian and non-Christian religions throughout the globe.

According to Catholic tradition, the church, while it is mysteriously the body of Christ and a sacramental people of faith on Earth, must remain a visible society and organized institution in order to best serve the various human needs of many peoples and intentionally share the gospel of Jesus (evangelize God's creation) in many cultures. Currently, Catholic leaders and theologians often point out that the church as institution must faithfully work hard to nurture and develop an interior, dynamic Christian spirituality among all its members in order to remain institutionally faithful to the vision of the ultimate reign of God and the counter-cultural, life-altering values proclaimed in the good news of Jesus.

Church teachers today note that the church community—the body of Christ and the people of God—has four basic Christian marks or characteristics: 1) it is one in faith; 2) it is holy, as Jesus of Nazareth, the founder of the Christian community, was holy; 3) it is catholic or universal; and 4) it is apostolic. The church community is thus to remain a true continuation of the apostolic community and fundamentally dedicated to the apostles' mission of proclaiming and spreading the gospel of Jesus to all individuals and to all cultures throughout the world.

The *Catechism of the Catholic Church* says that the church both inhabits and transcends the history of the world. It is a visible assembly and a spiritual communion, a complex mystery and reality combining human and divine elements. Ultimately, the Catechism notes, any study of the church community must lead one to the conclusion, using the words of Vatican II, that the church is in Jesus "a kind of sacrament or instrumental sign of intimate union with God and the unity of all humanity." Because the Creator wants the entire human community to form one people of God, this people should be called together, by church members today, into one body of Christ and be built up together into one temple of God's Spirit.

(See also Apostolic Succession; Catholic; Church, Images of; Community; Ecumenism; Evangelization; and People of God.)

ECUMENISM   and the ecumenical movement refer to the efforts by the Roman Catholic community and other Christian churches to work toward full unity among all baptized peoples around the globe. In recent decades Catholic leaders and others have spoken clearly and quite forcefully at times about the largely unfulfilled need in our age to overcome the basic differences, divisions, disagreements, and faith-related obstacles to full unity among many Christian congregations. The church strongly urges Catholic individuals and parishes to strive in many ways to overcome and resolve the vexing problems resulting from the continued separations among various Christian peoples. "Ecumenism" has Greek origins that refer to "of or from the whole world."

The major thrust toward ecumenism today among various non-Catholic, Christian churches worldwide began in 1910 in Edinburgh, Scotland. An extension of this expression of Christian concern for unity—the World Council of Churches, founded later in 1949—has worked since then to help further global ecumenical movements among the baptized.

In 1964 Roman Catholic leaders in attendance at the Second Vatican Council issued a landmark document called the Decree On Ecumenism. This groundbreaking statement outlined the basic charitable, concerned, and gospel-oriented attitudes that all Catholic peoples and parishes should have toward the modern ecumenical movement as a whole. Vatican II went on to identify various practical means by which the Catholic community today can work for ecumenical unity on Earth. Current thinking, cued by Vatican II, frequently notes that ecumenical work by Catholic individuals and communities is not merely an option or a secondary cause in the ongoing mission of Christian evangelization. It is instead a primary issue and duty for all members of the church.

Many emphasize that the movement toward ecumenism on the part of the Catholic community should be characterized by certain efforts that include 1) the elimination of words, judgments, actions, and labels directed toward other Christian congregations that make relationships with separated Christians more difficult; 2) dialogue with skilled experts and leaders of other Christian communities in the world; 3) cooperation and collaboration, whenever and wherever feasible, for the good of all the baptized and of all humankind; 4) common prayer with other Christians when possible and appropriate; and 5) self-examination, on the part of Catholic communities, about how they can help overcome Christian divisions—for which the Roman church bears some serious responsibility—in order to undertake with real vitality the foundational Christian mission to reform and renew a world troubled by human sinfulness, divisions, conflicts, and various estrangements from God.

In June 1993, the Vatican issued an important document called the "Directory for the Application of Principles and Norms on Ecumenism," an attempt by the church's Pontifical Council for Promoting Christian Unity to update and refine the contents of church statements since 1967 on the need for ultimate Christian unity. Many ecumenists believe this 100-page paper is the most significant Catholic position statement on ecumenism of the past decade. The Vatican has said recently that basic conversion and education are needed so that all members of the Roman church can truly recognize today the critical importance of Christian unity—a "priority for the church, not just a specialization."

Many officially-sponsored dialogues between representatives of the Catholic tradition and other Christian traditions continue at this time.

(See also Christian Unity Week, Ecclesiology, and Reformation.)

ELECTION, RITE OF   is a ritual element of a person's overall preparation for full entry (initiation) into the Christian community through the rite of Christian initiation of adults (RCIA). It is a public liturgical experience that leads into the phase of the RCIA process known as the period of enlightenment. The word "election" comes from Latin roots that refer to "choose" or "select."

The Bible describes various persons as specially "chosen" or "elected" by God (e.g., Abraham, Moses, David, Jesus of Nazareth). Being "chosen" by God was a privilege, in a sense, yet it also involved much personal responsibility and risk. Jesus chose disciples—real human beings—to develop his new people, just as Judaeo-Christian faith teaches that Yahweh chose a body of people called Israel for special favor and moral responsibility (Deuteronomy 7:6–9, Matthew 4:18–22, Acts 1:8). Members of the early post-resurrection community of the Lord, such as St. Paul, spoke of Christians as "chosen" ones, a new Israel, if they accepted fully the gospel message—whoever they might be, whatever their past. Other primitive Christian voices spoke of the community of Jesus' followers as God's own nation, one chosen to proclaim Christ's mercy, love, and light (1 Peter 2:9–10). In time, persons preparing spiritually for baptism, and thus reception into the church, engaged in a rather long period of catechetical and liturgical formation. Full members of the church challenged them to risk living the gospel's message and values and introduced them, in various ways, to Christian sacramental rituals. Those in preparation for full Christian initiation and church membership came to be-known as catechumens.

Today, contemporary catechumens (those not baptized) and candidates (those already baptized but not fully initiated) prepare for reception into the Catholic church through the Rites of Christian Initiation of Adults. On the first Sunday of Lent, they are affirmed at Mass by their sponsors and community, and they are then ritually enrolled in a book of the Elect. The gathered assembly prays for the newly elect and sends them forth to meet with the local bishop for the rite of Election. During this rite, the bishop receives the catechumens and candidates into the body of "the elect" and instructs them about what they should consider in order to be ready for full initiation into the Christian community at the Easter Vigil. From then on, those in this phase of the Christian initiation process are considered "called and chosen" by God to become full members of God's church.

(See also Catechumenate and the RCIA, Easter, Lent, and People of God.)

ENCYCLICALS are formal pastoral letters written by popes to all members of the church throughout the world. These pastoral messages typically offer guidelines on matters of Christian faith, morality, and church disciplines. "Encyclical" can be traced to both Latin and Greek terms that mean "in a circle," "general," and "common to all." Generally speaking, a papal encyclical gets its title informally from the first few words of its text.

The first papal encyclical was issued by Pope Benedict XIV in 1740. It was called *Ubi primum*. This letter to the global church community addressed the chief duties of Catholic leaders. Issuing encyclicals to the entire Catholic body around the world became a more common practice during the 19th century, especially during the time of Pope Pius IX, and that trend has continued to the present day.

Encyclical messages are formal statements by the leadership of the church community; thus in many cases Catholic individuals and local faith communities are encouraged to accept wholeheartedly the papal teachings they contain. Yet, not many encyclical letters are meant to be infallible statements. In fact, many of the authoritative teachings borne by papal encyclicals past, present, and future will have to be refined, restated, or more appropriately phrased for proper interpretations and proper understandings in diverse, evolving cultures and emerging communities in the Christian global body still to come.

The Catholic community affirms that the pope is the chief leader and pastoral guide for all members of the universal church. Therefore, according to Catholic tradition, encyclical teachings on Christian faith and morality have a special authority to which all the baptized should give particular recognition and honor. In 1950 Pius XII noted officially, in *Humani generis*, that encyclical "teachings belong to the ordinary magisterium, of which it is true to say: 'He who hears you, hears me' (Luke

10:16); for the most part, too, what is expounded...in encyclical letters already appertains to Catholic doctrine for other reasons." In its Dogmatic Constitution on the Church, Vatican II pointed out that the teachings of popes in encyclicals should be reverenced and adhered to in both one's heart and mind.

Some encyclical statements by the church's leadership are actually not written for a worldwide audience. These documents—called encyclical epistles—are addressed to limited regions of the Christian community or certain persons alone.

Since the time of Pope Leo XIII (1878–1903), over 150 official church encyclicals and limited encyclical epistles have been published. Pope John XXIII (1958–1963) issued eight, Paul VI (1963–1978) wrote seven, John Paul I who was pope for a very brief time in 1978 wrote none, and John Paul II, pope since late 1978, had written nine by the beginning of 1994.

(See also Doctrine, Infallibility, Magisterium, and Pope.)

Note of Interest: A *motu proprio*, also more formally called a *motu proprio et certa scientia*, is an official document issued by the pope. Usually the subject of such a papal declaration is a church administration issue or, on occasion, a special favor that the pope wishes to grant. A *motu proprio* is always created solely by the choice of the pope. The Latin term *motu proprio* refers to this. It means doing something "on one's own accord."

EPIPHANY   is the church's solemn feast day on which Catholics celebrate liturgically the manifestation of the divinity in Jesus of Nazareth. The solemnity of the Epiphany has traditionally been celebrated on January 6. One of the key events in the life of Jesus especially commemorated on this feast day is the visit by the magi (or wise men) to the newborn Jesus and to Mary, his mother, and Joseph, her husband (Matthew 2:1–12). "Epiphany" has Greek and Middle English roots that connote an appearance, a manifestation, or "to show forth."

First celebrated in the 3rd century, Epiphany was later discussed in the writings of the great Clement of Alexandria. (This 3rd-century date indicates that celebration of the Epiphany pre-dates the current Western church custom of observing Christmas.) Epiphany became popular in numerous local Christian communities, and its observance soon spread to all parts of the Christian world.

By the time of the Middle Ages it had become a common custom among Catholics in some places to have their households blessed in association with the Epiphany. A main part of the blessing ceremony of the time was the inscription (with chalk) of the names traditionally given to the wise men (magi)—Melchior, Balthasar, and Caspar—above the doors of Christian family homes. Epiphany was also dedicated to (focused on) several Christian themes besides the manifestation of the divinity in the child Jesus. These themes included celebration of the birth of Jesus of

Nazareth, in the town of Bethlehem, and Jesus' baptism by John at the beginning of his public ministry.

Through the centuries, it has become customary for the members of various religious orders to renew their personal vows of poverty, chastity, and obedience on or near Epiphany. In many countries today January 6 is the only date on which the solemnity of the Epiphany can be celebrated. In the Catholic community of the United States, however, it is now celebrated annually on the Sunday between January 2 and 8.

The Epiphany remains one of the most ancient and most traditional of Christian liturgical feasts. In some areas of the world this feast coincides nicely with various twelfth night parties and other traditional festivities.

(See also Christmas, Holy Family, and Liturgical Year.)

EPISTLE has Greek origins, *epistole*, which mean "letter" or a "message." The letters, or epistles, in the Christian Scriptures (i.e., the New Testament) are attributed to persons named Paul, John, Peter, Jude, and James. The epistles are very ancient statements of Christian belief. Some were written prior to the drafting of the gospels.

At times today "epistle" is still used in limited circumstances to describe the first or the second readings from the Bible during celebrations of the Catholic liturgy of the Word. Twenty-one short "books" in the Christian Scriptures can be legitimately referred to today as epistles. These epistles were addressed by their authors to various primitive Christian-era communities and individuals in order to instruct them about the basic beliefs of the followers of Jesus, to advise them practically about moral behaviors and relationships appropriate for Christians, to encourage and inspire them in faith, and to urge them to counter false religious doctrines that often cropped up.

Many think that the various epistles date back to at least the years 55 c.e. through the early 100s. Fourteen of the epistles in the Christian Scriptures are attributed to Saint Paul, though current biblical and historical research suggests that Paul himself most probably did not compose all fourteen. It is likely that the historical Paul did in fact compose the epistle to the Romans, 1 and 2 Corinthians, and the brief epistles to the Galatians, the Philippians, to Philemon, and 1 Thessalonians. Recent biblical and other scientific research endeavors have cast some doubt on his actual authorship of the epistles to the Colossians and the Ephesians, as well as the second letter to the Thessalonians. It is believed that persons other than Paul, perhaps close disciples and associates of his, actually wrote the epistles to the Hebrews, 1 and 2 Timothy, and Titus. These early-era Christian epistles are Pauline in style and intent, in that their authors clearly were influenced by Paul's remarkable preaching, teaching, and theological thought.

The seven epistles in the New Testament not attributed to the pauline tradition are the epistle of James, 1 and 2 Peter, the epistle of Jude, and 1, 2, and 3 John. These are often called the catholic letters of the Christian churches. Although various apostles of Jesus—Peter, James, and John—

are named as the authors of these early Christian tracts, these letters were probably written by various followers of Jesus of Nazareth who were familiar with the evangelizing efforts and thought of the original apostles.

(See also Bible, Books of; Inspiration; New Testament; and Paul.)

EUCHARIST   is one of the seven sacraments of the Catholic community. According to canon law, it is the "most august" of all the sacraments (canon 897). The term Eucharist is also used at times as a synonym for the Catholic communal ritual known as the Mass. The word comes from the Greek *eucharistia*, which means "thanksgiving." Members of the Catholic church maintain that the risen Jesus is fully and truly present in the Eucharist, in the forms of bread and wine, and that the eucharistic celebration is the central act of worship and communal prayer for all baptized persons. Thus Catholic peoples trust that the Eucharist is meant to be their essential spiritual food and drink, a spiritual nourishment provided to humanity by a loving God.

The Christian eucharistic celebration has deep roots in the Hebrew seder, a ritual meal commemorating the original passover and the exodus of the ancient Hebrews from slavery in Egypt. Christian communities believe that in the setting of a passover meal Jesus of Nazareth, in the company of his apostles (at their "last supper"), instituted the sacrament of the Eucharist. The Christian Scriptures indicate that Jesus, at that time, blessed, then broke, then shared bread with his close followers saying, "Take this and eat it, this is my body." Then he blessed and shared a cup of wine with them saying, "All of you must drink from it, for this is my blood." Jesus then commanded his followers to celebrate the Eucharist in his name and memory (Matthew 26:26–29, Luke 22:17–20).

Through the first few centuries of community life, Christians celebrated the Eucharist on Sundays and on a few other special occasions. At first, the Eucharist was held in the context of ordinary (agape) meals in Christian households. But by the 2nd century the practice of sharing the Eucharist ("breaking the bread") in this way had stopped and Christians had begun to gather for special eucharistic rituals in central locations on the Christian sabbath. (For more information on these elements of Christian history, see the articles on Agape and Church, as Home.) The Catholic eucharistic prayer (the canon) and the formal consecration of the bread and wine into the body and blood of Jesus Christ became central features of the Mass in succeeding centuries.

The Fourth Lateran Council in 1215 developed the term "transubstantiation" to properly describe the process of establishing the real presence of the risen Jesus in the Eucharist. In 1965, in the encyclical *Mysterium fidei*, Paul VI stressed that transubstantiation is to remain the preferred term among members of the Catholic community to indicate the change of bread and wine into the Eucharist, truly the body and blood of Jesus Christ, during the celebration of the Mass.

Vatican Council II in the 1960s urged Catholics and others to reflect deeply on the mystery of Jesus' real presence within the community of the baptized whenever they assemble for the Eucharist or for another purpose. The Eucharist is meant to be a meaningful ritual experience that transforms the Christian community, the body of Christ, into a people united in faith who proceed from worship to live, act, hope, and dream in a spirit of conversion and community—as the living, evolving, and sacramental presence of God's Spirit in the global human community.

The idea of the Eucharist (and the Mass) as a sacrifice remains a central aspect of Catholic tradition. In the Eucharist believers are united with the sufferings and self-sacrifice of Jesus on the cross who still today gives himself ceaselessly and faithfully to the Creator.

The church teaches that every Catholic who has received his or her first Eucharist (first communion) must receive the sacrament at least once, during the Easter season, every year (see the article on Easter Duty in this book). In addition, the Catholic community maintains that only presbyters and bishops may preside at the Eucharist and consecrate the elements of bread and wine into the body and blood of the Lord. Other church members take part today in eucharistic liturgies as members of the assembly, lectors, commentators, special ministers of the Eucharist, music ministers, ushers, and liturgical planners.

The Catholic community continues to emphasize that in the Eucharist Jesus Christ becomes fully and really present in the forms of ordinary bread and wine. Doctrines on these matters of faith have been stated or restated by the Councils of Trent, Constance, and Fourth Lateran, Vatican II, and also recently by Paul VI in the encyclical mentioned above. The *Catechism of the Catholic Church* refers to the Eucharist as a passover meal or paschal banquet, which is both a sacrificial memorial that continues Jesus' sacrifice on the cross and a holy banquet at which his followers—a true communion—share his body and blood. The Catechism notes too that each time it is celebrated, the sacrifice of the Mass must be wholly directed toward intimate union with Jesus, for to receive communion (the Eucharist) is to receive the God in Jesus who has offered himself for all humankind.

(See also Agape; Church, as Home; Eucharistic Prayer; Liturgy of the Word/Eucharist; Passover; and Transubstantiation.)

Note of Interest: The Catholic community calls each of its members to receive the Eucharist at least once a year (the Easter duty). To receive this sacrament at any time, however, one must be free from serious sin and believe in the real presence, being capable of distinguishing communion from ordinary bread and wine. All Catholics preparing to receive the Eucharist are expected to fast for a short period of time. No food or liquids (besides water) may be taken within one hour prior to personal reception the sacrament.

EUCHARISTIC PRAYER/CANON OF THE MASS   is the long prayer proclaimed at the heart or main section of the liturgy of the Eucharist in the Mass. This eucharistic prayer is sometimes still referred to as the canon of the Mass.

The Roman Canon, known today as Eucharistic Prayer I, probably was first formed in the 600s. It has remained intact, in today's basic form, since the 800s. This basic Roman canon can be prayed at Mass on any occasion. Since 1975, the church has added a number of additional eucharistic prayers, including three for use with Masses with children and two for liturgies with a theme of reconciliation.

The canon of the Mass calls to mind essential events in religious history and prayers for the living church, the dead, and the saints. Its proclamation begins immediately after a prayer called Holy, Holy, Holy Lord and is concluded just as the congregation prepares to join in the Lord's Prayer. During the eucharistic prayer, bread and wine are consecrated. The culmination of this prayer occurs when the presider holds up the consecrated bread and wine, saying "Through him, with him, and in him, etc." to which the assembly responds aloud, "Amen."

The eucharistic prayer emphasizes the death and resurrection of Jesus and our own self-sacrificing dyings-and-risings as Christians. The faith expressed in the eucharistic prayer is meant to encourage church members to choose ever-new life, love, and personal sacrifice in daily service to the human community.

Only the main presider and concelebrants are allowed to pronounce the eucharistic prayer at Mass. In 1987, the bishops of the United States re-emphasized that no unofficial form of eucharistic canon may be used in church liturgies. As noted, Eucharistic Prayer I can be used in any situation. Eucharistic Prayer II, the briefest canon, has its roots in the 3rd century and is well suited for daily Mass. Eucharistic Prayer III, with its fine remembrance of those who have died, is often chosen for use on Sundays and important feasts. Eucharistic Prayer IV, with its roots in primitive Christian communities and its emphasis on historical religious events, can be used effectively especially in worshiping groups aware of Scripture themes and church history.

(See also Eucharist, Liturgy of the Word/Eucharist, and Presbyter.)

EUTHANASIA   is the practice of directly killing human individuals or the overall process of allowing human beings to die by not following basic and normal medical procedures. Generally those who die as a result of euthanasia have suffered sicknesses or painful injuries to a hopeless degree. Euthanasia is often spoken of as a mercy killing. The word stems from both Latin and Greek origins that imply a "well (or painless) death." Catholic tradition, however, has long emphasized that euthanasia in most cases is really an act of murder.

In the history of the Christian community, and in church teaching contexts in particular, two central themes have emerged in serious discussions and debates on the practice of euthanasia. The first theme centers on the Christian doctrine that all the baptized should maintain ultimate respect for all human life and should therefore avoid every action that might destroy or hinder it in any way. The second key theme focuses on the Christian doctrine that a good God has created life and thus all human beings created by the one God have a special worth, goodness, and dignity that should not be extinguished prematurely.

Debates on "mercy killing" some years ago often revolved around distinctions between "putting people to death" as compared to "letting persons die." Purposely putting someone to death by physician-assisted suicide (which was much in the news in the U.S. in the early 1990s), by suffocation, or through an overdose of drugs, for example, has often been judged in recent decades to be an act of murder. However, some Catholic theologians have pointed out recently that church tradition seems to support the idea that it is not necessary in any situation to use extraordinary means simply to prolong the human existence of someone who has suffered a grievous illness or injury. Church authorities have commented formally during our time that the administration of powerful drugs to those suffering and dying—to ease severe pain—can at times hasten one's physical death, yet this medical and merciful practice is not necessarily a sign of euthanasia and may even be advisable in certain circumstances.

The moral issues associated with serious illnesses and euthanasia are very complex. Many church leaders and theologians have noted that official Catholic positions on the entire matter of euthanasia or on moral issues and practices related to it could be much refined or made more definite in the years ahead. The church's current teaching on euthanasia has been more clearly and fully developed since the 1960s, the time of Vatican II. For euthanasia to take place today, according to official Catholic thought, an intentional act must occur that is directly opposed to human life in some way.

The Catholic community, therefore, continues to stress that every case of euthanasia does great dishonor to the Creator of all life, and that all human beings today should actively search for ways to safeguard and respect the dignity of human life, not destroy it in any manner. The *Catechism of the Catholic Church* stresses that those who participate in ending the life of a disabled, sick, or dying human being—whatever the motive(s)—commit an act that is morally unacceptable. Thus any action or omission that causes physical death directly contradicts the fifth commandment ("you shall not commit murder") and seriously disregards the true dignity of every human person and the respect due to the living God.

(See also Commandments of God, Death/Dying, Morality, and Suicide.)

EVANGELIZATION　　is the entire faith-inspired process of witnessing to and sharing the good news of Jesus of Nazareth with others. The terms "evangelization," "evangelize," etc., have Greek roots that mean "messenger" or "one who announces." According to Christian tradition, evangelization is the foremost mission and duty of all the baptized.

Evangelizing activity occurs whenever and wherever persons who have never heard the gospel of Jesus, or persons who have been baptized but have become alienated from the Christian community, or persons who have come to believe in the Lord and the community that follows him, benefit in some way from the witness of committed Christians and become introduced (or reintroduced) to the saving power and values of Jesus' call to life-changing conversion.

The biblical and apostolic-era roots for the Christian mission to evangelize all peoples, places, and cultures can be discerned in many texts in the Christian Scriptures (Mark 16:15, Matthew 28:16–20, Luke 10:1–9, etc.) In 1975 Pope Paul VI developed a pastoral statement on modern evangelization for the worldwide Catholic community. This statement, *Evangelii nuntiandi*, stressed the need for a renewed willingness among contemporary Catholics to witness to and proclaim the good news of Christian hope to others, particularly in light of the many spiritual struggles, relationship troubles, cultural shifts, and everyday stresses that men and women experience in our time. *Evangelii nuntiandi* cited the Christian traditional viewpoint that all Christian witness, outreach, and gospel proclamation is dedicated to the conversion of others. Thus, the purpose of Christian evangelization is "interior change, and if it had to be expressed in one sentence the best way of stating it would be to say that the church evangelizes when [it] seeks to convert, solely through the divine power of the message [it] proclaims, both the personal and collective consciences of people, the activities in which they engage, and the lives and concrete [situations] which are theirs."

Evangelization is something every baptized person should do, simply by witnessing through everyday words, work, deeds, and lifestyles that somehow "speak" to others about Christian hope and Jesus' call to all human beings to join the great enterprise of preparing the way for the ultimate reign of God in creation. Many Catholics, however, seem to either fear or avoid using terms like outreach, proclamation, witness, and evangelization, thinking that these somehow should only be associated with street preachers, fundamentalist communities, TV televangelists, fringe Christian cults, and the like. An emerging Catholic perspective on evangelization is that the term is properly perceived when it is used to refer to a wholistic pastoral process of reaching out to others, in the name of Jesus and his community, to care for their needs, to befriend and serve them, to eventually share the good news of the gospel with them, and then to invite them to accept this gospel and enter (through baptism) or re-enter (if they have become alienated from the church) the living Christian community. Thus, the dynamics of Catholic evangelization include daily Christian witness, pastoral outreach, proclamation of the gospel, and invitation to Christian community. These dynamics should be infused into the church community's ongoing ministries of word, worship, community building, and social service.

Several significant new Catholic statements on the mission of evangelization have appeared in the U.S. in recent years. In 1993, the bishops of the United States issued a pastoral plan for the American Catholic community called "Go and Make Disciples." The National Federation for

Catholic Youth Ministry issued (also in 1993) its statement "The Challenge of Catholic Youth Evangelization: Called to Be Witnesses and Storytellers." Pope John Paul II has called often for a "new evangelization" and a "re-evangelization" by members of the worldwide Christian community. He has encouraged local Catholic communities to reach out to others from all races, cultures, and social heritages with the good news of Jesus, and to do so with new enthusiasm, a new certainty, new methods, and renewed expressions of Christian faith. This is needed by the spiritually-troubled human race because the world today eagerly awaits a true and inspiring sense of hope (a "new Advent" as it were) and wishes to oppose all things that threaten the spiritual and physical welfare of humanity and creation.

In recent years many parishes and dioceses have established evangelization teams and committees to pursue the goals of Christian faith sharing among those who live in or near their communities. The church, however, continues to urge all baptized persons to actively witness to their own Christian conversion and beliefs because, to paraphrase Paul VI, modern people today listen to living witnesses more readily than teachers, and if they listen to teachers and preachers at all it is because they are witnesses.

(See also Conversion, Gospel, Kerygma, Missions, and Witness.)

EXCOMMUNICATION   is the process of imposing a penalty or punishment on a baptized person that results in the dismissal (exclusion) of that person from union with the Catholic, eucharistic community. The word comes from Latin roots that basically mean to "expel from communion." This sanction or punishment is only placed on someone who has very seriously violated an important Catholic teaching or the Catholic Christian way of life. Excommunication is the church community's most severe penalty or censure.

There are several indications in the Christian Scriptures that some individuals were put outside primitive local communities of Jesus' followers. This process usually followed upon a gravely sinful choice or deed by someone baptized, who then refused all calls for repentance and reconciliation with the gospel way of life. Excommunication itself was mentioned first in 4th-century church documents. By the 6th century, one who sinned seriously was permanently alienated from the Eucharist and general church life unless he or she did extended public penance and was sacramentally reconciled. This sacramental reconciliation from sin could occur only once in life. Later, a disciplinary censure process was developed by the church and was applied to those who were fully alienated from the Christian community and adamantly opposed to repentance.

Today, some speak of the rarely-used process of excommunication as an enduring sign of the church's concern about the spiritual well-being of the people of God. It is a severe penalty that always has and always will be rooted in Christian hope. Every sinner is called to turn away from alienation and wrongdoing and toward Jesus and the gospel-based community. In essence, excommunication is designed both for the spiritual healing of one who has chosen a path opposed to church ways and the strengthening of the entire Christian body through the actual return of one who has very seriously strayed away.

Excommunication is never irreversible. The love and forgiveness of God, and of all God's people, is always extended to the one penalized. Currently, the official church believes excommunication should be used only in cases of absolute need (for very seriously wrong actions, words, or lifestyle choices). Absolution from this severe form of church exclusion may be offered only by a local bishop or, in certain cases, only by the pope. In the Code of Canon Law, Book VI, canons 1311–1399 specify the sanctions, penalties, and censure processes that the church imposes in certain situations. Typical human choices that result in automatic excommunication from the community of the baptized include abortion, heresy, causing a serious disruption in overall church unity (schism), apostasy, and violation of "the seal of confession."

(See also Apostasy, Hope, Reconciliation, and Sin.)

EXEGESIS   involves the examination of and explanation of a passage or portion of the Bible. The word is Greek and means "leading out." Thus, contemporary biblical exegesis is a bringing out (or leading out) of a biblical author's real thoughts, meanings, and purposes in writing. Exegesis is related directly to a science called hermeneutics, which is a disciplined interpretation of Scripture.

Christian biblical exegesis has a long history. Schools of Scripture study were begun in the communities of Alexandria and Antioch by the 3rd century. St. Jerome (d. 420) and St. Augustine (d. 430), among others, commented insightfully about the meaning of the sacred writings. After this, however, interest in biblical exegesis waned as a whole for a time. In the 1200s a new focus on analysis and interpretation of Hebrew Scriptures arose. By the 18th and 19th centuries, Catholic leaders felt particularly challenged to defend the divine inspiration of Scripture. In 1890, the Ecole Biblique was founded in Jerusalem. In 1909, the Pontifical Bible Institute was started in Rome. These Catholic schools were dedicated to the examination and interpretation of biblical books. Pope Leo XIII issued the encyclical *Providentissimus deus* in 1892, and, in 1943, Pius XII wrote *Divino afflante spiritu*. Each document strongly encouraged the use of biblical research, biblical criticism, and various sciences (e.g., history and archaeology) for better Catholic biblical interpretation and study.

Today, scholars speak of exegesis as the science of hermeneutics in action. A basic theological understanding that applies to this is that biblical texts were penned by human beings in an inerrant and inspired way. This understanding has led to much intriguing dialogue between Catholic and Jewish researchers and to 1) positive influences on Catholic catechetical and liturgical ministries (especially preaching of the Word), 2) exciting translations and new editions of the Scriptures, 3) further investigation of the Dead Sea Scrolls and other old texts, and 4) greater Catholic community renewal overall.

Biblical exegesis helps humankind respond better to God through God's revelation in biblical events, figures, and themes. Scholars are urged to investigate the meanings and purposes of the sacred writers of the Bible in order that all church members can better know that which God has communicated to humankind. Specific guidelines for modern exegesis were developed at Vatican Council II in its Dogmatic Constitution on Divine Revelation. In essence, authentic biblical exegesis will examine 1) the original languages in which a text was composed, 2) literary forms or genres used, 3) cultural and historical events surrounding biblical authors, 4) geographical details related to the text, 5) church doctrines related to the Bible, and 6) the quality of various translations of the biblical text(s) under consideration.

(See also Bible, Dead Sea Scrolls, Inspiration, and Revelation.)

EXORCISM   is the process of driving out evil spirits from possessed persons. An exorcist is an individual who performs rites of exorcism. The word *exorcism* comes from the Greek *exorkizein*, which means roughly "to drive away" by command. The exorcism rituals of the Catholic community include prayers and forceful commands demanding that evil spirits (sometimes also referred to as devils and demons) either leave the presence of persons possessed or stop troubling them altogether.

It is reported in the Christian Scriptures that Jesus of Nazareth powerfully commanded many evil spirits and demonic presences to leave people who were suffering. Some of Jesus' original followers also used spiritual powers to assist those troubled by evil spirits. Church teachings have noted that a devil—sometimes personified as Satan or Lucifer, but actually the overall powers of evil, sin, and darkness in human life—is a real (but spiritual) entity and remains humankind's greatest enemy or adversary, opposed to all forms of goodness and the spiritual well-being of men and women. The power of sin, however, cannot and will not prevail because all of humanity has definitively (once and for all) been redeemed by Jesus of Nazareth through his death and resurrection by God. Thus the powers of sin and evil have been conquered for all time. These concepts have provided the theological foundations for the ritual known as exorcism.

For centuries the order of exorcist was one of the minor orders received by all men preparing for the Catholic presbyterate (priesthood). However, the Catholic community declared in 1972 that this minor order, as well as some others, would no longer be received by those preparing for ordination. Officially speaking, Catholic church-sponsored exorcisms are very rare. Those that are performed are usually administered by presbyters who are the special delegates of the local bishop of the diocese in which the exorcism ritual takes place.

Modern scholars maintain that many cases supposed to be examples of demonic "possession" and illness today actually are caused by pathological (natural) factors rather than by supernatural forces and evil spirits. Church leaders today seem to recognize and generally accept that a person is truly possessed by supernatural evil only if there is absolutely no natural explanation for the spiritual or physical problems that the troubled individual experiences.

A Roman Catholic exorcism rite incorporates prayer for the one possessed and the use of sacramentals such as holy water and the crucifix. In the ritual of the sacrament of baptism, in a form of traditional exorcism, the Catholic community calls upon the one to be baptized to reject sin and evil (the devil) and all that is opposed to God's goodness and creation. The Catholic baptismal liturgy also contains exorcism prayers for the ongoing spiritual protection of those to be baptized. The Rite of Christian Initiation of Adults contains exorcism prayers for those seeking to enter the church through the sacraments of initiation. These prayers call all members of the Christian community to pray that those preparing for church membership might forever remain freed from sin, preserved from evil, and outside the direct influence of the devil.

(See also Baptism; Catechumenate and the RCIA; Devil; Election, Rite of; and Prayer.)

F

FAITH   is one of the three theological virtues (the others are hope and charity). The rich roots of the word "faith" lie in the Latin term *fides*, which means "belief" and "trust." In a general sense, faith can be described as a trust, a conviction, commitment to, a response to, or belief in someone or something. Religious faith can be defined, in a way, as trust in (or belief in), a response to, and commitment to the Creator God who has revealed many things throughout the history of the world to humankind. Some people use the word faith—referring to a religious faith—predominantly as a noun, as in "the faith," referring basically to belief in a set of essential doctrines, values, and ritual practices involved in the Christian way of life as a whole. Others comment today that faith, in a religious or spiritual sense, is in many ways more like a verb (i.e., a way of life or active lifestyle), as in "I live my faith" or "I am one ever-growing in, acting on, and ever-learning about our shared Christian faith tradition."

Jesus of Nazareth, who was the promised messiah of Israel and God's greatest revelation, called others to repentance (for the reign of God was at hand) and to faith in him, in order to truly believe and live his good news about salvation for all of humanity. Key beliefs and values in primitive Christian communities centered on Jesus' death and resurrection and on the import of his life-changing message for the whole of the human race. Great thinkers such as Saint Augustine (d. 430), and Saint Thomas Aquinas (13th century) have held that true Christian faith is like an inner light, a thorough conviction about God and the ways of God toward human beings and the church in particular.

In recent centuries the leadership of the Roman Catholic community has strongly emphasized that Catholic faith is an act of the intellect (the mind)—a reasonable response to God's revelation and church traditions—in order to offset certain influences in Christian life worldwide that were initiated with the Reformation in the 16th century. Some theologians continue to explain the nature of Christian faith, at least in great part, as an intellectual assent to divinely revealed truths—an act of the human will moved by God's grace. A number of other theologians and pastoral ministers, however, speak these days of the ancient Christian tradition that faith foremost is a gift (or grace) from God to which every human being must give a fundamental response of some sort. Therefore, because faith is not a seeable or touchable phenomenon, faith responses to the Creator and the faith community (people of God) that follows

Jesus are truly risks based upon some kind of conviction(s) that God is really disclosing an invitation to love and to faith. Thus, faith at its roots has to do with relationship—between God and human beings, and between believing members of the human community as a whole.

Today, faith growth is often seen as a dynamic process, something that evolves and changes as a person moves through his or her life-cycle. Thus the faith style of the child will be somewhat different from the faith style of the adolescent or young adult, which in turn should be somewhat less mature than the faith response of the maturing adult or senior citizen. This idea leads many to conclude that faith is a wholistic phenomenon: Yes, it involves an intellectual response (rational assent) to God's revelation and church doctrines and tradition, but it also truly encompasses the whole way of life one adopts in and through one's personal relationships with God and the world, and it encompasses one's choices, actions, and decisions (which either are or are not fundamentally in line with faith in the one, good Creator). This means that parents, catechists, and pastoral outreach workers must envision the task of "transmitting Christian faith and values" to young and old alike as a process of helping them "learn the basics of the faith" but also as a process of helping them become individuals who live the faith and act on their faith convictions—a Christian faith-ing lifestyle—in all their relationships and activities day by day.

Thus, as many theologians have said, the experience of Catholic Christian faith cannot simply be a "me and God" thing, a personal experience only. Faith in the Christian tradition is a personal and communal reality, a gift from God that challenges individuals to share in the faith life of all the baptized on the globe, i.e., the faith life of the entire people of God whom God is calling to friendship and happiness forever.

Vatican Council II in the 1960s taught that religious faith must be a free response. Individuals must be able to freely choose to commit themselves to God and the reign of God proclaimed by Jesus of Nazareth. Therefore, no one should ever be forced to believe in a religious tradition, doctrine, or historical figure. Council documents likewise stressed that all Christian individuals and local communities should give living witness daily to the whole world about the total trust in God that characterizes baptized persons, thereby also disclosing the shared hope and love to which people of faith are called by the gospel.

Noting the import of perseverance in Christian faith, the *Catechism of the Catholic Church* says that the gift of faith from God is the beginning of one's everlasting life (articles 163–165). The vision of life with the Creator "face to face" is the goal of the human journey: yet now, on Earth, as Paul said, we "walk by faith, not by sight," we perceive divine realities dimly and partially, and one's faith is often tested. Thus we should run the course of human life with Christian perseverance, looking to Jesus of Nazareth as a model and witness, "the pioneer and perfecter of our faith."

(See also Atheism, Deposit of Faith, Free Will, God, and Virtue.)

FAMILY MINISTRY   is a response by the contemporary Christian community that acknowledges the key role that the family of origin and family household plays in the transmission of Christian faith and values to all its members, especially the young. In a sense, then, family ministry—or better yet, attempts to incorporate a family perspective into each existing ministry endeavor in a local faith community—respects the reality that every Christian household is a domestic church or "church of the home" and tries to empower local families to fulfill their multifaceted baptismal mission: to share the good news of Jesus of Nazareth with all persons, to pray and worship regularly as a small community with the church body overall, to form and support its members in faith, and to reach out to serve the needs of others in the world, the wider "human family of God." The term "family" has Latin roots (*familia*) that point to concepts such as "servant" and "household." Recently the bishops of the global Catholic community have stressed that support for modern family life and for family ministry efforts must remain a major priority in all local church communities.

The Catholic emphasis on the notion of family as an *ecclesia domestica*, a domestic church, is not new; it is, in fact, very ancient. The ancient Hebrews viewed the family of origin as a force that helped shape the nation of Israel as a whole and the quality of its communal existence in particular. Among the Hebrews the heart of family life was imaged as a covenant-style love between persons. Family relationships thus were seen to be symbolic of the loving relationship between Yahweh and God's chosen people. The earliest followers of Jesus emphasized that family households were the key building blocks or cells of God's spiritual family on Earth. In a way, then, early Christian generations saw the combined Christian community, the church, as a "household" in which God's family dwelled. The earliest of Christian communal and ritual gatherings happened in ordinary homes—"house churches" or churches of the home.

Modern family life seems to have become more fragmented, hurried, individualistic, materialistic, and otherwise vulnerable. Major cultural shifts and upheavals have reinforced this perception: for example, the increase in divorce rates, both husbands and wives working outside the family household, increased births to unwed mothers, more frequent cohabitation among unmarried persons, economic limitations, and the availability of finely-tuned birth control methodologies. Some observers point out, however, that contemporary media and other "voices" in our pop culture have perpetuated a myth or stereotype of sorts that all of modern family life is therefore endangered in Western culture and that all families are stressed beyond help, dysfunctional, and in a state of total disintegration. These observers note that family life today is perhaps changing, diverse (in its family structures), and often harried and stress-inducing, but many family households (even many non-traditional households such as single-parent families, stepfamily systems, etc.) nevertheless remain strong and functional in their attempts to live and hand on a living, faith-filled way of life.

Recognizing some of these issues, an international synod of bishops met in Rome in 1980 to consider the role of the Christian family in the contemporary world. This synod proposed a Christian charter on family rights. It urged the church's membership to help modern family households to try to daily 1) live in contradiction to the strains of modern pop cultures, 2) become constructively critical of human injustices and human disregard for spiritual values, 3) affirm that valid marriages cannot simply be discarded or ignored through separation and divorce, and 4) choose a lifestyle consistent with its calling (mission) as a true church of the home, promoting growth in holiness for all family members according to the gospel of Jesus.

Vatican II underscored in the 1960s a long-held Christian community conviction that parents are actually the first and foremost educators (Christian formation ministers) of their children (for example, see the Council's Declaration on Christian Education, article 3). It urged local ministers to become partners with parents and grandparents of children in this important Christian effort.

In recent decades, therefore, Catholic leaders have urged local communities to offer direct support to mothers, fathers, and other family members. As a result a number of Catholic parishes and other types of small faith communities have begun to regularly sponsor family-centered catechesis programs and other family-related faith-formation ministries, such as family retreats, parish family gatherings, and family-oriented seasonal prayer/sacramental services. In 1981, in a statement titled "The Role of the Christian Family in the Modern World," Pope John Paul II challenged all Christian churches to support every family household today, whatever its composition, racial background, or economic or social status, and to help family units to witness to the gospel of Jesus of Nazareth.

In 1987, the Catholic bishops of the U.S. produced an official statement called "A Family Perspective in Church and Society." The bishops indicated that the late 20th-century ministry agenda related to modern family life will include 1) reflection by local pastoral staffs on the conditions and realities of family life in modern cultures, 2) extension of Christian hospitality by local faith communities to households/families of all kinds, and 3) new and creative steps to offer better support and better services that will help contemporary families build upon their strengths, move from crisis to growth, and be enabled to journey from stress to new life in the Lord. The bishops noted that this can best be done by having local churches incorporate "a family perspective, as a pastoral strategy, into all (present and future) policies, programs, ministries, and services."

More recently, in November 1993, the U.S. bishops published a new document on family life and ministry called "Follow the Way of Love: A Pastoral Message to Families." Designed as a U.S. Catholic contribution to the 1994 International Year of the Family, it noted that family life and family ministries participate "in the work of the Lord [as] a sharing in the mission of the church..."

(See also Agape; Church, as Home; Divorce; Holy Family; Matrimony; and Small Faith Communities.)

FASTING is the spiritual practice and self-disciplinary process of choosing to go without eating solid foods for designated periods of time. Members of the Catholic community in the United States are required to fast on certain days of the year—on Ash Wednesday and on Good Friday—if they are between the ages of 18 and 59. In current U.S. church law, this means that persons can eat only one full meal and two smaller snack-type meals on these days. The terms "fast" and "fasting" have Middle English origins (*festen*) that mean "abstain from food." Abstinence is not the same as fasting in Christian terminology. To abstain means to refrain from eating meat or meat products at certain times. (See the article on Abstinence in this book.)

Biblical evidence suggests that Jesus of Nazareth and his original disciples recognized the value of fasting. Among early generations of the baptized, prayer and fasting were often linked together for the purposes of doing penance for sinfulness and growth in Christian spirituality. The general idea of a Christian fast day that permits only one full meal per day dates back to the 5th century.

Originally both Wednesdays and Fridays all year long probably were marked by community members for spiritual fasts (and all Fridays soon became days on which all Christians also abstained from eating meat). In time, however, fasting became focused on Good Friday (actually the 40 hours surrounding the observance of Good Friday each year) and on the days prior to important liturgical feasts, such as Christmas, Easter, and the Assumption of Mary. Eventually the idea of a lenten fast among Christians was broadened by Catholic custom in Europe to incorporate all of the season of Lent, from Ash Wednesday through Holy Saturday (every day of Lent, in other words, except Sundays), a spiritual discipline that many older Catholics today can recall in great detail. In 1966 Pope Paul VI significantly relaxed many of the very strict church fasting and Friday abstinence rules, basically establishing Ash Wednesday and Good Friday as the only fast days at that time.

Current reflection on the meaning of Christian fasting seems to underscore the spiritual value of the practice and the practical help it can lend to persons who truly wish to grow in their relationship with God through penitential actions and self-discipline. Fasting is best done within a prayerful context that includes doing acts of charity (works of charity and mercy), daily prayer, almsgiving, and social action endeavors.

Official church rules regarding fasting and abstinence were "relaxed" in the 1960s for a special spiritual reason: namely to encourage members of the community of the baptized to become more personally responsible for meeting the general Christian gospel mandate to do penance for one's wrongdoing. Thus the Christian community expects all its members to do penitential works, and it is, in some ways, up to every church member and family household to decide if regular penance(s) will include fasting, abstinence, almsgiving, works of charity, prayer, devotions, or some other forms of spiritual development.

Catholic leaders continue to urge all Catholic individuals, families, and parishes to elect to fast regularly on their own, even though many of the fasting laws from the past have been relaxed. The obligation to do penance frequently, and particularly to fast on the appointed days of the church year, remains one of the church's precepts in the United States. Universal church rules regarding fasting, abstinence, and other penitential works can be found in the *Code of Canon Law*, canons 1249–1253.

(See also Abstinence; Almsgiving; Ash Wednesday; Church, Laws of; and Lent.)

FATHERS AND DOCTORS OF THE CHURCH were outstanding leaders, writers, teachers, and catechists during some of the early centuries of the Christian experience. The honorary titles of "Fathers of the Church" and "Doctors of the Church" do not mean exactly the same thing, but the officially recognized Fathers and Doctors do share some similar qualifications and characteristics. Thus both titles refer to spiritually-minded historical figures, all of them saints in Christian tradition, who proved to be great church writers, teachers, and theologians, and who became in their day memorable and outstanding witnesses to the gospel of Jesus and the way of life appropriate to his committed followers.

Four criteria have been used to establish one as an authentic Father of the Church: 1) one who was a teacher of correct doctrine, 2) who lived a Christian lifestyle dedicated to the Christian mission and to holiness, 3) who received the broad approval of Catholic community leadership, and 4) who can be linked to Christian antiquity (i.e., the earliest centuries of the post-apostolic era church body).

Officially speaking, the time of the great church fathers, called the Patristic Age, extended from the 1st century to basically the 8th. Certain historical persons closely associated with Christian literature and the dynamic growth period of Christian communities in the earliest generations of the church have been referred to often as Apostolic Fathers, a term (coined during the 17th century) indicating some kind of contact between these saints and the original apostles of Jesus or their immediate followers. In church tradition, the Apostolic Fathers include: Clement of Rome, Ignatius of Antioch, Polycarp, Papias, Justin Martyr, Irenaeus, and Clement of Alexandria. Listings of the latter church Fathers have typically included: Ambrose, Augustine, Jerome, Athanasius, Cyril of Alexandria, Cyril of Jerusalem, Ephraim, Hilary of Poitiers, Isidore of Seville, Leo the Great, Gregory the Great, Basil the Great, Gregory of Nazianzen, and John Chrysostom. The last of the great Fathers were Gregory the Great and Isidore of Seville in the Western Catholic church community and John of Damascus in the Eastern Catholic tradition.

Doctors of the Church have had to meet the same traditional criteria as Fathers of the Church through the centuries, but Doctors of the Christian community have not been expected to have had close linkages with Christian antiquity. Overall, church Doctors, both female and male persons, were learned and holy (saintly) Christian witnesses, most of whom were notable teachers of Christian doctrine. These individuals have been named Doctors of the Church through either explicit statements by church councils or by papal decrees.

Officially, there are 32 Doctors of the Church, some of which also qualify as Fathers of the Church. The most recently named Doctors of the Church are Teresa of Avila and Catherine of Siena, each named by Paul VI in 1970. These were the first women to be acclaimed as Doctors of the Church in Christian tradition.

The list of Doctors of the Church includes: Albert the Great; Alphonsus Liguori; Ambrose, also a Father of the Church; Anselm; Anthony of Padua; Athanasius, also a Father of the Church; Augustine, also a Father of the Church; Basil the Great, also a Father of the Church; Bede the Venerable; Bernard of Clairvaux; Bonaventure; Catherine of Siena; Cyril of Alexandria, also a Father of the Church; Cyril of Jerusalem, also a Father of the Church; Ephraim, also a Father of the Church; Francis de Sales; Gregory of Nazianzen, also a Father of the Church; Gregory the Great, also a Father of the Church; Hilary of Poitiers, also a Father of the Church; Isidore of Seville, also a Father of the Church; Jerome, also a Father of the Church; John Chrysostom, also a Father of the Church; John of Damascus, also a Father of the Church; John of the Cross; Lawrence of Brindisi; Leo the Great, also a Father of the Church; Peter Canisius; Peter Chrysologus, also a Father of the Church; Peter Damian; Robert Bellarmine; Teresa of Avila; and Thomas Aquinas.

(See also Doctrine; Saints, Communion of; Veneration; and Witness.)

FORTY HOURS DEVOTION   is a traditional form of Catholic communal worship that has afforded members of local faith communities a special chance to honor the real presence of Jesus Christ in the Eucharist. Where it still is observed, this type of devotion is usually held once a year in parish church settings. Traditionally, it has begun with a celebration of the Mass to which all parishioners and others are invited, followed by the placement of a large eucharistic host in an ornate container called a monstrance, which is then carried through the parish church building by the pastor or another presbyter in a solemn procession. This initial phase of the 40 Hours devotion traditionally has been concluded with the placement of the Eucharist on the main church altar for all to visit during the next forty hours or so. The entire devotional period is brought to a close by the pastor (or another local presbyter) and the parish assembly with a recital of certain ritual prayers, with the singing of Christian hymns, and with a parish-wide celebration of a Mass of "reposition."

The Forty Hours devotion was first conceived during the 14th century. It seems, however, that it was first fully held in Milan, Italy in 1527 or 1534. Pope Clement VIII declared in 1592 that it was to be held annually in all parishes in the diocese of Rome. This church custom then spread to other parts of the world. The idea of "forty hours" was decided upon because popular Christian notions have stressed that the body of the crucified Jesus of Nazareth lay in a tomb in Jerusalem forty hours before he was raised to new life by God on the first Easter Sunday.

Two main reasons have often been cited for the origination of the practice of the Forty Hours devotion: 1) to give members of various local faith communities a chance to pray for protection against troubles and 2) to allow time for the baptized to make amends and do penances for personal sins. In the 20th century this devotion has often taken on a main theme of veneration of Jesus in the Eucharist rather than making amends for personal faults and failings.

In 1973 the church officially decreed that the devotion should take place once a year in local parishes and that Catholics should be encouraged to spend periods of time during their parish's appointed 40 hour devotional period thinking about the mysteries of the incarnation of the Word of God, the Eucharist, and the saving and enduring presence of the risen Jesus in the church community on Earth. In recent years a simplified and shortened version of this devotion has been observed in U.S. Catholic parishes.

(See also Benediction, Devotion, Veneration, and Worship.)

FREE WILL/RELIGIOUS FREEDOM   is the natural human capacity to be responsible for one's personal decisions and actions. In exercising free will, individuals and communities make choices (voluntarily and freely) for good or evil. The concept of free will is at the foundation of all Christian morality and points to the essential dignity and uniqueness of every human being.

The idea that all human individuals enjoy the God-given freedom to make choices appeared in the writings of many early church writers and teachers, especially St. Augustine. To do God's will and to achieve full union and happiness with God in heaven deeply involves how one uses one's free will and God's gift of grace throughout one's lifetime. To freely work toward ultimate salvation and to seek God's ways in everyday life is a loving, mature human response to God's unmerited gifts of faith and grace.

Vatican Council II maintained that every human person in the world has a right to religious freedom. The council added that this unique freedom is based upon the authentic dignity of each man and woman, created in God's own image and likeness, and therefore is in accord with God's revelation.

Recent teachings in the Catholic community have stressed that all nations and governments should recognize religious freedom as a civil right for everyone. Thus every individual deserves true religious freedom. Whenever groups of individuals act in community for the common good of humankind, they should also be accorded religious liberty without question or restraint. A complete study of Vatican II's teachings on freedom and religious freedom can be found in its document Declaration on Religious Freedom. (Interestingly though, the conciliar statements did not directly address the issue of freedom in the Christian church itself.)

(See also Creation, Discernment, Faith, and Morality.)

FRUITS OF THE SPIRIT   are named in chapter five of the epistle to the Galatians in the Christian Scriptures (New Testament). According to Christian faith and tradition, the spiritual fruits of the Spirit of God enable human beings to live in a humble and unselfish manner. The fruits have been traditionally listed as: charity, joy, peace, patience, gentleness, goodness, mildness, faith, endurance, modesty, self-control, and chastity.

The spiritual fruits are grace (or gifts) from God that counter some of the sinful effects that humanity experiences by not following the Spirit's transcendent plan for human salvation and happiness. The epistle to the Galatians lists some of these sinful effects as lewd behavior, impure living, worshiping false gods, sorcery, hostility, frequent arguments, jealousies, rage and anger, selfishness, dissension, envy, drunken behavior, and sexual misconduct.

Through the ages, members of the Catholic community have been encouraged to remain always open, in prayer and in personal lifestyle, to the fruits of God's Spirit in order that they may continue to grow and mature in Christian faith, holiness, and active Christian witness.

(See also Epistle, Faith, Grace, Holiness, and Trinity.)

FUNDAMENTALISM   is a 20th-century religious movement primarily in North America that focuses on the Bible as the ultimate guide to Christian faith and life. It is a very conservative wing of Christian evangelicalism. Fundamentalist believers strongly emphasize a literal understanding of the Bible. They believe that the Bible is humankind's error-free religious truth and authority from God.

Fundamentalists tend to reject contemporary biblical exegesis and focus on personal holiness (piety) in a way that downplays the need for any Christian social action. They likewise tend to look to biblical prophecy and a coming apocalypse (a future second coming and reign of the Lord Jesus) in a way that views human experience and modern cultures as basically evil and sinfully degenerating until Jesus' triumphant return. Strident fundamentalist congregations see most other Christian churches as too liberal or worldly. Fundamentalist worship centers on a revivalist Christian spirit and intense Bible preaching.

Fundamentalism originated in Christian evangelicalism in England in the 1730s and in America's "Great Awakening" of the 1740s. The term was first used in the early 1920s. It referred to conservative Christians who believed strongly in the teachings of publications called *The Fundamentals*, little booklets that taught fundamental truths, such as the full unerring authority of Scripture, and pointed out the mistakes of liberal "enemies" of Christianity (e.g., atheism, naturalism, socialism, Roman Catholicism, and Mormonism).

Fundamentalists soon began to exercise great influence in various Christian congregations in the northeastern and southern United States, and in American politics, eventually spreading across the continent. In the 1940s, some fundamentalist Christians began calling themselves "evangelicals." They proved to be a counterpart to fundamentalist hardliners. Evangelicals have basically been able since then to coexist peacefully with mainline Protestant churches. Several have become famous (e.g., Billy Graham, an evangelical TV televangelist and world-traveling missionary, and Jimmy Carter, a "born-again" evangelical Christian, who became the U.S. President in 1976). A number of archconservative, fundamentalist TV preachers and Christian televangelism in general were quite prominent in U.S. presidential politics and social debates in the 1980s and early 1990s. Notable figures included Jerry Falwell and Pat Robertson.

Unlike Catholics, many fundamentalists believe in the absolute necessity of being "born again"—of experiencing an emotional and very sudden life-changing moment of being "saved" by Jesus Christ, and accepting him as one's personal Lord and Savior. Also, unlike Catholic Christians, fundamentalist believers tend not to recognize the worth of biblical exegesis or accept the work of Bible scholars on elements of myth and symbolism in the Word of God. And fundamentalist emphasis on personal faith experience and piety—to the virtual exclusion of Christian social doctrine and communal Christian service—lies in stark contrast to the recent social teachings of the Catholic community and Catholics' long-term faith in God's loving and universal offer of grace, mercy, and forgiveness.

Fundamentalists and modern evangelicals, numbering some 45 million Americans in recent times, continue to have noticeable influence on Protestantism in the U.S. Many fundamentalists, in particular, continue to express unshakable belief about the literal truth of the Bible and their religious convictions. Some individuals and congregations testify to the need (mission) to impose fundamentalist beliefs and practices on others so they too can be "born again," be "baptized in the Spirit," and possibly avoid eternal damnation.

In recent decades, an evangelical branch of Christianity called pentecostalism has arisen in America. Pentecostalist Christians are very flamboyant evangelicals, noted for charismatic-type traits like prophecy, healing, fiery preaching, speaking in tongues, and intense faith testimonies. Pentecostals number about two million today. They tend to be staunchly fundamentalist in their beliefs and profess rigid codes of moral behavior.

(See also Bible, Exegesis, Grace, and Inspiration.)

G

GIFTS OF THE SPIRIT   are seven unique gifts offered to all of humankind by the Spirit of God. The seven gifts are identified in the book of Isaiah (Isaiah 11:2–3) in the Hebrew Scriptures (Old Testament). Traditionally, the gifts have been identified as: 1) wisdom, which bestows an ability to personally discern God's will for one's life; 2) understanding, which helps persons know that which God has revealed; 3) knowledge, which aids members of the human community in their desire to know and believe in things as they really are; 4) fortitude, which provides persons with special strength and courage needed to face various human troubles, questions, and struggles; 5) counsel, the gift that helps humanity decide what to do and what to choose in problem situations; 6) piety, which assists persons in their attempts to reverently approach God as loving and good Parent and Creator; and 7) fear of the Lord, which teaches the human community that God is transcendent, all good, and loving; thus Christian peoples trust that God is deserving of human beings' complete reverence, awe, and adoration, while remaining a close Spiritual Companion, Guide, and all-loving Parent to all humans.

Christian faith and tradition emphasize that human beings are infused with the gifts of the Spirit of the Creator, by God's grace, in and through the sacrament of baptism, and that these gifts are strengthened by the experience of the sacrament of confirmation. The Catholic community believes that the seven gifts of the Spirit strengthen human beings in their efforts to lead faith-filled and moral lifestyles in line with the Creator's transcendent plan for human salvation and happiness. Scripture scholars often point out that the number seven was frequently used symbolically by biblical authors to indicate perfection, fullness, or completion in God.

(See also Baptism, Discernment, Exegesis, Revelation, and Trinity.)

GOD   in Christian thought is the one, spiritual, perfect, and infinite Being—a holy One without limitation—who "always was and always will be." The word *god* has origins in Teutonic and Middle English languages. Christian monotheism stresses that God is the mysterious but supreme and holy Being who alone is creator and ruler of the entire universe. Some other adjectives traditionally used to describe this one Creator are all-good, all-loving, self-sufficient, all-knowing, uncaused, everlasting, and the final end or horizon of all of human existence.

Humankind's awareness of and appreciation of God has developed over the centuries. Both Jews and Christians believe that God loves human beings and all of creation unconditionally. Jesus of Nazareth spoke of God as a personal, loving Parent —"abba," which basically means "daddy"—a God nearby and understanding of human experience, not a stern, other-worldly judge. The Christian community teaches that there is but one, true, caring, and loving God (e.g., see 1 John 4:7–13) but three expressions of this one God: Father, Son, and Spirit (the Trinity). This God has loved humanity so much that the Son (the Word), Jesus of Nazareth, the Christ, became human. Jesus has been called the ultimate love and revelation of the Creator.

In the 13th century, St. Thomas Aquinas developed a number of rational proofs for the existence of this invisible, untouchable God. He and others since then have tried to fully describe the infinite God's everlasting attributes by using terms like: almighty, compassionate, eternal, faithful, good, holy, immanent, immortal, incomprehensible, ineffable, just, loving, merciful, most high, mysterious, omnipotent, omniscient (all-knowing), patient, present, provident, simplicity, sovereign, supreme, transcendent, ubiquitous, unchangeable, and unseen.

In recent decades, church teachers have noted with Thomas Aquinas that reason and reflection on human life can lead one toward belief in the one God. One should live in a way always open to discoveries about God, and prayerfully search in all things, at all times, for what God wants us to do with our lives. Doubts or questions about the actual existence of God seem to be quite natural or normal, although painful, in some human lives. Doubts about the reality of God or God's care can eventually lead persons to strong faith. In fact, many faith-filled Catholics and other persons of yesterday and today have experienced powerful doubts about God and have searched hard in life for signs of God's presence. Contemporary believers emphasize the power of Christian prayer—a form of spiritual communication by which people can seek to "talk things over" with the all-knowing, ever-present God—at any time, through any joyful experience or depth of trouble and doubt.

Catholic teachings stress that human beings, along with all creation, are dependent on the one Creator God. God is a good and personal Being, not an impersonal cosmic force. God loves all persons and all things, and seeks a real love relationship with each person, each culture, and all of humanity. God, the supreme being, is distinct from the world (God is transcendent), yet God is likewise mysteriously present and active everywhere in human lives and in all of reality (God is immanent), in the form of God's loving Spirit, leading humanity and creation, as a whole, toward the great horizon envisioned by the Creator—the reign or kingdom of the one, good God. Catholics trust that it is absolutely necessary that one believe personally in the existence of the Almighty and the divinity of the human revelation of God—Jesus Christ.

(See also Creation, Monotheism, Pantheism, Revelation, Trinity, and Yahweh.)

GODPARENTS   also sometimes called Christian sponsors or baptismal sponsors, are those persons (sponsors) who assist adults in Christian initiation process, or who (godparents), along with the parents, present an infant for baptism. According to current church law and pastoral practice, there can be up to two godparents present at each baptism of an infant. In special circumstances, however, there can be one Catholic godparent present and one non-Catholic baptized person present who serves as a witness to the baptism. Godparents today are challenged to accept the important role of caring for the baptized person's ongoing spiritual welfare and Christian formation if his or her parents or guardians cannot or will not do so for some particular reason.

The pastoral practice of having a fully initiated member of the Christian community act as a spiritual friend and guide to someone preparing for baptism and full membership in that community is an ancient tradition. Current church law requires that a godparent or sponsor who is Catholic must be 16 years of age or older, must have received the sacraments of baptism, confirmation, and Eucharist, must be active in practicing his or her Catholic way of life, and should be fully willing to assume the rather important role that godparents must play in the spiritual lives of those Christians they sponsor.

Godparents and sponsors visibly represent the whole faith community of the baptized and give witness to the love and support this Christian community in Jesus is willing to pledge to the newly initiated. Recent Catholic thinking about infant baptism, however, has served to re-emphasize that, ultimately, the role of all godparents is secondary to that of parents and families of origin. Thus godparents and sponsors in the present day appropriately serve as representatives of the community of Christ who perform certain ritual functions during sacramental ceremonies and act as a lifelong connection to the Christian community for the one baptized. The Code of Canon Law indicates that those who "undertake the office of sponsor (along with the parents of the one to be initiated) are to be properly instructed in the meaning of the sacrament and the obligations which are attached to it..." (canon 851). Ideally, one male or one female sponsor or one of each sex is to be employed in the baptism of another (canon 873).

The Code adds that a "baptized person who belongs to a non-Catholic ecclesial community may not be admitted [to the role of godparent/ sponsor] except as a witness to baptism and together with a Catholic sponsor" (canon 874). Generally speaking, it is expected by the church community that godparents will offer wise and practical life-guidance, spiritual assistance, and a wholesome formation overall for the one baptized on an ongoing basis whenever these are called for.

(See also Baptism, Catechumenate and the RCIA, Confirmation, and Sacraments.)

Note of Interest: Confirmation Sponsors. When an adolescent or adult is receiving baptism or confirmation or both through the Rite of Christian Initiation of Adults (RCIA), no godparents participate in the celebration. One person, a baptized and active Catholic, of the same sex as the candidate for initiation or full communion, is present at the ceremony as a sponsor. This sponsor is called by the entire people of God to be a witness to Christian faith and an example of how to live a Christian life for the newly initiated at all times. The Code of Canon Law speaks of sponsors for those to be confirmed. It says that, "as far as possible, a sponsor for the one to be confirmed should be present" for the sacramental ritual and adds that the sponsor should try to see "that the confirmed person acts as a true witness to Christ and fulfills the obligations connected with this sacrament" (canon 892). Therefore, the confirmation sponsor must fulfill the same conditions as the baptismal sponsor/godparent and "it is desirable that the one who undertook the role of sponsor at baptism be a sponsor for confirmation" (canon 893).

GOSPEL   is a traditional Christian term referring to the good news of salvation proclaimed to humankind by Jesus of Nazareth and the community that follows him. The word can be used to mean one or more of the following things: 1) the entire ministry and teachings of Jesus, 2) one of the four versions of the good news story written by the original evangelists, and 3) the proclamation of part of one of the four gospel versions during a Catholic Christian liturgy of the Word or other ritual. The word *gospel* is derived from the Anglo-Saxon *godspell*, which fundamentally means a "god story."

While there truly is only one gospel, there are four versions of the Christian good news (gospel) in the Christian Scriptures (New Testament). The authors of the four gospel versions, often referred to as evangelists or evangelizers, were not attempting to write a complete biography or history of the life, preaching, and ministry of Jesus of Nazareth. Rather, they wrote about significant events in Jesus' life and the personal encounters, spiritual teachings and sayings, and stories of his that the earliest followers of Jesus had remembered and wished to have handed on to their successors. At the heart of each version of the gospel story is the crucial story of the suffering, death and, resurrection of Jesus of Nazareth.

Historical evidence and current research suggest that each of the four gospels was written sometime between the years 65 and 100 c.e. It is generally held that the gospel of Mark was the first gospel to be written, followed closely by Matthew, Luke, and John, in that order.

(See also Evangelization, Exegesis, Jesus of Nazareth, New Testament, Parable, and Synoptics.)

GRACE   is God's free, unmerited, loving gift of God's own life and presence to individuals and to the human community as a whole. Through a loving and open response in faith to this gift, human beings and human cultures are transformed and share dynamically in God's life and love. They also become more and more like Jesus of Nazareth, the "pioneer and perfecter" of the proper human response to God's grace, as the *Catechism of the Catholic Church* states. The gift of grace is the precondition to eternal salvation (i.e., the foundation of an everlasting relationship and happiness with the Creator). The word derives from the Latin *gratia*, which means "favor" and "free gift."

The church teaches that human beings receive grace as a totally free gift from God through the saving work and witness of Jesus, and that this gift transforms (or elevates) human nature to a new, higher level of existence. In the Christian Scriptures, grace is conceived as the key principle and source of Christian life and spirit. That is, grace impels the followers (individuals and communities) of Jesus of Nazareth to be like him, to do good works, and to act with righteousness.

Since the beginning of the Christian community's story, the people of God have been plagued by heresies and misunderstandings about the nature and experience of God's grace. St. Augustine (5th century) pointed out that grace is a gift completely unmerited by humanity. The Catholic community of the Middle Ages struggled with false teachings (and to a degree continues to address these teachings) on predestination, stating quite clearly that grace, salvation, and everlasting happiness are meant for all persons—not simply for a pre-chosen few selected personally by God for ultimate happiness. By the time of the Council of Trent (16th century), the Catholic church was teaching that, through the powerful gift from God known as grace, human beings are fundamentally transformed interiorly by God's own Spirit of love.

The question of how men and women remain free and natural beings, even as they participate in God's self-communication of life and love through grace, has been posed and studied in recent decades. Some think of grace as a gift of God's Spirit that can transform one's life, relationships, and free human journey for the better and that can profoundly urge (call) human beings and communities to change for the better. Other theological ideas highlight the notion that grace is like a relationship. A good and loving God offers the opportunity, universally, to all individuals, communities, and cultures, for a friendship (ongoing relationship) with God, to which every human being or community must give an essential yes or no response on an ongoing basis. This concept of grace as a divinely-initiated relationship—ultimately a matter of faith—is the basis on which persons today can choose to develop a deep, ongoing connection with their God and by which they can find strength to avoid sin and do the right things in life, thus following the path carved out for all of humanity by Jesus of Nazareth and his original followers.

Today the church understands grace as God's gratuitous love given to the entire human community, past and present (and future). Thus grace is not a "thing" or a heavenly substance of any sort that can be measured, quantified, or piled up like a spiritual bank account that will be one's ticket to heaven. Rather, it is spoken of dynamically as a divine life source, a source of God's revelation, life, and love communicated to and offered to all human beings freely by a God who longs for human beings and communities to love God back in all ways at all times.

Vatican II documents note that the Spirit of God dwells in and with humanity, and in the church community in a unique way, through the gift of grace. Catholic tradition underscores that the one God makes a free and loving offer of God's own life to all persons and cultures in order that they might respond in some way in faith. The loving relationship between the Creator and those who lovingly respond to the unmerited gift of grace can be deepened, day by day, through prayer, devotions, the sacraments, loving attention to human relationships, and the completion of works of charity and justice.

Sometimes grace is still described (as in the new *Catechism of the Catholic Church*) as actual, sanctifying, created, and uncreated—phrases that stem from scholarly, theological studies of the nature of grace from centuries past. The church calls all members of the people of God to reflect seriously and prayerfully on the mystery of God's divine gift of grace.

(See also Conversion, Creation, Faith, God, and Revelation.)

H

HEAVEN according to Christian tradition is that state of being or spiritual condition enjoyed by all who have achieved the happiness and perfection of everlasting salvation. Christians believe that those in heaven enjoy the beatific vision, a complete and perfected happiness with God, the loving Creator of all life. The term stems from the Middle English *heven*.

Parts of the Christian Scriptures (New Testament) speak of the human potential to see God in the blessedness of life-after-death. This vision of God is mentioned in the beatitudes and in the writings of Saint Paul, who claimed that believers would eventually see God "face to face" (Matthew 5:8; 2 Corinthians 3:12–18). The first letter of John says that men and women will see God. It indicates that people of faith will be transformed and become glorious like God in heavenly happiness. The New Testament also describes heaven as eternal life.

Major church teachings on heaven have been included in the doctrinal statement *Benedictus deus* by Pope Benedict XII, published in 1336, and the authoritative statements of the Council of Florence (1439). These teachings point out that all who die worthy of heaven, and without any need of purgatory, see God clearly and immediately after death. Recently, Pius XII (in 1943) and then Paul VI (in 1968) have re-emphasized the church's long-standing doctrine on heaven.

Some contemporary theologians have described heaven as a way of spiritual life or a spiritual condition from which the Word of God—known in history as Jesus of Nazareth—came and to which the eternal Word has returned. All who choose freely to live according to the vision of God's reign and the life values Jesus proclaimed, thus achieving the fullness of salvation, will eventually join the Word "face to face" in heavenly happiness. Others stress additionally that heaven should be imaged as a state of being, a condition of existence full of joy and light, rather than as a material place (in the geographical sense).

Catholic thinking emphasizes that heaven must be seen as complete union with God, a beatific or blessed, everlasting relationship in God's actual presence. Thus heaven is the antithesis of the everlasting alienation from God and the resulting loneliness, separation, and loss known as hell.

The church community clings to its teachings on heaven as a great source of human hope. Catholic teachings often present heaven as a true goal of all human life and as unselfish, perfect, and total union with God.

Catholic tradition maintains that each human person is judged at the time of death as to whether he or she has, fundamentally, through life either accepted and responded to God's gift of grace and life or has inclined basically toward sinfulness. This judgment is called the particular judgment. Catholic teachings hold also that, at the moment of the second coming of the Word to all of humankind (the *parousia*), all who have lived will be judged as worthy or unworthy of salvation and eternal life (heaven) in the eternal reign of God. This is referred to as the final judgment of the human community.

(See also Grace, Hell, Parousia, Purgatory, Reign of God, and Salvation.)

HEBREWS is one of the terms traditionally used by the Christian community and others to identify the ancient members of the nation of Israel, God's original chosen people. Two more common, modern words used to identify those who have descended from the Hebrews are Jews and Israelites. "Hebrew" was most often used in biblical times to refer to those members of the Israelite nation who spoke the Aramaic language and adhered strictly to ancient Jewish customs, laws, and spiritual traditions. The Catholic community and other Christian traditions fondly remember the ancient Hebrews to this day as the descendants of the great patriarch Abraham—and, therefore, the spiritual ancestors of all Christian peoples and communities, chosen specially by Yahweh among all the peoples of the world—who then tried to live up to a loving and lasting covenant that had been made by God with God's chosen ones. The Hebrew Scriptures (Old Testament), the Christian Scriptures (New Testament), and Christian tradition overall indicate that the Yahweh known to the ancient Hebrews is in fact the same one, loving God in whom the baptized have believed throughout the Christian era.

(See also Anti-Semitism, Catholic-Jewish Relations, Covenant, Judaism, Patriarchy, People of God, and Zionism.)

HELL is the spiritual state or condition of everlasting alienation from God. Tradition teaches that a human being's own free, complete, and deliberate life-choice of sinfulness and evil leads that person to the experience of hell. Christian belief says that hell begins right after physical death for those who die estranged from the divine by sin, and that the experience of sorrow in hell will last forever. The term has Middle English and other roots—words like *helle* and *helan*—that refer to "cover" and "concealment."

The term "hell" does not appear in the Hebrew Scriptures (Old Testament), yet a roughly equivalent term, *gehenna*, does appear. *Gehenna* in Hebrew thought was an unholy place, an actual geographical spot in ancient Israel, wherein the corpses of those who had revolted against Yahweh were thrown. In some ancient Jewish documents, *Gehenna* is pictured as a dark and fearsome place, an environment full of fire in which unfortunate, evil-doing human beings were chained and suffering. *Gehenna* is mentioned at times in the Christian Scriptures of the Bible

(New Testament), particularly by Jesus. It is depicted there as a place of fire and suffering in which there is much pain and many tears.

A great creedal statement, produced by Christian community leaders in the late 400s, claimed that hell, a state of eternal damnation and punishment for human sinfulness, truly exists. The Catholic belief in hell was upheld by the Fourth Lateran Council in 1215, by the Second Council of Lyons in 1274, by other key church councils, and by Pope Benedict in 1336.

Hell was not directly mentioned by the Second Vatican Council in the 1960s, nor has it been much discussed critically and officially by recent Catholic community leaders. Some conservative theologians and catechists still describe hell as a place of fire and unending punishment and torment. But some modern thinkers now maintain that the New Testament only assumes, but cannot empirically confirm, the existence of a spiritual state or condition called hell for some individuals who have died. Some contemporary thinkers believe that Jesus of Nazareth may have used very dramatic, hellish imagery drawn from Hebrew traditions to strongly urge his listeners to turn away from sinfulness and hardheartedness and to turn toward (and be converted to) his message about the reign of God-at-hand.

Neither Jesus of Nazareth nor anyone else in the Christian community has ever taught, definitively, that a specific human being or group has been permanently banished to hell. Some writers and thinkers go so far in our day as to suggest that the notion of eternal damnation is just out of the question for a God who is an all-good and all-loving Creator. Others emphasize that heaven and hell are something like two poles or opposite ends of an issue related to acceptance or fundamental rejection of God's offer to humanity of life, love, and loving relationship: Thus men and women are free to respond daily to God's grace (and thus, strive for the pole called heaven) or they can lean freely toward sinfulness and total separation from God and others (and move toward the other pole, hell).

The official Catholic tradition stresses that God does not dispatch persons to eternal unhappiness and alienation in hell. Human beings, throughout their lifetimes, either fundamentally respond to God's gift of grace and strive spiritually for salvation in a positive way or they fundamentally reject God's free gift of life and love, and thus opt for unending sorrow and a painful existence without relationship to God or relationship to the graced human community.

Hell is often pictured as the unspeakable torment of complete loneliness and loss. The Catholic church still teaches that there is a devil, a powerful adversary to humankind, who is like the prince of hell, and that those who die after choosing a lifestyle that has rejected totally the gift of grace are judged worthy of the experience of hell. The gospel of Matthew, in chapter 25, speaks of a final judgment at the second coming (the parousia) at which all who have lived on Earth through the ages will be either welcomed into the everlasting happiness of heaven, as members of God's perfected reign, or bound to an eternal state or condition known as hell.

(See also Devil, Free Will, Heaven, Parousia, and Sin.)

HERMIT is one who chooses to live in total isolation (i.e., fully removed from society) in order to focus on a way of life dedicated to quiet prayer, penance, and other spiritual-growth endeavors. The word has Greek roots meaning solitude and "desert place." There have been female and male hermits since the earliest Christian times, and some choose to practice the lifestyle of the Christian hermit to this day.

Catholic tradition holds that the Christian witness of hermits is of great value to the whole church community. Hermits' lives testify to the human and Christian search for God and to the need to contemplate great mysteries that God has revealed and placed at the core of human existence. In a sense, a Christian hermit is a sign of hope affirming God's ongoing care for humanity and a sign of the church today still gazing, in sincere prayer, toward the loving Horizon of all creation.

(See also Prayer, Religious Orders.)

Note of Interest: A monk is a member of a Christian religious community of men who live apart from the social world. The term "monk" is from a Latin word for "one who lives alone." In the 3rd century some men in the Middle East entered the desert to lead solitary lives of Christian prayer and conversion. These original Christian hermits soon had many followers. Eventually, some banded together to form small, religious communities. This development began the rise of Christian monasticism, a communal lifestyle of religious orders of men and women that emphasized solitude, reflective prayer, worship, and work. Great orders of monks still in existence include the Benedictines, Cistercians, Trappists, Carthusians, and others. The teachings of Vatican II urged contemporary monks to devote themselves to Christian prayer and worship, within the seclusion of the monastery life, or to take up meaningful and prophetic works of charity in the wider world, in addition to their ongoing prayer and worship of God.

HOLINESS is a way of life characterized by a state of being sanctified and thus dedicated in a very special way to God. The holy man or woman, according to Christian tradition, is one who possesses God's gift of grace and is committed, actively and unselfishly, to love of God, to moral goodness, and to bettering the world for all persons. The Catholic community believes that God is all-perfect and all-holy, that Jesus of Nazareth—the perfect model of holiness for Christian peoples and cultures—was dedicated to the Creator in a completely holy manner, and that all members of the people of God are called to ultimate Christian holiness.

The words "holy" and "holiness" have Middle English roots in *holi*, meaning "to be consecrated, sacred, or set apart" for God. In the Hebrew Scriptures, Yahweh (God) speaks of Godself as the Holy One (Isaiah 40:25; Jeremiah 50:29). Many generations of Hebrew and Jewish people believed that a truly holy man or woman was someone with a life mission, completely dedicated to serving Yahweh, and that the sacred nation of Israel, the nation set apart and selected by Yahweh to be God's specially chosen people, was likewise very holy (Leviticus 17–26).

The Catholic community affirms that God is infinitely perfect and all-holy, completely and spiritually pure and unchangeable, totally separate from evil, and the source of all goodness and grace (holiness) in human existence and in creation. God demands a lifestyle that gives witness to growth in Christian-style holiness from all members of the community of the baptized worldwide and ultimately from all members of the human race.

The Catholic church teaches that the risen Jesus is and was historically a uniquely holy person in his commitment to God, his love for God's definitive salvation plan, called the reign of God, and his care for all people. Christian tradition calls and challenges all men and women to be devoted to the Creator as Jesus of Nazareth was, and to imitate the lifestyle of holiness and charity apparent in the life-stories of Jesus, Mary, the mother of Jesus, and all the saints—witnesses to the ways of God's holiness who have passed through the human journey into heaven. Catholics trust that the church, while populated by fallible human beings and groups, is truly sacramental and holy in that it is a living sign of God's care for humanity and a particular dwelling of the Spirit of Jesus on Earth. Catholic teachers likewise stress that each baptized person has a holiness-oriented mission to share with all communities and cultures the gospel of salvation that urges them toward a life of conversion and Christian holiness. The universal church community has the same mission.

Vatican Council II maintained that Catholic Christians can progress in holiness particularly through prayer, devotions, and reception of the sacraments, especially the Eucharist. Catholic commentaries since the 1960s have also noted that by doing one's life work in the marketplace (and by freely engaging in Christian acts of charity and mercy), in the name of Jesus of Nazareth, a contemporary disciple of Jesus can develop dynamically in holiness and find ways to better cope with the human trials, troubles, and problems that go with modern life. Those Catholics (whether clergy, religious, or laity) who practice the evangelical counsels (vows) of poverty, chastity, and obedience are spoken of in traditional Catholic terms as outstanding gospel-committed witnesses to and examples of holiness.

Current church documents emphasize that all Christians and others have a duty to work together in harmony to make the entire people of God on Earth, the human community worldwide, more holy and a more perfect sign of how Jesus would want human beings and cultures to live in this world.

(See also God; Grace; Morality; Paraclete; Saints, Communion of; and Virtue.)

Note of Interest: Authentic Christian spirituality involves a whole way of life. It gives active witness to the dynamic Spirit that motivates and inspires, and it is in harmony with the goals of the people of God and body of Christ. To be a spiritual human being is to admit that there is more to existence than what is encountered through the senses. It is to trust and pray that God is present to humanity and creation through the gift of grace. It is to be constantly open to God in order to understand who we are and what God asks of us. Some signs of living spirituality in the Christian community are liturgical renewal, commitment to liberation and social justice issues, renewed honor given to Scripture, ecumenical developments, and increased desire for personal, prayerful experiences of the Spirit.

HOLY DAYS   also called "holy days of obligation" are special feast days on the church's liturgical calendar. On these annual feast days, Catholics who have reached at least seven years of age are expected to attend a celebration of the Eucharist (Mass) and to avoid all unnecessary work.

For some time now, six holy days have been celebrated by the Catholic church in the United States. They are: the Solemnity of Mary, Mother of God (January 1), the Ascension of the Lord Jesus (40 days after Easter Sunday), the Assumption of the Blessed Virgin Mary (August 15), All Saints' Day (November 1), the Immaculate Conception of Mary (December 8), and Christmas Day (December 25). These particular Christian solemnities (a solemnity is the highest rank of feast in the liturgical calendar) were established as U.S. holy days by the third Plenary Council of Baltimore, during the 19th century. Four other holy days are celebrated in certain parts of the world, according to general Catholic discipline, but not in the United States. These include: Epiphany (traditionally January 6), Saint Joseph's Day (March 19), Corpus Christi (a movable solemnity), and the solemnity of the apostles Peter and Paul (June 29).

In the United States, since 1993, the obligation to attend a eucharistic celebration has been relaxed any time that January 1, August 15, or November 1 falls on a Saturday or a Monday. However, it is still expected that all persons in the Catholic community will honor traditional holy day practices.

(See also Church, Laws of; and Liturgical Year.)

HOLY FAMILY, FEAST OF   is the day on which the Catholic community honors Jesus, Mary, and Joseph as a family. This feast is usually celebrated each year on the Sunday between December 25 and January 1. Traditional Christian devotion to the holy family of Jesus of Nazareth became very popular among church members during the 17th century. In 1921, Pope Benedict XV stated that through this feast the universal church community should most reverently honor and remember the holy family. Earlier, Pope Leo XIII had blessed and dedicated all Christian families to the holy family.

The Catholic church teaches that members of Catholic families ought to look to the life shared by Jesus, Mary, and Joseph—a domestic community rooted in faith and love—as a perfect example of the virtue-filled, spiritual, and holy lifestyle to which every family household should strive. Thus every modern family of origin should therefore try to be like the holy family—an *ecclesia domestica* or "church of the home"—accepting its mission to live as Christian witnesses.

(See also Church, as Home; Family Ministry; Jesus of Nazareth; Joseph; and Mary.)

HOLY SEE   refers to the official network of Vatican agencies, departments, officials, and diplomats—the Roman Curia—authorized by the pope to assist him in the central administration and government of the global Roman Catholic church. The term can likewise be used to identify the diocese of Rome, the home diocese of the Roman pontiff. "See" is a church term meaning "diocese." *Curia* is a Latin word that implies a "court" and "center of government." Catholics trust that the agencies and officials in the Roman Curia will act faithfully and effectively in the name of the universal church and in harmony with the authority of the pope.

The present structure of the Holy See, or Roman Curia, evolved very gradually in church history from various clergy groups and advisory bodies that helped different popes guide church affairs. By the 4th century, a central church government called the Apostolic Chancery had been created. The current Roman Curia somewhat resembles the institutional Catholic church organization of the mid-1500s. The Curia was officially established by Pope Pius X in 1908. Paul VI's great reform and reorganization of the Holy See took effect in March 1968. In 1988, John Paul II made further changes in the structure and operations of the Holy See as a whole. As of 1989, modern reorganizations of the Holy See had led to major curial departments that included a Secretariat of State, nine Congregations (governing agencies), three Tribunals (church courts), twelve Councils (agencies to promote the church and its services), and three Special Service Offices. The modern reforms also officially authorized numerous non-curial committees, commissions, and institutes that today assist in the mission of the Holy See. Representatives, apostolic delegates, and diplomats from Rome can be found in countries around the world. In the U.S., the office of the Apostolic Nunciature is located in Washington, D.C.

(See also Ecclesiology, and Vatican.)

HOLY WATER   is a sacramental of the church community, one often used by Catholic people as they enter and leave church buildings. In using holy water, Catholics customarily dip the fingers of their right hand into a font or bowl that contains holy water and then make the sign of the cross on themselves. Holy water is ordinary water that has been blessed by a priest. During this blessing, a special prayer is said expressing the Christian hope that all who use holy water will remain free from sinfulness and human evil.

Holy water was originally intended to remind Catholic church members of the waters of baptism. The use of holy water was meant to encourage the baptized to lead holy lives dedicated to serving God. Sometimes holy water is used during official church ritual ceremonies, for example in the sprinkling rite and blessing of the assembly during some celebrations of the Eucharist.

(See also Baptism, Holiness, Sacramentals, and Vestibule.)

HOLY WEEK   is the week leading up to Easter Sunday. It begins with Passion (Palm) Sunday and is considered the most holy of all the weeks during the entire church year. Holy Week was called Passion Week for many years because Christians are called to deeply ponder the death and resurrection of Jesus Christ during this sacred time.

A very early mention of this particularly holy period can be found in the writings of Saint Athanasius. By the 3rd century, the holy week celebration was begun by Christian communities actually on Good Friday and concluded with Easter celebrations. By the 6th century, however, Holy Thursday memorial services had been added to Christian holy week observances, and some local customs involving holy week, as a whole, had been stretched to the include a full week of devotional practices. In 1955 Pope Pius XII noted that all local Catholic communities and all individual church members should honor Holy Week because of its importance to the Christian faith overall.

On Passion (Palm) Sunday Catholics receive pieces of blessed palm branches to help them recall Jesus of Nazareth's entry into the city of Jerusalem and his eventual death and resurrection to new life there. On Holy Thursday Christian communities remember the last supper of Jesus with his apostles—and center their attention on his gift of the Eucharist to humankind. (It is also traditionally a day to honor the institution of the Christian priesthood.) On Good Friday Christians remember the suffering and death of Jesus of Nazareth through the communal/ritual proclamation of Bible passages, a litany of special prayers, and ritual veneration of the cross of Christ. On the night of Holy Saturday, the great Easter Vigil is celebrated; a paschal candle is lit in every local Catholic community worldwide to symbolize the light of the risen One in the human community and creation. The baptized renew their baptismal commitment, and those seeking full initiation are then baptized, confirmed, and share in the Eucharist for the first time.

(See also Easter, Lent, Liturgical Year, Passover, and Triduum.)

HOMILY   is a talk, an oral reflection on the proclaimed Scriptures, delivered during the course of a Catholic liturgical celebration. The word is derived from a Greek term that means "being together." Homilies are commentaries on biblical readings that help people apply Scripture to their daily lives. During celebrations of the Eucharist in Catholic communities, the homily follows the gospel reading.

From the ancient writings of Justin Martyr, which include interesting accounts of primitive Christian community practices, scholars and others now know that homilies were given during the earliest agape-meal eucharistic ("breaking of the bread") rituals. These talks were delivered most often in a friendly, warm, conversational tone and style. In later centuries in Catholic life, homilies became more like formal speeches on Christian doctrine and church laws and disciplines, and homilies thus were frequently not much related to the themes of liturgical celebration of the day or to the Scriptures proclaimed. The Council of Trent (1545–1563) taught that presbyters must give sermons related to the Scripture texts read at Mass. But the real meaning of the homily as a familiar discourse and faith sharing did not really catch on again until the 20th century.

Vatican Council II taught in the 1960s that homilies should be given during eucharistic celebrations on Sundays, holy days, on the feast days of saints, and on other important church feasts. The council noted that ideally every eucharistic liturgy (Mass) should have some kind of homily presentation.

The Catholic community now stresses that homilies are meant to instruct the baptized and the faithful in Jesus about God's revelation in the Word, but homilies should also be given in order to encourage participants in Christian rituals to be more committed to a life of holiness and thus to the gospel of Jesus. At Mass the homily is a link between the liturgy of the Word and the liturgy of the Eucharist. Brief homilies are also included in communal celebrations of the other sacraments, including baptism, reconciliation, anointing, and matrimony.

(See also Agape, Bible, and Liturgy of the Word/Eucharist.)

HOPE is one of the three theological virtues (the others are faith and charity). Hope is a gift from God helping us to center daily life confidently on the idea that God offers everlasting holiness and salvation to all members of the human community. Therefore, in the Christian vision of reality, hope entails a joy-filled expectation of perfect happiness and peace in God's loving, heavenly presence forever. The word "hope" stems from a Middle English term that refers basically to "expectation."

The traditional notion of gospel-based hope is rooted in the message, values, and resurrection of Jesus , and is addressed in several epistles in the Christian Scriptures, particularly in the letter to the Romans and in the letters to the Corinthians. Christian tradition has long noted that hope is a constructive habit by which an individual trusts that the Creator will grant life everlasting and the means by which one can naturally attain it. This view of hope has usually centered though on the individual alone who seeks freedom from sin and personal salvation in heaven.

Recent theological thinking tends to stress that while individuals should yearn for life everlasting with the Holy in heaven, they should also hope for and pray for the liberation of all of humanity from sinfulness, for the continued perfection of God's reign on Earth, and for the second coming of Jesus (the *parousia*). The loss or absence of hope in life is frequently described as despair. Despair is experienced whenever individuals and communities either forget or fail to accept that God loves all of creation continually, that God never abandons human beings, and that God remains merciful and forgiving in all cases, at all times.

Some Christians believe that the gift of hope is especially needed by Christians today because of the anxieties, insecurities, discouragements, and frustrations that go hand in hand with much of modern life. Thus while all the baptized are called to strive personally for full and final union—eternal happiness—with God in a life beyond the present, the Catholic community nevertheless teaches that all peoples and cultures ought to work tirelessly and hopefully to solve the many problems that trouble humanity in the here and now.

Because Jesus of Nazareth has risen from death to new life, the Catholic story stresses that people of faith should be able to face death with great hope and courage and look to unending joy in heaven with great expectation. Catholics are particularly urged by church community leaders to pray for hope and confidence in God's promise of salvation, especially when tempted toward selfishness and personal sin or when suffering physical or psychological problems.

(See also Heaven, Reign of God, Salvation, and Virtue.)

HUMANISM   is a system of thought centering on human perfection or on the welfare of humanity as a whole through personal self-perfection. Humanists concentrate on those things that help a person become more completely human: more good, more knowledgeable, and more whole in his or her ability to experience life, love, and other emotions.

The cultural movement known as humanism began in 14th-century Europe at the dawn of the Renaissance. It emphasized the value of human insight and experience rather than Christian teachings and values. Later, a Marxist humanism stressed human self-creation and full human realization (self-fulfillment) through work and proper social order. The church quickly criticized such secular humanisms. It affirmed the need for the revelation of God in Jesus and the vision of God's reign, rather than mere human efforts for the true and final fulfillment of human beings.

Theologians today sometimes speak of the need for a universal Christian humanization of reality. They say this would, through increased knowledge, enablement, freedom, and respect for all, bring the whole of creation, especially human beings, progressively nearer to completion in the reign of God and toward self-fulfillment and perfected holiness for all peoples. However, the denial of God and alienation from the Christian way of life and institutional religion are fairly common results of a contemporary scientific humanism. Christians should struggle, these theologians say, to communicate to all that all persons and things are created in the image of a good God and that all well-intentioned human efforts at personal and social development contribute in some way to the Christian mission of reform and renewal of creation.

In his encyclical *Populorum progressio* (1967), Paul VI taught that the church must work for the full development of all human beings. A few years earlier Vatican II had acknowledged the broad birth of a "new humanism" (Christian-like in spirit) in the world today by which the human person should be defined, first and foremost, by his or her duties to others and to society as a whole. John Paul II has echoed this in recent writings such as the exhortation *Christifideles laici* (1988) and the encyclical *Redemptoris missio* (1990).

Church leaders say that an excessive humanism raises up false trust in humanity's ability to control all things and to order the world through technology, scientific discoveries, and individualistic freedoms. They call for an authentic, new Christian humanization process that promotes the full development of individuals and human communities who, by the gifts of God's creation and grace, are called in all ways to become co-creators with God (and to overcome the many effects of human sinfulness) so that all people in all times will work toward the betterment of self, others, and the world in hope for the coming of God's eternal reign.

(See also Creation, Free Will, Grace, and Reign of God.)

HUMILITY   is a moral virtue that helps individuals, communities, or groups to be honest and discerning about their abilities and achievements and to avoid self-centered pride. Christian humility leads persons toward recognition that members of the human community will always be dependent upon God, the Creator of all life, and that all human beings should praise God for the good things that they are called to do with their life. The terms "humble" and "humility" have Latin roots *(humilis* and *humilitas)* which suggest smallness, lowness, and "of Earth."

Catholic tradition maintains that selfish human pride is the direct opposite of sincere humility. In light of Christian teaching, persons who are humble thank God for the unique gifts and talents they have been given by God's grace and for the daily opportunities they have to use these gifts to assist others. However, persons often fail (a result of human sinfulness and pride) to be thankful for their gifts and choose to act pridefully independent of their Creator and others. Church teachings stress that Christian humility is a sincere imitation of Jesus of Nazareth, one who was always humble and who sought no empty and self-centered honors from others. Christian tradition teaches that Jesus wanted only to do God's will and to please God, thus all his followers should walk in his footsteps.

Many of the saints were very humble persons, remaining good role models or Christian witnesses for all those who wish to be truly humble Christians today. John Paul II has recently described humility as "submission to the power of truth and love." He added that humility is a Christian "rejection of appearance and superficiality" in this life.

(See also Discernment, Fruits of the Spirit, Jesus of Nazareth, and Virtue.)

I

ICONS   are colorful paintings or other flat-surface images of Jesus Christ, Mary, or various Christian saints in the style of the Eastern Orthodox (Byzantine) Church. The word "icon" is derived from the Greek *eikon* meaning "image." Icons are religious pictures that are used instead of statues by Eastern rite Catholics.

The universal church has a rich history of using statues, icons, and other artistic images. Homage to Mary and the saints was begun among the very earliest followers of Jesus. Eventually church members created paintings, statues, and mosaics in their honor. The Seventh Ecumenical Council, which met in Nicaea in the year 787, taught that veneration of Mary and the saints is different from worship of God and that veneration of them, through statues or icons, is not worship of a picture or idol. It represents instead a very deep level of respect and reverence for the Christian faith and Christian life witness of the person(s) depicted.

Icons are frequently enhanced by excellent use of color and fine design methods, particularly those done in the style of the Byzantine art high period of the 10th to 12th centuries. The church continues to emphasize the spiritual value in honoring and imitating the lives of Jesus, Mary, and the saints through the prayerful use of icons and similar church sacramentals. Today, Eastern-style religious icons can typically be found in Byzantine liturgical settings, in honored places in Christian family households, and in church-related shops where they can be purchased for use in prayer devotions, personal spiritual growth purposes, or as gifts for others.

(See also Devotions, and Sacramentals.)

IMMACULATE CONCEPTION   is a dogma of the Catholic church. This dogma teaches that Mary, the mother of Jesus of Nazareth, and wife of a carpenter named Joseph, was in fact conceived in complete holiness, that is, without original sin. The solemnity of the Immaculate Conception is celebrated annually on December 8. It is a holy day of obligation.

The Bible does not specifically refer to an immaculate conception of Mary, but the faith beliefs summarized by the term have long been elements of the church community's faith tradition. On December 8, 1854, Pope Pius IX formally and dogmatically defined *ex cathedra* the doctrine of the Immaculate Conception. His action was a culmination of 900 years of tradition in which the Roman church had maintained liturgical celebrations that focused on belief in Mary's sinless life and holy life-condition. In 1846 Mary, imaged as the Immaculate Conception, had been declared the patroness of the United States. Even so, much heated debate regarding the Immaculate Conception took place during the Middle Ages, and the Catholic communities of the Eastern church have not subscribed to this fundamental, dogmatic but, to some, controversial teaching about Mary.

Today the church officially holds that Jesus and Mary were the only two persons in history to be conceived in complete holiness and grace—in other words, free from the effects of original sin. Official church doctrine on the Immaculate Conception has been sketched out formally by the papal document *Ineffabilis deus*. However, more recently, reflections on the life and lasting importance of Mary's witness to all of humankind have been published in the U.S. bishops' document "Behold Your Mother: Woman of Faith" (1973), *Marialis cultus*, by Paul VI (1974), and the encyclical *Mater redemptoris*, written by Pope John Paul II in 1987.

(See also Holy Days, Holy Family, Mary, and Original Sin.)

INCENSE   is a substance that produces a sweet-smelling smoke when it is burned. In many cases, the incense used in Christian worship is made from plants and resins that are processed into sandy granules, powder, or little cubes or bricks. The term has Latin origins that mean "to set on fire."

History indicates that incense was used by ancient peoples in the Near East as a perfume to honor their gods and as a ritual substance to drive away demons. The Israelites used incense for communal prayer and rituals, especially to show reverence for God and to thank God for many blessings (Exodus 30:34ff.).

It seems that incense was not regularly used in Christian worship for the first 400 years of Christian life, largely because of its connections to Roman cult worship. Once the Christian religion was mainstreamed in the Roman Empire, however, use of incense seemed much more appropriate. By the year 500 or so, incense was being used commonly in Christian funerals and as a sign of respect for church elders (e.g., bishops presiding at Mass were "incensed" with sweet white smoke). As the years went by, many elements within Christian worship services were honored with incense to show they were sacred to the community. Things incensed included: the book of Scripture readings, the altar of sacrifice, the gifts of bread and wine, the presider and dignitaries present, the Easter candle, and the whole congregation—all of which symbolize the presence of the Spirit of Jesus in some way. This tradition goes on today within liturgies on particularly solemn Catholic feasts.

In all, incense remains a symbol of Christian prayer rising to God, with the help of the Spirit. It also serves to remind Catholics that they should show deep respect to persons and things dedicated to the Christian journey toward holiness. In worship settings, the smoke of Christian incense ascends, bearing church members' prayers and the "sweet" results of Christians' good works to the dwelling of the Creator, far beyond the natural reaches of this world.

(See also Prayer, Sacramentals, and Worship.)

INDULGENCES are partial or total remissions of punishments due for sins that already have been forgiven. Indulgence has Latin (*indulgentia*) and Middle English roots referring to "yielding to the wishes of" another and "gentleness." The church community says that it can grant indulgences to individuals because of the super-abundance of merits gained for humanity by Jesus of Nazareth and because of the great spiritual bounty available to humankind through the cumulative Christian prayer, works, and witness of the entire communion of saints.

The practice of granting indulgences (though stretching back to the early days of the Christian church, at least in principle) got much emphasis from Pope Urban II during the 11th century, the time of the great Crusades. By the 13th century the church community had begun formally to accept that indulgences could be gained overall through the redemptive efforts of Jesus and the spiritual and prayerful works of the saints. Pope Clement VI incorporated the concept of indulgences into church law in 1343. In 1476 Pope Sixtus IV declared that the spiritual merits gained by individuals on Earth and in heaven can assist those in purgatory. Church leaders then began to dispense various kinds of indulgences from an official thesaurus—a church "treasury" as it were, of Christian graces and merits.

Institutional processes involved in granting indulgences to church members and communities were frequently abused during certain times. Martin Luther, for example, bitterly complained in the early 16th century about Catholics who sold indulgences. In the middle of the 16th century the Council of Trent declared that church doctrines on indulgences were legitimate, but did acknowledge that certain abuses had crept into Catholic practices and policies. In 1950 an official Catholic listing of indulgences was published by the Vatican.

At that time (mid-20th century) a new theory on indulgences was developed by European thinkers. It stressed that the whole people of God can and should prayerfully intervene on behalf of the repentant sinner who seeks a church indulgence. Thus legalistic approaches to dispensing indulgences and official indexes for remissions of punishments due (for example, seven years and 500 days) should thus no longer be emphasized. Rather, theologians began to claim that proper emphasis should now be placed upon voluntary works of charity and voluntary prayerful penances that can be done by all the baptized in a spirit of Christian faith and hope.

The church officially continues to recognize two kinds of indulgences: partial indulgences, through which part of one's temporal punishment for sinfulness is remitted, and plenary indulgences, through which all of one's temporal punishment due is wiped away forever. Of course, certain traditional conditions must be met in each case for an indulgence to be granted. The Catholic community continues to trust that indulgences can be gained through Christian works and prayer, for one's personal spiritual benefit and for those whose souls are in purgatory.

In 1967 Paul VI issued a document called "The Doctrine and Practice of Indulgences." His work underscored the value that the contemporary Christian community as a whole places on the doctrine of the communion of saints. In 1968 an official *Handbook of Indulgences* was published by the church. This statement placed great emphasis on the personal and voluntary works of charity and prayer that can be done today among the baptized. In 1985 the Holy See issued a decree granting permission to diocesan bishops to offer a papal blessing, with a plenary indulgence attached, three times a year (on church feasts of their choice) to all who cannot be physically present but who follow along, by television or radio signal, with the rituals at which the blessing is imparted. In 1986 the Catholic church announced publication of a simplified handbook of indulgences (*Enchiridion Indulgentiarum*) in line with the 1983 revisions to the Code of Canon Law.

(See also Prayer, Purgatory, Reconciliation, Reformation, and Sin.)

Note of Interest: The Code of Canon Law says that an "indulgence is a remission before God of the temporal punishment for sin...already forgiven, which a properly disposed member of the Christian faithful obtains under certain and definite conditions with the help of the church which...dispenses and applies authoritatively the treasury of the satisfactions of Christ and the saints." The canons that relate directly to church doctrine on plenary and partial indulgences can be found in sections 992–997 of the Code.)

INFALLIBILITY   is a charism or gift given to the church by the Spirit of God. Essentially, infallibility means that the Christian community will be protected forever by the Spirit from great error on matters of Christian faith and on matters pertaining to the moral life of the baptized. More narrowly, infallibility can also be described as a dogma of the Catholic church that states that 1) the pope can speak *ex cathedra* (i.e., using his full authority as the legitimate successor of the apostle Peter), or 2) the Catholic bishops as a "college" or unified body, in union with the pope (as occurs in an ecumenical council), may teach infallibly, without essential error, on matters of Christian faith and morality.

The term has Latin roots, basically meaning "not able to deceive" in any manner. Catholic teaching on this issue is rooted in long-held Christian convictions that Jesus of Nazareth willed (intended) that the community of those who followed him would possess a spirit of truth or infallibility. The Christian community has believed since the apostolic era that the risen Jesus has sent (and continues to send) his living Spirit to guide the community of the baptized in truth and to help those faithful to his gospel speak truthfully and courageously as genuine witnesses for him (John 16:13; Luke 10:16).

By the end of the 2nd century, church members had begun to greatly rely upon those communities originally founded by the actual apostles of Jesus or their very close disciples to faithfully and accurately hand on the doctrines and practices that traced back to gospel-era Christian life. From the 4th century on, however, special reverence began to be shown for the church of Rome, known as "St. Peter's community," the center of the Christian way and traditional site for the preservation of Christian truths. This special reverence for the community at Rome was extended through the Middles Ages and beyond, even though different centuries and struggles brought many challenges to the primacy of the bishop of Rome (the pope) from Eastern-world Christians, Protestant reformers in the 16th century, and others.

In time, Catholic peoples began to accept that the pope should have something akin to the ultimate word or decision pertaining to issues and questions related directly to Christian faith and morals. Thomas Aquinas, in the 13th century, even went so far as to urge local Christian communities to adhere to the pope's choices and decisions because "he cannot err." (It is worth noting that "infallibility" was coined by Guido Terreni a short time later, in the 1300s.) On July 18, 1870 the First Vatican Council declared infallibility to be a dogma of the Catholic body world-wide, claiming that whatever the pope proclaims *ex cathedra* (from the chair of Peter) must be held in faith by the universal church. In 1964 Vatican II chose to simply reaffirm this doctrine, but council leaders made it very clear that the bishops and pope in unity, with a single teaching voice or as a "college" of Christian teachers, can also define Christian doctrine in an infallible way.

Papal infallibility has often been interpreted to mean that the pope is incapable of any human error or that everything he says is immune from mistake. In fact, however, the pope (or the whole college of bishops united with the pope) can speak infallibly only on matters directly touching upon Christian faith and morals, only when the pope clearly claims to be teaching *ex cathedra*, and only when explicitly stating that a doctrine proclaimed is to be binding absolutely on the global church community. In recent decades, some Christians have suggested that such teaching statements should be referred to as irreformable, rather than infallible, to stress that the method by which great truths (doctrinal formulas) are expressed may be subject to some revision and discussion over time, but the essence of a Christian truth expressed in irreformable teaching can never be fundamentally altered.

In ecumenical dialogues in recent days the "indefectibility" of the church community has been much discussed. Indefectibility emphasizes that the Spirit of the risen Jesus has guided and will guide the people of God at all times. The Spirit, therefore, will not let the Christian community go astray, in a fundamental way, from the basic vision of the gospel or the essential life and mission of those who have for centuries wanted to follow Jesus' values and vision.

Vatican II said some thirty years ago that the pope cannot proclaim or elaborate on Christian teachings, values, and practices as a private person. Rather, he can do so only as the ultimate teacher for the people of God worldwide. Therefore, in the Catholic perspective on faith, the charism of infallibility is present in the pope in a unique way. However, as previously noted, the council likewise clarified how Christian teachings may sometimes be expressed by the universal college of bishops.

Papal infallibility has been formally exercised only twice in relatively recent times: on the topics of the Immaculate Conception (by Pope Pius IX in 1854) and the Assumption of Mary (defined by Pope Pius XII in 1950).

(See also Apostolic Succession, Collegiality, Deposit of Faith, Dogma, Magisterium, and Pope.)

INQUIRY has Latin roots meaning "search" or to "seek after." Inquiry is the first period or phase of a faith-formation process known as the Rite of Christian Initiation of Adults, today more commonly known as the RCIA. The period of inquiry is one's initial step toward baptism and full initiation into the Catholic community.

The Rite of Christian initiation of Adults is a contemporary model of the wholistic faith-formation process that the earliest followers of Jesus employed to help new members (converts) enter the catechumenate and join the emerging Christian community. In recent years, the period of inquiry has sometimes been also referred to as the pre-catechumenate.

The inquiry period usually occurs within the scope of a local parish's ministry. It often takes shape as a series of group meetings for all persons—inquirers—interested in the Catholic faith. These meetings tend to focus on the various teachings, spiritual practices, values, and rituals of Catholic Christian tradition. For example, inquirers learn about the meaning of the Mass, a Catholic reading of the Bible, how Catholics pray, the importance of Christian witness and service, and central doctrines of the church. In many cases, inquirers also begin to experience a sense of community and sacramental ritual in Catholic settings.

The period of inquiry is not a time for pressure or commitments. At its best, it should spark inquirers to search freely and deeply through faith-related questions, share their life stories and struggles with others, learn from the stories and faithful life choices of co-searchers, and reflect on whether or not the way of the Catholic church will help them on their life journey toward God.

The spirit of Christian inquiry should not be limited to only certain persons or a certain stage of the Christian initiation process. In fact, the spirit of inquiry—the human struggle to grow in faith, to freely change one's selfish or sinful ways, to search for God's revelation, and to understand how to live a fully loving Christian life—should continue throughout one's life.

(See also Baptism, Catechumenate and RCIA, and Election.)

INSPIRATION is the mysterious process by which the Spirit of God has guided human beings in the actual composition of biblical writings. The Christian community maintains that the sacred and canonical books of the Bible have God as their principal and divine author/inspirer and that God has influenced and guided human writers in order that certain divine revelations would be communicated to humankind. The term stems from the Latin *inspirare*, which means "to blow upon" or "breathe into."

The Catholic concept of biblical inspiration springs from a belief expressed in the Hebrew Scriptures that Yahweh has communicated with humanity directly through such historical figures as Abraham, Moses, the prophets of Israel, and others. The Israelite community believed that the sacred writings in the Hebrew Scriptures were divinely inspired, especially the five volumes of the Law—the Pentateuch (the first five books of the Bible). Early Christian communities believed that the Bible had its origins and authority in the holy inspiration of God's Spirit. During the Middle Ages the notion that the Creator had somehow dictated Scripture—communicated directly to human writers what should be written, word for word—gained great acceptance among church members.

Church history shows that a huge debate ensued in the 19th century about how God had in fact inspired the human writers of biblical books. Vatican Council I declared in 1870 that the church should accept all biblical books as sacred—since God is their true author and they were created through the help of the Spirit's unique inspiration. In 1893 Pope Leo XIII stated in his encyclical *Providentissimus deus* that God "incited (human authors) to write, and assisted them in writing so that they correctly conceived, accurately wrote down, and truthfully expressed all that God intended and only what [God] intended." Catholics refer to the notions of divine revelation and inspiration when they speak of the Scriptures as "the Word of God."

Catholic thinking acknowledges today that biblical texts were composed by ordinary human beings, individuals who were free to communicate/compose through their own natural gifts and talents. Study of the books of the Bible indicates that biblical authors used various literary forms and figures of speech, histories, symbols, metaphors, and allusions in order to express certain points.

The church community believes that the sacred Scriptures are essential to the preaching, teaching, and ongoing life of the entire people of God. Biblical texts firmly, faithfully, and without error reveal God's inspired and saving Word for the sake of humanity. Through the assistance of biblical exegesis by Scripture scholars and teachers, the church community is responsible for interpreting and proclaiming the timeless and inspired insights in the books of the Bible.

Vatican Council II noted in the 1960s in its Dogmatic Constitution on Divine Revelation that God chose human persons and "made use of their [natural human] powers and abilities, so that with [God] acting in them and through them, they, as true authors, put to writing everything and only those things which [God] wanted" to have expressed.

The *Catechism of the Catholic Church* points out that, in a way, the process of inspiration continues in our day. Christianity essentially is a religion of the incarnate and living Word of God. Thus the Bible must not become an unused and dead letter. All Catholics rather should strive to have the eternal Word of a living God open their minds to the Spirit in order to best understand the Scriptures and God's loving revelation to humanity overall.

(See also Bible; Bible, Books of; Exegesis; Pentateuch; and Revelation.)

Note of Interest: Inerrancy refers to the inability of the Bible to be in fundamental error because God has divinely inspired the human writers of scriptural texts. In the Catholic view of things this does not imply that the human writers involved in composing Scripture were without error themselves or incapable of making any mistakes. Yet the concept of inerrancy does imply that even though historical, limited writers were capable of committing errors or of including merely personal opinions in their work on biblical passages, their limitations did not affect the essential expression of God's revelation in Scripture.

ISAIAH   was the first among the major Israelite prophets. The name *Isaiah* basically means "Yahweh is salvation." One of the books of the Hebrew Scriptures, the book of Isaiah, bears his name. Some historical evidence indicates that Isaiah was probably born in the city of Jerusalem about 760 b.c.e. It is quite likely that he served as a prophet to the nation of Israel from about 742 to 701 b.c.e. Isaiah spoke to God's chosen people about the evils of human immorality and sin. He announced that there were enemies who wanted to attack and conquer the Israelites.

The book of Isaiah is the longest book of prophecy in the Hebrew Scriptures. It contains a collection of sayings and poems by the historical Isaiah himself, plus some writings from a number of his most dedicated followers. Isaiah boldly proclaimed a coming destruction of Israel while also foreseeing that a remnant of people faithful to the Creator of humankind would rise to restore God's chosen nation. Isaiah was probably a well-educated, intelligent family man who lived about the same time as the Hebrew prophets Amos and Hosea.

In recent years, scholars have shed much light on the actual composition of the biblical text that bears Isaiah's name. The first part of the book of Isaiah was probably based on the historical prophet's actual statements and sayings, for example, his prophecies about Emmanuel and the virgin birth of the promised messiah of Israel (Isaiah 6–12, especially 7:14). However, another author-poet probably composed the current chapters 40–55; thus this section of the biblical text is often referred to as Deutero-Isaiah. Chapters 56–66 probably were composed by a third composition source, a group of Isaiah's followers now sometimes referred to as "the school of Isaiah."

Isaiah the prophet is honored by Christians because he prophetically called for true reform among the people of God. Isaiah is also fondly remembered for his lasting and bold messages of hope about a faithful few—a remnant of people (a humble community)—who would remain forever Yahweh's chosen nation despite the great sufferings and struggles that would in time befall the human community.

One of Isaiah's most timeless statements—one still embraced closely by the contemporary Catholic community—concerns a king for Israel who would descend from David's family line; Christians have applied this prophecy about a royal (kingly) messiah to Jesus of Nazareth.

(See also Bible, Jesus of Nazareth, Messiah, Old Testament, Option for the Poor, and Prophet.)

J

JESUS OF NAZARETH   is the person at the heart and center of Christian faith. Catholics believe that Jesus was the promised messiah, "the Christ," and the eternal Word of God who was incarnated ("made flesh") in order to lead humanity toward hope in God and toward eternal salvation. The name *Jesus* (Hebrew equivalent: *Yeshua*) is Aramaic at heart. It means "Yahweh saves" or "Yahweh is salvation," emphasizing the saving love expressed by God through the incarnation of the eternal Word.

Jesus was a real person, a Nazorean (from the Israelite town of Nazareth) according to the Christian Scriptures, and he was actually born about 6 or 7 years b.c.e., as best as scholars can tell. Jesus was the son of Mary, and his stepfather was named Joseph. For 30 years or so, he lived uneventfully as a carpenter, yet many now think he was gradually becoming aware of a significant holy mission he was to perform. Much of Jesus' eventual 2–3 year long public ministry—urgently announcing the need for human repentance and healing and the inception of the eternal reign of God—was conducted in Galilee and Jerusalem. He suffered a tortuous death but was miraculously raised from death by God. Historical evidence suggests his death and resurrection may have happened about 27–29 c.e.

The Bible implies that Jesus of Nazareth publicly spoke of himself as the Son of Man and saw himself in the tradition of great Hebrew prophets. He was obviously a man very knowledgeable about the Hebrew Scriptures and, as biblical testimony shows, he seemingly was much influenced by the ministry of the prophet Isaiah. The contemporary dialogue about the "Jesus of history" and "Christ of faith" focuses frequently on the way Jesus of Nazareth was historically, in the flesh (which we will never fully grasp due to limited historical sources), and the way Jesus was later viewed and worshiped as Jesus the Christ—the holy and anointed messiah and risen Lord over creation—in light of post-resurrection faith.

Many commentators theorize that the human, pre-Easter Jesus of Nazareth had a very limited awareness of his divine nature and his messianic and Christological significance for humankind and all of human history. His self-chosen messianic title Son of Man, as some scholars interpret it, means simply the "human one." It is at root a self-effacing, humble term. In March 1992, however, Cardinal Joseph Ratzinger noted official church concerns that modern religious educators often stress the historic, human traits of Jesus of Nazareth only to undercatechize on

Christ's eternal and divine nature. He called for a new balance in catechesis on both the human and divine expressions of the Word of God's existence as found in authentic Catholic tradition.

Over the centuries the church has taught that the one God became human—was made flesh and fully human—and that as a divine person, the human expression of the Word, called Jesus, had united divine and human natures (a "hypostatic union"). The church has likewise declared that Jesus of Nazareth was conceived (miraculously) by the power of God's Spirit, and he lived, died, and is risen from the dead. As the eternal redeemer and mediator for all of humankind, the risen Jesus continues to offer unending salvation to all through his ever-present, loving Spirit.

The church stresses that Jesus Christ, both God and human—a person who was prayerfully obedient and had total faith in God, and love for all persons—was the messiah, the anointed Son of God. The teaching that Jesus was divine and human, and that he is the one, true Son of God, is central and dogmatic to all of Christian belief. Vatican II stressed that Jesus Christ is present through the Spirit in the church community throughout the world. As a divine gift to humanity, he remains the ultimate sacrament of encounter between the unseen God and humanity. Jesus Christ—a man among humans and God's own divine Son—is thus often called by Catholics the perfected and most complete divine revelation of all. As the new Adam, Jesus the Christ is the spiritual head of the body of Christ and of the mystery called the church.

(See also Annunciation; Christmas; Christology; Councils, Christological; Holy Family; Jesus, Titles of; Messiah; Redeemer; and Resurrection.)

JESUS, TITLES OF   are some of the various names and phrases that have been used in Christian tradition to describe Jesus of Nazareth. Each of these titles or descriptions provides a unique perspective on Jesus and communicates something about Christian belief in him. Traditional titles include:

Christ or *Jesus Christ*—to be completely accurate, the proper expression should be "Jesus the Christ" (thus: Jesus, the messiah). Though it has become fairly common to hear Jesus of Nazareth called Jesus Christ, Christ was not in any way his historical surname. The name Jesus (in Hebrew *Yeshua*) essentially means "Yahweh is salvation." Yeshua was a common name during the time of Jesus of Nazareth. The title Christ, from the Greek term *christos*, essentially means "the anointed one." Jesus was first called the Christ because his earliest generations of followers believed that he was indeed the true messiah, the anointed one sent by God, and long-awaited by God's salvation-hungry chosen people.

Savior is an English word derived from a Latin expression of the name Jesus (i.e., "Yahweh is salvation"). Savior, therefore, expresses the foundational Christian belief that God's loving and eternal plan of salvation for creation was brought to fulfillment through Jesus of Nazareth.

Lord is the way that the apostles and other followers of Jesus in primitive Christian communities referred to the risen Jesus after the Easter-Pentecost event. The word Lord stems from the Greek term *kyrios*, which was used by early Christian generations to express the absolute majesty of the risen Jesus, the Son of God and equal to the Creator of humankind. For example, see the early Christian hymn in Philippians 2:6–11, especially its final line.

Redeemer is a traditional title for Jesus of Nazareth. It indicates that, by sacrificing his human life (through his ministry and his suffering and death) and in being raised in glory by God from the dead, Jesus has definitively brought about universal salvation for all of humankind. Thus the term implies that in his death and resurrection Jesus has fulfilled God's revelation of the reign of God and has made possible true freedom and hope for all persons.

Son of God is a post-resurrection title that acknowledges that the historical Jesus of Nazareth was in fact the one, eternal, only-begotten Word of God, and that Jesus was in fact truly God and truly human. While in some ways all human persons are the "sons and daughters" of the Creator, the traditional Christian term Son of God gives Christian communities the chance to identify Jesus as the divine and human person who perfectly reflected God's glory and through whom the Creator has definitively spoken (John 1:1, Romans 9:5, and Hebrews 4).

Son of Man is now widely recognized as a messianic title current among Israelites at the time of Jesus of Nazareth. This title appears over 70 times in the four gospels contained in the Christian Scriptures. Scripture scholars think that Jesus actually used the phrase Son of Man, in essence a humble and self-effacing term, in speaking of himself (Mark 10:33 and Luke 9:20–22).

Lamb of God is a title used to describe Jesus in the gospel of John (John 1:29). Jesus' original disciples recognized the sacrificial nature of his life, ministry, and death. Because the paschal lamb was a traditional symbol of sacrifice to God during ancient Hebrew times, Jesus began to be referred to as the true Lamb of God in the communities and rituals of his earliest followers.

New Adam indicates that the risen Jesus of Nazareth was considered from earliest Christian times to be the first member, the head as it were, of a whole new generation of humankind. In the Christian Scriptures, Jesus (like a new Adam) is called "the firstborn of all creatures"—the one who has responded most fully and most perfectly to God's loving revelation. Thus, in traditional Christian terms, through the "old Adam" the evils and despair of human sin first entered human experience, yet in the New Adam (Jesus of Nazareth) true hope and salvation have been made available to all persons, communities, and human cultures for all time (1 Corinthians 15, Colossians 1:15).

New Moses reveals what Jesus has accomplished for the sake of humankind. Through Moses, the great Hebrew leader, the old law and the old covenant between God and humanity were established. Through

Jesus of Nazareth, however, a new law and a new covenant—in fact a new people of God—have been established once and for all (Hebrews 3:1–6 and 8:7–13).

Mediator describes the risen Jesus of Nazareth as the one who stands between God and humankind and has preserved humanity from utter estrangement from the Creator. The term is rooted in a Latin term for middle. Mediator refers to one who stands between two parties, an intercessor who tries to reconcile the parties. In Christian concepts and teachings, then, Jesus is imaged as an ideal go-between who has brought about a reconciliation and a lasting peace in the relationship between God and God's true people (1 Timothy 2:5).

Emmanuel is a prophetic name or title applied to Jesus of Nazareth, basically meaning God-with-us (Isaiah 7:14 and Matthew 1:22–23).

Servant is a traditional term expressing a basic Christian belief that Jesus was a humble person who sought tirelessly to help and serve others lovingly rather than be served himself. Christians believe that Jesus of Nazareth was a living and true expression of the living God (God's own Son and Word), yet the Word became "empty," as it were, to become human. In post-resurrection days, the initial followers of the risen Jesus viewed him essentially as the living Word who became a servant of God and humankind and who humbly accepted even death on a cross for the sake of others (Philippians 2:7–8). Jesus was therefore a "suffering servant" for all peoples, according to the Christian story, the one who has been exalted and glorified by the Creator in heaven.

Word indicates that Jesus, the living Word "spoken by the Father" in human history, is the most perfect and definitive revelation (self-communication) ever to come to humanity from the divine. Thus Jesus of Nazareth was and is God's own personal and most loving expression to human beings. In Christian doctrine, the eternal Word is sometimes imaged as the eternal *logos*—the Word that became flesh (John 1:1–18).

Rabbi is a Hebrew title that basically means "teacher." It is widely believed that Jesus of Nazareth was accorded this title by at least some of his original followers because he proved to be a wise and knowledgeable person. Thus some people were willing to listen to him and to be guided by his teachings (John 20:16; Mark 9:38, 10:20).

Good Shepherd traces its origins to the Hebrew Scriptures in which Yahweh is compared to a shepherd who shows great care and pastoral concern for his chosen sheep—the people of the nation of Israel (Jeremiah 23 and Ezekiel 34:11–16). The gospels show Jesus of Nazareth referring to himself as a good shepherd who guides the flock of God's chosen people and is even willing to lay down his life for the sheep in his care (John 10:1–18).

High Priest is how the letter to the Hebrews depicts the risen Jesus glorified in the heavenly state and functioning as God's high priest over all of creation (Hebrews 4:14–5:10 and 8:1–6).

(See also Christology, Jesus of Nazareth, Kenosis, Messiah, Redemption, and Revelation.)

JOHN   is known in Christian tradition as the son of Zebedee and one of the original apostles of Jesus of Nazareth. According to the Christian Scriptures, John was a young man called along with his brother James to leave behind his work as a fisherman to follow a rabbi (teacher) called Jesus. John is traditionally named as the author of the fourth gospel as well as three brief epistles. Most Catholic Scripture scholars, however, consider it unlikely that either the gospel of John or the Johannine letters were directly composed by the apostle John.

The gospel of John was probably composed by a disciple of the apostle John. This gospel was perhaps further refined by another person who was primarily an editor of the work. Many commentators seem to agree today that the gospel of John was produced in Asia Minor about the years 90–100 c.e. It is historically noteworthy, however, that the Christian belief that attributes composition of this gospel to the historical John goes all the way back to the time of the great early Christian witness Irenaeus (died c. 200) and perhaps even St. Polycarp (died c. 155), a man who may have actually met John before John's death. Biblical studies have indicated that the original writer of the gospel of John likely also composed the first epistle of John in the Christian Scriptures. However, some other person(s), maybe an elder or presbyter in an early Christian assembly, probably wrote the second and third letters of John.

Contemporary commentators say that the gospel of John was written to show that Jesus of Nazareth was revealed in glory as the messiah, the long expected-one of Israel and the divine Son of God. They add that this gospel must have evolved slowly from very ancient Christian preachings and teachings, but ones quite different theologically from the traditions/ background of the synoptic versions of the gospel (Mark, Matthew, and Luke). This would help explain how some events in the life and ministry of Jesus came to be reported in John but are missing from the synoptic gospels.

John is often referred to (perhaps a bit improperly) as the most theological of the four gospels. The gospel of John describes how the divine and eternal Word of God, known to humanity as Jesus the Christ, shared his light and life and glory with all of humanity, and how he invited people to respond to the God revealed in him in faith. Some of his hearers chose to believe; yet some could not accept ultimate faith in God and they rejected the glorious light and life of the Christ.

According to Catholic tradition, the historical apostle John did not die a martyr, as did the other original apostles of Jesus. The Catholic community celebrates the feast day of St. John the evangelist each year on December 27.

(See also Apostles; Epistle; Gospel; Jesus, Titles of; Messiah; and Synoptics.)

JOHN PAUL II   was elected to the papacy on October 16, 1978, soon after the death of Pope John Paul I. John Paul II is the first non-Italian pope since Adrian VI in 1522–1523.

Pope John Paul II was born on May 18, 1920 in Wadowice, Poland. His baptismal name is Karol Wojtyla. After his ordination to the presbyterate, Fr. Wojtyla received a doctorate in theology and went on to teach seminary courses in morality and ethics. He is credited with writing many essays and articles for publication during that period of his life and ministry. Pius XII named him a bishop in 1958. He later became archbishop, and then cardinal, of the Archdiocese of Krakow in Poland. Archbishop Wojtyla helped represent the Polish Catholic community at the Second Vatican Council in the 1960s. He spoke often then, and has since then, in favor of basic human rights. As Pope, John Paul II has frequently supported Vatican II's advocacy for the dignity and rights of every human person and he has written in progressive terms about social questions and issues. In particular he has challenged modern church members to unite as a true global community of faithful Christians.

John Paul II, like Paul VI and John Paul I before him, has taught that evangelization is the special mission and duty of every member and local community in the modern church worldwide. He has urged the entire body of Catholic bishops and cardinals to work together in a true spirit of collegiality in order to better serve the entire people of God. He has become known for his many trips (pilgrimages) around the world to visit Christians and others in the Americas, Europe, Africa, and Asia, and for the great personal character, faith in God, congeniality, strength, warmth, and humor he has given witness to on his journeys. His teachings as the overall leader of the worldwide Catholic Christian body are seen by many today as very firm, very traditional, and to some very conservative, yet nevertheless often full of courageous expressions and textured theological thoughts.

John Paul II is the author of many speeches and texts, exhortations, encyclicals, and other official church documents. His major encyclicals include *Redemptor hominis* (On the redemption and dignity of the human race), 1979; *Dives in misericordia* (On the mercy of God), 1980; *Laborem exercens* (On human work), 1981; *Slavorum apostoli* (Commemoration of Sts. Cyril and Methodius), 1985; *Dominum et vivificantem* (On the Holy Spirit in the church and the world), 1986; *Redemptoris mater* (On the role of Mary), 1987; *Sollicitudo rei socialis* (On social concerns), 1987; *Redemptoris missio* (On the church's missionary mandate), 1991; and *Centesimus annus* (On the centenary of *Rerum novarum* and on social concerns), 1991.

(See also Encyclical, Pope, and Vatican.)

JOSEPH the husband of Mary in Christian tradition, is known as a humble, ordinary Jewish carpenter who became the foster father of Jesus of Nazareth. Joseph is mentioned in the Christian Scriptures in the gospels of Matthew and Luke. The name Joseph is a shortened expression of the traditional Hebrew name *Jehoseph*, which basically means "may Yahweh give an increase."

Christian traditions have held that the historical Joseph was a distant descendant of the great Hebrew king David. They also indicate that once

Joseph and Mary were engaged, Joseph then learned that she was pregnant and would give birth to a child that was not his. Joseph wanted to hide his bride away to protect her from public shame, but a divine message from God urged him not to do so. It is a tradition of the Catholic community that Joseph was present at the birth of Jesus in a village called Bethlehem and that he died sometime before Jesus began his public ministry.

Contemporary perspectives suggest that Joseph, who is referred to as a carpenter, may actually have been a handyman who did various kinds of jobs. Traditionally he has been described as a rather old man, yet recent studies of biblical times in the land of Israel indicate that Jewish males commonly married before or quite near their twentieth birthday.

For five centuries the feast day of Saint Joseph has been celebrated by the global church on March 19. In 1870 Pope Pius IX named Saint Joseph the patron or protector of the Catholic church worldwide and of all human workers. In 1955 Pius XII announced that the feast of Saint Joseph the Worker would be celebrated annually on May 1.

(See also Annunciation, Holy Family, Jesus of Nazareth, and Mary.)

JUDAISM   is the religion of the Hebrew Bible and of the contemporary Jewish community. Those who follow Judaism believe in a transcendent God, the revelation of God in the Torah (Pentateuch or Law), the prophets, and the sacred history of the Hebrew nation throughout the centuries. In Judaism, all persons are thought to be part of a human family (a brother- and sisterhood of sorts) under one loving Parent called God. The moral expectations placed on persons stem from the teachings of God's law in the Torah. The worship of Judaism centers on prayer, reading of the Scriptures, observance of the sabbath, and observance of certain religious festivals. Judaism maintains certain kinds of messianic expectations aimed at fulfillment of God's covenant with humanity, the ultimate judgment by God of human beings, and the establishment of God's everlasting reign.

(See also Anti-Semitism, Covenant, Diaspora, Hebrews, Patriarchs/ Patriarchy, Pentateuch, Reign of God, Sabbath, and Zionism.)

K

KENOSIS   is a biblical and theological term of Greek origin. It refers to "empty" or an "emptying." Fundamentally, *kenosis* in the Christian sense means that the divine Word of God, the second person of the holy Trinity, became human and was made known to humanity as Jesus of Nazareth. Thus, the Word did not cling to divinity and all its heavenly glory. The Word became fully incarnate (was "made flesh and blood")— empty of God-like splendor—and fully, humbly open to human life and death.

The New Testament gives evidence that the earliest followers of Jesus grasped the basics of this great mystery, the mystery of the incarnation. A profound hymn-like meditation on Jesus the Christ can be found in Philippians 2:6–11—the humble, suffering human servant made glorious by God. For centuries, Christians have found in this passage a powerful witness to both the complete humanity and divinity of Jesus.

Many today believe that the divine Word either surrendered— became emptied of—or relinquished divine awareness and omnipotence through the incarnation. According to such kenotic theologies, if the Word did not become empty of divine self-awareness, then the idea of a truly and fully human life for Jesus of Nazareth and of the agony involved in his choice to humbly sacrifice himself and suffer death on behalf of others do not make much sense.

Catholic tradition holds that the divine Word of God freely became fully human. Yet, the divine nature of Jesus of Nazareth was not readily observable to those who saw him in the flesh. Jesus came to be honored as the glorious Christ only later, in light of post-resurrection (post-Easter) faith. The Word became human in all ways, walking humbly and obediently like a servant of God, to the point of painful death for others. For this, the self-emptying Word was raised from death by God and is now proclaimed Lord of glory over all creation. (See also Christology; Councils, Christological; Jesus of Nazareth; Jesus, Titles of; and Trinity.)

KERYGMA   is the verbal and public proclamation of the gospel message of salvation in Jesus Christ during the post-resurrection era of the apostles. Put a slightly different way, the Christian *kerygma* was the earliest actual publicly-spoken "word of salvation" about Jesus and the reign of God that he announced. The word is Greek and means "preaching." It appears about 60 times in the books of the New Testament (Christian Scriptures). In context, it refers often to proclamation of the life-altering reign of God on Earth.

According to biblical evidence, the *kerygma* was the spirited public, spoken witness of Jesus' original followers that, in Jesus of Nazareth, the Word of God incarnate, hope and salvation are possible for all persons. Thus, historical evidence suggests that the apostolic-era *kerygma* focused on Jesus' own call to conversion and the powerful themes and figures in the Old Testament (Hebrew Scriptures) that prepared the way for his proclamation of God's never-ending reign. The central aim of the apostolic-style *kerygma* was to cause individuals (or whole communities and cultures) to change their ways and believe wholeheartedly in the risen Jesus' message, or to cause those who already believed to become more firm in faith.

Several key notions about the original Christian *kerygma* have been much discussed in recent times. The proclamation of the saving Word was meant for all persons, in all times and places, not just a chosen few (Luke 10:1–9). Thus, the sharing of the *kerygma* was and is the essential witness and the mission of all the baptized (Mark 16:15, Acts 8:4). In all, *kerygma* implies both the verbal sharing (spoken message) of the Word of God and the manner (lifestyle and method) by which the Christian proclamation is shared with others. Therefore, the essential proclamation of the gospel is communicated even to this day—as in apostolic-era days—through the words and daily deeds ("the wordless witness") of members of the Christian church. Elements of this *kerygma* are infused today in the evangelization strategies, catechetical programs, liturgical preaching and reading of God's Word, and all the daily activities of the contemporary Christian community.

The core of the testimony given by the original followers of Jesus centered on his life, death, and resurrection and the conversion to which the Jesus-experience calls all human beings (Acts 2:22–24, Galatians 1:1–4). As the *kerygma* was further developed and shared, more of the message and ministry of Jesus was explained, as was the radical idea that all of those who had faith in him were to share actively in his ongoing mission to bring the reign of God to complete fulfillment in creation. The Catholic community believes this *kerygma* lives on today through the power of Jesus' Spirit and through the "living proclamation" of the word of Christian salvation by evangelizers and others as they reach out to share the Christian challenge to believe, accept, and live the message and values of Jesus in the here-and-now and for all time.

Catholics today sometimes hear about a branch of theology called *kerygmatic theology*. Kerygmatic theology is a systematic reflection on and a carefully ordered, insightful presentation of all the data in Judaeo-Christian history and in the revelation of Jesus Christ that help humans grasp the depths of the "good news of salvation."

(See also Apostles, Conversion, Evangelization, Reign of God, and Witness.)

KOINONIA   is a Greek word that roughly means "fellowship." The term used in English to approximate *koinonia* is community.

In recent years, the word *koinonia* has begun to appear in various Catholic and other Christian resources, especially in books for catechetical ministers and other pastoral ministry and pastoral theology texts. The experience of *koinonia* among Christians is enabled by the presence of the Spirit of the risen Jesus, a gift that bonded the followers of Jesus of Nazareth together originally at Pentecost. In general, *koinonia* is used to describe the people of God and, more specifically, the body of Christ, the experience of church community.

A contemporary emphasis on Christian initiation and the ongoing faith formation of church members underscores that *koinonia* (community building) is an essential form of church ministry. In fact, it is one of the Christian tradition's interlocking (or interdependent), foundational ministries that, when provided together in a comprehensive manner to inquirers and the baptized, serves the pastoral needs of men, women, and young people. The interlocking, foundational ministries of the church are proclamation and teaching of the Christian message (*didache*), "fellowship" or community in the Spirit (*koinonia*), prayer and worship (*leitourgia*), and service to the people of God and the whole world (*diakonia*).

(See also Community, Didache, Pentecost, and People of God.)

L

LAICIZATION is the process by which someone who has received the sacrament of order is relieved, by Catholic authorities, of the duties and tasks of the Catholic priesthood. In essence, then, laicization means the process by which one is returned to the laity's way of life in the Christian faith community.

The process begins when an ordained man freely forwards a request for laicization to the local bishop. The bishop takes the matter under review and, whenever appropriate, forwards the presbyter's request to the Holy See for final review and final approval or denial of the request, according to the norms and procedures outlined in the Code of Canon Law. The department of the Holy See (or Roman Curia) that deals today with cases of laicization is the Congregation for Divine Worship and the Discipline of the Sacraments. (A similar process is put in place when members of religious orders wish to be relieved of the vows they have taken. Requests for laicization in such cases are forwarded to Rome via religious community superiors and are reviewed by the Congregation for Institutes of Consecrated Life and Societies of Apostolic Life.)

For a period of time in the 1970s and 1980s, the laicization process was streamlined and seemed to move much more quickly than in previous years. Pope John Paul II, however, expressed concern regarding this. He greatly slowed the process down so that church authorities could study ways by which it could be better handled in the future.

The church teaches that once any person enters the presbyterate, he remains a priest always, even though he is discharged from priestly activity—just as once someone is baptized, he or she is always baptized. Order is a sacrament by which a permanent relationship is established between the ordained and the community of Jesus Christ. Since ordination is a ministry call to render particular Christian services to God's people and the world at large, the empowerment to offer those special Christian services is never lost or "taken away" by the church. Thus, even if one has left active priestly ministry (has been laicized), he can still render priestly services (e.g., hear individuals' confessions, celebrate the Eucharist, anoint the dying) in cases of dire need.

(See also Holy See, Order, Presbyter, Religious Orders, and Vows.)

Note of Interest: The Code of Canon Law and the *Catechism of the Catholic Church* each mention that the share in Jesus' ministry conferred through the sacrament of order is a gift "granted once and for all." Thus, reception of order is neither temporary nor repeatable. The Code emphasizes that a validly ordained man may for just reasons be discharged from the obligations and functions of ordination or may be forbidden to exercise them but he cannot become a layperson again in the strict sense of the term. The character of ordination is permanent. The vocation and ministry conferred mark the ordained person for life.

LAITY are those baptized members of the people of God who have neither received the sacrament of order nor become members of religious orders. Vatican Council II emphasized that laypersons, both women and men, are called to take part in the timeless Christian evangelizing mission and likewise are "called to the fullness of the Christian life and to the perfection of charity," like all the baptized have been since the beginning of the Christian experience. Put another way, by the spiritual gift and power of baptism, every layperson has a responsibility to give daily witness in words and deeds to the good news of Jesus of Nazareth, to participate in the mission to reform and renew the created order, and to foster the actual building of the reign of God in the world, every day, to the best of their abilities. The origins of the term *laity* can be found in the Greek *laikos* and *laos*, meaning respectively "belonging to the people" and "people."

In Catholic communities today, a common truth expressed is that there are no second class citizens, no "haves and have nots," no better-than-thou members of the people of God. Thus the church now stresses that laypersons (laity), religious community members, and the ordained alike should all be treated with great respect and dignity, for each plays an important role and is called to particular duties in the mission of those who follow the risen Jesus. In the 1960s, Vatican II, in its Decree on the Apostolate of the Laity, encouraged all laypersons to recognize and use their God-given, unique gifts and witness in seeking to evangelize the entire human community.

In recent decades, many lay members of local Catholic communities have become very active in various church ministries and pastoral programs. Thus in parishes and other local settings (e.g., retreat centers, social service shelters, and houses of prayer) lay men and lay women have become pastoral associates, catechists, school teachers, directors of religious education, youth ministry coordinators, liturgy and music coordinators and ministers, justice and peace outreach ministers, parish administrators, ministers of greeting and hospitality, ministers to the separated and divorced, leaders in parents' organizations, small community conveners, adult education and Bible study leaders, RENEW (parish outreach and renewal) team members, parish council participants, family ministry coordinators, and staff (volunteer, professional, or paraprofessional) for various other local ministry endeavors. Of course some laypersons also work for Catholic dioceses, for example in pastoral ministry offices, in administration and finance bureaus, and on assorted diocesan councils/diocesan boards.

In 1980 Pope John Paul II noted that the laity have a true vocation and participate in the church's mission in diverse ways. In October 1987, the seventh ordinary assembly of the synod of Catholic bishops noted that the majority of the Christian laity live out their vocation as followers and disciples of Christ in all spheres of life [called] "the world": the family, the marketplace, the local community, and the like. To permeate this day-to-day living with the spirit of Christ has always been the primary task of the lay faithful; and it should be with still greater force their challenge today. It is in this way that they sanctify the world and collaborate in the realization of the reign of God. As a response to this synod's insights, Pope John Paul published in 1989 a meditative reflection called *Christifideles laici* ("Lay Members of Christ's Faithful People"), on the call of laywomen and laymen today in the real conditions of the spiritually-troubled, changing modern world.

The Vatican formally established the Pontifical Council of the Laity in 1976, headquartered with the Holy See offices in Rome. The rights and obligations of all lay members of the global Catholic community and the contours of their traditional apostolate are spelled out in the Code of Canon Law, canons 208–231. In the U.S. the National Association for Lay Ministry, founded in 1977, is based currently in Chanhasset, Minnesota. The National Center for the Laity, also founded in 1977, is based in Chicago. Many other lay-serving agencies and organizations in the United States are listed in the annual *Catholic Almanac*, edited by Felician Foy, O.F.M.

(See also Discipleship, Evangelization, Lay Ministries, Parish, People of God, and Witness.)

LAY MINISTRIES are forms of officially recognized Christian service rendered within and to the church community by baptized persons, as a direct ministry response to their call to witness to belief in the good news of Jesus. Some generally accepted lay ministries are: 1) ministry of hospitality, 2) ministry of the word, 3) ministry of the bread and cup, and 4) ministry of music.

In the very early days of the Christian experience, the apostles and other disciples of the risen Jesus simply could not perform all the ministry tasks and human services required by the growing, diverse gospel community. Church historians and commentators believe that at first deacons and deaconesses were chosen to help community-leadership care for the sick and poor, preach the Word (the *kerygma*), and assist at baptisms and other rituals, such as "the breaking of the bread" (the Eucharist) and agape meals in house churches. Scholars say that other gifted and talented persons were soon being called to ministerial service and to assist presbyters and elders in primitive Christian communities when particular needs arose. Gradually, however, lay ministries diminished as such roles were typically and officially subsumed into the responsibilities of bishops, pastors, other presbyters, and members of religious orders.

Since the time of Vatican Council II, 1962–1965, there has been a renewed interest among Catholics in the notion of a baptism call to all

Christians and in the ministries that the intellectually, culturally, and socially diverse Catholic population of the world can offer to the human family of the Creator (1 Corinthians 12:4–11). In 1972 Paul VI issued an apostolic letter, *Ministeria quaedam*, which provided for reform of liturgical ministries in the church. This document abolished various minor orders in the church and opened up two liturgical ministries to the laity: ministry of "reader" and ministry of "acolyte." New rites for the official institution of persons into these ministries were then developed. Paul VI also left open the possibility for additional lay ministries, such as the ministry of catechesis, to be recognized by the Holy See in the future. The individual tasks of four primary lay ministries often acknowledged in local Catholic communities today are:

Minister of Hospitality, often called an usher, welcomes those who enter the church for worship services. He or she sees that worshipers are seated and that the building remains comfortable throughout the celebration. Sometimes this person also assists with the presentation of the gifts at Mass, collects money contributions from the assembly, distributes parish bulletins and other materials, and sees that the church building is kept neat and orderly after every ceremony. These ministers also sometimes help to count financial offerings given in support of the church. Through his or her friendly manner and welcoming attitude, the minister of hospitality is meant to give witness to a positive Christian spirit for the worshipers who gather for celebration.

Minister of the Word, also called a reader or lector, proclaims the first or second reading during the Eucharist, but never the gospel reading, which must be done by a presbyter or deacon. Study, practice, and prayer help persons to be good and effective ministers of the Word for the people of God.

Minister of the Bread and Cup, also referred to as a special minister of the Eucharist, helps to distribute communion during Mass. He or she might also take the Eucharist to the sick, the dying, or to shut-ins who can't get to the church for worship. Local pastors and parochial vicars must petition the local bishop before persons can be commissioned as ministers of the bread and cup. These persons must also participate in a rite of institution in order to serve the worshiping community.

Minster of Music assumes one or more of several possible roles: musician, choir director, song leader, or cantor. Because liturgical music enhances the community's expression of faith and spiritual reverence for God, the minister of music helps worshipers rediscover and deepen faith commitment through musical expressions.

(See also Deacon, Laity, Ministry, Presbyters, and Worship.)

LECTIONARY is a book of Scripture readings used during the liturgy of the Word in Catholic worship. The Lectionary provides the Bible passages that are proclaimed aloud by lectors (readers) and presiders at Mass over a multi-year cycle. The term is from a Latin word meaning a "gathering or selection of readings."

The Hebrew Scriptures say that the original people of God assembled with Moses at Mount Sinai, heard the word of the Lord proclaimed, accepted its truth, and then entered into a covenant relationship with their God. To this day, Catholic worship follows this pattern through its liturgy of the Word. Believers assemble to hear the saving Word, accept its challenge, and go on to share in the Eucharist, the ultimate sign of the new covenant, made in Jesus Christ, between an ever-loving Creator and the new people of God. By the 2nd century, the rudiments of the liturgy of the Word, as Catholics know it today, were firmly in place: Hymns were sung, psalms were prayed, readings from the Old Testament (Hebrew Scriptures) and New Testament (Christian Scriptures) were proclaimed aloud, and presiders or others preached their faith witness. These basics have remained constant for many centuries. In 1969, the church published the first English-language Lectionary. A revised official Catholic edition was released in 1981.

The Lectionary is a rich ritual resource that helps people of faith hear and accept the revelation of God in the Word. It is a very practical sign or symbol of God's never-ending desire to communicate with humanity, and the Christian community in particular, through the life-changing message and challenge of Jesus of Nazareth. Hearing God's Word in Scripture, with open hearts, is itself an act of faith and worship.

The church community now listens to three Scripture readings on Sunday: an Old Testament passage (a reading from Acts during the Easter season), a passage from one of the letters or from the book of Revelation in the Christian Scriptures, and a passage from one of the gospels. Only two readings are proclaimed on most weekdays. All readings at Mass should be proclaimed from one prominent place in the congregation—a place at which all worshipers can center on hearing the dynamic Word of God. Gospel passages are read aloud by presbyters or deacons. Lectors (lay men or women) read aloud the other biblical selections at Mass. Everyone in the congregation at Catholic worship is urged strongly to listen very carefully to the Word and reflect on its implications for authentic Christian life.

In some Catholic communities, the Sunday biblical readings form the basic curriculum and discussion-focus for the praxis of small Christian communities, for adult religious education, for catechumenate groups, and for adolescent religious education. Such ministry efforts today are sometimes called lectionary-based catechesis.

(See also Bible, Epistle, Gospel, Lay Ministries, Liturgy of the Word/ Eucharist, and Revelation.)

LENT   is a season of the liturgical year. It begins on Ash Wednesday and concludes with the beginning of the Triduum (the evening of Holy Thursday). The word comes from the Middle English *lente* and the German *lenz*, meaning "spring."

Lent is a time for repentance, spiritual renewal, and *metanoia* (i.e., conversion or re-conversion to an authentic Christian way of life). Therefore,

Lent is a most appropriate time for Christian prayer, fasting, almsgiving, other penances, and works of charity. Lent is a time, therefore, for all the baptized to turn away from sinfulness and human evil in order to respond to the gospel and to experience a change of heart in preparation for the joyous Christian celebration of Easter.

In Christian history, Lent has been a time dedicated to remembrance of the forty days that Jesus of Nazareth spent fasting and and praying in the desert to prepare for his ministry and his radical call to humanity to repent and believe in the reign of God. Before Lent was officially observed for a full 40 days, Christian communities observed weekly days of fasting and penances, usually the Wednesdays and Fridays of each week. (For more information, see the article on Days of Prayer in this book.) Like springtime itself, each lenten season can and should be a time for spiritual rebirth and renewal for both individuals and whole communities and cultures.

Vatican Council II noted that, during Lent, it is particularly appropriate for Christians to reflect on God's revelation in the Bible, the Word of the Creator, and to participate in Scripture-centered prayer. In recent years Pope John Paul II has called Christians worldwide to make the most of this traditionally penitential season through the long-revered Christian practices of prayer, fasting, and almsgiving.

Note of Interest: Current church laws seem to require very little in terms of penitential practices compared to what was required in the past. In the U.S., all Fridays of Lent are to be days of abstinence: No meat or meat products may be eaten on these days. Ash Wednesday and Good Friday are also to be observed as days of abstinence, but they are days for fasting too: Only one full meal and two smaller meals may be consumed. Lenten regulations and rules vary from country to country.

(See also Abstinence, Almsgiving, Ash Wednesday, Conversion, Fasting, Holy Week, Liturgical Year, and Triduum.)

LIMBO according to some theologians, is the condition or state of being that is shared by all those who have died deserving neither the full experience of heaven nor the everlasting sorrow of hell. The term has Latin roots (*limbus*) that mean "on the border" or on the edge. Thus, limbo was often thought of as an experience on the edges or fringes of heaven.

In essence, the idea of limbo is rooted in the prayer called the Apostles Creed, particularly its phrase about Jesus after death: "He descended into hell." For centuries, many church members have believed in a spiritual place or state of being in which the souls of those who had been faithful to God were resting easily and enjoying fundamental happiness until Jesus, through his death and resurrection, liberated them from this limbo ("He descended into hell") and conducted them into heaven's glory. This limbo has sometimes been called the *limbus patrum*. Another limbo-related Christian belief has been that the souls of all unbaptized, little children, and others who never did sin seriously, enjoy a spiritual condition of basic happiness, even though they do not participate in the fullness of heaven. This has sometimes been called the *limbus infantum*.

Early church thinkers often rejected the idea that the souls of innocent little children suffered alienation from God or other pain. In the 5th century, however, St. Augustine said all the unbaptized (including children), after death, were destined for a diminished but real experience of hell. Later, St. Anselm in the 1100s taught about a place of natural happiness for the unbaptized that kept them essentially outside of heaven.

In 1794, Pope Pius VI taught that the souls of the unbaptized are not condemned to hell. Rather, a Catholic can believe in a spiritual condition of happiness called limbo (not heaven) in which no pain is suffered. However, limbo was not then and is not now an essential element in Catholic belief.

Current thinking often notes that we in fact know very little about the destiny of the souls of unbaptized persons. Many contemporary theologians stress that one need not be baptized in order to become a child of God's grace or an heir of heaven. For example, some might responsibly speculate that the dying but unbaptized person is given a moment for a fundamental choice for goodness or for alienation from God at the point of death. Others say that the dying individual's life experience, no matter how long or very brief, is a testimony to whether or not he or she lived in basic harmony with God's will for humanity. In each case, what follows is that eternal happiness with God becomes available to all humans who have lived, even if only for a few seconds or so.

The magisterium of the church has never elaborated on the pronouncement by Pius VI on the idea of limbo. Vatican II seemed to reflect thinking that says God loves all persons universally, and strongly wills that all will be fully happy on Earth today and in the glory we call heaven forever. Therefore, much current Catholic opinion says that the Creator must care deeply and everlastingly for the unbaptized in some way. The church officially continues to emphasize the goodness of baptism for infants and all those in danger of death, so they will in fact become members of the Christian community plus share immediately in Jesus' death and resurrection and the reign of God he announced.

(See also Baptism, Grace, Heaven, Hell, and Original Sin.)

LITANY   is a word with Greek roots meaning "to pray" and, more specifically, "to ask in earnest." A litany is a Christian form of prayer centering on a series of invocations and responses (for example: "St. John," "Pray for us," "St. Joseph," "Pray for us," etc.).

Originally, litanies were short prayer petitions or invocations repeated over and over (e.g., "Lord, have mercy" or "Lord, hear our prayer"). Remnants of ancient Christian litanies remain in the Mass—in the *Kyrie* (Lord, have mercy) and Lamb of God. During the high Middle Ages, litanies were used to venerate and pray to Christian saints. Litanies began to be incorporated into church processions and other church rituals, such as Benediction and the Forty Hours devotion.

Early and unedited versions of litanies included extremely long lists of earnest invocations to Jesus, Mary, and the saints, but they remained popular devotions in Europe and elsewhere nevertheless. One of the oldest of these lengthy litanies is the Litany of the Saints. In the later Middle Ages, a selection of litanies invoking the spiritual help of Mary, the Mother of Jesus, became popular. In 1587, Sixtus V approved a Marian litany made popular by St. Peter Canisius in Italy. It is today called the Litany of the Blessed Virgin Mary.

Litanies are both prayer devotions and sacramentals in the Catholic community. They are used today in communal church worship, at the Easter Vigil liturgy, at ordinations, and by assemblies at church devotions. Some Catholics pray litanies in their private prayer. Among all litanies that have been constructed, only a few are now approved for use in Catholic public worship. These include the Litany of the Saints, the Litany of the Blessed Virgin Mary, the Litany of the Sacred Heart, the Litany of the Precious Blood, and the Litany of St. Joseph.

(See also Devotion, Prayer, Sacramentals, and Veneration.)

LITURGICAL YEAR   is the cycle of seasons and feasts celebrated by the Roman Catholic church, and other Christian churches, during the course of a twelve-month period. This traditional cycle is sometimes also referred to as the church year, the liturgical calendar, and the Roman calendar. The cycle begins on the first Sunday of Advent (close to the beginning of December) and includes five major seasons: Advent, Christmas, Lent, Easter, and Ordinary Time. The Paschal Triduum, the holy three-day celebration of the passion, death, and resurrection of the Lord, forms a bridge between Lent and Easter and is the center and high point of the liturgical year.

Feasts are Christian celebrations held on specific days to honor the risen Jesus, Mary, or one or more of the saints. Feasts are grouped into three categories, by order of importance: 1) solemnities, 2) feasts, and 3) memorials. An inclusive Roman church calendar of feast days was published by Pope Pius V in 1568. Since then many feasts and celebrations have been added to the Roman liturgical cycle. Vatican Council II indicated in the 1960s that the total number of feasts on the calendar overall should be limited, in order to give central Christian traditions, feasts, and seasons proper celebratory focus.

The liturgical calendar is a Christian response rooted in the deep human need for faith in an ever-present, caring Creator and for order, stability (repetition), life-inspiring changes, and life-giving memories. Observance of the Christian mysteries expressed through major Christian feasts and seasons can lead individuals and entire local communities toward greater faith and witness through spiritual "practices for soul and body" (e.g., prayer, fasting, almsgiving, abstinence, works of stewardship and charity, and celebration) and through catechetical instruction within the liturgy.

The entire Catholic cycle of the liturgical year centers on the mission and ministry of salvation conducted by Jesus of Nazareth, and in a special way on his paschal mystery (suffering, death, and resurrection). The Roman liturgical year also offers Catholics and others a meaningful opportunity to remember and honor Mary, the mother of Jesus, other saints, and key events in the history of the evangelizing community that has followed the risen Jesus for almost twenty centuries. The liturgical calendar/year is not a mere recollection or representation of past events. It is a living, ongoing celebration of Jesus alive and present within his community.

The revised (and current) calendar for Roman Catholic communities was officially approved by Pope Paul VI in 1969, and the U.S. bishops ratified it in 1972. By the conclusion of 1992, a number of celebrations commemorating certain U.S.-related Christian saints and witnesses had been placed on the annual "particular calendar" of the U.S. Catholic community (but not on the general Roman cycle).

The seasons of the Roman liturgical calendar include:

Advent: From the Sunday nearest to November 30, the feast of Saint Andrew, until Dec. 24.

Christmas: from the vigil of Christmas (Dec. 24) until the Sunday after Epiphany (January 6).

Lent: Ash Wednesday until Holy Thursday evening, the day before Good Friday.

The sacred *Triduum* begins on Holy Thursday evening and closes with evening prayer on Easter Sunday.

Easter: Easter Sunday until Pentecost (50 days total).

Ordinary Time: begins on the Monday after the first Sunday following January 6 and concludes on Mardi Gras, the day prior to Ash Wednesday; it then proceeds anew on the Monday after Pentecost and ends with the day before the First Sunday of Advent.

(See also Advent; Christmas; Easter; Holy Days; Lent; Prayer; Saints, Communion of; Triduum; and Worship.)

LITURGY OF THE HOURS   often also called the Divine Office is the official daily prayer of the church. The liturgy of the hours helps the church praise the Creator and dedicate all the elements of everyday life to Christian holiness. The usage of the term "hours" implies certain set periods or times of prayer which occur around the clock.

The Didache urged Jesus' followers to pray daily—morning, noon, and night. By the year 300, community leaders were urging all the members of the Christian body to gather for prayer in the morning and the evening. Soon these public prayer services became widespread and popular. Among those who later lived hermit-like in monasteries, regular community prayer gatherings (up to seven per day) took place. Their "prayer of the hours" eventually came to be known as the Divine Office. Over time, as the hours of prayer multiplied and the liturgy of the hours grew in complexity, the participation of lay persons gradually diminished until the prayer became almost the exclusive domain of the clergy and members of male and female religious orders.

Today, the ideal is still that Christians are called to pray very regularly and humbly worship the Creator. Whether or not one uses the actual liturgy of the hours, whether or not one is ordained, all the baptized should establish some personal habits or patterns of life that lead regularly to prayer and various spiritual-growth disciplines.

The original office, known as the Roman Breviary, was last revised in 1965–70. The resulting liturgy of the hours was finally published in official English translation in 1975. It appeared as four volumes with thousands of pages. The revised format provides readings and reflections from the Bible; morning and evening prayers; daytime prayers for mid-morning, midday and mid-afternoon worship; night prayers, and some non-biblical prayer sources, including the works of early church leaders and saints.

(See Devotion, Didache, Holiness, Prayer, Sacramental, and Worship.)

LITURGY OF THE WORD/EUCHARIST   are the two main parts of the eucharistic celebration (also called the Mass) in Catholic worship. The term "liturgy" has its origins in the Greek *leitourgia* which refers to "public service" and, in some ways, "work" of the people gathered. In Catholic rituals, the liturgy of the Word centers on the proclamation of the word of the Creator (Scripture). The liturgy of the Eucharist includes the eucharistic prayer (the canon of the Mass), the consecration of bread and wine, the Lord's Prayer, and the sharing of the Eucharist by all assembled. In other eras, these two key movements or parts of the Catholic community's traditional Mass were referred to as the Mass of Catechumens and Mass of the Faithful.

During the liturgy of the Word, Scripture verses are proclaimed from a liturgical resource book known as the Lectionary. When there are three biblical readings, on Sundays, for example, the first reading is taken from the Hebrew Scriptures (except during the Easter season, when it is taken from the Acts of the Apostles), the second is taken from the Christian Scriptures—an epistle or the book of Revelation (the Apocalypse), and the third reading, also taken from the Christian Scriptures (New Testament) is always a gospel passage. In Catholic eucharistic worship, a homily based on these Scripture readings follows, and all assembled then profess their faith in response to God's Word by praying the Nicene Creed. The liturgy of the Word concludes with prayers of the faithful, also referred to as general intercessions, in which the worshiping assembly prays for the needs of the church, for public authorities and the salvation of the world, for those oppressed by any need, and for the local community.

The liturgy of the Eucharist generally has begun in Catholic ritual tradition with the presentation and preparation of the gifts of bread and wine and has proceeded with the eucharistic prayer (canon of the Mass), including the consecration (Jesus becomes fully present under the forms of ordinary bread and wine), the doxology, and then the great Amen response of faith by the whole assembly, followed by the communion rite, including the Lord's Prayer, the sign of peace shared by all, and the reception of the Eucharist (communion) in the forms of bread and wine.

The detailed order of the Eucharist (the Mass) is:

Introductory Rites: Entrance song, Greeting of the assembly, Introductory comments, Penitential rite (or sprinkling rite), Glory to God hymn of praise, and Opening prayer.

Liturgy of the Word: First reading, Responsorial psalm, second reading, Gospel procession and acclamation, and then the Gospel reading, Homily, Creed—profession of Christian faith, and prayers of the faithful.

Liturgy of the Eucharist: Presentation of the gifts, Offering of the gifts, Prayer over the gifts, Eucharistic prayer (including Preface; Holy, Holy, Holy Lord; Doxology; Great Amen).

Communion Rite: Lord's prayer, Prayer for deliverance (embolism), Prayer for and shared sign of peace, Lamb of God and the breaking of the consecrated bread, Communion, Communion song, Hymn or recitation of Bible verses, Prayer after Communion.

Concluding Rite: Announcements, Blessing of the assembly, and the General dismissal.

(See also Agape; Altar; Bible; Church, as Home; Eucharist; Eucharistic Prayer; Homily; Lectionary; Sacramentary; Transubstantiation; and Worship.)

LUKE in Christian tradition is credited as one of the four evangelists in the Christian Scriptures (New Testament). He is considered the author of a two-volume work: the gospel of Luke and the Acts of the Apostles. The gospel of Luke is one of the synoptic gospels, perhaps written in the city of Rome (the exact place of composition remains unknown) sometime between 75–85 c.e.

Ancient Christian stories and traditions say that Luke was a Greek man and a gentile (i.e., a non-Jewish person) who may have been a physician (Colossians 4:14) and a good friend and one-time traveling companion of St. Paul. These stories also tell us that he remained unmarried throughout his life and was in his eighties when he died somewhere in the Middle East.

The gospel of Luke reveals that Jesus of Nazareth radically cared for the poor, the suffering, the lowly, and the sinners of this world. The gospel was probably written as a faith statement—a *kerygma*—about Jesus, intended more for gentiles interested in the emerging Christian community than for those of Jewish background. This author/evangelist used the gospel of Mark as one of his most important resources.

Catholic teachings stress that the gospel of Luke shows the true love and healing compassion which Jesus of Nazareth had for all women and men and particularly for all persons burdened by sin, illness, and other kinds of suffering. Catholic bible-study specialists have also stressed that the good news according to Luke shows Jesus, in the light of post-Easter faith, to be a bold proclaimer of a vision of salvation for all humanity, a vision that Christians have learned to name the reign of God over creation. The Lucan gospel also includes some unique introductory information about the conception, birth, and childhood of Jesus of Nazareth and some stories with a focus on women.

The Catholic community honors Saint Luke with an annual feast day on October 18.

(See also Acts of the Apostles, Gospel, Kerygma, Option for the Poor, and Synoptics.)

M

MAGISTERIUM is the teaching authority or teaching office of the universal Catholic community (the "teacher of truth" according to a phrase from the Second Vatican Council). The term can also be used accurately to refer to the body (or "college") of Catholic episcopal-level leaders/teachers who define and comment on official Christian doctrine. Magisterium derives from the Latin word *magister*, which means "teacher." Catholic tradition maintains that the members of the church's magisterium have the call and the responsibility to elaborate on matters pertaining directly to Catholic Christian beliefs and moral values in an authoritative and authentic manner.

According to Christian tradition, the very first followers of Jesus of Nazareth who received this special authority were Peter and the other original apostles. Gradually through the early centuries of Christian life, catechists, teachers, deacons, and presbyters became directly subject to Christian episcopal authority (i.e., the spiritual leadership and authority of their pope and local bishops). By the onset of the Middle Ages, whenever apostasies or false teachings (heresies) challenged the truth or authority of the gospel or the church community's various beliefs, values, and practices, bishops often became the authentic and authoritative (magisterial) Christian teachers in their dioceses. By the 13th century the pope had become *the* magisterial teacher in the Christian world, often simply expecting Christian church members to fully accept and assent (without any question) to the doctrinal statements he proclaimed.

Over the ages, something like two unequal classes of people developed in the institutional church: those who were learned and literate enough to teach and lead others (e.g., teachers, presbyters, and bishops) and those who were the lowly learners and the led (all baptized others). In recent years this artificial caste-like (separation) system among the members of the community of the baptized has begun to radically change, at least on many local-church levels and in many types of Christian communities. Every person, baptized or not, is called by a loving and creative God to become a lifelong learner and something of a teacher to others based upon their accumulated human-life experience and Christian-life wisdom.

The recent emphasis on collegiality in the church community worldwide is helping all the people of God to be more open to numerous points of view, and to rely less on strictly-imposed authoritative statements about how to live and worship faithfully. From this point of view, the term magisterium at its best can—and perhaps should—be used to refer to the whole faith-filled community of the baptized and not merely to the ordained or, more narrowly, to certain hierarchical teachers and theologians in Catholic institutions.

Still, however, the word *magisterium* is usually used to focus Catholics' attention today on the official teaching ministry of the pope united with all other Catholic bishops. Paul VI addressed this issue by stating that, officially speaking, magisterium refers to the "subordinate and faithful echo and secure interpreter of the divine word." Thus the magisterium of the church does not really reveal new doctrinal truths "nor is it superior to sacred Scripture"; its power to teach infallibly extends only as far as the Scriptures and Christian tradition and the experience of the church overall have revealed God's will to the human community.

Over the centuries magisterial teachings have been expressed in the various creeds, doctrines, liturgical practices, decrees of ecumenical councils, encyclicals, and synods recognized by the Catholic church. The baptized are called by church authorities to give full assent to the teachings and proclamations that are authoritatively Catholic and magisterial; however, in certain circumstances, after authentic reflection, prudent study, discernment, and prayer, Catholic individuals or groups may have to choose to follow their consciences, even if this means basic dissent from officially-accepted concepts.

An elaboration on the church community's current thoughts on the nature of the magisterium can be found in the *Catechism of the Catholic Church*, sections 84–90.

(See also Apostasy, Apostolic Succession, Bishop, Deposit of Faith, Diocese, Doctrine, Infallibility, and Pope.)

MARK is credited as the chief author of the first-composed and the shortest of the four gospels in the Christian Scriptures. The gospel of Mark was probably written around 65–70 c.e., soon after the death of the apostle Peter. The gospel of Mark is placed second in the canon of gospel versions in the New Testament, between the gospels of Matthew and Luke.

Early Christian traditions tell us that Mark was a Jew from Jerusalem, perhaps sometimes called John Mark. Such sources also indicate that Mark was a close follower of the apostle Peter—Mark has traditionally been known as "the interpreter of Peter"—and that he also knew the historical Paul (perhaps, as is reported in the Acts of the Apostles, Mark even went along with Paul while Paul conducted his first missionary journey). Historical traditions indicate that Mark later wrote his gospel in Rome, then died as a martyr in Alexandria after founding a Christian community in that area.

Many scholars today suggest that the gospel of Mark was written either for one specific primitive Christian community or perhaps a community primarily made up of gentiles—non-Jewish individuals—who were interested in baptism and the gospel. It is generally thought that the gospel of Mark was intended to show how Jesus of Nazareth was indeed the long-awaited and promised messiah of Israel, truly the resurrected Son of God, who offers all of humanity hope in an eternal salvation. The gospel seems to dwell on the daily actions and details of the public life, preaching, and healing ministry of Jesus of Nazareth in order to make Jesus' key and life-changing point clear. Because it is short compared to other gospel versions (and perhaps because it concludes rather abruptly, making it seem somewhat incomplete to some) the gospel according to Mark is at times criticized, erroneously, as not being as refined or theologically sophisticated as the other New Testament-era works known as Matthew, Luke, and John.

The Catholic community believes that the author of Mark was inspired by God and by Christian faith to reveal the good news that all persons, in all places, cultures, and eras, have been called by God through the suffering, death, and resurrection of Jesus of Nazareth to an eternal happiness in the unending reign of God. The most proper response, according to Mark's gospel, to Jesus' mission, message, and values is authentic Christian conversion and discipleship, despite the human fears, sufferings, or misunderstandings that might result. The Catholic community celebrates a feast day of St. Mark on April 25.

(See also Conversion, Discipleship, Gospel, Messiah, and Synoptics.)

MARTYR   is one who has freely chosen to give up his or her life for the sake of Christian faith. Many martyrs have died in terrible persecutions rather than deny the faith and values essential to the way of life revealed by Jesus. The word is a Greek term meaning "witness."

Many of the earliest followers of Jesus died in Roman persecutions. Their total and painful life sacrifice was seen by other Christians as an imitation of (i.e., a witness to) the mystery of the terrible suffering and death of Jesus of Nazareth.

Some believe a man named Stephen was the first Christian martyr (Acts 6–7). Others died between the years 67–313 because they openly practiced the culturally-forbidden Christian way of life and worship. Friends gathered at their graves to pray and celebrate their Christian victory over death. In time, altars (and later entire church buildings) for the communal celebration of the liturgy of the word and Eucharist were constructed over martyrs' graves. A bishop of Smyrna named Polycarp (died in 155) was likely the first Christian martyr to have a cult following. In the 3rd century, Origen wrote that a life of total Christian self-sacrifice and service was like an "unbloody martyrdom." Clement of Alexandria taught that every Christian's death is a type of martyrdom if it is experienced with total faith in Jesus.

A radical martyr is one who has given up his or her life to profess deep Christian trust in God. Yet anyone who has died naturally but has lived a way of life devoted to extraordinary, charitable Christian witness and full self-sacrifice is a martyr in a real sense as well. All Christians should try not to cling to self-centered, materialistic values. Instead, they should try to imitate Jesus to the limit, as the original martyrs did.

Catholics believe that martyrs and other saints have achieved full union and happiness with God in heaven. Thus they are the human beings and Christian witnesses that all Christians should strive to imitate. Catholics are urged to pray to the martyrs and other saints for help, just as we might ask for the prayers and assistance of Christian persons on Earth. Because martyrdom is an ideal that leads toward full unity with the Creator, there clearly is a very close relationship in Catholic belief between the suffering, death, and resurrection of Jesus and the painful life-to-death experience of Christian martyrs.

Vatican II taught that all martyrdom (self-sacrificing) experiences help transform church members into the image of the risen Jesus. In many ways, disorder, human sinfulness, and evil cause various degrees of persecution for the people of God, and thus martyrdom experiences continue in the U.S. and around the globe to this day.

(See also Apostasy, Canonization, Death/Dying, Heaven, and Saints.)

Note of Interest: The Roman Martyrology is an up-to-date listing of Christian martyrs and other saints. It remains the official Roman Catholic catalogue of saints honored by the church. Additions are made to this martyrology via beatifications and canonizations, which are prepared by the Roman Curia department called the Congregation for the Cause of Saints. There are more than 5000 names listed currently in the Roman Martyrology.

MARY   is the mother of Jesus, the wife of Joseph, and the greatest of all the saints. Catholics believe that Mary remains a genuine witness and model of faithful living for all Christian individuals and communities for all time. Mary is often called the Blessed Virgin because she freely and completely responded to the will of the Creator and conceived Jesus of Nazareth by the sheer power of God's Spirit. Christian tradition maintains that this humble, loving Jewish woman continued to seek to do God's will throughout her life. The Catholic church believes that Mary was conceived without sin (that she was the "Immaculate Conception" and was thus redeemed from the moment she came to be) and that she was at some point in time miraculously assumed into heaven with body and soul united.

Since 1964, Mary has been officially honored by the Catholic community as the mother of the global people of God. Historical traditions indicate, though they cannot be proven, that Mary was the daughter of Jewish parents named Joachim and Anne. Quite likely she was born about the year 18 b.c.e. either in Jerusalem or in the province called Galilee. The Christian Scriptures reveal, and Christian doctrine teaches, that Mary conceived a son named Jesus through the power of the Spirit (Luke 1:26–38, Matthew 1:18–25) then married a carpenter (perhaps more like a handyman) named Joseph, an upright Jewish man from Nazareth.

Not much else is really known about the historical Mary. The Christian Scriptures mention her in the infancy narratives of the gospels and describe how she attended a wedding at Cana with Jesus, was present at the crucifixion of her son, and was present with Jesus' close followers for the powerful and spirited experience of Pentecost. The Catholic community, in light of its Easter (post-resurrection) faith, has always accorded Mary a special place of honor in the traditional Christian story overall as the mother of God and as a faithful witness to what total Christian surrender to Jesus' compelling good news of salvation is all about.

For centuries in Christian tradition, Mary has been referred to as a new Eve. The first Eve helped bring personal sin and death to the world, but Mary, the mother of Jesus, proved to be the bearer of a new kind of everlasting life and grace for all of humanity. In 431 c.e., the Council of Ephesus identified Mary as the true mother of God and a model of Christian living in her total surrender to the will of the Creator.

Belief in the mysterious assumption of the historical Mary, body and soul, into heaven was in fact widespread among certain Christian churches by the 700s. By the mid-800s, the church was celebrating the annunciation to Mary (about Jesus' miraculous birth), Mary's ritual purification, Mary's assumption into heaven, and the birth of the historical Mary on certain liturgical feast days. The earliest celebrations of Mary's immaculate conception became popular about 150 years later. Centuries later, in 1950, a Catholic dogma on the assumption of Mary was formally defined by church authority. Soon after, in 1953, Pius XII declared a Marian Year for the entire church community. A dogma on the Immaculate Conception of the mother of God was proclaimed on December 8, 1854.

Mary was an ordinary human person—a very young woman when Jesus was conceived, perhaps only 14 years of age or so—who was greatly challenged to have a simple but profound and counter-cultural trust in her God. Some modern biblical students have wondered anew if Mary and Joseph actually had other children once Jesus was born; they point, for example, to a reference in Acts 1:14 about brothers of Jesus. Debates aside, however, the church community has traditionally perceived Mary, the mother of Jesus, to be one who symbolically remained ever-virginally pure and gave her complete assent and her heart to the Creator—thus in a way (as Vatican II noted) she deserves to be called also the mother of the timeless Christian community and people of God.

Mary is reverenced, even by some non-Christians, for her courageous ability to withstand even the deepest and most mysterious of human sufferings and doubts and yet remain essentially faithful to God. She is therefore someone to whom modern, harried individuals and communities can look—someone with whom they can have a spiritual relationship—while trying to cope with all the troubles and surprises that contemporary life can serve up.

While many non-Catholic Christians and others still criticize what is thought to be a Catholic "cult of Mary," theologians and other church leaders today continue to point out that the baptized truly are not called to worship Mary. They are called to remember and venerate her as a key member of the "communion of saints," an ever-relevant Christian witness from the historical past, for her actual life and witness always pointed to the God revealed to her in a special way. The Catholic community thus believes that Mary is a living symbol of the way in which every person should respond faithfully to God's gifts of life and grace. She is to be given very special honor among all believers because of her unique relationship to Jesus of Nazareth. Catholic teachers sometimes speak of Mary as an archetype or faith-prototype for the body of Christ, the people of God, who constantly intercedes in prayer to God on behalf of all faithful human beings. Catholic emphasis clearly is placed on the fact that the historical Mary was a human being, not a superhuman goddess, and that her profound faith and holiness make her worthy of imitation by all of humanity.

In 1970 the Catholic bishops of the United States issued a testimony to Mary's lasting import called "Behold Your Mother." In 1987 Pope John Paul II wrote an encyclical, *Redemptoris mater*, on Mary's role in the mystery of the incarnation and the mystery of the church. The *Catechism of the Catholic Church* describes various aspects of traditional doctrine on Mary in sections 487–511. The Catechism notes that in Mary's virginal motherhood she cooperated with freedom and obedience in humanity's salvation, thus becoming a new Eve, a mother of all the living.

(See also Annunciation, Assumption, Immaculate Conception, Jesus of Nazareth, Holy Family, and Witness.)

MATRIMONY is one of the seven sacraments of the Catholic Christian community. Through this sacramental experience, a man and a woman are united in a loving covenant as husband and wife. Married couples are called, therefore, by the people of God to be visible signs of the ongoing, loving relationship that exists between the risen Jesus of Nazareth and the community that follows him, the church.

According to church law, certain conditions must be met in order for a Christian marriage to be considered valid. A man and a woman must each be of legal age and neither can have been married previously (unless an official annulment of the previous marriage has been granted by church authority). Other general conditions for a valid marriage include: Both partners must be choosing marriage freely (without duress or constraint); both must be able and willing to have sexual intercourse; both must be willing to have children, if possible; and the man and woman to be joined in marriage must not have a direct family (blood) relationship.

The term "marriage" stems from the ancient Latin *maritus*, meaning "husband." The term "matrimony" also has Latin origins, *matrimonium*, meaning "mother."

Nuptial celebrations of the Eucharist in which marital covenants were formed and blessed were being held by Christian assemblies as early as the 4th century. By the time of the Middle Ages, Catholic authorities had declared that a presbyter (priest) should be present at all marriage ceremonies as an official representative of the church community. At that time the church also began to stress officially that marriages were more like legal contracts than covenant-love relationships. It was not until the 1440s that Catholicism, through the Council of Florence, declared that matrimony should be truly regarded as one of seven sacraments. The Council of Trent, in the middle of the 16th century, reaffirmed that matrimony is a sacrament that, in order to be valid, must take place in the presence of a Catholic presbyter.

Jesus of Nazareth proclaimed that a legitimate covenant bond between a man and woman in marriage could not simply be abolished. St. Paul wrote about married life, likening marriage to the permanently-framed relationship that mysteriously but genuinely exists between the risen One and the community that believes in his good news message and values (for example, see Ephesians 5).

Given the difficulties and many stresses too frequently encountered by couples in marital relationships and family households in general today, what should be the true meaning of Christian marriage? Some maintain that it should primarily be imaged and lived as an essential way in society to personally give love, receive love, and grow in love (e.g., Genesis 2:18–25). Others express the opinion that co-creation of children and family should be imaged as the primary aim of a marital covenant. Still others recognize other practical, financial, or socially creative purposes as the chief reasons for marriage in our world today, such as the formation of family units or support communities (in Christian traditional terms, the formation of "churches of the home").

The Catholic community emphasizes that a valid marriage relationship is a permanent union (a relational and covenantal bond) between two parties, male and female, until the death of one of the marital partners. Catholics believe that in matrimony a man and a woman enter into a covenant by giving the sacrament to each other (thus the marriage partners can be called the ordinary ministers of this sacrament). A presbyter or deacon must act as an official witness on behalf of the Christian community at each Catholic marriage, and the others assembled for the ceremony (whether or not it occurs within a celebration of the Eucharist) affirm that a loving union and covenant has been established in Jesus.

This sacrament is primarily intended to help men and women to love faithfully, in a covenantal way, to grow personally and spiritually as individuals and as a couple, to strive for holiness as Jesus of Nazareth did, and to co-create and raise children (if the couple can give birth to children) as members of the Christian community in the world. A Catholic perspective on matrimony and marital lifestyles affirms that women and men are equal partners in their relationships, that both are free human beings created by a loving God and endowed with personal rights and dignity. The Catholic community today strongly encourages married couples to love deeply and to witness to a caring God's continuing love, support, and concern for humanity's welfare. By becoming considerate and loving parents, by forming a Christian family household, and by encouraging participation in socially responsible activities and careers for all family members, married people cooperate in God's ongoing work of creation (as co-creators) in an important way.

Official church disciplines (canons) regarding the sacrament of matrimony can be found in Book IV of the Code of Canon Law, canons 1055–1165. The *Catechism of the Catholic Church* contains an elaborate section on marriage (sections 1601–1666). It makes many assertions about matrimony based upon a foundational theology, affirming that the vocation of marriage is written in the very nature of humanity. Thus marriage is not purely a human (legal) institution. It is intimately connected to the well-being of the human person, the human family (society), and the spiritual growth of young people through Christian family life.

(See also Annulment; Church, as Home; Covenant; Divorce; Family Ministry; and Sacrament.)

MATTHEW is one of the original apostles of Jesus of Nazareth and is traditionally named as the author of the gospel of Matthew. The name Matthew has ancient Hebrew origins meaning "gift of Yahweh."

The text of the gospel according to Matthew indicates that Matthew was a tax collector. Not much else is known about his life. Ancient Christian stories say he died a martyr, and a particular Christian tradition claims that some relics of his body were discovered in Salerno in the year 1080.

Many scholars now hold that the gospel of Matthew was written by a now-unknown follower of the risen Jesus of Nazareth in a combined Jewish-and-gentile community, such as Antioch, in Syria, about 85–90 c.e. (Some now think the gospel bears Matthew's name because the original apostle was instrumental in founding this primitive Christian community.) Some speculate that the theological perceptions and sophisticated knowledge of both the Greek language and Jewish law in the gospel indicate it was written by a well-trained Jewish person who had converted to the Christian way. Probably two key resources used in the construction of the Matthean gospel story were the gospel of Mark and an earlier primitive post-resurrection writing, now commonly known as Q (*quelle*, the source).

The gospel of Matthew may have been a favorite among many early Christian worship assemblies, being used often in eucharistic celebrations and as a basis for early Christian preaching and catechesis. Scripture commentators have noted that this gospel contains three main story-movements or parts: 1) the presentation of Jesus of Nazareth; 2) the ministry of Jesus to the nation of Israel; and 3) the journey of Jesus to Jerusalem and his resulting death and resurrection. In focusing on the life and ministry of Jesus of Nazareth in the overall context of salvation history, Matthew depicts Jesus as the true fulfillment of Israel, the promised messiah or anointed one, who remains at the center of all proclamations about the reign of God. Matthew's gospel, written for a culture full of both Jews and gentiles—and perhaps one quite full of resulting tensions and dissensions and hostilities—claims that the life, ministry, death, and resurrection of Jesus (claimed by his followers to be the Son of God) is of unquestioned, life-changing, decisive significance for humanity as a whole. In the gospel story, Jesus, the messiah and teacher, is very much like a new Moses who forges a new type of covenant between a loving God and the people of God.

Matthew's gospel has been referred to as the gospel of the kingdom or the reign of God (the Greek equivalent of the word "kingdom" appears in it many times). Many believe that this gospel clearly was meant to illustrate that the mission of all Jesus' disciples in the world is an extension of Jesus' own mission and ministry "to the lost sheep of the house of Israel" (Matthew 10:6, 15:24)—in which the eschatological nearness of the reign of God must be urgently proclaimed. Consequently, in Matthew's gospel, true disciples are dedicated, like Jesus, to suffering servanthood. They are persons who, despite limited vision or misunderstandings, nevertheless freely "take up the cross and follow" the risen One, the divinely revealed Son of God (Matthew 16:24). The Catholic community celebrates a feast of Saint Matthew every year on September 21.

(See also Gospel, Kerygma, Messiah, Reign of God, and Synoptics.)

MEDALS are sacramentals of the Catholic community made from metallic substances that usually have a religious picture or words on them. Some Catholics wear medals on neck chains or carry them in purses or pockets. The term comes from the Latin *metallum*, "metal."

Religious medals and images were used by early Christian communities; medals with depictions of the apostles Peter and Paul and other martyrs have been discovered, some dating back to the 2nd century of the common era. By the 4th century, medals were given to the newly baptized. Medals pressed to honor the popes were first made in the 15th century. And an official church blessing for sacramental medals was instituted by Pope Pius V in the 1500s. Some Catholics and others believe that an apparition (a private revelation) of Mary, the mother of Jesus of Nazareth, appeared to Catherine Labouré in 1830 in France and told Catherine that a Miraculous Medal of the Immaculate Conception should be created so that devotion to Mary would be promoted.

Christian devotion and prayer via medals does not seem attractive to everyone, but many Catholics over the centuries have chosen to believe that religious medals can help those who wear them express Christian faith and a living spirituality. Medals are not to be considered lucky charms or magical items that have special, superstitious powers.

There are many kinds of religious medals still recognized in various ways by the global Catholic community today—for example, the miraculous medal, the scapular medallion, various papal medals, and American Catholic medals. A favorite medal in parts of the Catholic world still is the aforementioned scapular, which was promoted by Pope Pius X in 1910 (rooted in an 11th-century tradition dating to the ministry of St. Peter Damian). The traditional scapular has a picture of Jesus (as the Sacred Heart) on one side and an image of Mary on the other.

Medals can still be specially blessed by presbyters, and some church indulgences may be granted to persons who wear or carry certain devotional Catholic medals such as: 1) the miraculous medal, 2) the medal of the child Jesus, 3) the medal of Our Lady of Guadalupe, 4) the medal of Saint Benedict, and 5) the medal of Saint Bernard.

(See also Apparitions, Devotions, Indulgences, Sacramentals, and Veneration.)

MESSIAH   is a derivation of a Hebrew term, *masiah*, which essentially means "the anointed." The comparable Greek word is *christos*, which translates into English as "the Christ." Christians believe that Jesus of Nazareth, who was raised from death by God, was and is the promised one from the Creator, the messiah, the one chosen to reveal decisively the life-altering good news of salvation and the nearness of the reign of God to all of humanity.

The nation of Israel waited many centuries for a messiah, a figure promised by Yahweh, who would be a strong military leader and a kingly savior capable of defeating the Israelites' foes and restoring the kingdom of God's chosen ones to power and greatness. For the Hebrews, *masiah* had connotations of an anointed king, one appointed by divine command, the adopted son of Yahweh, and the holy one who was the instrument of God's justice for the human community. Sources show that the Jews, therefore, imaged this much-anticipated leader as something of a superhuman and royal person.

The intense, burning hope in Israel for a strong, warlike messiah had probably begun to wane somewhat toward the close of the pre-Christian era. The heart of biblical messianism was the notion that God would choose to intervene personally in human history and cultures by sending a savior to deliver the people of God from sinfulness, suffering, and injustices. The Hebrews sometimes imaged the messiah as a prophetic figure, a Moses-like presence, or a suffering one, anointed by Yahweh to proclaim good news of salvation and hope to the lowly and the oppressed (Isaiah 61:1 and Luke 4:18).

Christian communities believe that Jesus of Nazareth, a self-sacrificing and service-oriented suffering leader, the definitive Word of hope to humankind, should be identified as the messiah from God. Some of his original hearers and followers found his model of messianic witness surprising and difficult to comprehend, because it was radically different from the traditional Jewish expectation of a powerful, royal messiah-conqueror. Some scholars say that the historical Jesus probably did not claim a divine mantle for himself such as Son of God; they think he was quite probably more comfortable with the self-effacing, humble title Son of Man, by which he identified himself as an important spiritual guide and humble leader for the people of God, a suffering servant sent by a loving Creator to care for God's chosen ones on earth.

Early Christians, including the anonymous authors of the four gospels (the evangelists), recognized and proclaimed that the risen Jesus was indeed the promised messiah from God. The gospels indicate that Jesus of Nazareth did claim to be the promised messiah (e.g., Mark 14:61ff., Matthew 26:63ff., and John 10:24).

The four gospels express the belief that Jesus' true messianic mission was to be a humble, spiritual guide and divine witness—one who suffered and was then raised from death by God for all peoples, communities, and cultures in order to lead them toward hope in a life-giving, ever-present, everlasting reign of God. Traditional usage by Catholic communities of the name Jesus Christ really means "Jesus, the anointed one" or "Jesus the Messiah." Thus the word Christ, of course, was not a personal last name for Jesus of Nazareth.

(See also Anointing; Christology; Gospel; Hope; Jesus of Nazareth; and Jesus, Titles of.)

MINISTRY   is any form of active Christian service, designated or commissioned by the church, to aid the Christian community in meeting the diverse needs of humanity and to help the people of God fulfill its evangelizing mission to proclaim good news of salvation and hope in Jesus. The term has some roots in the Latin term *ministrare*, "to minister" or "to serve."

The mission of the Christian community and the community's diverse ministries are not the same thing. Ministries exist to help the church fulfill its mission. Their reason for being and their true source is the universal mission given to the followers of Jesus to reach out and share his gospel message (to extend his divinely-received mission and Word) in all communities and cultures, to call all humanity to Christian conversion and genuine adoption of Christian lifestyles (Mark 16:15, Matthew 28:16–20, Luke 10:1–9).

The church today recognizes ministries offered to the people of God and the world at large by both ordained ministers and non-ordained lay ministers. Contemporary Christian theologies emphasize that all baptized members have a certain right and responsibility to be persons of service and ministry to others, and thus should informally and generally give daily witness to participation in the evangelizing, Christian mission. However some individuals and groups feel particularly called to do Christian ministry, and thus they seek the responsibility for various kinds of ministry in their local faith communities.

The original apostles and disciples and their immediate successors surely considered themselves persons engaged in a mission and conversion-oriented service to others (Mark 10:45, Acts 1:17). A Christian Scriptures word for such human service is the Greek *diakonia*: actions performed that build up the body of the risen One. Paul believed that the Spirit of Jesus gives many gifts (charisms) to individual members of the baptized community to enable them to minister to others in diverse and humble, selfless ways (Ephesians 4:7–11; 1 Corinthians 12:4–11).

From the 2nd century onward the definition of Christian ministry and who should normally be engaged in ministry seems to have progressively narrowed. Catholic leaders began to emphasize that ministry at all levels could only be legitimately performed by ordained men representing the institutional church, and by certain members of religious communities. In fact the term "ministry" gradually acquired connotations of power, influence, and authority in the Roman Catholic church.

Since the 1960s, and the Second Vatican Council especially, the original meaning and forms of Christian ministry have been actively reclaimed in Catholic communities, particularly for laypersons. Many individuals have begun to feel called to participate actively in a very broad variety of ministries now regularly open to the people of God. Catholics authentically express the belief that it is the power of the Spirit that calls and empowers individuals for evangelization and ministry, not some institutional church authority; rightly though, it is the church community, the living, witnessing people of God, that commissions persons and groups to do their ministries in the church and in the marketplace in the name of Jesus' living body on earth.

In 1972 Paul VI wrote an apostolic letter, *Ministeria quaedam*, saying that Catholics should no longer see certain ministries as mere steps ascending toward reception of the sacrament of order. Pope Paul declared that two ministry forms—those of reader and acolyte—were to be seen as valid lay ministries, and he left open whether or not other official ministries would be opened for laypersons (e.g., the ministry of catechesis). Vatican II taught that there is a wide variety of ministries, all of which work for the good of the whole human community and toward a common vision: the conversion of humankind in Jesus and the realization of the reign of God in creation.

The *Catechism of the Catholic Church*, published in the early 1990s, and the U.S. bishops' National Catechetical Directory: Sharing the Light of Faith (1977) indicate that Christian tradition reveals that the interlocking and interdependent ministries of word, community-building, worship, and service bind all the baptized into relationship, and that all other expressions of Christian ministry somehow fall within their scope.

(See also Baptism, Laity, Lay Ministries, Order, and People of God.)

MIRACLES are marvelous events or extraordinary, observable moments that cannot be fully explained by natural laws and circumstances and in which God's unlimited, caring power and saving presence to humanity are manifested in a purposeful and striking way. Catholic tradition emphasizes that Jesus of Nazareth had miraculous powers and, by the power of God's loving Spirit, was empowered to perform a number of miraculous signs and works, such as healing the sick, calming a raging sea, feeding a large gathering of individuals (with very little food available), and raising back to life some persons who had already died. The word derives from the Latin words *miraculum*, "a marvel," and *mirari*, "to wonder."

Many religions and cultures have spoken of miracles and wondrous signs attributable directly to transcendent powers. The Hebrew Scriptures report various kinds of miraculous events, through which Yahweh revealed a choice of or support for certain individuals or groups. For example, the Bible says that Abraham, Jacob, Moses, and Elijah each were gifted with direct revelations from God. Plagues befell those who persecuted God's chosen ones, and miraculous healings, stunning visions, and mysterious deliverances were granted to some in need. The Christian Scriptures indicate that the apostles, other disciples, and eventually the primitive Christian communities all came to truly understand who Jesus of Nazareth was, and what his divinely-inspired mission (to announce and inaugurate the everlasting reign of God) was about, through the miraculous signs and wonders he worked. The gospel of John (20:30–31) says that true believers recognized in particular signs (e.g., healings) that Jesus of Nazareth had been revealed to be the anointed one, the messiah, through whom all people of God can now have life and hope. The Acts of the Apostles says that many close followers of the risen Jesus worked miraculous signs during the apostolic era.

Much of contemporary Catholic teaching on miracles can be traced back to the First Vatican Council (1870). Vatican I declared that the miraculous deeds performed by Jesus of Nazareth were signs of God's revelation in him. Vatican II later recognized Jesus' miracles in its document *Dei verbum* (Dogmatic Constitution on Divine Revelation). It identified the contemporary Catholic teaching that certain marvelous, miraculous events (or signs) did occur during Jesus' earthly ministry, but that it is difficult to identify or prove in a scientific way just what happened during these events.

Some people today choose to dismiss the whole notion of biblical miracles, saying they didn't really occur. Others interpret them fundamentally, saying they happened exactly as reported in Scripture. And still others seem to hold that it's not important if they actually took place or not; what really counts is faith in God's saving power, care, and revelation, which the biblical miracle stories express.

The Catholic community teaches that Jesus of Nazareth worked miracles and that biblical miracle stories can help deepen the faith of the baptized. The gospels indicate that miracles were an essential element in Jesus' disclosure of the reign of God and the timeless good news of hope in it (Matthew 11:4–5). Among the many miracles reported in the church's story, the greatest miraculous event was the resurrection of Jesus by God.

(See also Faith, Gospel, Reign of God, and Revelation.)

MISSAL   more properly titled the Roman Missal, is a liturgical book containing the texts used in the celebration of the Mass along with various guidelines about the ritual. The Roman Missal comes to us today actually in two volumes, the Roman Missal—commonly known in this country as the Sacramentary (containing the prayers and rubrics for the celebration of Mass), and the Lectionary (containing the Scripture readings used at Mass). The Latin root of the English word "missal" means "dismissal" of those assembled or present.

Various regional sacramentaries have been developed throughout the history of the church. The first universal Roman Catholic missal book, however, was commissioned by the Council of Trent and published by Pope Pius V in 1570. A revised version of this Sacramentary was published, in Latin, by the Holy See (the official church) in 1970. This was the first substantial revision and liturgical update of the Roman Missal in four centuries. The English translation of the new Sacramentary was ready by July 1974. Its use in the United States was made mandatory by the Catholic church in December of 1974.

The word *missal* can also refer to small but elaborate booklets used by those who attend Mass. These became popular in the early decades of the 20th century when the Mass was celebrated in Latin. These small missals, which translated the Mass into the vernacular language, were used by worshipers to better follow the actions and texts used by the priest presider. Today, simpler, updated variations of earlier English-language missals, called missalettes, can be found in many Catholic churches.

(See also Eucharistic Prayer, Lectionary, and Liturgy of the Word/ Eucharist.)

MISSIONS   are places around the world where the Christian gospel has not become either widely known or accepted. Missions comes from the Latin *missio,* meaning "sending."

The Christian community professes that the people of God have an urgent mission, received from the risen Jesus personally (Mark 16:15), to spread his good news message, values, and witness—to disclose the nearness of the marvelous reign of God—throughout all parts of the world. The Catholic church and other Christian communities have long chosen to establish and support particular missions, at various geographical locations around the globe, in order that the good news of salvation for all humanity, in Jesus of Nazareth, can be shared and so that acts of charity, compassion, healing, and mercy can be offered to various individuals, communities, peoples, and cultures.

Current Catholic thought teaches that every person baptized is called, through commitment to the Spirit of the risen One, to do his or her part in fulfilling this overall mission of Christian evangelization. Certain dedicated and enthusiastic individuals experience a call, in the name of the Christian community, to become missionaries to many emerging missions and Christian settlements in countries and territories in all parts of the world. The gospels indicate though that all followers of Jesus should be dedicated to the work of witnessing to and sharing the message of repentance, conversion, and good news in the reign of God, announced by Jesus of Nazareth, with all peoples and cultures (Luke 10:1–9, Matthew 28:16–20). The Christian community has, therefore, attempted to preach the gospel, to spread the teachings of Christian faith, and to offer healing and help to all individuals and places encountered.

Christian missionary activity has often led to great physical suffering and personal sacrifice on the parts of countless dedicated missionaries. Some have been tortured, imprisoned, or killed. Catholics and other Christians recognize that the apostles and others in the apostolic era were missionary in a special sense and that Christian tradition teaches that the fiery preacher and witness Paul was a particularly striking model of Christian missionary work (his missionary travels and ministry of evangelization are described at length in the biblical book called the Acts of the Apostles).

Catholic tradition emphasizes that the entire church is called to become truly catholic—a universal community that invites all men and women from all races, cultures, and religious backgrounds to join its living, growing, worshiping, and evangelizing body. Such a global "catholicity" for all the people of God remains a goal and an ideal, something to be reached for, just like the reign of God in creation.

Another key Catholic concern regarding Christian missionary activity and evangelization pertains to the experience of the baptized in the U.S. and other Western (traditionally Christian) countries. Too often in the world of pop culture today the lifestyles of the baptized frequently do not differ much from the lifestyles of the non-baptized. Therefore the idea or image of "missionary" activity needs to be reinterpreted radically, according to some observers—it can and should happen in the neighborhoods, schools, family households, churches, and workplaces of all the baptized today too, not just in obscure, foreign lands among those who are ungospeled.

In recent years John Paul II has called for a new evangelization—or better, a re-evangelization—of all people of God. As he said in August 1993, the Western society of today must evolve from a "culture of death" to a "culture of new life" through the liberating message of Jesus of Nazareth. The pope has noted that every baptized person should "not be afraid to go out on the streets and into public places like the first apostles…this is not time to be ashamed of the gospel….Do not be afraid to break out of comfortable and routine modes of living in order to take up the challenge of making Christ known in the modern metropolis…invite everyone you meet to the banquet which God has prepared for [God's] people."

In this age the Catholic community still strives to reach all parts of the world in order to effectively preach the gospel, spread the spirit of Christianity, and bring help and healing to all human cultures. Various means by which Catholic missionaries participate in this foundational evangelizing work include: service in foreign countries and cultures; service among unchurched peoples and among non-practicing and alienated baptized individuals and groups; evangelizing witness and outreach to others wherever and whenever the opportunity arises in a spirit of re-evangelization; and making financial contributions, donating medical supplies, and other needed goods. Catholic tradition holds that personal prayer, acts of worship to God, and personal sacrifice for the building up of the reign of God in creation are other acts that can support missionary works.

Vatican II issued its Decree on the Church's Missionary Activity, attempting to express the contemporary church community's belief that it is missionary by nature and that every baptized person has a fundamental responsibility to do his or her part in sharing the good news of Jesus in the world. The council added that church missions, at home and abroad, must center urgently on effective evangelization and on planting the Christian message of good news and hope in Jesus among all those peoples and groups where it has not yet taken root.

The church annually observes a World Mission Day. On one of these days recently, Pope John Paul II noted that a gospel-based church community without a missionary commitment is an incomplete Christian community, a sick or dysfunctional church. He called upon all people of God to reflect deeply and critically on the true mission of the entire community of the Christ and on how evangelization can and should be accomplished in the future.

(See also Catholic, Evangelization, Inquiry, Witness, and Works of Mercy.)

MONOTHEISM   is belief in the existence of only one God and the worship of that God. The word comes from two Greek terms: *monos,* which means "single," and *theos,* which means "god." Monotheism is often contrasted with polytheism—belief in and worship of many different gods. *Polytheism* derives from the Greek *polus,* meaning "many," and *theos,* meaning "god."

Jewish and Christian traditions alike have maintained that there is but one, true God and that this God has freely chosen to reveal Godself (i.e., make a loving self-communication) to all peoples and cultures in the world. The Hebrews of old had faith in Yahweh, the God of the patriarchs, the one God revealed to Abraham, who brought the chosen people out of slavery in Egypt, made them a great nation, and initiated a loving covenant-relationship with them. The monotheistic tradition of the Israelite people stood in stark contrast to the polytheistic beliefs and practices of many of their neighbors, e.g., the Babylonians, Egyptians, Phoenicians, and others. Christian peoples, notably all Catholic communities, are monotheistic. Christian tradition has long emphasized that a new covenant between the one Creator God and all of humanity has been established through God's most definitive and complete revelation, the Word, known in history as Jesus of Nazareth. Christians say firmly that God is the only God, and no other gods should be placed before this God, for to place another god before the one God is to commit the sin of idolatry.

The Catholic community trusts firmly that God is the infinite and one loving Creator, the origin and single source of all that exists. This one God is transcendent, distinct from this world, and wholly other, yet somehow also mysteriously and personally present to, or in relationship with, individuals and the whole world.

(See also Christian, God, Revelation, Trinity, and Yahweh.)

MONSIGNOR   is an honorary title given to a priest for distinguished pastoral service and leadership or to recognize his pastoral significance to the local-level church community. The term essentially means "my lord." Over the years, a priest/pastor has been named a monsignor by a decree of the pope, at the special request of the local bishop. It is also still used as a title for Catholic bishops in some parts of the world.

Today there is no official or necessary relationship between the honorary title monsignor and the priest's individual and actual ministry to the church in the world. Today, in fact, most dioceses seem to be actively de-emphasizing the use of this title in order to better reclaim and focus on the heart of all ministry—genuine self-sacrifice and unselfish Christian service for all—by the ordained as well as all other baptized individuals in the faith community.

(See also Ministry, Order, and Presbyters.)

MORALITY   for Christian individuals and communities, centers upon the new command that Jesus of Nazareth handed on to his followers in the gospels: "Love one another as I have loved you." Christian doctrine maintains that human words and deeds are most truly gospel-oriented, and therefore fundamentally Christian, when they are based on this precept. "Morality" derives from the Latin *moralis*, which means "custom."

During biblical times the Hebrews adhered to a covenant relationship established between Yahweh and the people of Israel. They were guided in their daily lives as a faith community by this covenant and the precepts and practical life-rules in the Torah (the Pentateuch), also called the law of Moses, which includes the ten commandments of God (Deuteronomy 5:6–21). Christian communities believe that Jesus of Nazareth, a man well-versed in the Mosaic law and other aspects of the Torah, did not intend to do away with this traditional law. Rather he fulfilled and perfected the law and the original covenant between the Creator and all of humanity.

The Christian moral code is founded on the two great commandments of the old law: 1) love your God with your whole heart, whole soul, whole mind, and whole strength; and 2) love your neighbor as yourself (Mark 12:30–31, Luke 10:27, Matthew 22:36–40). These commands were part of the law of Moses and the overall moral code of Israel (Deuteronomy 6:5, Leviticus 19:18). Jesus of Nazareth emphasized, though, a new dimension to the traditional, legalistic Hebrew requirements of the law of love: he proclaimed that each of his followers must be ever-willing to give up his or her life in love for God's sake and for the sake of other human beings.

The gospels contain no systematic moral or ethical codes. Over many centuries the Catholic community and tradition has probed Jesus' teachings and values to determine what is moral and what seems counter to the spirit of Christian morality, based on Jesus' new covenant and command to love.

The communal dimension of Christian morality—as compared with a purely personalistic or individualistic view of moral behavior—has been much discussed and explored in recent years. Today Christians are challenged to view Christian life as a call to love God, through the revelation of Jesus the Word, and as a daily call to love and concern for others, especially the poor, the suffering, the oppressed, and the lonely. Therefore, all of Christian morality has a social dimension—the destinies of all human individuals, groups, and cultures are somehow linked or bound in relationship within creation in a significant way. Thus, to be moral, Christian peoples must seek first to freely do God's will while recognizing their responsibility and freedom to serve all others caringly.

Catholics are urged to rely on certain specific guidelines that will assist Christians in living morally as faithful Christian witnesses. These life-guidelines include: Jesus' commands to love, service, and self-sacrifice; the decalogue (the ten commandments); the beatitudes; the corporal and spiritual works of mercy; and traditional Christian teachings on the virtues and the precepts of the church. The Catholic community's basic moral teachings are reflected upon in detail in the *Catechism of the Catholic Church*, Book 3, articles 1691-2550.

(See also Beatitudes, Charity, Commandments of God, Covenant, Free Will, Option for the Poor, and Works of Mercy.)

MOSES   was a great leader of the Hebrews and one of the founders of the nation of Israel. The Hebrew Scriptures colorfully describe how Moses received a private revelation from the one God, led the Hebrew people out of slavery in Egypt and through the desert toward a promised land, and helped them to respond to an offer of a covenant-love relationship with God. The name seems to have Egyptian (*mesu*) and Hebrew roots (*moseh*), meaning "one drawn out" and "one who is born."

The books of Exodus and Deuteronomy, in the Hebrew Scriptures, seem to have been edited into something like a semi-biography of the historical Moses. Moses, the son of Hebrew parents, lived about 1200 years before the birth of Jesus of Nazareth. The book of Exodus describes how as a baby Moses was hidden in a basket by his mother and sister, then placed in a river so that the Egyptians would not find him and kill him. Moses was saved by an Egyptian princess and grew up in a royal palace. Moses got older and killed an Egyptian to defend the life of an oppressed Hebrew man. He fled to the land of Midian where he became a shepherd. One day, near Mount Horeb, Moses encountered Yahweh (God) in a burning bush. God commissioned him to return to Egypt to ask pharaoh to free the Hebrews from slavery. Moses and Aaron gave pharaoh God's message, but pharaoh refused to free the Hebrews. God then sent plagues to punish Egypt. Eventually with Moses as leader, the Hebrews escaped from Egypt (their escape has traditionally been called "the exodus") and they went journeying into the desert in search of their promised land. While in the desert Moses committed the people in his care to observance of the great commandments of God (the decalogue) at Mount Sinai. Later he helped the chosen people of Yahweh seal a covenant relationship with their God.

Christian communities see Moses as a great lawgiver who taught God's people about the love and concern of the Creator for them. Moses is venerated as a great patriarchal leader who unified the ancient Hebrew people, prefiguring the spiritually great nation of Israel. Vatican II pointed out that, through Moses, the one God promised to care for and guide people as long as humanity remained fundamentally faithful to its relationship with and commitment to the Lord.

(See also Commandments of God, Covenant, Passover, Patriarch/ Patriarchy, Pentateuch, and Zionism.)

MYSTICISM   is the personal journey by which one seeks to experience deep spiritual union with the divine through prayerful contemplation. True mysticism results in an intense awareness of God's loving presence. The word has roots in the Greek *mystikos*, which implies certain "secret, sacred rituals." In general, mystical experiences lead a person to a spiritual consciousness or wisdom that comes from spiritual illumination much beyond the ordinary powers of the human mind and feelings. The great mystics in church life and history include such saints as Teresa of Avila, John of the Cross, Catherine of Siena, Catherine of Genoa, and Gertrude the Great.

St. John of the Cross claimed that mysticism is a special gift from God. One therefore can never experience it only through common prayer rituals. St. Teresa referred to phases or stages of mystical growth through prayer and contemplation. These include: 1) quiet prayer, 2) union with God in prayer, 3) ecstasy (a condition beyond the human senses), and 4) enlightenment and full identification (union) with God's loving presence.

Current ideas about mysticism underscore that it is for the many, not just a chosen few. Ultimately, mysticism is a depth experience of God's life and grace. A mystic is one who seeks a deep, intense spiritual relationship with God through meditative prayer. Only some great mystics experience a powerful, peak awareness of the Creator in ecstasy. All persons, however, can experience relationship with God through grace every day. Thus, any experience of God—in person-to-person love and kindness, in the wonders of the natural world, in the heart of meaningful prayer or liturgy—is mystical in essence.

The form of Catholic moral theology called mystical theology focuses on the realities and mysteries associated with deep, intense Christian contemplation and the spiritual means humans use to strive for perfect holiness.

(See also Devotion, Grace, Holiness, and Prayer.)

N

NEW TESTAMENT also known to many today as the Christian Scriptures, is that portion of the Bible that tells about the life, death, and resurrection of Jesus of Nazareth and about the beginnings of the Christian community's mission to the worldwide human family, the people of God on Earth. The Christian Scriptures contain the four gospels plus a number of other sacred Christian writings: the Acts of the Apostles, the epistles, and the book of Revelation (also called the Apocalypse). There are 27 "books" in the New Testament. "Testament" stems from the Latin *testamentum*, which means "covenant" or "agreement." "Scripture" comes from the Latin *scriptura*, which means "writing."

By the end of the 4th century the present 27 books (and only these 27) had been confirmed by the church community as the official canon or body of writings to be included in the New Testament. In the year 405 Pope Innocent I confirmed this. The Council of Trent (16th century) stated authoritatively that the four gospels, the epistles, Acts, and Revelation constitute the complete body of the Christian Scriptures (New Testament) of the Bible.

The gospel writers—traditionally named by Christian communities as Matthew, Mark, Luke, and John—attempted to reveal the importance of (i.e., give a living faith-testimony to) the life, ministry, death, and miraculous resurrection of Jesus of Nazareth for the salvation of all of humanity. Thus the gospels included in the New Testament were probably not composed as complete biographies of Jesus. Scholars also note that the epistles, the book of Acts, and Revelation show how the earliest generations of Christians developed their understandings about the risen Jesus as the Son of God, about their call to proceed with and extend his incarnational, urgent mission, and about how followers of Jesus are called to live in this world.

(See also Apocalypse; Bible, Books of; Epistle; Evangelization; Gospel; Inspiration; and Missions.)

NOVENA is a nine-day period of devotional prayer that uses set formulas of petition usually addressed to Mary, the mother of Jesus, or to one of the other members of the communion of saints in heaven. Catholics pray novenas to gain particular favors from the divine, especially when they have pressing and urgent needs. Novenas may be made publicly or privately.

Early Christians adopted and adapted a Roman (pagan) custom called the *novendialia*, which was a nine-day period of sorrow and prayer observed after the death of a loved one. Christian novenas were modeled on the apostles' nine days of fervent prayer and waiting in an upper room after the surprising resurrection and ascension of Jesus of Nazareth. This nine-day period stretched from the feast of the Ascension, a Thursday, until Pentecost Sunday. The Christian Scriptures report that the close followers of the risen One prayed and stayed together, waiting for the gift of the Spirit whom Jesus had promised to send. By the time of the high Middle Ages novenas had become frequent, prayerful nine-day preparations for important feasts such as Christmas. Eventually novenas became much more centered on prayers of petition directed to the Blessed Virgin and the saints.

Even though novena-style prayer is believed by some to lead to special favors and God's grace, novenas are not qualitatively or quantitatively better than other forms of Christian prayer and devotion.

(See also Ascension, Devotions, Indulgences, Pentecost, and Prayer.)

O

OFFERTORY is more appropriately called "preparation and presentation of the gifts" of bread and wine. It is a ritual element within the liturgy of the Eucharist, the second main part of the Catholic celebration of Mass. An ancient Christian liturgical term, "offertory," has a Latin origin, meaning a "place of offerings."

The idea of praising God with thankful hearts through sacrificial gifts has many roots in the Judaeo-Christian tradition (e.g., Psalm 50:14). Early members of the post-resurrection community of Jesus began to consecrate gifts of bread and wine at their agape eucharistic meals to symbolize their willingness to sacrifice (offer) their whole lives to God, just as Jesus of Nazareth had blessed Passover seder symbols of ordinary bread and wine at the Last Supper to ritualize his complete sacrificial offering of his body and blood for the reign of God. Catholic tradition has emphasized that the gifts of bread and wine offered to God in the liturgy are transformed into the real presence of Jesus, and that through him, with him, and in him, worshipers humbly offer all they have—their entire Christian lives—to the Creator.

During the preparation and presentation of the gifts at Mass, several worshipers carry the bread and wine from the midst of the assembly to the presider. He accepts these items and then says prayers over the bread and wine. Church members are urged to pray that they will be deeply identified with these gifts and the real presence of Christ so that they will become deeply united with their loving God. On Sundays and certain holy feasts, a collection of voluntary gifts of money is gathered from members of the congregation. These financial offerings are then used by the church to maintain the ministries of the Catholic community and to reach out, in charitable service, to spread the gospel and care for human needs.

(See also Altar, Liturgy of the Word/Eucharist, Passover, Transubstantiation, and Worship.)

OLD TESTAMENT also known to many today as the Hebrew Scriptures, is that portion of the Bible that reveals how God (Yahweh) was first disclosed to humankind, how God initiated a basic covenant-love relationship with a chosen people (the Hebrews), and how God set in motion a great plan for the salvation of the entire human race, which Christians believe was eventually fulfilled by a divinely-sent messiah known as Jesus of Nazareth, the Christ. The Hebrew Scriptures is a collection of 46 "books," written over a period of 900 years. "Testament" derives from the Latin *testamentum*, which means "covenant" or "agreement." "Scripture" stems from the Latin word *scriptura*, which means "writing."

Some of the major events described in Old Testament writings include the creation of the world, Moses' call and his exodus from Egypt with the Hebrews out of slavery and toward the promised land, the formation of a series of covenant agreements/renewed relationships established between Yahweh and the chosen people, and the delivery of many prophetic, life-altering messages delivered to the troubled but blessed nation of Israel by the biblical prophets. Some of the great historical figures introduced in the Hebrew Scriptures include Abraham, Sarah, Moses, David, Jeremiah, Isaiah, Elijah, Esther, Ruth, and many others. Portions of the Hebrew Scriptures traditionally have been incorporated into Catholic worship services, especially in the liturgy of the Word.

The Old Testament (Hebrew Scriptures) as a whole was compiled by many, many authors and editors, over many centuries. The Hebrew Scriptures were long thought to have three major parts: the five books of the Law, or Pentateuch; the Prophets, containing 21 books; and the Writings, a set of 13 books. Some Bible students now say, however, that the Old Testament should be thought of as having four basic sections or themes: the Law, the Prophets, the Historical Works, and the Wisdom Books (see elaboration on this in the article Bible, Books of in this volume).

The Catholic community recognizes another set of seven books that Scripture scholars call the deutero-canonicals. These writings include Tobit, Judith, Wisdom of Solomon, Ecclesiastes, Baruch, 1 Maccabees, and 2 Maccabees. This is how the Catholic tradition counts 46 books or writings in the Old Testament. Some other Christian congregations and traditions do not recognize or include the deutero-canonical books in their versions of the Bible.

The church believes that the Old Testament is an important collection of inspired writings that disclose God's revelation to the whole of humanity.

(See also Bible; Bible, Books of; Covenant; Hebrews; Inspiration; Messiah; Pentateuch; Prophet; and Yahweh.)

OPTION FOR THE POOR   is a phrase generated in 1979 by a pastoral statement of the Latin American bishops at the Third General Conference of the Latin American Episcopate (CELAM). The bishops noted that a "preferential option for the poor" (and a related option for youth) must guide pastoral planning and ministry priorities in the present era. The word "poor" traces to the French *pauvreté*, "poverty." While there are many ways to be poor (e.g., economically poor or spiritually poor), the church chooses to view the poor as a resource, not a problem, and a dynamic hope for the world, not a sign of hopelessness or despair.

The Hebrew word for the poorest of the human community is *anawim*. The *anawim* were the lowest in social status (God's little ones) and the most meek and disadvantaged among those left behind in Israel after the Babylonian exiles. The Judaeo-Christian tradition teaches that from the *anawim*—the poorest and most oppressed of the poor among the people of God—God would raise up a messiah and a great people who would show creation the way toward the ultimate reign of God.

Christian history has spoken of poverty both as a problem to be overcome and as a blessing from the Creator. It is a social trouble—whether one is economically poor or spiritually destitute—in that one has human needs not being met. It is a blessing or virtue, according to Christian tradition, in that it can lead to a lifestyle (or state of mind) by which individuals view material goods properly as gifts from a good Creator and things to be used to support and enrich the lives of others. Thus true Christian poverty is spiritual detachment from materialism and consumerism. It properly should lead one to loving attachment to and faith in God.

Some recent thought on this subject points out that the baptized (and all of humanity) have a mission to improve the world and thus must be focused first on the poor, disadvantaged, and oppressed. It is right for Christians to want for all people what they most want for themselves—life, freedom, food, shelter, good health, civil rights, education, meaningful work, and developing cultures. But because there are so many impoverished peoples in a world full of resources, prophetic Christian voices today say, it is scandal for Christians to do nothing when others are tormented by hunger, diseases, and other miseries.

Catholics believe that Jesus of Nazareth cared deeply for outcasts, the marginalized, the poor, and the alienated in Israelite society. Thus, he identified with and "opted for the poor" (Matthew 5:3–12). Because "the poor" are spiritually linked to Jesus' own human suffering, Catholics should see the face of Jesus in the poor and oppressed of today and feel a new urgency to reach out to them.

Such insights have greatly influenced recent teachings of the U.S. bishops, as in their prophetic 1987 letter "Economic Justice for All." In 1993, Pope John Paul said all Christians must in faith either live a "spirit of poverty" or "betray the gospel." This does not mean one must live "radical poverty (and renounce) all property," but one must be moderate in consumption and use of material things in order to be centered on service to God and those in need.

(See also Beatitudes, Messiah, Reign of God, and Works of Mercy.)

ORDER   is a sacrament in the Catholic community through which a person (male) enters the ordained ministry. Through the sacrament of order, members of the Catholic experience worldwide seek to guarantee that the mission of gospel proclamation will be continued and extended, the sacraments will be celebrated in Christian communities, and the spiritual needs of all people of God will continue to be served. When conferring this sacrament of order, a Catholic bishop imposes (i.e., extends his) hands over the deacon or presbyter candidates, anoints them with blessed oil (chrism), and prays that they might receive the gift of the Spirit of the risen Jesus.

Historical reflections on the tradition of ordination in Christianity have noted that the Christian Scriptures (New Testament) do not present a perfectly-defined model for leadership in the early, local Christian communities. It seems there were numerous ministries: prophets, apostles, preachers, teachers, healers, elders, administrators, deacons, and overseers. (For more information, see the articles in this book on Bishop, Deacon, and Presbyter.) Ignatius of Antioch, in the early 2nd century, indicated that a general pastoral practice emerging among Christian bodies was for episcopal elders/overseers (bishops) and presbyters (priest-like ministers) to preside at celebrations of the Eucharist. Ignatius added that without bishops, presbyters, and deacons the church community would not exist. By the end of the 2nd century only those named ("ordained" or selected) by local Christian bishops could preside at the eucharistic sacrifice (the Mass) in cases where bishops had to be absent. Some historians believe that prior to that time various members of Christian worship assemblies were asked to preside as eucharistic celebrants.

About the year 230 Tertullian wrote about a type of order that applied to clergymen of the time: This order, according to the ancient writer, proposed three categories of church ministers—bishop (overseer), presbyter (priest), and deacon (helper, server). The church overall, however, did not develop an officially-written declaration requiring ordination in order to preside at the Eucharist until the year 1208. Further decrees on this matter were made definitively by the general councils of Florence (1439) and Trent (1563).

The three degrees or stages of Christian order—episcopate, presbyterate, and diaconate—have been reaffirmed in the Catholic community in many ways, notably through the Second Vatican Council (1962–1965) and through the *Catechism of the Catholic Church*. Vatican II said that ministerial priesthood (presbyterate) is actually a sharing in the priesthood of the episcopate (the bishops), the authority of which rests in Jesus himself. Therefore, presbyters and deacons are called to work with their bishops, to participate in the mission of building up, sanctifying, and watching over (pastor-ing) the body of Christ and people of God. The primary responsibility of priests, according to the recent authoritative decrees of Vatican II, is proclaiming the good news of Christian liberation and salvation through personal witness, through missionary work, and through catechesis (teaching). Candidates for Catholic ordination attend seminaries to prepare for this ministry. In the early 1970s the Vatican officially issued a number of revised rites for ordination to the ministerial presbyterate.

Today the church teaches that those who are ordained as deacons, presbyters, and bishops participate in the priestly, prophetic, and kingly offices of Jesus, the Savior and Light of humanity. The sacrament of order may be received only once. The local bishop ordinarily administers the sacrament to men who have prepared for the diaconate or priesthood.

In recent years a tradition of calling and ordaining certain persons to the permanent diaconate has been renewed by the church. (There remains also a transitional diaconate, for those who intend to become presbyters.) Some of the historical minor degrees of order (for example, porter, exorcist, and subdeacon) were terminated by Paul VI, in 1972.

Some men today are ordained to be diocesan priests. They receive the sacrament from their local bishop to ministerially serve in a local diocese, most often in a parish community as a pastor or parochial vicar. There are religious priests who are ordained members of religious communities (for example, the Jesuits or the Franciscans), under the jurisdiction of religious superiors. These presbyters serve in many different capacities, in many different countries and cultures around the globe; they often take the three traditional Christian vows of poverty, chastity, and obedience as guides for life.

The Code of Canon Law summarizes Catholic rules and disciplines associated with the sacrament of order in canons 1008–1054. The *Catechism of the Catholic Church* speaks of order as a sacrament the in service of Christian communion. It calls order the sacrament of apostolic ministry, going beyond simple election, designation, delegation, or institution by the community, because in it the Catholic Christian community confers a gift of the Spirit that permits the exercise of a sacred power that can only come through Jesus Christ and his faithful followers.

In April 1992 Pope John Paul II published an apostolic reflection on the formation of priests for the ministerial priesthood. This exhortation followed upon the 1990 general synod of Catholic bishops on the same topic. The text of John Paul II's reflections can be found under the title *Pastores dabo vobis* ("I will give you shepherds").

(See also Bishop, Diocese, Ministry, Parochial Vicar, Presbyters, and Religious Orders.)

ORIGINAL SIN   is the basic condition or state into which every member of the human race (with two exceptions—Jesus and Mary) is born. The Christian doctrine on original sin teaches that every person is born into a world greatly affected by sinfulness, and that each person has an inclination to personal sin. Original sin (also called "the sin of Adam") is the result of the selfish choices made by some of the first humans to seek their own goals and desires rather than to do the will of the Creator God. In the book of Genesis, the story of Adam and Eve illustrates symbolically how sinfulness became part of the human story overall (Genesis 2:15–17, 3:1–24), and how the free choices of humans beings, not God, are responsible for all sin and suffering in the human community. With self-centered personal choice and the resulting alienation or estrangement from God, personal sin was introduced into the human experience.

The term "original sin" is not found in Scripture. It is a theological phrase developed during the early centuries of Christianity. Theologians like Augustine (d. 430) and Thomas Aquinas (d. 1274) wrote about the Christian doctrine of original sin. The Council of Trent, in the year 1547, formally taught that original sin came into the world through the sin of Adam, and thus each human being inherits death and sinfulness. Yet Trent also noted that humanity has been fully redeemed by Jesus of Nazareth, but the human community nevertheless still suffers the many withering effects of original sin.

Catholic Christians emphasize that grace and salvation are offered to all persons by the Creator through the saving and redemptive life, death, and resurrection of Jesus. All Christians must engage in a lifelong, daily effort to remain open to God's revelation (to remain faithful to relationship or friendship with the Creator) and the call of the gospel to conversion—to daily choose a Christian lifestyle and values, in order to overcome the cumulative effects of and inclinations toward human sinfulness.

Vatican II taught that through original sin humanity has inclinations toward evil. Thus human freedom was abused in history and the original blessedness or harmony between God and a grace-filled human community was deeply disrupted. As a result, much of human conduct, many personal human choices, and many human desires and aims are grounded in selfish thought and sinfulness (personal sin). Also, many human institutions and group endeavors are hindered by sinful attitudes and values (social sin). Catholics recognize that all sinfulness—personal or social—causes humanity to be estranged from its covenant relationship of love and faithfulness to God.

Two important Bible passages about original sin are 1 Corinthians 15:21 and Romans 5:12–21. A substantial reflection on the nature of human sinfulness can be found in the *Catechism of the Catholic Church*, Book Three, on the human vocation to live in Jesus Christ (articles 1846–1876). The Catechism notes that sin creates a human attachment to sinfulness. "It engenders vices by repetition." It results from perverse inclinations that obscure one's conscience and corrupt personal judgments about good and evil. Thus sin tends to reproduce and reinforce itself in the human community overall, and in personal lives in particular, but it cannot destroy the moral sense of Christian life in its root (article 1865).

(See also Adam and Eve, Creation, Creation Theology, Free Will/Freedom, Morality, and Sin.)

ORTHODOXY refers to soundness of Christian belief and consonance with authentic Christian tradition. The roots of the term are Greek. Basically, it means "rightness of belief" or "rightness of opinion." Orthodoxy is seen as one of the great characteristics of the Catholic church. In other words, the official church authority (magisterium) and the Christian community of the faithful (the people of God) are guided today, as always, by the Spirit of the risen Jesus and are given the ability to wisely and freely distinguish genuine Christian doctrine from error.

Orthodoxy for Catholics means consistency with Catholic Christian teachings, faith traditions, and the enduring values of Christianity as they are expressed in the Scriptures, the works and life-witness of great teachers and leaders of the church, official church doctrines, and sacred liturgy. Orthodoxy is complemented by Christian orthopraxis—that is, rightness of Christian lifestyle, moral choices, and overall behavior. In other words, the orthodoxy of the individual believer's life, or of the entire Christian community, must express itself in the *orthopraxis* of Christian moral action, which gives witness to a true, gospel-rooted faith and hope in the reign of God to come.

The church today challenges its members to live in such a way that they blend orthodoxy (right belief in the gospel of Jesus and his church), with personal theological reflection, reflection on Christianity's challenge for all life choices, and the appropriate, radical Christian orthopraxis (lifestyle). Thus, Catholics today are urged to weave authentic and faithful commitment to the church community with self-giving sacrifice and service to the reign of God—without which intellectual belief in the story of Jesus Christ and his followers is incomplete.

(See also Doctrine, Magisterium, Theology, Tradition, and Witness.)

P

PANTHEISM   is a word with two Greek roots meaning "all is God." Pantheism is a worldview or system of belief that sees everything—the material universe and all things spiritual—in unity or harmony with a cosmic God. Put another way, pantheists see the universe as a whole as God and material things in the universe as manifestations of the cosmic One.

The great philosophers Kant, Hegel, and Schopenhauer created thoughtful works on the nature of human experience essentially in line with pantheistic thought. Catholic doctrine, however, has consistently opposed pantheism. Pius IX condemned it in 1864 in his *Syllabus of Errors*. Vatican I spoke against it. So did Pius X.

Some pantheists say the cosmic deity has been absorbed into and can be found through the world of the senses—in persons, places, sights, and sounds, etc. Others claim that cosmic evolution is still occurring. Thus humankind and the material world are progressing dynamically toward full union (a oneness) with the cosmic God known only slightly today in immanent reality.

The church's essential problem with pantheism is that Catholic Christian belief stresses that God, while both immanent and transcendent to us, is different from the material universe. God created the universe to reveal divine goodness and glory. Thus the Creator and the created are not identical, but they are capable of being in loving relationship with each other thanks to God's love and revelation. Christians trust that this God-human relationship can lead to full union with the Creator, but each person must personally and freely choose to have faith in God and live in a spirit of charity with others in order to achieve holiness and union (salvation) with the one God.

(See also Creation, Creation Theology, God, Grace, Heaven, and Revelation.)

PARABLES   are brief, fictional stories told to make an important point or to illustrate a great moral truth. The roots of "parable" are Greek and Latin (e.g., *parabole* and *parabola*) and mean "to throw beside" or "to compare."

Biblical texts disclose that Jesus of Nazareth employed parables often as he taught about the wonders of the reign of God. There are almost 80 parables in the Christian Scriptures. These parables include proverb-sayings, metaphors, allegories, and stories to make certain points. Christian commentators have tried to classify New Testament parables but often to no avail. Early church thinkers noted three levels of meaning in Jesus' parables: the literal, moral, and spiritual. In more recent times, however, Bible scholars have noted that each parable has a basic moral insight or moral comparison. Therefore, the emphasis in recent Bible studies has been on finding the key point (or meaning) of every parable without getting overly focused on the parables' many details.

Some parables (e.g., the Mustard Seed) can be found in all four gospels. Some can be located in three gospel versions (e.g., the Lost Sheep). Some can be found in two (e.g., parable of the Talents), and quite a few can be discovered in only one (e.g., the Prodigal Son: Luke 15:11–31, and the Unforgiving Servant: Matthew 18:23–35).

Current reflection on Jesus' parables centers on several themes. Readers are urged to focus on the conclusion of each parable to seek its main thrust or teaching. They are likewise urged to reflect on whom or what gets the most attention in the story: The main characters or symbols usually embody a parable's moral point. Scholars stress that knowing what a parable meant to its original gospel-era hearers will give it greater vitality today. Additionally, knowing about the original Christian community/audience of a gospel writer—and how this might have influenced the gospel writer's drafting of individual parables—can lead to new insights into Jesus' proclamation of God's mysterious reign.

(See also Exegesis, and Gospel.)

PARACLETE   is a biblical term found only in the gospel of John. It has Greek and Latin roots that refer to one "called to one's side" and thus an advocate, helper, and consoling one. Today, it is a title Catholics give to the Spirit of Jesus, the third person of the Trinity.

In Hebrew tradition, a paraclete was one who was called in to be a mediator or intercessor to plead the cause of another. The word has legal or courtroom overtones. The Spirit-advocate (paraclete) is like a defending counsel who leads the whole community of Jesus' followers always toward greater appreciation of God's truth and glory as revealed in the post-Easter, risen Jesus. The Spirit of Jesus thus is depicted as the constant spiritual companion and counsel of all disciples, up to this day and forever.

Current understandings about the theology of John's gospel stress that in reality the risen Jesus and the Paraclete (his abiding Spirit) are the same. The Spirit is goodness, the force against evil in our world (Revelation 12:10). The gift of the Paraclete, after the resurrection, is somewhat akin to the second coming of Jesus in glory.

There are five paraclete sayings in the gospel of John: 14:15–17; 14:25–26; 15:26; 16:4–11; and 16:12–15. These sayings provide the one catechesis on the Spirit of God to be found in the Christian Scriptures. The Spirit was and is a gift from Jesus that teaches true disciples about the Christian message and values (John 14:26; 15:26; and 16:13–14). The Paraclete helps the baptized extend the Christian mission to proclaim Jesus' "good news" (the gospel) to all parts of the globe (John 16:8). The

Holy Spirit will remain with all disciples forever (John 16:7), but in an interior (or invisible) and spiritual manner (John 14:17). Even though the world might judge Jesus and his followers in a negative way—even condemn them in the "courts" of world opinion—the ever-present Paraclete will be by their sides, consoling and defending them, ultimately overturning the world's negative judgments and persecutions in God's court of glory.

(See also Disciples, God, Parousia, and Trinity.)

PARISH is a local community of Catholic Christians who share a common faith and participate in common Christian worship and service. The term refers to a geographical territory within a Catholic diocese that is headed by a presbyter known as the pastor, one who, in turn, is under the jurisdiction of the local bishop. The word stems from the Greek *paroikos*, which indicates "dwelling near."

The chief presbyter or pastor is the spiritual leader of the local parish community, often acting as its overall administrator as well. In addition to the pastor, many parishes also have one or more parochial vicars (associate pastors) assigned by the bishop, who usually assist the head presbyter in serving the needs of the individuals and families in the faith community. Pastors and other presbyters in local parishes are not only spiritual leaders. They are also servants of the people of God—leading and serving parishioners sacramentally (e.g., in presiding at worship rituals like the Eucharist) and handing on the cumulative teachings, values, and practices of the Catholic tradition.

Christian tradition also stresses that all the baptized are full members of the people of God—and thus they have, according to the gift of the Spirit, a right and a responsibility, a true Christian calling, to become involved in all the ministries and the outreach that the parish community attempts. In recent decades laypersons and religious have assumed much more active roles in diverse forms of local-level Christian ministry (e.g., pastoral associates, directors of religious education, youth ministry coordinators, lectors, special ministers of the Eucharist, and outreach team members), sharing in the evangelizing work and mission of the community as a whole and taking up leadership and decision-making responsibilities through parish councils, boards, committees, etc.

In many respects, then, the parish is not so much a geographical entity as it is a community, on the grass-roots level, of the people of God exercising its calling to gather persons to worship God and to follow Jesus. It is a community of baptized persons and households of the baptized choosing to take part in the mission, ministry, and assorted tasks of gospel proclamation and service to humanity that the risen Jesus has handed on to his faithful followers.

Because of modern cultural developments and many contemporary life-pressures and changes, countless Catholic individuals and families today find that traditional large and formal parishes do not meet their spiritual needs in a very satisfying manner. Some seek out smaller faith-community groups and neighborhood-style, household-based cluster communities for regular meetings focused on various aspects of Christian life, such as Christian support, prayer, Christian education, Bible study/discussion, and Christian service opportunities. In many cases these small communities have developed on the model of the *communidades de base*, which have sprung up in Latin America and other places around the globe in recent decades.

Vatican II taught in the mid-1960s that renewed efforts must be made to encourage a sense of living community in local parishes, especially through the celebration of the Eucharist. The church's norms and laws directly pertaining to the administration of and ministry of parish life are detailed in the Code of Canon Law in canons 515–552.

(See also Bishop, Community, Diocese, Koinonia, Ministry, Parochial Vicar, Presbyters, and Small Faith Communities.)

PAROCHIAL VICAR is a term often used in Catholic communities today rather than the title "associate pastor." "Parochial" essentially refers to "parish." A *vicar* in church life is one appointed by a bishop or pastor to act in his name, as his associate, by exercising a jurisdiction over some aspect of the Christian body. A parochial vicar is assigned to a parish by a bishop. He is a priest who is called to render various ministries and other services overall (or one specialized ministry only) as a co-worker with the pastor, yet one subject to the pastor's authority. Over the years, parish communities have often had one, two, or more parochial vicars appointed to meet the needs of the local faith community.

Essentially, the parochial vicar of today is 1) expected to assist the pastor in the development of new ministries, 2) consult and co-work with the pastor and other local ministry teams/councils on parish ministries in existence, 3) collaborate with the pastor on the overall pastoral care offered to all parishioners, 4) reside in the parish territory and help develop a spirit of community among the pastor, himself, and other parochial vicars in the parish. Another part of the parochial vicar's ministry, according to canon law, is to guide the parish as an interim pastor whenever a pastorate becomes vacant.

Parochial vicars are assigned by the local bishop and can be removed from parishes only by the bishop for just reasons. Canons 541–545 of the Code of Canon Law describe the essential duties and responsibilities of parochial vicars today.

(See also Order, Parish, Pastoral Council, and Presbyters.)

Note of Interest: A pastoral associate is a layperson, female or male, who is a pastoral ministry leader in a parish. Pastoral associates are sometimes also given titles such as pastoral minister, pastoral life coordinator, pastoral administrator, or minister of Christian formation. Pastoral associates, while not ordained, often perform many of the pastoral duties of the parochial vicar (associate pastor) when none are available to a parish. In many cases today a pastoral associate also assumes many of the central leadership duties of the pastor and parochial vicars in those communities that are "priestless" by necessity. Pastoral associates cannot preside at the Eucharist, absolve persons from sin, and perform other sacramental functions. They can, however, provide many valuable ministry services, some of which include: leading prayer services and communion services, helping with annulments, providing spiritual direction and pastoral counseling, coordinating catechetical programs, coordinating the life of small Christian communities, and managing various parish affairs (e.g., budgets, finances, councils, and local staff members and ministry volunteers).

PAROUSIA   is a Greek word meaning "presence" or "arrival. " It refers to the second coming of the risen Jesus at the end of time (the conclusion of salvation history) and the beginning of the eternal reign of God.

The *parousia* is referred to a number of times in the Christian Scriptures. The gospels report that Jesus of Nazareth warned his listeners to be watchful for the end of natural time, and in the meantime to be faithful witnesses to his values and message of good news. He revealed that the Son of God would return to Earth in glory at an unknown date and time in the future of humanity (only the Creator knows exactly when that will occur). Early communities who followed the risen One assumed that this "second coming" of Jesus (in post-resurrection faith they had clearly come to believe in the risen Jesus as God's divine Son) would take place very soon after Jesus' ascension to heaven. Paul wrote to the faithful that the much-awaited *parousia* was indeed coming, but he warned fellow Christians not to use this Christian hope and promise as an excuse to be lazy about how they lived.

Over the centuries, the Catholic community has continued to teach that the *parousia* will occur, and when it does it will fully confirm the triumph of the good news of salvation for all peoples and cultures. In the *parousia*, a general judgment of the living and the dead will take place, and the complete, definitive establishment of the loving God's eternal reign (through the transformation of the universe into a new dwelling and a whole new creation centered on freedom, justice, and peace) will come about.

Through the doctrine of the second coming, and through active use of the timeless image of the *parousia*, the Catholic tradition attempts to reveal that the essential Christian mission, message, and way of life are hope-filled. During the Catholic eucharistic liturgy (right after the consecration of bread and wine), Catholic worshiping assemblies express belief that Jesus the risen One will come again in glory.

The branch of Catholic theology known as eschatology is a study of "the last things"—the nature of human passage from life through death, heaven and hell, the second coming of Jesus the Christ, the resurrection of the body, the final judgment, and the proclamation and definitive, once-and-for-all establishment of the reign of God. Catholics believe that certain biblical passages directly refer to the *parousia*: Matthew 24:3–14; Luke 21:27–29; John 14:13; Acts 1:11; 1 Corinthians 15:23; Titus 2:13; and 1

Thessalonians 4:15–17.

(See also Ascension, Creation, Death/Dying, Hope, Reign of God, and Resurrection.)

PASCHAL CANDLE   is a large candle that is blessed and lighted during the annual Easter Vigil in Catholic worshiping communities. The paschal candle is a symbol of the risen Jesus of Nazareth—the light of the world. From Easter Sunday to Pentecost it is kept in the sanctuary area of Catholic churches and lighted for all celebrations of the Eucharist during this 50-day period. After Pentecost, the candle is placed near the baptismal font and is lit at celebrations of baptism, and at funerals as well.

Traditionally, the paschal candle has five large grains of incense imbedded in it and arranged in the form of a cross. These five grains of incense represent the five major wounds suffered by Jesus of Nazareth when he was crucified. At the top of the candle is an Alpha (beginning) sign and at the bottom is an Omega (end) sign, which are meant to show that Jesus, the risen One and the Christ, is really present to humanity and to every Christian community in the world as the spiritual beginning and end of all existence. Also traced on the paschal candle, on the four angles of the cross symbol, are numbers indicating the year it is being used.

(See also Altar, Candles, Holy Week, Incense, Sanctuary.)

PASCHAL LAMB   is one of the many titles given to Jesus of Nazareth, known to Catholics and other Christian communities worldwide as the lamb of God, the risen One, the Christ. The term comes from a Scripture story about the exodus of the Hebrews from slavery in Egypt. According to God's instructions, the Hebrew households in Egypt slaughtered lambs, prepared them, and then ate them on the night of their passover from slavery to freedom. According to the law of Moses, special sacrificial lambs were then to be killed and consumed annually, at a certain time, to remember and celebrate the original Hebrew passover. This annual ceremony is still celebrated in Jewish communities today. It reminds the Jewish people of the quick and unpleasant journey out of Egypt and God's saving work on behalf of human life and freedom. Catholic Christians are urged to think of Jesus as a paschal lamb because he willingly and freely gave up his life for the salvation (passover) of all humanity to new life in God.

Just as the Hebrews were saved from slavery in Egypt by God, Christians now trust that the death and resurrection of Jesus of Nazareth won hope and freedom for all peoples and cultures, for all time, from the slavery of sin, unhappiness, and despair.

(See also Eucharist; Jesus of Nazareth; Jesus, Titles of; Paschal Mystery; and Passover.)

PASCHAL MYSTERY   refers to the deep spiritual mysteries associated with the suffering, death, and resurrection to glorious new life of Jesus of Nazareth. This Christian phrase implies the universal redemption of all of humankind brought about by the self-sacrifice and re-sulting glorification of Jesus Christ. *Pasch* is a Hebrew and Greek expres-sion for "pass over." "Paschal" essentially means "related to the Passover."

The book of Exodus (chapter 12) describes the original passover/paschal feast and the Hebrews' festive joy over their divine salvation from slavery. The passover feast included the killing (sacrifice) of a lamb, which was then eaten with bitter herbs and unleavened bread. Christians believe that the original passover pre-figured both Jesus of Nazareth's self-sacrifice (his "passover" from human life, suffering, and death to new life and glory in God) and the celebration of the eucharistic sacrifice. Put another way, Christian tradition holds that Jesus' paschal mystery experience is the New Testament-era's central passover.

Current thinking on this subject has continued to emphasize the sav-ing value of the human suffering and total self-sacrifice of Jesus. Church members, however, are also called to focus on the importance of the res-urrection and the ascension as powerful Christian signs that all people are meant to be fully united with God forever, as Jesus was and is. This salvation is for all individuals but also for the human community as a whole and the entire universe too. Thus, all Christians and others are challenged by the paschal mystery—the universal redemption—to be faithful stewards who care for and co-create all of God's creation.

The global Catholic community trusts that humankind and the entire cosmos have been saved according to God's plan. This is best revealed in the paschal mystery of Jesus the Christ. In some ways, the paschal mys-tery is carried on today in the lives of all the baptized—in their daily re-lationships, joys, sufferings, struggles, prayers, and Christian hope. It is especially evident when Christians celebrate the Eucharist and when Christians act in self-sacrificing, service-oriented ways to meet the world's needs. As Jesus of Nazareth did, all Christians are called to give their all for the gospel in order to work toward the reign of God over hu-manity.

(See also Jesus of Nazareth; Jesus, Titles of; Paschal Lamb; Passover; and Redemption.)

PASSOVER   is a seven-day Jewish festival, also known as the *pasch*, during which Jewish communities worldwide recall and celebrate how Yahweh (God) helped the Hebrew people escape slavery in Egypt. The annual Passover feast begins on the 14th day of the Jewish month *Nisan* and centers on a special meal, the seder supper. The Hebrew seder meal originally included the eating of a young lamb sacrificed especially for the occasion. During the course of this festive meal, the story of the ex-odus—called *Haggadah*—is read to those gathered at the table. Jewish people celebrate the passover as a reminder that God's love and un-limited power secured their freedom from Egyptian tyranny.

Since the earliest days, the Christian story and vision have em-phasized that Jesus of Nazareth gave his life in sacrifice—like the

Passover lambs—in order that all of humanity might have true hope and true freedom and salvation over slavery to sinfulness and evil. Christians often refer to the risen Jesus as the "Lamb of God" and have likened his suffering, death, and resurrection to the original passover of the Hebrews, calling the Jesus-experience the paschal mystery.

The first Eucharist celebration took place on Holy Thursday—at a traditional Jewish passover meal, held by Jesus of Nazareth and some of his original disciples, which is now referred to in Christian traditions as the Last Supper. The Christian Scriptures (New Testament) and various Christian teachings say that during this last supper celebration Jesus asked something very special of his followers: He requested that they forever honor and remember his passover from death to new life in God through celebration of the sacrament called Eucharist. Therefore, as Yahweh commanded the Hebrew people to forever remember their original passover from slavery to freedom by God's love and power, so Jesus—the new Moses and the definitive Word of God—commands all generations of his followers to remember and celebrate his new passover.

(See also Eucharist, Hebrews, Jesus of Nazareth, Moses, Paschal Lamb, Paschal Mystery, Triduum, and Yahweh.)

Note of Interest: No passover discussion would be complete without some mention of the "tenth plague" suffered by the Egyptians before the Hebrew exodus from slavery, which is reported in the book of Exodus, in the Hebrew Scriptures (Old Testament) of the Bible. On the night of the first Passover ritual meal, the Hebrews sprinkled some of the blood of slaughtered paschal lambs on their doorposts (Exodus 12:21–32). The Lord Yahweh then came upon the land of Egypt and killed the firstborn male in every non-Hebrew household. Even the first son of Egypt's pharaoh was slain. But the Lord mysteriously "passed over" Hebrew homes, sparing their firstborn sons, because of the sign of the lamb's blood on their doorways. Scripture indicates that it was this event that persuaded pharaoh to allow the Hebrews to leave the land of Egypt.

PASTORAL COUNCIL   is a group assembled to provide consultation, advice, or decision-making help on the overall life and ministry of a particular Christian congregation. The contemporary word "council" is derived from Latin and Middle English expressions for "assembly."

The Second Vatican Council called for the formation of diocesan-level pastoral councils in its Decree on the Apostolate of the Laity. Each diocese should have a consultative body of clergy, religious, and laypersons convened at least once a year by the local bishop to help the bishop "examine and consider all that relates to diocesan pastoral work." A council should "offer practical suggestions on these matters" to better accomplish the Christian mission to spread the gospel.

Speaking practically, a diocesan council tends to review the efforts of diocesan pastoral offices, develop guidelines on various matters, formulate church policies, help grass-roots parish councils, and deal with pastoral planning issues. Special concerns include church finances,

Catholic schools, liturgical and sacramental practices, youth and family ministry matters, social action needs, statistics and trends, and religious vocations. In essence, the diocesan pastoral council is designed to provide insights and practical planning helps necessary to empower the whole Catholic community to develop its pastoral agenda systematically and effectively.

The Decree on the Apostolate of the Laity also called for the development of grass-roots level pastoral councils in parishes. A parish pastoral council is an assembly of people in the local faith community—priests and laypersons—dedicated to helping all baptized persons "to collaborate energetically in every apostolic and missionary undertaking sponsored" by the parish. Parish council members—whether elected or appointed—have a special share in the people of God's pastoral mission to evangelize the world. Though tensions and conflicts sometimes crop up in the deliberations of parish-level pastoral councils, many commentators and observers say that parish councils' reflections on vital grass-roots faith concerns, the decisions they render in collaboration with pastors, and the Christian witness they give to entire communities make the great effort to form and maintain them worthwhile.

Today, parish councils should help unify the local faith community, share in responsibility for decision making on parish pastoral matters, and set mission statements, goals, objectives, and other pastoral-planning elements in place in their local church congregations. In the Code of Canon Law, canons 511–514 specify guidelines for starting and maintaining diocesan-level councils. Canon 536 discusses the need for parish council organizations.

(See also Bishop, Diocese, and Parish.)

PATRIARCH/PATRIARCHY   are terms with origins in the Greek *patria* and Latin *patriarcha*, which refer to a parent (male) or a headship who guides a family. "Patriarch" can be used in Catholic language in three ways. 1) Biblical patriarchs were the heads of the tribes of ancient Israel (e.g., Abraham, Isaac, and Jacob). Biblical patriarchy was the era in which patriarchs held power over the ancient Hebrews. 2) "Patriarch of the West" is a title held by the pope, the bishop of Rome. Current church patriarchy, then, is composed of the pope, cardinals, eastern Catholic patriarchs, bishops, and apostolic vicars around the globe. 3) "Patriarch" is also used to designate a bishop in the Eastern church who is in union with the universal Catholic community.

Patriarchs in Scripture were the ancestors of the Israelites (Genesis 12–50). They were male (e.g., Abraham) and female (matriarchs such as Sarah, Hagar, Rachel, Rebekah, Leah, and Zilpah). All popes to a great degree (and all bishops to a lesser extent) have had patriarchal responsibility for the universal Christian community. Other patriarchates have existed since the early church. In 325, the Council of Nicaea recognized three Catholic church patriarchs—the bishops of Alexandria, Antioch, and Rome. In 381 and 451, other councils added the bishops of

Constantinople and Jerusalem to the church's patriarchy.

Today, a Catholic patriarch is a bishop, subject only to the pope, who is the spiritual leader of Catholic peoples who participate in a certain rite of worship. Eastern patriarchs include: the patriarch of Alexandria (the Coptic rite); three patriarchs of Antioch (the Syrian, Maronite, and Greek Melkite rites); the patriarch of Babylonia (the Chaldean rite); and the patriarch of Sis/Cilicia (the Armenian rite). The Western patriarch is the bishop of Rome (the Roman rite). Like the pope, an Eastern patriarch is the head of all other bishops, metropolitans, clergy, and laypersons who use a certain worship rite. Patriarchs in the East are selected by the other bishops within their worldwide ritual community.

Vatican II described the catholicity of Eastern patriarchy in its Decree on Eastern Catholic Churches. Today, the church emphasizes that all patriarchates and patriarchs are equal in power and dignity, even though some patriarchates pre-date others. They should be given "exceptional respect" by the whole Catholic body according to Catholic tradition.

(See also Abraham, Bishop, Catholic, Diocese, and Pope.)

PAUL   is the great Christian saint, preacher, and writer often called the apostle to the gentiles. He is perhaps best known as the author of fourteen epistles—or letters—that can be found in the Christian Scriptures (the New Testament).

Paul was a Jew. He was born into the Israelite tribe of Benjamin, but because his home city was Tarsus, in the ancient hellenistic province of Cilicia, he was also a Roman citizen (Acts 16:37). Historical evidence suggests that Paul was probably born about the same time as Jesus of Nazareth. He was named Saul by his family. As he grew up, he studied the Hebrew Scriptures, especially the law of Moses. Saul then became a lawyer and a Pharisee. According to his own story, he proved also to be a skilled tentmaker.

Saul was very active in persecuting the early followers of Jesus, because he believed they were violating Jewish law. During a trip to the city of Damascus (he was chasing down Jewish Christians who had fled there), Saul had a striking and life-altering vision of the risen Jesus (Acts 9:3–20, 1 Corinthians 15:1–11). After this experience he stopped persecuting the followers of Jesus. He became a fiery convert to Christianity and began using the name Paul. Later he made at least three long missionary journeys (seeing himself as God's chosen apostle to the gentiles) to spread the good news of hope and salvation for all of humanity (Jews and gentiles alike). Paul was persecuted often; he spent many months in prison for the cause of evangelization. Tradition says that Paul was martyred, beheaded in Rome about 65 c.e. in the persecutions of the Roman emperor Nero.

The two best sources to find out about Paul—his life, his teachings, his theological outlooks—are the book of Acts of the Apostles and the Pauline epistles in the Christian Scriptures.

Although Paul was not one of the original apostles of the historical

Jesus of Nazareth, he nevertheless does deserve the title "apostle" to the gentiles in that he was a living witness to a personal encounter with the risen Jesus. Paul is one of the most important of early church figures. The Catholic community annually honors him twice during the liturgical calendar, on two feast days, January 25 and June 29.

(See also Acts of the Apostles, Apostles, Epistle, Martyr, New Testament, and Pentateuch.)

PENTATEUCH is one of the terms used to refer to the first five books of the Bible. The two other terms frequently used are the "Law" and the "Torah" (Hebrew). "Pentateuch" is derived from the Greek *pentateuchos*, which means "five volumes of work (or scrolls)." The Pentateuch is composed of the books of Genesis, Exodus, Leviticus, Numbers, and Deuteronomy.

For a long time many thought that Moses, the great leader of the ancient Hebrew community, was the actual author of the five books included in the Pentateuch. They have often been referred to as the "five books of Moses," "the law of Moses," or the "Mosaic books." Biblical exegesis has shown, however, that the books of the Pentateuch could not have been composed by the historical Moses; they were edited into their present form by anonymous authors long after the lifetime of Moses and only after centuries of oral and written developments. (It is possible, however, to say Moses is the "author" of the Pentateuch in that his life, ministry, and teaching provided the initial impetus for its formation.)

The Pentateuch opens with accounts of the creation of the world by God and the earliest history of the human race. It then goes on to describe God's call to Abraham and the other patriarchs, the call of Moses, the exodus of the Hebrews from oppression in Egypt, the covenant-relationship established between Yahweh and the Israelites (the chosen people of God) under Moses' guidance, and the initial formation of the great Israelite nation. The Pentateuch also contains religious laws and guidelines for the Hebrew people.

The Pentateuch is a very significant portion of the Hebrew Scriptures (Old Testament) and a central and sacred part of Jewish life and faith even to this day. The church recognizes that the Pentateuch describes its own spiritual roots as a people of God in the Judaeo-Christian tradition, as well as the original covenant between God (Yahweh) and humanity, which was fulfilled through a new covenant in a type of new Moses, Jesus of Nazareth.

Some commentators say the real thrust of the Pentateuch is the set of divine promises made to humanity by God in the book of Genesis (Genesis 12:1–3), and echoed many times in the other books of the Torah ("I will make you a great nation"; "I will bless you"; and the promised land is the "land I will give you"). Other themes prominent in the spiritual heritage of the Pentateuch are the nature of the divine-human relationship, the notion of a "promised land" for God's chosen people/community on Earth, and the covenant as a basis for Jewish and

Christian worship of God. These promises and themes have never been fully realized by humanity. Thus they continue to point all people of God toward a more hopeful, salvific future in God the Creator for all of humanity.

Here is a brief description of the five books of the Pentateuch.

Genesis describes the creation of the world and of the earliest members of the human race. It contains stories about the patriarchs and the events that lead to enslavement of the Hebrew people in Egypt.

Exodus describes the first passover meal of the Hebrews and the passing over from oppression to freedom, with Moses leading the Hebrew people. The story of the mosaic covenant and the development of the Israelites into a nation are also included.

Leviticus centers on Israel's holiness and on liturgical worship requirements.

Numbers shows how the Israelites were organized and the role of authority in the Jewish nation.

Deuteronomy explains and describes the ways in which the Israelites should relate to one another and how the chosen people must relate to God.

(See also Bible, Covenant, Creation, Exegesis, Moses, Old Testament, Patriarchy, and Yahweh.)

PENTECOST is celebrated fifty days after Easter in remembrance of the outpouring of the Spirit of the risen Jesus of Nazareth on his first followers, the disciples and apostles. The story of the Pentecost-event is recorded in the Acts of the Apostles (chapter 2). Pentecost is often referred to as the birthday of the church. The term is Greek in nature, meaning "the 50th day" or more simply "fiftieth."

The first records of the Christian celebration of a liturgical feast of Pentecost date back to the 3rd century, but it seems that Pentecost celebrations were held by Christian communities long before that time. Pentecost was originally a Jewish harvest festival held some fifty days after passover (Exodus 34:22). The earliest followers of Jesus of Nazareth believed that the Spirit of the risen One had mysteriously but powerfully empowered Peter and other original followers of Jesus to boldly proclaim the good news of hope and salvation in Jesus the Christ. Through the faith animated by the pentecostal outpouring of the gift of the Spirit, many faith-filled followers were made bold enough to undertake the global mission of evangelization entrusted to them and began to baptize many individuals and households, beginning with many gathered in Jerusalem for an annual harvest feast.

One of the key themes of the biblical story of Pentecost is that people within Israel as well as neighbors from distant lands, speaking foreign languages, found a certain unity in the gospel. The original Pentecost-event filled ("fired up") the followers of the risen Jesus with his Spirit of courage, so that they could faithfully try to fulfill the great mission they had received from him (Matthew 28:16–20). Members of Catholic worshiping communities are reminded every year at Pentecost that the Spirit of the risen Jesus continues to guide the baptized and the people of God everywhere. Catholics believe that all baptized persons, like the apostles and all other first Christians, have personally and communally received the gift of the Spirit of Jesus, that they too have received the evangelizing call to witness daily and share the Christian good news to all peoples and cultures.

In the Catholic tradition, Pentecost is a movable feast on the church's official calendar. (It is not celebrated on the same date each year.) Catholic teachings emphasize that this feast remains a true annual celebration of the gift of the Spirit and the Christian community's lasting, hopeful presence in the modern world.

Some Catholic peoples still refer to Pentecost as Whitsunday. Traditional Catholic devotions called novenas are compared to the nine-day period of intense prayer, petition to God, and hopeful waiting observed by Jesus Christ's followers before the original Pentecost-event.

(See also Baptism, Confirmation, Discipleship, Evangelization, Liturgical Year, Novena, and Trinity.)

PEOPLE OF GOD   is a term used to describe the community of the baptized, the followers of Jesus of Nazareth. It was popularized by Vatican II in the 1960s.

Christians believe that Israel—beginning with its ancestral ancient people called the Hebrews—was chosen by Yahweh to be God's chosen people. The Israelites saw their nation as a unified people, a "corporate personality," a community of the faithful dedicated to the loving God, Yahweh, with whom they had a covenant relationship. The chief expression of this covenant relationship between Yahweh and the chosen people is described in the books of Exodus (6:7–8) and Leviticus (26:9–12). Christian tradition maintains that Jesus of Nazareth, the eternal Word and the definitive human sign (revelation) of the living God, liberated humanity, the all-inclusive people of God, once and for all from human sinfulness and evil and established a new Christian people of God, the community of the baptized. The earliest communities of the risen Jesus saw themselves as God's truly chosen community, a holy nation, a people unified in faith in Jesus and his resurrection (1 Peter 2:9–10).

The church today often uses the term "people of God" to symbolize that it is a single people, a true community, that has a single mission of evangelization: to proclaim the liberating good news of salvation in Jesus of Nazareth to all people of God. The baptized are called to remain faithful daily to the teachings, witness, and counter-cultural lifestyle of the Lord, which speaks boldly of radical Christian hope, trust in the nearness of the reign of God (which has already begun), and love for the whole human family of God and creation. The unity of the new Christian people of God has several sources: the deep unity of the Father, Son, and Spirit, the divine Trinity; the life, ministry, and gospel-story of Jesus of Nazareth; and a living faith rooted in the gift of the Spirit through baptism.

Vatican II taught that the church—the true people of God—was founded by Jesus and should give all humans a witness to and a foretaste of the wondrous, peaceful reign of God. Vatican II also noted that all people of God must strive constantly to create—in their own hearts and souls and in their local communities and cultures—an earthly dwelling-place suitable for the dynamic Spirit of God. Therefore the followers of Jesus have sometimes been characterized in the ideal as the light of the world and salt of the earth—a people who prove every day to be "instruments of salvation" sent to reach out to others to form a human community truly dedicated to love of God and hope in Jesus.

(See also Church, Images of; Community; Covenant; Ecclesiology; Hebrews; and Trinity.)

Note of Interest: The *Catechism of the Catholic Church* reminds readers that the universal people of God is marked by certain characteristics that distinguish it from other political and cultural groups in human history: It is a people of God; one becomes a member not by physical birth alone but by water (baptism) and the Spirit; it has the anointed messiah, the risen Jesus, as its head; it has a life-condition—freedom in the Spirit of God; it has a law in Jesus' commandment to love others as he has loved all of humanity; it has a mission to be light to the world and the salt of the earth in preparation for full realization of the reign of God; and it has a true destiny in that this reign of God, in some ways already here and now, must be extended more and more until, at the end of time, it will be completed as a universal people of God to the fullest extent in the Creator (article 782).

PETER   is one of the original apostles of Jesus of Nazareth, the one generally considered the overall leader of the followers of the risen One after the ascension of the Lord and the experience of Pentecost. The name Peter is derived from the Greek version (*petros*) of the Aramaic word *Cephas*, which means "rock" or "stone." Saint Peter is honored as the first pope, and his successors, the bishops of Rome, have traditionally become pope for the global Catholic Christian community.

Scripture tells us that Peter's name was actually Simon or Simeon. He was the son of a man named Jonah and a brother to the apostle Andrew. Quite likely, according to biblical evidence, Simon Peter was a lower class (economically poor) fisherman from the territory of Galilee and was one of the first disciples called to follow Jesus of Nazareth. (The gospels indicate that it was Jesus who gave Simon his new name, Peter—Mark 3:16, Matthew 16:18, John 1:42). Simon Peter was a married man; Peter's wife eventually traveled with him during at least some of his evangelizing journeys (1 Corinthians 9:5).

Peter is named as the first male disciple to see the risen One after the resurrection (Luke 24:34, 1 Corinthians 15:5). He also seems to have quickly assumed a position of real leadership in the post-Easter Christian community (Acts 1–12, 15; Galatians 1:18–19; Galatians 2:1–10). But after Chapter 15 in the book of Acts he basically disappears from the narrative-story about the emerging, primitive Christian community. Many scholars now think that the apostle James became sole leader of the foundational Jerusalem community of the risen One, the gifted preacher Paul became the primary missionary "apostle to the gentiles," and Simon Peter went on missionary travels that ended with a sojourn in Rome shortly before his death as a martyr. If this is so, some speculate that Peter probably died at the hands of the Roman emperor Nero about 64–65 c.e. A non-biblical Christian tradition claims that his body is buried at the present site of St. Peter's Basilica at the Vatican (in Rome).

Many primitive Christian writings are credited to (but were not actually written by) Simon Peter: the letters of Peter in the Christian Scriptures, an extra-biblical gospel of Peter, and even a book of Acts according to St. Peter. This all probably serves to underscore that the traditions, stories, and the actual witness of Peter's life were of great import to the earliest generations of followers of Jesus. Many historians believe that early Christians came to depend on Peter in a way for strong, rock-like authoritative leadership in the name of the Lord (Matthew 16:17–19). He clearly had a position of moral leadership at the landmark council of early community Christian leaders in the year 52, in the city of Jerusalem. In fact, as some note often today, Simon Peter is mentioned in the Christian Scriptures more often than any other original apostle or disciple of Jesus of Nazareth.

Recently some very serious study of the key gospel passage about Simon Peter and his authority in the emerging church (Matthew 16:17–19) has raised new questions. For example: Is the "rock" spoken about actually Simon Peter, or is it his faith-filled confession of Jesus? Was the traditional "power of the keys" to the reign of God actually meant to symbolize the power of welcoming others into the Christian community through evangelizing activity, or was it symbolic of the power of institutional church authority and discipline? Is this power given to Peter and his papal successors alone or to all members of the community of the baptized? Were the words attributed to Jesus of Nazareth in Matthew 16:17–19 actually spoken by Jesus before his death and resurrection, or by the risen Jesus, or were they only penned much later to explain the actual position of community leadership that the historical Peter eventually achieved?

Catholic tradition maintains that Peter received authority to direct and guide the early Christian community personally from Jesus of Nazareth and that Peter's true successor, the bishop of Rome, has the ultimate authority to teach, govern, and guide the entire people of God. The Roman Catholic liturgical calendar has two feast days on which Saint Peter is specially honored, February 22 and June 29.

(See also Apostles, Apostolic Succession, Discipleship, Martyr, Pentecost, and Pope.)

PILGRIMAGE is a journey. A pilgrim is one who makes a journey. In a Christian sense, a spiritual pilgrim is one who journeys to a sacred location (e.g., a Christian shrine) for the purpose of spiritual development and growth in Christian holiness.

A pilgrimage symbolizes the great march of the people of God into the everlasting reign of God (Hebrews 11:8–16; Revelation 7:1–12). It is a way to walk a journey similar to that of the ancient Hebrews—from slavery in Egypt to happiness in the promised land. The spiritual pilgrimage has also been likened to the challenging journey of Jesus and his disciples toward Jerusalem and the Easter experience (Luke 19:28–38). Pilgrimages have been made by church members for centuries. Pilgrimage, for example, was a key motif for the Christian and human life journey in Chaucer's famous *Canterbury Tales.*

All of Christian existence is meant to be a pilgrimage, a lifelong journey toward holiness and deeper faith in God. True Christian pilgrimages are devoted to prayer, spiritual contemplation, interpersonal faith discussions, reception of the sacraments, and related spiritual activities. All our Christian days are to be imbued with these religious elements as well.

Catholics believe that a spiritual pilgrimage is much more than a tourist trip. And it must be undertaken for reasons deeper than simple curiosity or an enhanced personal reputation. A pilgrim journeys to a Christian shrine or other holy place to grow in holiness and undertake devotions that honor Mary and the saints, to do penances, to give thanks to God, to complete a vow, or to ask for divine help. Pope John Paul II has said that the key reason to go on a pilgrimage is to encounter Jesus Christ in some way: Christ is the goal of every life journey, the model for the church's pilgrim journey overall, and source of all Catholic holiness.

(See also Devotions, Discipleship, Holiness, Indulgences, Prayer, and Shrine.)

POPE   is the title given to the Catholic bishop of Rome, the successor of Saint Peter and supreme leader of the global Catholic community. The word can be traced both to the Latin *papa* and the Greek *pappas*, which mean "father." The pope, or holy father, as he is sometimes called, has the foremost authority among the Catholics of the world to teach on matters of Christian faith and morality and to otherwise guide and direct the affairs of the church on Earth.

The Christian Scriptures indicate that the apostle Peter was entrusted with a special authority by Jesus of Nazareth and by very early followers of the risen One to guide the primitive Christian community on the whole and to speak with some special authority (Matthew 16:17–19, John 21:15–17, and Acts 2:14 ff). Through the ages Peter's successors, the bishops of Rome, have held the title pope, and they have been entrusted by the worldwide Catholic community with the responsibility to faithfully proclaim and preserve the gospel message and guide the people of God.

The Catholic community's rules by which popes have been elected have changed a number of times over the centuries. For example, Paul VI revised papal election laws in 1975. He decreed that all cardinals under the age of 80 should come together in Rome for a conclave to choose a new pope whenever this becomes necessary.

The pope is known as the bishop of Rome, the Vicar of Christ, the Roman Pontiff, the Holy Father, and the Servant of the Servants of God. The Catholic tradition has chosen to use the term "pontiff" because this word denotes a kind of bridge—thus the pope is seen as kind of human symbolic bridge who is meant to help God and the human family draw closer and closer together. Catholics today believe that the pope should follow upon Peter's powerful witness. He should therefore remain a strong, trusted, spiritual leader, yet also a humble servant and shepherd.

Building on evidence from the Bible and many centuries of Christian tradition, the Catholic community maintains that the pope holds power in the church as its chief pastor. In fact, Catholic doctrine on papal primacy, officially defined by Vatican I in 1870, was reaffirmed by the Second Vatican Council during the 1960s.

In all, there have been 265 popes, nine of whom have lived in the present century. Once a man is elected to the papacy—also called the chair of Peter—he remains pope for the rest of his life. The most recent popes include: Leo XIII, (St.) Pius X, Benedict XV, Pius XI, Pius XII, John XXIII, Paul VI, John Paul I, and John Paul II.

(See also Apostolic Succession, Cardinal, Collegiality, Infallibility, Peter, Vatican Council I.)

Note of Interest: At least 37 persons who had no right to the title or office have claimed to be the authentic pope, overall leader of the church. These persons are sometimes described as the "anti-popes." A very traditional church prayer for the papacy refers to the pope as the "appointed successor to Saint Peter...the visible center and foundation of unity in faith and love."

PRAYER   is communication with God and an awareness of the Creator's powerful and loving presence. Prayer can be silent or verbal, formal or informal, private or communal. The gospels point out that Jesus prayed to God frequently and that he went off to quiet, deserted places to pray before crucial events in his life and ministry. The word *prayer* has both Latin and French origins meaning "to entreat" or to ask (or to beg). In Christian tradition the faith community has come to describe prayer as the raising of one's human heart and mind to God. There are four basic types of Christian prayer: petition, adoration, thanksgiving, and contrition.

Prayer is a response to God: a basic openness to and communication with God, within a dialogue initiated by the Creator. Thus many Christians see prayer as a gift from God and a powerful, effective way to deepen the covenant relationship between a loving God and humankind. The prayerful person is one who freely responds to God's offer of relationship and open communication. Prayer is therefore a response made in Christian faith and hope; essentially it is a true surrender to God's love. The human response to God in prayer—the response to God's invitation to a deeper relationship with God—is like a hunger, a powerful longing to be with God in an intimate way and to spiritually converse with God.

In the Catholic tradition there are many, many possible ways to pray: including participation in the worship of the church community (e.g., the eucharistic liturgy and the liturgy of the hours), joining Bible studies, local prayer groups, and spiritual renewal movements such as Renew, and quiet prayerful reflection alone or in communal settings with others. Prayer of petition asks something of God; it centers on human needs. Prayer of adoration offers praise to the Creator. Prayer of thanksgiving expresses gratitude, humility, and awareness of God's greatness. Prayer of contrition focuses on human failures and sinfulness but also on a loving God's ever-present offer of mercy and forgiveness to the sinful human community.

All of Book Four within the *Catechism of the Catholic Church* is devoted to Christian prayer. In attempting to address the question "What is prayer?" it quotes St. Thérèse of Lisieux: "For me prayer is a surge of the heart; it is a simple look turned toward heaven, it is a cry of recognition and love, embracing both trial and joy." The Catechism notes that through prayer one can better live out one's vital, personal, conscious, and responsible relationship with the living and true God (article 2558). It further notes that prayer is God's gift implanted into human hearts, an expression of a covenant between the divine and humanity, and a form of "communion"—because prayer is the cultivation of a habit of being in the presence of God and in close relationship with the Holy (articles 2558–2565).

(See also Covenant, Days of Prayer, God, Liturgy of the Hours, and Worship.)

Note of Interest: A retreat is a period of time used to step away from the routine activities of daily life. The individual retreatant (or a retreat group) seeks renewed spiritual focus, peacefulness, and commitment to the Christian way through growth in faith, prayer, sacramental liturgy, Scripture reading, meditation, prayer, faith-centered discussions, and other quiet reflection.

The Christian practice of making retreats traces back to the wilderness experiences of biblical figures. Jesus spent time in the desert to reflect upon his life and ministry. Great saints such as Ignatius Loyola, Francis de Sales, and Vincent de Paul also spent time in "desert prayer." In 1922 Pope Pius XI endorsed the opening of retreat houses for individuals and groups that wished to deepen their Christian spirituality and strengthen their abilities to daily live the Christian faith through retreat experiences. During the 1960s Vatican Council II urged Catholic bishops to stress the value of retreats for presbyters, members of religious orders, and all laypersons. The council declared that periods of recollection and spiritual exercises renew and revitalize the life activities, careers, and family life of all Christian witnesses. There are many kinds of retreats today, including traditional silent retreats, retreats for adolescents, retreats for young adults, family retreats, parish renewals and missions, and Cursillo, Charismatic Renewal, and Marriage Encounter retreats.

PRESBYTERS   also more commonly known as priests, are men who receive the sacrament of order and are thus ordained by their local bishop to serve as spiritual leaders in the local Catholic community. "Presbyter" is derived from Greek expressions for "old" or "elder." Early presbyters (*presbyteroi*) were distinguished from overseers (*episcopoi*) and deacons (*diakonia*). These primitive Christian ministry categories are now the three divisions of the Catholic sacrament of order: bishops, priests, and deacons.

There were many spiritual gifts and ministries needed among primitive Christian community members (e.g., see Acts 13:1, Ephesians 4:11–13, and 1 Corinthians 12:28–30). Christian ministries evolved slowly. Some scholars believe that women were active in primitive gospel-era ministries for years as co-disciples and presiders in house-church rituals for the Eucharist. In post-apostolic communities, elders (presbyters) and overseers (bishops) were selected to serve the gospel and placed in office through prayer and a laying on of hands by Christians (Acts 14:23 and 15–22). These elders then cared pastorally for the baptized, presided at the Eucharist, managed (governed) community affairs, catechized, and completed works of mercy for the poor and needy. In essence, they were ministers who remained in one church locale to carry on in the tradition of the original disciples of Jesus. In all likelihood, early presbyters were responsible to an overall council (presbytery) of elders and overseers (Acts 20:28). By the 3rd century, according to Hippolytus, presbyters were being regularly ordained by local bishops in collaboration with groups of presbyters.

The church teaches that presbyters (priests) have a share in the full Christian priesthood of Catholic bishops. In its Decree on the Ministry and Life of Priests, in the 1960s, Vatican II called presbyters a college in a diocese committed, with their local bishop, to building up the body of Christ, particularly through the celebration of the Eucharist and other sacraments, the proclamation of the gospel, and direct outreach to meet human needs. More recently, the *Catechism of the Catholic Church* has spoken of presbyters as the special co-workers of bishops who carry on the mission of the original apostles and who, in a sense, make the Spirit of Jesus Christ, the apostles, bishops, and the gospel present in local congregations.

All the baptized are part of a universal priesthood according to Catholic Christian tradition (1 Peter 2:5, 9), because all Christians—not just the ordained—are challenged and gifted (chosen) by the Spirit of Jesus to serve the church and all of humankind. Recent interfaith discussions among Catholics and other Christians on ordination to ministry and the Christian presbyterate have centered on: 1) the universal call to ministry of all the baptized; 2) how presbyters (priests and other ministers) speak to the world in Jesus' name; 3) how various local-level presiders should perform ritually, give spiritual direction, and do works of mercy for people in need; and 4) how all the ordained—female or male, whatever their Christian tradition—must exemplify the call to gospel witness and service.

(See also Bishop, Discipleship, Ministry, Order, and Parochial Vicar.)

Note of Interest: A presider is one who leads a Christian assembly in some form of prayer and worship, e.g., the Eucharist, the liturgy of the hours, litanies, liturgies of the Word, prayer services, and so on. The Latin root of "preside" means "sit before." In Catholic worship, only priests or bishops can preside at the Eucharist (Mass) and other sacraments. However, deacons and lay ministers—both female and male— may preside at various other forms of communal prayer rituals. For more information on this, see the note on pastoral associates in the article on Parochial Vicar.

PROPHET   is a person called by God to deliver divinely-revealed messages to humankind. The statements and symbolic actions of the biblical prophets often centered on hopes, promises, and warnings about the covenant established between God (Yahweh) and the chosen people. In a sense, biblical prophets were called to read the signs of their times and constantly remind the Hebrew community to be faithful to its relationship with Yahweh. Our word "prophet" has Greek origins meaning "one who speaks before others."

Historical and scriptural evidence suggests that the most important biblical prophets lived between 900 and 500 b.c.e. This significant period of prophetic activity probably was mostly concluded by the time the Israelites were freed from Babylonian captivity in 538 b.c.e. After the time of the prophets, the Hebrew people seem to have been guided more by God's revelation in the written Word than by the words and deeds of human prophets.

The Catholic community believes that the Spirit of the Creator did indeed inspire the prophets to perform their ministry, and that God truly spoke through the biblical prophets to the nation of Israel and can therefore speak meaningfully through them to this day to the human family. Some of the prophets suffered awful persecutions and some even died at the hands of their enemies.

Many Scripture students say clearly that John the Baptist, a kinsman of Jesus of Nazareth, who announced the need for repentance and the coming of the reign of God, was a prophetic figure in the Christian Scriptures. Some think that the historical Jesus too was considered a striking prophet by some of the people of his time, but it seems that Jesus never specifically claimed to be a prophet along the lines of the rich Hebrew tradition of prophecy.

New Testament writings (Christian Scriptures) seem to suggest that the first communities of Jesus' followers also indeed had prophets. For instance Paul noted that prophecy is a special gift from God (1 Corinthians 12:28, 14:1ff., Ephesians 4:11). This form of prophecy may have taken shape as a clear perception on the part of an individual of an insight or "truth" from the divine that could then be shared in an understandable way with the rest of the Christian assembly. This kind of prophecy probably receded into the background of Christian community life over the decades as ministry became more institutionalized and Christian communities as a whole began to rely more and more on preachers, scholars, and catechists.

There were three major prophets in the Hebrew tradition through the pre-Christian era: Isaiah, Jeremiah, and Ezekiel. And there were a number of minor prophets, such as Amos, Hosea, Joel, Micah, Baruch, and Zechariah. Portions of the biblical books of the prophets are frequently read during Catholic celebrations of the Eucharist and at other sacramental liturgies.

(See also Bible, Old Testament, and Revelation.)

PURGATORY   is a spiritual state or condition into which the souls of persons who have died enter to be purified of the effects of unforgiven sin or to endure a form of temporal purification and punishment for sins already forgiven. Catholic tradition maintains that the spiritual preparation experience called purgatory is for those considered not yet worthy of the fullness of heavenly happiness. The word "purgatory" is based on a Latin term that basically means "cleansing."

Early generations of Christians prayed zealously for those who had gone to a "place of tears" after death. The actual word "purgatory" has been used by church members in the Roman tradition since the Middle Ages. The Council of Lyons (1274) and the Council of Florence (1439) declared that souls in purgatory need the prayers and good works of those who still live on Earth. The Council of Trent in the 16th century stated clearly that offering prayers and receiving the Eucharist for the sake of those in purgatory greatly helps those souls in preparation for heaven.

The Catholic community's belief in purgatory is rooted in Catholic tradition only—there is no clear basis in the Christian Scriptures (although 2 Maccabees 12:38ff. is often cited) for the doctrine on purgatory. Nevertheless the church has traditionally taught that the souls in purgatory are the souls of persons who have died fundamentally worthy of the full happiness of heaven (in the state of grace), but who have not perfectly atoned for their personal sins. Thus they must undergo a time of painful separation from God, but those in purgatory do experience a basic sense of hope and joy as they prepare for complete and happy life in God in heaven. One line of theological thinking in church history, especially in more contemporary times, has held that these souls still cling in some ways to their sinful human patterns, faults, and self-centered failings and thus cannot fully be free to enjoy full union and spiritual focus with God. The process of pain and separation from God that souls endure has sometimes been compared to a burning or searing fire.

The *Catechism of the Catholic Church* says that all who die in God's friendship are assured of eternal salvation. But those not yet perfectly purified undergo a post-death purification so as to achieve the necessary holiness to enter heaven. The Catechism adds that from the beginning of the Christian experience the baptized have honored the memory of the dead and offered prayers and sacrifices on their behalf (articles 1030–1032).

(See also All Souls Day; Almsgiving; Heaven; Saints, Communion of; and Sin.)

R

RECONCILIATION   is one of the seven sacraments of the Catholic community. Sometimes this sacrament is called penance or confession. The word refers to healing the rift between a sinful human being and God (and others in the human community). It comes from the Latin *reconciliare* —to conciliate or to "restore to friendship." The word "penance," which comes from the Latin *poenitentia*, means "contrition" and "repentance for wrongdoing."

Through the sacrament of reconciliation sinful persons express their sorrow and contrition for personal wrongdoing after baptism in order to be reconciled to—restored to full and healthy friendship or relationship with—the loving and merciful God and the Christian community. To receive forgiveness for sinful wrongdoing through this sacrament, one must have true sorrow, be willing to confess one's sins to a Catholic priest, make reparation for sin, and receive absolution. The words used by the priest to absolve (forgive) sins are "I absolve you from your sins in the name of the Father, and of the Son, and of the Holy Spirit."

A basis for the sacrament of reconciliation can be found in the Christian Scriptures in the gospel of John (20:22–23). Christian communities in all eras have firmly believed that Jesus of Nazareth cared deeply about sinners, outcasts, and the alienated, and that he called all persons, especially the sinners and the most downtrodden of his time, to experience conversion (turn away) from sin and evil in order to turn their lives fully toward his good news of hope.

The first followers of the risen Jesus preached that human sinfulness could be forgiven and that an eternal salvation and lasting hope were offered to all of humanity through Jesus, the messiah, the risen Christ. By the 6th century, however, severe public penances were being administered by church authorities for the sins of murder, heresy, and adultery. Lesser penances, such as fasting, prayer, almsgiving, and charitable works, were assigned for less grievous personal sins. During this era members of the Christian community could receive the sacrament of penance only once during their lifetime. By the 7th century, however, Christians were permitted to confess their sins more frequently—to a bishop or presbyter, who acted more as a harsh judge than a pastoral healer or reconciler. The penances assigned soon became a strictly private matter. Emphasis was placed on various listings or codes of penances to be assigned for the many kinds of sins.

By the 14th century, great stress was being placed on making satisfaction for one's sins. Belief that penance was a sacrament of reconciliation—a pastorally-caring restoration of friendship between the sinner, a loving God, and the forgiving Christian community—had waned. In 1439 the Council of Florence formally declared that penance was one of the seven sacraments. Florence also noted that to be sacramentally forgiven one must express contrition for personal sinfulness, confess to a priest, and make satisfaction, also known as "reparation," by doing a penance. In 1551 the Council of Trent formally noted that the Catholic community has come to believe that this sacrament was in fact instituted by Jesus Christ.

In recent decades the idea has been reemphasized that penance is a means of reconciliation between God, the people of God, and the individual sinner. Through this sacrament the unconditional mercy of a loving, forgiving Creator is extended to the individual sinner. But through the celebration of penance the entire people of God likewise comes to recognize that it too is constantly in need of God's grace and that the entire community of the baptized must daily undergo the process of Christian change, reform, and radical conversion.

The Second Vatican Council, in the 1960s, called for a revision of the rite of reconciliation. Vatican II taught that sacramental penance aids Christians in their desire for ongoing conversion to authentic Christian living.

The usual minister of the sacrament of reconciliation is a presbyter or bishop. Since 1974, with the Vatican's publication of the document *Ordo paenitentiae*, the church community has provided local Catholics three forms for the celebration of reconciliation: 1) traditional private confession to a priest and subsequent absolution; 2) communal penance service (including a liturgy of the Word and individual confession, followed by absolution), and 3) communal penance with general absolution (does not require private confession to a presbyter and therefore is used rather infrequently). The Code of Canon Law details church disciplines and rules regarding the sacrament of penance in canons 959–991.

The *Catechism of the Catholic Church* explores many aspects of this sacramental experience—its history and current pastoral practices in particular—beginning with article 1422. In April 1992, Pope John Paul II acknowledged that many modern church members have either stopped taking part in this sacrament or find the pastoral practice of personally confessing to a priest hard to accept. He noted that "The sense of sin has been weakened [and] many find difficulty in accepting the church's mediation in being reconciled to God."

(See also Actual Sin, Grace, Sacrament, and Sin.)

REDEMPTION   is the process by which humanity is brought back, through the self-sacrificing, salvific deeds of Jesus of Nazareth, into fullness of relationship with the Creator. The Catholic community recognizes and affirms, therefore, that Jesus is the redeemer of humankind, the one who offers the human community a path toward freedom from sin and the way toward eternal salvation. The world also awaits a kind of final redemption-to-come—a conversion of all creation from sinfulness and human selfishness to the immeasurable goodness of God and the perfected and never-to-end reign of God. The term has roots in the Latin *redemptio*, essentially "a buying back."

Christian redemption and everlasting salvation are offered to every member of the human race through the free, self-sacrificing, and therefore saving deeds of Jesus of Nazareth and through the outpouring of his Spirit on the entire human community. The gifts of Jesus' witness and his living Spirit are meant for all individuals and cultures, and all are correspondingly free to accept or reject these redemptive gifts. God became human to do for humanity something that humanity could not do for itself: craft a way, on the whole, to overcome the power of human sinfulness, pride, and selfishness. Thus the essence of the redemption is God's great love for human beings. And each human being, group, and culture remain in need of Jesus' liberating witness, values, teachings, and good news of hope because each person remains capable of alienation from God's love, which sinfulness is.

The Catholic community emphasizes that God became human in order to definitively redeem the whole human community for all time. Thus the incarnate God, known as Jesus of Nazareth, sought to establish the reign of God firmly within the global human community and to reconcile forever the Creator and the entire human race. The church is a kind of sacrament of salvation, a living community with an evangelizing mission to help make the everlasting, salvation-centered reign of God a perfected reality in creation. This faith community—or sacrament of salvation—is to be dedicated to the end of time to spreading the liberating good news (gospel) of Jesus of Nazareth and to responsible stewardship of the entire world.

The particular branch of Catholic theology called soteriology is the study of the salvation of humanity. Soteriology centers on Jesus' redemptive suffering, death, resurrection, and his eventual exaltation as the Christ by God.

(See also Christology, Kenosis, Messiah, Paschal Mystery, Reign of God, Salvation, and Stewardship.)

REFORMATION   describes the long-term process of disintegration (division) and turmoil experienced by Christian churches throughout the Western world in the 16th century and beyond. Many view the Reformation as religious in nature. In actuality, however, many complex cultural forces in Europe—humanist, political, social, intellectual, artistic, and Christian—came together to influence the impassioned calls for official church reform.

In 1517 in Germany, an Augustinian presbyter named Martin Luther began publicly addressing and publishing his many doctrinal disagreements with the official church. He was excommunicated from the church for heresy in 1521. In effect, this process began the Reformation. Other key European reform leaders included Ulrich Zwingli, a Swiss priest, John Calvin, also in Switzerland, and John Knox, who established Presbyterianism in Scotland. Later reformers included John Wesley, founder of Methodism in the 18th century, and Roger Williams, in America, who helped begin the Baptist community in the 1600s.

Reformers generally spoke of the need to overcome church apathy, corruptions, and grave scandals in order to return to the original spirit and practice of Christianity enjoyed by the earliest of gospel-focused communities. Some of the central doctrinal dissents of the various reformers—for example, *sola scriptura* (the Bible is the only true guide to Christian faith), the rejection of the ultimate authority of the pope and bishops, denial of the real presence of Jesus in the Eucharist, concern over other sacramental practices (e.g., individual confession/absolution), and harsh criticism of certain church teachings on indulgences—were indirectly shaped by the teachings of John Wycliff, a 14th-century priest in England, and John Hus, a 15th-century preacher in Bohemia.

The Reformation brought about the division of millions of the baptized. Reform communities were sometimes extreme in their reactions, but Catholic leaders often blindly turned away from legitimate calls for needed changes. While the immediate official Catholic response to the reformers was a Counter-Reformation, heralded by the Council of Trent, and a continuation of some religious practices decried by the Protestants, more recently there have been concerted efforts at Catholic reform. The influence of Christian ecumenists has helped many see that the Reformation process overall was made necessary because of many sinful tendencies among church members and that all people of God deeply need one another. Thus, all Christians (Catholics included) should work to end the "family squabbles" and separateness caused by the Reformation in order to restore full Christian unity around the world. Catholics believe that prayer with other Christians, loving and generous service, and dialogue will help lead toward the goal of true renewed unity among all churches and all the baptized.

Catholics and Protestants share one faith, one Lord, one baptism, and many hopes. Vatican II noted therefore, in the 1960s, in its Decree on Ecumenism that prejudices and separations tracing to the Reformation openly contradict the will of Christ, scandalize the world, and damage the preaching of the gospel. Many official inter-faith dialogues and reports between the Catholic community and other Christian church groups have been produced in the last thirty years. In May 1992, John Paul II said to a mixed Christian audience that "many are the spiritual treasures we share. Among them the Holy Scriptures occupy an eminent place...[the] great task and the need for a renewed evangelization of humanity are inseparable aspects of our duty to be faithful and humble messengers of the Word of God."

(See also Apostasy, Christian Unity Week, Ecumenism, Humanism, Indulgences, and Trent.)

REIGN OF GOD   is God's saving kingdom or rule over all humanity and the universe. Many today believe the expression "kingdom of God," as found in the gospels, is better translated as "reign of God"—a dynamic event or process by which God exercises saving grace and fulfillment for all human beings and all material creation in a new way.

The roots of the idea of the reign of God can be found in the Hebrew Scriptures. The Hebrew people looked forward to a powerful and political kingdom of God that would be founded by and led by a royal messiah. During his public ministry Jesus of Nazareth taught that the reign of God was already among and within all persons who repented, changed their ways, believed in God, and followed him. This mystery was made clear to his closest followers, the apostles and disciples, after Jesus was raised from the dead and after they received the gift of the Spirit at Pentecost. The phrase "kingdom of God" can be found in over 150 places in the Christian Scriptures, especially in the synoptic gospels. The meaning of this symbol of the kingdom of God is explained in particular in many gospel parables.

The terms "reign" and "kingdom" are important in Catholic language. The church is often referred to as the new kingdom or new reign of God, a new Israel and new people of the Creator. Theologians continue to emphasize that the entire Christian community needs to express and re-express the good news of God's reign, as proclaimed by Jesus of Nazareth, in every time and every culture. The reign of God, however, is not identical to the church. Vatican II claimed that the church has received a mission to proclaim God's reign from the apostles. It is the duty of the entire people of God to make the church a living reality, "a budding forth" of the dynamic event of grace called the kingdom.

Catholic tradition stresses the idea that the reign of God is "already at hand" and that this proclamation held a central place in the teachings of Jesus of Nazareth and his disciples. Vatican II noted that the church today must work to remain a visible sign of community and Christian holiness in order to become more perfect, from age to age, until the end of the world, the time in which the true reign of God will be fully realized. In addition, the expression "reign of God" explicitly underscores God's care for, and divine activity at the center of, all human life. Thus the reign of God is made present in relationships and communities today whenever human beings care for one another, in harmony with the Christian spirit, and wherever peoples and cultures are being healed, set free from oppressions, freed from dehumanizing forces, or otherwise made whole. The *Catechism of the Catholic Church* summarizes key church beliefs regarding the reign of God in articles 2816-2821.

(See Ecclesiology, Evangelization, Messiah, Parousia, and People of God.)

RELIGIOUS ORDERS   are communities of Christian women or men who seek to live as active witnesses to the good news of Jesus Christ and who have pledged to observe the vows of poverty, chastity, and obedience. Persons who enter religious community life are often called sisters or nuns, brothers, or religious priests. Religious orders tend to follow specific codes for daily living and rules for life that help them offer Christian service to the baptized and to the entire human family of God.

In the 3rd century of the common era, some men in the Middle East went to the desert to lead solitary lives of prayer, spiritual discipline, and ongoing Christian conversion. These individuals, known as hermits, soon had many followers. Eventually some of these followers banded together to form religious life communities. Christian history suggests that this development led directly to the rise of a community-oriented monasticism, an alternative or countercultural lifestyle that stressed community living, prayer, reflection, and much solitude. Those who chose to live the monastic life in early monasteries were influenced by the Rule of St. Benedict, which dates to the 6th century. Formal religious orders began to emerge in the 11th century. In succeeding centuries members of religious orders turned more toward the Christian church community as a whole, and the secular world too, to offer genuine Christian service to others.

Women and men who live in religious communities feel called to become dedicated to Jesus and the gospel, to personally become living reminders of the risen One who is still present to the people of God today. Some persons who prepare for the presbyterate (or priesthood) choose to join a religious order, to live in a religious community, and observe the traditional evangelical counsels (vows) of poverty, chastity and obedience. They are called "religious priests" or "order priests."

Vatican II called for a true renewal of religious life in its Decree on the Appropriate Renewal of Religious Life (*Perfectae caritatis*). The Council suggested that this spiritual renewal should center on the original inspiration, purpose, or the charism of each religious community tradition and involve appropriate adjustments to the changing circumstances of modern life. Pope Paul VI, in August 1966, issued sweeping guidelines for the renewal of religious life in the worldwide Catholic body in his document *Ecclesiae sanctae*. In September 1992, the findings of an authoritative, three-year study of the future of religious communities of men and women concluded that they each need to be faithful to their founding purpose or charism and responsive to real human needs. The study noted that some orders have in recent years increasingly shifted members into individual and parish-centered ministries but the result has sometimes been loss of corporate identity and corporate witness for the religious order, leading to a depletion of their communal vitality.

Some religious orders embrace a primarily contemplative life. In these orders, contacts outside the religious community are kept to a minimum; members usually focus on prayer, penances, and solitude. Other religious communities urge their members to undertake ministries in the church and in the wider marketplace so they can offer active Christian service to help build the reign of God among the wider family of the Creator.

Vatican II taught that observing the evangelical counsels is an answer to "a divine call to live for God alone not only by dying to sin but also by renouncing the standards of the world. [Religious] have handed over their entire lives to God's service in an act of special consecration deeply rooted in their baptismal consecration and which provides an ampler manifestation of it." More recently, Pope John Paul has spoken with high regard about religious orders in his document *Redemptoris missio* (1990), calling them "religious families" of God giving active Christian witness to the world.

While there are many conferences and institutes that support and guide the progress of religious life and religious orders in the U.S. and around the globe today, the agency at the Vatican that oversees Catholic religious orders is the Congregation for Institutes of Consecrated Life and Societies of Apostolic Life.

(See also Celibacy, Hermit, Ministry, and Vows.)

RESURRECTION   is the event at the heart and core of all Christian beliefs and practices. In the resurrection, Christians trust that the crucified Jesus of Nazareth was raised to new life by God and thus has entered a glorified spiritual state, victorious for all time over human death. Jesus died, was raised miraculously by the Creator from the dead, has ascended to the fullness of life with God, and will come back at the end of time (in the *parousia*). The resurrection of Jesus is celebrated annually by Christians around the world on Easter Sunday—the high point or summit of the church's liturgical year.

All four gospel versions in the Christian Scriptures (the New Testament) note that Jesus of Nazareth actually, physically died on a cross and soon after returned to the presence of his community of close followers, the disciples. The Bible testifies to the ancient Christian belief that the risen Jesus appeared first to the apostles and then to other followers. At a time soon after the resurrection he ascended to heaven, after which his community of followers prayerfully but anxiously awaited the sending of his gift of the Spirit.

Catholic tradition firmly maintains that the crucified Jesus of Nazareth was raised from death by God and, in the process, the human Jesus was likewise fully and spiritually transformed—glorified by God in a spiritual way. The cross and the resurrection of Jesus Christ are therefore at the very center and the heart of all Christian faith and evangelization.

Faith in the miraculous resurrection of the Lord and true faith in the good news of salvation that Jesus proclaimed were what impelled the earliest generations of Christians to spread the gospel, baptize others, and claim that Jesus the Christ and the reign of God, through his gift of the Spirit, were living and present ("at hand") in creation. Belief in the actual resurrection of Jesus thus caused the early Christians to declare the divinity of Jesus—to begin to view him in faith as the one, true Son of God. So in accord with this line of theological thought, once believers began to fully comprehend the meaning of Jesus' resurrection from death, they became transformed into hope-filled, committed bearers of the gospel's good news message of hope for all of humanity. The first disciples began to recognize that the resurrection and spiritual transformation of their self-sacrificing, service-oriented Teacher was in a way the destiny that also awaited them, and all Christian believers, in faith.

Some current theological speculation centers on the historical resurrection event itself. What exactly was it? Thinkers sometimes now point out that because there were no known eyewitnesses to the raising of the crucified Jesus from the dead, it is possible to think of the resurrection as an a-historical event—in other words, a transhistorical, meta-historical, or supernatural event. Thus perhaps the spiritual resurrection of Jesus of Nazareth was something then that occurred far beyond the limits of natural time and natural space—and so remains beyond what human observers might usually define as an identifiable and actual historical event. For example, some Bible students and teachers claim that gospel writers used a word for "appeared" (regarding the post-Easter Jesus) that connotes a strong, interior (or inward), spiritual sense of the risen One's presence, as compared to a word for "appeared" that would have indicated a physical or bodily presence.

The Catholic Christian community maintains its foundational belief in the resurrection of Jesus, recognizing that faith in the resurrection is at the very center of Christian doctrine, values, rituals, and practices. The church teaches that the crucified Jesus was raised from the dead and glorified, as the one messiah and Christ, by the Creator. By Jesus' mysterious resurrection all members of the human community have been raised to a new level of spiritual life and glory in him forever. The Catholic tradition offers the good news that Jesus proclaimed before his death and resurrection, and likewise offers the sacrament of baptism to all human beings, in order to call them to Christian conversion and to lasting belief in the resurrected Christ. The church teaches that Catholic Christians truly participate in the sacrifice, death, and resurrection of Jesus whenever and wherever the Eucharist is celebrated and whenever they look forward to his return in glory in the *parousia* to fully establish the everlasting reign of God.

Some significant passages in the New Testament that clearly mention the resurrection of Jesus include: Mark 16:1–8, 9–20; Matthew 28:1–28; Luke 24:1–53; John 20:1–29, 21:1–23; Acts 2:14–36, 3:12–26, 4:8–12, 5:29–32, 10:34–43; Romans 1:1–5, 8:34, 10:8–9; 1 Corinthians 12:3, 15:3–5; 1 Thessalonians 1:9–10; Philippians 2:6–11; Colossians 1:15–20; Ephesians 1:20–22; 1 Peter 1:18–22; Hebrew 1:3–4.

(See also Ascension, Christology, Easter, Exegesis, Faith, Jesus of Nazareth, Miracles, Parousia, and Reign of God.)

REVELATION   is God's free and loving self-communication, especially through Jesus of Nazareth but also in many other ways—through creation, through human history, through other human beings and cultures, and through God's own words and deeds directed toward the spiritual well-being and salvation of all of humanity. The word stems from the Latin *revelatio*, which means "unveiling" or an "uncovering."

The Catholic Christian community teaches that God is a good and loving Creator who has revealed Godself and has thus been offering or giving Godself to all people and all cultures and communities in many ways throughout human history. God is revealed through creation, through the words and actions of human beings, through various events in creation history, and through the entire people of God, the worldwide community of the baptized.

In the mid-1500s, the Council of Trent said that there are two sources of divine revelation: Scripture and tradition. Later, in the 1960s, another ecumenical council, Vatican II, clarified the Catholic notion of revelation by saying that there is but one divine Source of revelation (like one stream of life-giving water) with the Scriptures and church tradition forming two key avenues by which God's divine revelation can be proclaimed. Vatican II likewise taught that all baptized persons must become aware of the "signs of the times" in modern cultures and in modern human relationships to better understand how the Spirit of God continues to reach out to humanity and the world: through the ordinary experiences and witness of men and women, through great non-Catholic and non-Christian religions and spiritual traditions, and through all the events of contemporary times. Such signs of the times in our world must be perceived, interpreted, and eventually understood in terms of the hope-filled gospel message revealed by Jesus of Nazareth. In this sense, Christian revelation can be viewed as a dynamic and ongoing process as opposed to something totally finished and complete. In other words, the fullness of God's self-disclosure to the human community has been uncovered irrevocably or definitively to humankind in history, yet God continues to offer the gift of Godself and the path of salvation to all peoples, at all times and in all places, to this day. The Catholic community teaches today that revealed religious truths and values originate in God's loving goodness and divine wisdom.

Through his life, words, and deeds, Jesus of Nazareth—God's most complete and definitive revelation about hope and salvation for the entire human community—fulfilled and perfected God's self-communication in history. Catholic doctrine stresses that through Scripture and sacred tradition in particular, divine revelation is handed on to all generations of humanity, that God continues to dwell (God's reign is "at hand") among the people of God, and that God continues to invite all persons and communities to respond in faith to divine revelation.

The *Catechism of the Catholic Church* summarizes Catholic beliefs about divine revelation in articles 50–141. The Catechism indicates that human beings can know God with certainty through creation and through ways people cannot reach at all by natural human powers alone. Thus, through a completely free and loving decision, the Creator has revealed and given Godself to us by making known the mystery of salvation in

Jesus the Christ on behalf of everyone. In other words, the Catechism notes, God has fully revealed a wonderful saving plan for creation by sending God's own Son into the natural world and by sending God's own Spirit into human hearts (article 50).

(See also Bible, Deposit of Faith, Faith, Grace, and Tradition.)

ROSARY is a Catholic prayer devotion dedicated to the honor of Mary, the mother of Jesus of Nazareth, which centers on a ring of beads used to say decades (groups of 10) of the prayer called the Hail Mary. An Our Father opens each prayer-decade and the prayer known as the Glory Be is used to close each prayer-decade (see the Catholic Prayers section at the end of this book). The rosary can be prayed aloud or in silence, in private or in communal settings. In the United States the rosary is usually begun with the Apostles Creed, an Our Father, three Hail Mary prayers, and then one Glory Be. After five or more decades of Hail Marys have been said, a prayer called Hail Holy Queen is typically recited and is sometimes accompanied by the prayer of the feast of the Rosary. The term *rosary* has Latin roots that alternately imply a bed of roses, a garland of flowers, and a collection of nice quotations. It came to be used by Catholic communities as a variation on a traditional title for Mary, the "mystical rose" of God.

The Christian roots of the rosary lie in a daily prayer devotion of 150 Our Fathers, later 150 simpler Hail Marys, observed by some Christians in the early Middle Ages. The largely illiterate Christian population of the time used strings of beads to keep count of their 150 prayers. In more recent Christian history, the type of rosary most Catholic communities in the Western world have used is the Dominican rosary. Some traditional legendary material indicates that Saint Dominic (d. 1221) received this particular devotional rosary from an apparition of Mary, the Blessed Virgin. This Catholic story can be traced, according to some sources, to Alan de la Roche in the 15th century.

With the establishment of an official Catholic rosary confraternity, plus the establishment of numerous papal indulgences for praying the rosary, the rosary became a highly popular devotion in many places. By 1573 an official feast of the rosary was declared and made part of the annual Catholic liturgical cycle.

Some students of Christian tradition continue to question and examine the true Christian origins of the rosary as we know it today. For example, the claim that Dominic received his rosary directly through a mystical appearance of the Blessed Virgin has been much disputed. Some historical commentaries point out that the five-decade version of the rosary seems more like a modified (or simplified) version of the 150 Hail Marys prayer tradition from the Middle Ages.

Whatever its origins, those who choose to pray with the Catholic rosary beads see this devotion as an authentic meditative type of prayer and worship. Many popes have encouraged Catholics in local communities to pray the rosary. Pope Pius XI granted a full (or plenary) indulgence to all who pray the rosary in the presence of the Eucharist. Pius XII recommended that Catholics pray the rosary devoutly and often. October has annually been seen as a month of the holy rosary by the Catholic community since the 16th century. The feast of Our Lady of the Rosary was permanently placed on the church's liturgical calendar in 1716. This feast is still celebrated every year on October 7.

See page 267 for a list of the mysteries of the rosary.

(See also Devotion, Indulgences, Mary, Prayer, and Sacramentals.)

RUBRICS   is a word employed by the Catholic church to indicate the forms, directions, and particular instructions that guide the proper use of a church ritual. The term comes from the Latin *rubrica*, a red color used in ink. In ancient days, a rubric was a rule or instruction penned into a legal volume in red ink.

In 1570, the Roman Missal began with instructions for the proper conduct of the Mass. The newer Missal or Sacramentary prepared under the guidance of Paul VI, and published in 1969, also detailed the rubrics of the Catholic liturgy but also included reasons behind the ceremonial functions and gestures that it proposed.

Of course, the Mass is much more than a set of rules and ceremonial forms. Regarding rubrics as a whole, the church stresses that when any communal worship is celebrated, much more is required than just accurate fulfillment of laws. However, rules and directives on how to conduct various liturgical services are helpful. A traditional Catholic saying, in paraphrase, is "if you need to understand the black (the prayers in the Sacramentary), read the words in red (the rubrics of church worship)."

(See also Missal, Worship.)

S

SABBATH/SUNDAY   is a day of the week on which human labor is to be set aside in favor of rest, recreation, and worship of God. The Hebrew *shabbat* means essentially to "bring labor to an end" and "to rest." "Sunday" comes from the Germanic *sonntag*, a day for worship of the sun. The sabbath is observed by Jews and Christians worldwide in accord with the divine command, "Remember to keep the sabbath day holy" (Exodus 20:8).

Sabbath is rooted in an ancient Hebrew belief (dating from the 8th century b.c.e.) in a weekly period dedicated to joy, rest, and prayer (Genesis 2:1–3). The Jewish tradition of the sabbath sees it as a day for worship in an assembly at the synagogue, for feasting and fun with family members, and for release from strenuous physical efforts. The Jewish sabbath begins at Friday sunset and ends at Saturday nightfall.

The earliest Christian believers were Jews who observed the sabbath, the seventh day of the week, according to the Law of God. However they began to gather in various households after Saturday sunset, then eventually at Sunday dawn, before weekly work began, in order to pray, eat an agape meal, and celebrate "the breaking of the bread" (the Eucharist). They did so on Sunday because it was the weekly anniversary of Jesus (the Son of God) being raised from death to Easter life (see Acts 20:7–11). By the 2nd century, the weekly eucharistic ritual had been fully moved to Sunday morning and separated from agape suppers (see 1 Corinthians 11). Christian church members eventually saw Sunday as the key day for worship assemblies to share the word and the Eucharist. In time, Sunday liturgy for Catholics came to be known as the "Sunday obligation."

In our day, many recognize that each Sunday is like a Christian mini-Easter. The day came to be called Sun-day (in harmony with pagan, pre-Christian rituals) because the natural sun is life giving and forever full of light and energy. However, Christians called it Sunday also because it is the Lord's Day: Jesus is the light of revelation to humanity (John 8:12, 9:5) and a life-giving Son for all (John 1:9).

Today, many Catholic individuals and families observe the Sunday sabbath as a family and recreational time—a time for togetherness, worship, and common meals. Catholics still proclaim the value of sabbath worship and recreation. A current church law says keep holy the day of the Lord by participation in Mass on Sunday and by refraining from Sunday activities that hinder the renewal of one's body and soul. Catholics can attend Mass in accord with church tradition on Saturday evening (the Sunday vigil) or any time on Sunday.

(See also Agape; Church, as Home; Commandments of God; Eucharist; and Worship.)

SACRAMENTALS   are Christian objects, prayers, or blessings that are identified by the contemporary Catholic community as sacred to Christian spirituality and tradition in a unique way (sacred in the sense of the Latin term *sacrare*, "to be set apart" or consecrated for a special purpose). Catholic sacramentals include the Bible, holy water, Christian medals, the rosary, the sign of the cross, blessed palm, ashes (used on Ash Wednesday), the crucifix, chrism (oil for anointing), candles, holy pictures, statues and icons, the way of the cross, grace (prayer) before meals, and more.

Some of the things that today are known as sacramentals were called sacraments before the Catholic community formally defined that there are only seven sacraments in the Roman Catholic tradition: baptism, confirmation, Eucharist, penance, anointing, order, and matrimony. The notion that there would be only seven sacraments recognized by the Catholic community was formally prescribed by the Council of Trent in the 1540s; of course, Trent was building upon official teachings by the earlier councils of Lyons II in 1274 and Florence in 1439.

Christian sacramentals are sacred signs and symbols that help human individuals and communities to recognize that the risen Jesus is always present to the world through his gracious Spirit. In the 1960s, Vatican II noted that sacramentals bear a strong resemblance to the sacraments. In other words, the many sacramentals available to the baptized and to others signify spiritual effects and a Christian holiness that can be obtained through the intercession of the community of faith. The Catholic tradition teaches that through various sacramentals people can become more open to growth in Christian holiness and therefore in their ability to respond actively to God's gifts of love and life. The *Catechism of the Catholic Church* summarizes the traditional Catholic insights on sacramentals in articles 1667ff. It points out specifically that, through the liturgy of the sacraments and sacramentals, members of the Christian community are enabled to see that almost everything that happens in human life and creation is sanctified by God's grace and loving power (article 1670).

(See also Devotion, Grace, Sacrament, and Worship.)

SACRAMENTS   are sacred, visible signs of God's loving grace and presence to humanity. Sacraments manifest the faith of the Christian community on Earth. The Catholic tradition remembers and honors Jesus as the greatest sacrament of all time, the most loving and definitive sign of the relationship (or encounter) between the unseen God and the whole of humanity. Catholic tradition also maintains that the church community itself is a kind of universal sacrament of salvation for all peoples and cultures in the world. The word comes from two Latin words: *sacramentum*, "solemn obligation," and *sacrare*, "to set apart as holy and sacred." The Roman Catholic community holds that there are seven ritual sacraments: baptism, confirmation, Eucharist, reconciliation, matrimony, order, and anointing of the sick.

Since ancient times various peoples and cultures have used special rituals and religious symbols to signify their belief in something greater than human life and natural human powers. Jesus used prayer, natural symbols, and simple ceremonies to express his unique relationship with Abba, the Creator in heaven. The Christian community sees Jesus of Nazareth as the founder of the Christian church in the world and as the divine one who instituted various sacraments, signs of salvation in and through his gospel of hope. In the 4th century, Saint Augustine described sacrament as a "visible sign of invisible grace" in the revelation of Jesus. Later, in the 13th century, Saint Thomas Aquinas taught that a sacramental sign 1) expresses the Christian faith of those who receive it, 2) expresses true worship of the divine, 3) indicates the true unity and faith of the entire church body around the world, and 4) exists as an effective sign of God's revelation and ongoing presence in and through the Spirit of the risen Jesus.

Sometimes, as some observers note, people wrongly consider sacraments to be "magical" signs and actions that mysteriously cause grace within humanity. Sacramental signs, however, do not have any magical effects. Rather, sacraments are free gifts offered by a loving Creator to the human community. And in celebrating and receiving these sacramental gifts from a loving and present God Christians freely choose to accept God's self-communication (revelation) in and through Jesus the Christ and to respond to God in Christian faith.

The Roman Catholic community decided officially at the Council of Trent (1547) that there are seven sacraments. This doctrine was based upon previous teachings and clarifications of sacramental theology made by the Second Council of Lyons (1274) and the Council of Florence (1439). This implies, of course, that for well over 1000 years the church community functioned without a definition of the exact number of Christian sacraments. In fact, many sacred or "sacramental" rituals and symbols were used by local Christian communities in the early centuries of church life; many of these are now called Catholic Christian sacramentals.

The idea that sacraments are special, grace-filled encounters between God and humanity has received much emphasis recently. It has helped pave the way for many interesting and hopeful ecumenical dialogues about Christian sacramental theologies, between representatives of the Catholic community and other Christian congregations, such as Lutherans and Anglicans. Catholic thinking has reemphasized that in each sacramental action members of the believing community truly encounter the risen Jesus—the most perfect and definitive revelation of God—in an intimate way and are thus drawn into closer relationship with him. Catholic theologians have also stressed recently that in and through the sacraments the baptized are invited to celebrate their own faith stories and the faith story of Jesus' community.

Some theologians today discuss the effects of sacramental participation. They note that each sacramental celebration can help make church members more like Jesus of Nazareth, one who was always centered on doing God's will and sought tirelessly to bring the reign of God to fulfillment. Recent ecumenical reflections between Catholic and Protestant thinkers have brought to light anew that the Christian Scriptures (the New Testament) seem to clearly identify two sacraments—baptism and the Eucharist—whereas Catholic Christian tradition has long maintained a larger sacramental system (i.e., that confirmation, reconciliation, matrimony, holy orders, and anointing of the sick are also sacraments).

In the 1960s Vatican II taught that the purpose of the sacraments is to sanctify people, thus building up the body of Christ around the globe. Catholic communities view the seven sacraments as signs of faith-filled life in the risen Jesus which presuppose active response to one's baptism and which nourish, strengthen, and express maturing trust in the Creator.

The *Catechism of the Catholic Church* notes the importance of sacraments to the worldwide church community. It says that, in this age of the Christian church, Jesus Christ lives and acts through the sacraments, in what the common faith tradition calls "the sacramental economy" (article 1076). Put another way, Catholic Christians believe that Jesus instituted the seven sacraments and continues to reach out to humanity through them. They are sacred signs, symbols, and rituals for Catholic communities that "touch all the stages and all the important moments of Christian life" and resemble those of natural life; it is necessary, therefore, to view the sacramental system as an organic whole (not just as a collection of separate rituals) in which each sacramental sign has a vital place in Christian existence (article 1210).

(See also Baptism, Eucharist, Faith, Grace, Holiness, Revelation, and Worship.)

SACRISTY   is a practical and simple room in a church building wherein vestments and other items used in Catholic worship (e.g., chalices, candles, ciboria, eucharistic hosts and wine, cruets, monstrances, incense, etc.) are kept. Those involved as ministers in Catholic eucharistic celebrations (the Mass) and other worship services often vest in the sacristy area. The word derives from two Latin terms—*sacristia* and *sacrum*—both of which basically mean "sacred" or "holy."

SAINTS, COMMUNION OF   is the community or family of the entire people of God. This communion or family of saints includes all those enjoying the marvelous presence of God in heaven, the members of God's people being prepared in purgatory for the fullness of happiness in the presence of the Creator, and those faithful to God on Earth. "Saint" is a derivation of the Latin word *sanctus*. Essentially it refers to one who is "consecrated," a truly holy or godly person. Many early followers of the risen Jesus of Nazareth (Saint Paul is one example) referred to other believers as saints, but eventually the words saint and saints were typically and somewhat inaccurately applied only to those who had passed over in death into the spiritual condition of complete salvation and joy with Jesus in heaven.

The phrase "communion of saints" is very ancient, dating back to primitive Christian communities. It signifies the deep relationship in Jesus, the Son of God and the Christ, and the deep hope and salvation shared by all of God's people. Later it came to signify the relationship shared by all those who remained faithful to God in life on Earth and in the spiritual life beyond Earth, in purgatory and in heaven. These three groups have been called at times, in Catholic terminology, the church militant, the church suffering, and the church triumphant. The Catholic tradition teaches that saints in heaven can intercede (pray and advocate to God the Creator) on behalf of those on Earth. Thus many Catholic Christians have learned to pray to saints in heaven for spiritual help. Catholic tradition has equally held that the members of the communion of saints on Earth can assist those experiencing purgatory through prayer, fasting, almsgiving, and other good works.

Vatican II stated that the Christian worship of the baptized is enriched by their participation in the communion of saints. Recent Catholic thinking on the "communion of saints" has reemphasized that the "communion" is a true union (a dynamic relationship) between all members of the people of God, the living and the dead.

The communion of saints is remembered and celebrated in every celebration of the Eucharist. The church honors and venerates Mary, the mother of Jesus of Nazareth, and the many other saints because they are truly authentic Christian witnesses, models who have walked the path of Christian life and grace to the fullest and who can be emulated. However, Catholics are usually quick to point out they do not worship the saints in any way.

(See also Canonization, Heaven, Martyr, Purgatory, Reign of God, Veneration, and Witness.)

Note of Interest: The *Catechism of the Catholic Church* discusses the traditions and beliefs regarding the communion of saints in articles 946–962. In particular the Catechism points out in article 957 that Catholic Christian tradition cultivates the memory of the saints in heaven not only to benefit from their example, but still more so that through them the union of the whole church in the Spirit may be strengthened. For just as Christian communion among our fellow pilgrims brings us closer to Christ, so our communion with the saints in heaven joins us to Jesus Christ, the source and the head of God's family from whom all life and grace flow.

SALVATION   implies a permanent union with God and union with all others who are united in loving relationship with their Creator. The salvation of the entire human community for all time, in all places and cultures, was the goal of the redeeming work of Jesus of Nazareth.

Christians believe that salvation is truly a gift from God, freely offered and meant to be freely accepted by all human individuals and communities. Therefore no human being can earn or gain eternal salvation in God on his or her own. The word comes from the Latin term *salus*, which means "health." The church stresses that one should strive for personal salvation (unending personal or individual union with God in heaven in the future) after death, but one also should seek salvation for all of humanity through love of God and neighbor and Christian service/stewardship for the global community of humankind. This ultimate or full salvation of creation has often been referred to as the perfected kingdom of God, or the "reign of God," which will be characterized by an end to human sinfulness and the life of joy and fulfillment for the whole world for which Christians pray.

(See also Grace, Heaven, Jesus of Nazareth, Parousia, Redemption, and Reign of God.)

Note of Interest: Catholics and other Christian communities sometimes speak about a "salvation history." Salvation history can be defined as the story of God's saving efforts to lead humanity toward the perfected reign of God and thus toward eternal salvation—happiness, peace, and justice in God's true presence. From a Catholic perspective, salvation history includes all of creation since the beginning of time, the events of the Hebrew Scriptures era, the incarnation through Jesus of Nazareth (God's greatest and most definitive revelation), the history and evangelizing mission of the Christian community, and the *parousia* to come.

SANCTUARY   is the area in Catholic church buildings wherein the main altar is placed. In the sanctuary priests and bishops preside over Christian assemblies in various forms of prayer and worship, especially at celebrations of the Eucharist (the Mass). The Word of God is also usually proclaimed from the sanctuary, from a book called the Lectionary, by lay ministers in the Christian congregation called readers or lectors. The word has roots in the Latin *sanctuarium*, a holy place or a shrine. For a long time the sanctuary was clearly divided from the rest of the church worship space by being elevated in some way or by a line of demarcation such as a traditional communion railing. In general accord with the renewal of the Christian liturgy since the time of Vatican II (1960s), the sanctuary area and the main altar of the church have often been situated more to the center (the midst) of the worshiping community, rather than to one end of the church building's interior.

(See also Altar, Lectionary, Presbyters, Sacristy, Shrine, and Vestibule.)

SCANDAL   is some form of behavior—words, deeds, or attitudes—which leads persons toward immorality, wrongdoing, or sinfulness. The word *scandal* has Greek origins that combine to imply a downfall, to "stumble against," and a snare.

Scandal is referred to at times in the Bible. The gospel of Luke indicates that Jesus spoke strongly against scandalous behavior (17:1–2). In church tradition, a direct form of scandal has been considered a deliberate choice to cause others to do wrong. An indirect form of scandal has been seen as anything that urges others toward sinful behavior in a non-deliberate way.

Catholics understand that each baptized person is called to act as a witness to gospel values and lifestyle at all times. Therefore, all forms of scandal are seriously wrong. One who acts scandalously, and thus tempts others to sin through his or her words and deeds, should try to make sincere amends for the bad example, undo all wrongs if possible, and change his or her lifestyle in some demonstrable way. Christian tradition maintains that any baptized individual rightly accused of serious public scandal ought to publicly speak against his or her wrongdoing, then show signs that he or she will convert to a genuine Christian lifestyle.

(See also Morality, Sin, and Witness.)

SEXISM is a form of prejudice by which someone believes that certain human beings are either inferior or superior to others on the basis of their sex. In itself, prejudice (from the Latin roots for "pre-judgment") is expressed in biased opinions, attitudes, or choices without proper reflection on the facts necessary for a fair, unselfish determination. Thus sexism is an unreasonable outlook on or objection to a person because she is female or he is male. Sexism—along with other "isms" like racism, ageism, legalism, or nationalism—can lead to unfair discriminations against individuals, groups, and cultural communities.

The church teaches that every vestige of sexism, racism, or religious discrimination must be vigorously opposed. Christians believe that treating someone or some group unfairly or oppressively is wrong because it fails to properly show the respect and dignity due all persons created by the one good God and seeks likewise to deny them their natural rights. It is directly counter to Christian charity and justice. In 1965, Vatican II stated that "any discrimination against people or any harassment of them on [any] basis" is "foreign to the mind of Christ..." (see *Nostra aetate*).

Recent discussions regarding sexism have often focused on sexist male attitudes toward women. In certain cases, however, sexist behavior can be also directed toward men. Many have criticized denigrating and sexist practices in the mainstream culture such as unfair and unequal pay scales for men and women, non-promotion in one's career because of one's sex, and poor work policies concerning maternal and paternal leave.

During recent decades there has been much energy spent by many to especially help women assume more equal and more involved roles in church life as a whole. Some critics strongly speak against a modern church community (with many male leaders) that displays signs of treating women as inferior.

Catholics believe that segregations or mindsets that cause one to feel superior to others are seriously wrong, counter to Christian love and justice, and in need of immediate transformation in our society. "Every type of discrimination," according to Vatican II, "whether social or cultural...is to be overcome and eradicated as contrary" to the Creator's dream of the just and peaceful reign of God. In the eyes of the Creator "...there is neither male nor female, for all are one in Christ Jesus" (Galatians 3:28).

(See also Anti-Semitism, Charity, and Social Justice.)

SHRINE   is a sacred site (a spot set aside) for prayer and religious devotions. Both simple and ornate Catholic shrines are usually displays of various objects (e.g., pictures, icons, crosses, statues, and other items) that inspire spiritual responses, honor Mary and the saints, or recall a great belief or event in Christian history. The term comes from Latin (*scrinium*) and Anglo-Saxon (*scrin*). It means "box" or "chest" (as in *coffer*).

The ancient roots of Christian shrines lie in the Ark of the Covenant described in the Hebrew Scriptures. In Christian history, the term has often been used broadly to indicate a place to which Christian pilgrims journey (e.g., Fatima in Portugal, Guadalupe in Mexico, and St. Anne de Beaupré in Quebec, Canada). However, more simple, local shrines have often been built in homes, in forests or other outdoor sites, in schools, and in local churches for personal and family-style devotions. The church in the past has sometimes spoken of the "crowned shrine." This is an ornate shrine approved by the Holy See as a proper place for pilgrimages and publicly-held Catholic worship, and it is often a site of a reported divine apparition or a miracle. The actual shrines named above are examples of such shrines. Recently, John Paul II prayed at the shrine of Our Lady of Coromoto, in Caracas, the patroness of all of Venezuela.

Shrines can be places at which Catholics experience deep, spiritual feelings and intense prayer. In the case of official church shrines 1) some are associated with holy relics (e.g., the Cathedral of Turin, Italy, which reportedly holds the shroud (or burial cloth) of Jesus of Nazareth; 2) some are dedicated to Mary, the Mother of God (e.g., Our Lady of Lourdes, in France); 3) many focus on the saints (e.g., the tombs of St. Peter and St. Paul in Rome and the Italian shrine of St. Nicholas of Myra, the Christian model of our cultural Santa Claus beliefs); and 4) some center on Catholic beliefs and traditions (e.g., the Shrine of the Immaculate Conception, in Washington, D.C.).

(See also Devotion, Pilgrimage, Saints, Sanctuary, and Veneration.)

SIN   is a conscious turning away from God's loving offer of friendship/relationship, which leads to a weakening or total breakdown of one's relationship with God and with others. Within the biblical perspective, sinfulness means to miss the mark. Thus through personal sin a man or woman fails to respond properly to God's offer of love and lasting friendship.

Although it is not known exactly how sin became part of the human condition, the story of Adam and Eve in the book of Genesis explains that human beings freely chose sinfulness and that God is not responsible for it. The Hebrew Scriptures thus describe sin as the failure to live by the covenant-love relationship established between Yahweh and the chosen people.

In the Christian Scriptures the gospels indicate that human sin is a real threat to humanity's physical and spiritual well-being and that Jesus of Nazareth, the promised messiah sent by the Creator to the whole human community, has overcome human sinfulness once and for all through his life, death, and resurrection. Other writings in the Christian Scriptures, for example the writings attributed to Saint Paul, emphasize that those who have faith in the resurrected Jesus can die to sin through his life, death, and promise of hope to humanity.

The Christian community has spoken at times, over the centuries, of two basic kinds of sin after baptism—mortal sin and venial sin—which can be forgiven in the sacrament of reconciliation. Mortal sin, the more grievous of the two, involves full consent of the will, sufficient reflection, and serious matter. The sin of Adam, the effects of which all men and women in the human race suffer, has frequently been identified as original sin. Sin has often been seen as a transgression (a breaking) of the laws of God. More recently, however, some theologians have begun to re-image sinfulness as a kind of alienation or estrangement from God or as a weakening of or complete turning away from a personal relationship with the Creator. Some theologians today maintain that sin is essentially a failure to respond to God's great love. In such reflection on sin and God's grace, emphasis is usually placed on the interior, spiritual attitudes and motives of the person who has sinned, not so much on the gravity of the actual deeds committed or the rules or laws broken.

Contemporary Catholic thought often notes that all sin ultimately is rooted in personal choices. In all, however, sin can be either personal or social in its effects. Thus personal sin is something freely chosen and done by accountable and free persons, while social sin is an evil that somehow creeps into entire organizations, structures, communities, or societies as a result of human choices, actions, inactions, and attitudes, doing harm to individuals as well as whole communities.

The church sees human sin as both a reality and a mystery—no definition or phrase fully sums up or expresses just what sin really is. Catholic pastoral leaders and teachers alike maintain that the Christian way of life should be characterized by ongoing conversion away from sinfulness and self-centeredness and toward acceptance (through the gospel of hope in Jesus of Nazareth) of God's loving offer of friendship.

The Catholic community today actively seeks to help men and women live as maturing, loving people of God who turn away from sinfulness and evil in every way. It teaches humanity that sinfulness must be viewed within the perspective of a person's entire lifestyle, choices, personal changes, and conversions. Above all, it teaches that God is merciful and that God loves sinners, always ready to forgive mercifully if someone is truly sorry.

The *Catechism of the Catholic Church* focuses on the Catholic tradition on sin and God's mercy in articles 1846–1876. It stresses that in the human community sin creates an attachment to sin: It tends to reproduce and reinforce itself. And so sin is an offense against natural reasoning powers, against truth, and against right conscience. Sin is a failure of authentic love for both God and neighbor caused by a disordered attachment to the things of this world. Sinfulness, the Catechism adds, wounds human nature and injures human solidarity, and, in fact, may be defined as an act, a word, or a desire "contrary to the eternal law" (article 1849).

(See also Actual Sin, Covenant, Original Sin, and Reconciliation.)

SMALL FAITH COMMUNITIES   are base communities of Christians who gather together on a regular basis for shared prayer, Scripture reflection, active participation in worship rituals, catechesis, and active discussion on human and social problems in need of Christian action.

The practice of Christians gathering together for spiritual growth and mutual support dates back to the days of the original followers of Jesus of Nazareth. The Bible implies that they had become community with Jesus. Once he had been raised from the dead and had sent the gift of the Spirit to them, they gathered with others who believed in Jesus' message in order to share their faith, pray together, break bread together (in the Eucharist and in agape meals), and support one another in their dynamic mission to reach out with the good news of the cross and resurrection to all peoples and cultures. As the Christian way became rooted in many places, and in many small groups founded by Jesus' disciples, Christianity became a network of these communities. In other words, it became an overall, multinational community of small communities. In recent decades, people around the globe have sought a similar lively, involving experience of basic Christian community.

Small faith communities have been forming among the baptized throughout the United States in recent years. Inspired by the *communidades de base*, which have sprung up in Latin America, Asia, Africa, and other locales, they have often been seen as attractive, personal alternatives—in which real spiritual bonding and gospel inspiration can be experienced—to the larger, more impersonal model of church that can often be found in large-scale, large-population parishes.

Many believe that small faith communities respond to spiritual hungers that individuals and families often experience today, e.g., a hunger for meaningful relationships, for meaningful worship, and for active Christian service. Thus basic Christian communities tend to be composed of persons who deeply value close personal relationships, the felt experience of gospel-based community, the opportunity to minister to others, and the faith-sharing that springs from deep, communal experiences of prayer and the sacraments. Some pastoral leaders are actively encouraging pastoral teams in some of today's parishes to consider re-visioning their overall communities into a neighborhood-based network of communities—a "community of small Christian communities"—to better meet the spiritual needs of the broad Catholic population.

Small faith communities, therefore, are grass-roots level gatherings of church members, in communion with the larger Catholic body, motivated by the desire to share Christian faith and witness and usually interested in working in their larger neighborhood/civic communities for Christian transformation of society. The formation of small communities is often inspired by real dissatisfactions among church members with large, impersonal models of parish life, a shortage of ordained ministers, and the isolation they sometimes encounter in contemporary urban, suburban, and rural settings.

In 1975, Paul VI said in *Evangelii nuntiandi* that the name small ecclesial communities could only be given to those basic communities that develop in unity with the church overall, "having solidarity" with it and nourished by its leaders and authentic traditions. He added that small communities can be places of genuine evangelization for the benefit of bigger parishes and "a hope for the universal Church." In 1990, in *Redemptoris missio*, Pope John Paul II spoke of such communities as "a force for evangelization" and a "a solid starting point for a new society based on a civilization of love."

(See also Agape; Church, as Home; Community; Evangelization; and Parish.)

SOCIAL JUSTICE   is basic respect for human beings coupled with concern for and action on behalf of human rights. Pope John XXIII declared in 1961 that human beings are the cause, foundation, and reason why all social institutions exist. The Catholic community therefore affirms and defends the ultimate dignity and rights of every human person. "Justice" stems from the Latin *justitia*— whatever is "rightful" or "lawful." In effect, Christian social justice means the total ongoing Christian mission to proclaim and live the gospel command to love God, neighbor, and all of God's great creation.

Catholic Christian tradition on social justice has been evolving in recent decades. Tradition maintains that true Christian social justice is an active effort to reform and re-shape human societies, governments, institutions, and structures that deny the basic rights of human beings. Christian social justice doctrine stems from the words and deeds of the Hebrew prophets but especially from the prophetic life, ministry, and death and resurrection of Jesus of Nazareth.

Contemporary Catholic social doctrine has made great strides since the late 19th century, particularly since the time of Pope Leo XIII. Since then, a number of important Christian social teachings, encyclicals, and synod statements have been developed and handed on to the human community by church leaders. In our time the Catholic church has taught that the drive for justice in the world is at the very center of the Christian evangelizing mission and a gospel-centered existence.

The cause of Christian social justice seeks to make the world more generally aware of how humanity can best be served by its many products, processes, and progressive achievements. The Catholic encyclicals that have dealt with social justice themes in recent decades include: *Rerum novarum* (1891), *Quadragesimo anno* (1931), *Mater et magistra* (1961), *Pacem in terris* (1963), *Populorum progressio* (1967), *Redemptor hominis* (1979), *Laborem exercens* (1981), *Sollicitudo rei socialis* (1987), and *Redemptoris missio* (1990). Vatican Council II's landmark document, Pastoral Constitution on the Church in the Modern World (*Gaudium et spes*), spoke in the 1960s of the need for social justice. John Paul II has repeatedly said in recent years that all people of God must seek basic human rights and an end to oppression because this is fundamental to the Christian duty of evangelization.

Essential Catholic notions regarding social justice, respect for human beings, equality among human individuals, differences among human beings, Christian stewardship of God's creation, and human solidarity in God's grace and the risen Jesus are explored in the *Catechism of the Catholic Church*, articles 1928–1948. The Catechism points out that the community of the baptized, and society as a whole, safeguard social justice by fulfilling the conditions that permit people to obtain what is due to each, according to the common good of humanity and the proper exercise of authority.

(See also Charity, Evangelization, Morality, Prophet, Stewardship, and Works of Mercy.)

SPECIAL MINISTERS OF THE EUCHARIST   also called extraordinary ministers of the Eucharist are non-ordained persons who receive special permission to distribute the Eucharist to others because there are not enough priests and deacons to perform this ministry in a local community. Special ministers may be female or male, laypersons or members of religious communities.

In 1966, the church began to allow local Catholic leaders to use the services of special ministers of the Eucharist. By 1971, the U.S. bishops had begun to commission these extraordinary ministers. In March, 1973, with the publication by Paul VI of the document *Immensae caritatis*, the Vatican authorized guidelines for the selection and approval of lay women and lay men as special ministers of the Eucharist.

Special ministers are usually appointed by the pastor or parochial vicar of a parish with the approval of the local bishop. In February 1988, the U.S. bishops noted that "when ordinary ministers (bishops, priests, deacons) are present during a eucharistic celebration, whether they are participating in it or not...they are to assist in the distribution of communion. Accordingly, if the ordinary ministers are in sufficient number, special ministers of the Eucharist are not allowed to distribute communion at that celebration." The Code of Canon Law says that the special minister of the Eucharist should be an acolyte or other member of the Christian faithful who, when the necessity of the church warrants it, can be commissioned to serve in certain ministries, e.g., exercise the ministry of the Word, preside over liturgical prayer, and "distribute holy communion in accord with the prescriptions of law." Canons 230 and 910 detail church guidelines regarding special ministers of the Eucharist.

(See Eucharist, Lay Ministries.)

STEWARDSHIP   is based on the social justice concept that Earth and the totality of material creation belong to God (Psalm 24:1). God has given human beings all that they have; it is all to be cared for ("held in trust") and shared with others—with other human beings alive today and all those in generations to come. The Old English word *styward* —a "keeper," guard, or watchperson—gives us the origins of today's term "stewardship."

The Christian concept of stewardship is rooted in the notions that God is good, that all God has created is good (Genesis 1:31), and that Christian charity is something to be lived in the spirit of the Beatitudes (Matthew 5:3–10) and the traditional works of mercy (Matthew 25:31–46). Since divine love has created all that is, all human beings, especially followers of Jesus, must be responsible, sharing stewards of all the Creator has made (Genesis 1:28). The very early Christian community recognized that the mission to spread the gospel included self-sacrifice, compassion, and sharing one's material abundance (1 John 3:17–18).

Some people today believe that church leaders and pastoral ministers should not critique current socio-economic conditions in the U.S. and the world because they are not economists or sociologists. Recent Catholic thinking, however, has underscored that the Christian moral command "Love your neighbor" demands commitment by every baptized person to the common good of all humanity and the whole globe. Every economic decision and each business and government must be aimed at uplifting the dignity and value of the human being and basic human rights—for example, the right to life, adequate shelter, nutrition, medical care, employment, and education. Catholics in particular were challenged to reflect on such matters by the U.S. bishops' 1987 pastoral statement "Economic Justice for All."

Vatican II, Paul VI, and John Paul II have all commented prophetically on the increasing gaps between the "haves" and "have nots" among the nations of the world. In 1988, John Paul II stressed that human and social development are other words for peace. Christian solidarity with Earth (and the one human community) means "the goods of creation are meant for all" and must be distributed in fairness to the world's needy peoples.

Catholics perceive stewardship as a set of moral imperatives and justice-related tasks. The church calls for gospel-inspired personal and structural transformations worldwide to overcome the ill effects of modern individualisms, materialism, and selfish, wasteful consumerisms.

Because there is one good Creator and one human family in God, Catholic doctrine today says that all property and the world's environment have a Christian "social mortgage." All people deserve respect and must have a share in all worldly resources because human beings (the center of creation) must be co-creators to continue the development of God's world. In 1991, John Paul II taught that the ultimate goal of all stewardship is to help peoples seek God and live in accord with the Creator.

(See also Beatitudes, Charity, Morality, Social Justice, and Works of Mercy.)

STIPEND is a free-will contribution to the support of a church official or the church community in general. More specifically, in Catholic tradition, a stipend has been a small donation of money given to a pastor or parochial vicar so a Mass will be dedicated to the cause(s) or intention(s) named by the contributor. "Stipend" comes from Latin origins that indicate a small pay-out or financial tribute for services rendered.

Both pagan and Israelite priests sometimes were given fees and other goods for their services (e.g., see Leviticus 5:13, 6:8–10). Among the earliest Christians, some of the bread and wine and material goods for needy persons donated at the offertory in local Eucharist celebrations were dedicated to the daily support of church presbyters. By the 500s, so-called "private masses" for particular individuals' intentions were occurring. By the 11th century, private masses coupled with small financial stipends for certain intentions had become common. Over time these Mass intentions usually dealt with hope for the spiritual well-being of someone who had died, hope for good health, thanksgiving to God, and special private (unnamed) causes.

The church stresses that the practice of stipending church services should be absolutely abuse- and scandal-free. Church law cautions that all Catholic stipend customs should be handled with great care and regulation. There should be no hint, for example, that one is buying a Mass or buying God's favor. Each presbyter has a serious obligation to render the spiritual services requested. The Christian community, in fact, has a duty to serve the needs and requests of all persons regardless of their economic or social status. The Catholic community in general believes that money freely donated should go into general parish funds to support the church community rather than into the personal accounts of the ordained.

Some today question the purpose of mass stipends overall. Instead, their local faith communities tend to maintain a book of prayer needs/intentions in which anyone can request spiritual help for just causes. In 1991, Pope John Paul II declared that 1) only one stipend offering can be assigned to any Mass, 2) priests must celebrate a Eucharist that focuses on the donor's true intention, 3) the priest who accepts a stipend should soon celebrate and preside at the Mass, or personally see that another priest will do so soon, and 4) local presbyters may combine very similar intentions by separate donors, but only when the permission to do so is granted by the actual contributors. The Code of Canon Law details church regulations on stipends in canons 945–958.

(See also Offertory, Presbyter, and Scandal.)

SUICIDE   is the intentional taking of one's own life. The term has two Latin roots, *sui* and *cidium* which mean "self-killing" or "to kill oneself." The Catholic community has long held that willful suicide is a violation of the fifth commandment of God ("You shall not kill") because only the Creator can decide how long a person should live. The Christian community has traditionally condemned suicide. Today, however, it recognizes that suicide is often the direct or indirect result of depression, desperation, or despair. Also, the church honors and upholds the idea that a human being may sacrifice his or her life for a good cause, as did Jesus of Nazareth—as in "laying down one's life for another" (John 15:13)—and thus not be guilty of personal suicide, even though the choice directly leads to one's death.

Suicide affects many different age groups in North America— especially adolescents and the elderly, people from many different social and economic backgrounds, and in fact many human cultures around the globe. Many note that numerous suicides and suicide attempts could be prevented through proper psychological care and other medical and supportive treatments for the suicidal person. Christian pastoral ministers and counselors say that many experiences and conditions lead individuals, and sometimes whole groups or communities, toward suicide. For example, these include: long-standing personal or family problems that seem overwhelming, family changes or stresses, changes or breakups in relationships, the death of another, major life failures, anxieties, depression, life and career crises, drug and alcohol dependency, old age, and terminal illnesses.

In recent years, there has been some reflection and debate in Christian circles on the notion of "physician-assisted suicide"—i.e., a doctor is present with a terminally ill, physically suffering patient in order to help him or her die (in a process called euthanasia). While not endorsed in any way by the Roman Catholic community (the *Catechism of the Catholic Church* refers to such things as contrary to the moral law, in article 2282), "physician-assisted suicide" and other issues related to the contemporary experience of human suffering/pain, illness, death, and suicide are being reflected on and discussed deeply and carefully by Christian moral theologians, pastoral counselors, pastoral ministers, members of the medical field, and others. The Catholic community recognizes that suicide causes tremendous suffering in modern families and that it weakens the entire human, social community within which the victim lived. Repeated, serious failure to care for one's own health and/ or one's psychological and spiritual well-being in general can be considered suicidal when taken to the extreme.

In May 1980, Pope John Paul II taught that no one may dispose of human life at will since life is a precious gift from God. John Paul noted that intentionally causing one's own death is as wrong as murder. It is in effect a human choice that adds up to a rejection of God's divine plan for the individual and for humanity as a whole.

A balanced Catholic perspective on suicide identifies suicidal actions and choices as failures to love one's self and God and as a denial of the instinct to live, yet it likewise calls all the people of God to a pastoral stance, that is, to an understanding that at times psychological and other factors can hinder or totally remove one's personal responsibility for the suicidal choice. The *Catechism of the Catholic Church* speaks of suicide in its reflections on the fifth commandment and on respect for human life, articles 2280–2283. The text of the Catechism maintains the each person is responsible for his or her life before the Creator of all life and that suicide contradicts the natural human inclination to preserve and perpetuate human life, something fundamentally contrary to love for the living God. The text also offers consolation and insight to some regarding human suicide by noting that the Catholic community today should not despair about the salvation of those who have killed themselves. In ways known only to God, God can provide opportunities for saving repentance. Thus the people of God today are urged to pray for all who have taken their own lives and to have hope for them (article 2283).

Pope John Paul II has upheld the traditional Christian belief that the baptized must distinguish between suicide and sacrificing one's life for another. The many reasons for which a Christian may sacrifice himself or herself (i.e., give up his or her life through death for someone else) include: 1) to express charitable service of one's fellow human beings, 2) to give glory to God the Creator of all life and goodness, and 3) for the eternal salvation of other individuals and communities.

(See also Commandments of God, Death/Dying, Euthanasia, Martyr, and Morality.)

SYNOD OF BISHOPS   is a meeting of some Catholic bishops—with representatives attending from around the globe—regularly convened by the pope to discuss important, contemporary issues in Christian life and ministry. The essential role of the synod of bishops is to advise the pope about how best to handle the important Christian matters being considered at individual synodal gatherings. The term comes from the Latin *synodus*, which means "a general meeting." Larger-in-scope and more critical gatherings of church leaders have been called councils (or ecumenical councils, such as Vatican II: the Second Vatican Council) whereas smaller, more limited-in-scope meetings of bishops have typically been known as synods.

Synodal-style meetings have been held by the baptized since at least the 2nd century. By the 3rd century such gatherings were being held in many parts of the Christian world. The general Council of Nicaea (325) set down rules and guidelines for synod meetings. In the 16th century the general Council of Trent came up with additional rules that required regular, even yearly synodal sessions in the Catholic community. Quite recently, on September 15, 1965, Pope Paul VI permanently established the current synod of bishops for the universal church through his document (a *motu proprio*) called *Apostolica sollicitudo*. Vatican Council II declared that it is vitally important for bishops to work together in a collegial way in order to guide and teach the people of God. Church leaders at Vatican II in the 1960s noted that Catholic bishops today have a particular, continuing, and serious duty to discuss and act upon the many pressing problems and spiritual issues affecting the lives of Catholic communities and other cultures in our time.

The pope, the bishop of Rome, is the official president of the synod of bishops. Thus all meetings of the synod are held under the pope's authority. Those in attendance at synodal gatherings are simply asked to advise the church community's overall leadership on important issues by providing information, opinions, and research that will help the pope in particular to effectively lead and serve the global Catholic community. Catholics are urged to reflect upon and accept the various teachings issued by the Catholic leadership once it has received the research, suggestions, and basic guidance provided by synod meetings.

Church laws pertaining to the administration of such synods, based upon the *motu proprio* by Paul VI, can be found in the current Code of Canon Law, canons 342–348. For example, church rules now require the pope to convene general meetings of the synod every three years. The following list gives the dates and topics of the 11 synods of bishops since 1967: 1) 1967—Strengthening of the Catholic Faith; 2) 1969—Bishop-Pope Relationships; 3) 1971—Priesthood and Justice; 4) 1974—Evangelization; 5) 1977—Catechetics; 6) 1980—Family Life; 7) 1983—Reconciliation; 8) 1985—Review of Vatican II; 9) 1987—Vocation and Mission of the Laity; 10) 1990—Formation of Presbyters; and 11) 1994—Religious Orders: The Consecrated Life and its Role in the World.

(See also Bishop, Collegiality, Diocese, Encyclical, Magisterium, and Pope.)

Note of Interest: Another type of synod is the diocesan synod, a meeting of selected clergy, religious, and laypersons called by the local bishop of a Catholic diocese. During diocesan synods participants consider the needs of their local church community and advise their bishop on ways to best meet these needs. The bishop is then free to act or not to act on the local synod's suggestions. Church law states that each diocese should have such a synod meeting every ten years.

SYNOPTICS   is a term commonly used to describe the gospels of Mark, Matthew, and Luke. These gospels are called synoptic because when the texts are laid side by side and "seen together," it becomes evident that they include and report many of the same sayings and events in the life and work of Jesus of Nazareth. The term has roots in the Greek *synoptikos*, meaning "to see the whole together" or through one eye.

Although not all biblical scholars agree, it is commonly accepted that the gospel of Mark was composed first, about 65–70 c.e., in or around the city of Rome, traditionally thought to be the Christian home community of the apostle Peter. The gospels known as Matthew and Luke were then composed later in the 1st century, with the direct assistance of two resources: the gospel of Mark and a document commonly referred to as Q for *quelle*, a source (perhaps a number of brief written resources) about the Jesus story and tradition.

(See also Exegesis, Gospel, Luke, Mark, Matthew, and New Testament.)

T

TABERNACLE   is a container found in a Catholic church building in which the consecrated Eucharist is reserved. The Eucharist is reserved so that it can be brought to the sick and the dying. By reserving the sacrament in tabernacles members of local faith communities also acknowledge and honor the continuing presence of Jesus Christ; some even make private, devotional visits to their church in order to pray to the Lord near the tabernacle.

"Tabernacle" comes from the Latin *tabernaculum*, referring to "a tent" or "a hut." The tabernacle was used by the ancient Hebrew community to symbolize the holy yet invisible presence of Yahweh (God) in their midst. (See, for example, Exodus 25–27.)

Tabernacles were not used in early Christian communities. After the liturgical ritual known as "breaking of the bread" (which evolved into the celebration of the Eucharist known as the Mass), leftover consecrated eucharistic bread was taken to private households so that Christian families could consume it during the week and share it with family members who were too ill to come to the eucharistic gathering. In later times, the ornate container (the tabernacle) in which the blessed sacrament was reserved in Christian church buildings was usually placed near or (later) on the main altar. In some instances, the tabernacle was hung above the main altar.

Catholic tabernacles can be round, rectangular, or square and are made of fireproof and burglar proof materials. Tabernacles are often decorated today with precious metals, stylish woods, jewels, and beautiful types of stone. Today in new church buildings and in renovations of existing buildings, the eucharistic tabernacle is often prominently placed in a chapel (i.e., away from the main altar and sanctuary) suitable for prayer and devotions for individuals and small gatherings.

Local Catholic communities are encouraged to make it clear that all church members can make devotional visits to pray to the Lord in a private, personal way. A Catholic custom calls for candles to burn at all times near tabernacles in which the blessed Eucharist is reserved; the flame on the candle is symbolic of the presence of the risen Jesus.

(See also Agape, Altar, Candles, Devotion, Eucharist, and Sanctuary.)

THEOLOGY   is a conscious attempt to bring thoughtful and insightful expression to the human search for faith in the Creator. For centuries theology has been defined in the Christian community (in Saint Anselm's words) as "faith seeking understanding." The living and personal trust in God to which human beings give free assent is interpreted and explained through theology. The term stems from the Latin *theologia*, that is, "knowledge of God."

Christian theology originated with the first disciples of Jesus of Nazareth; their personal faith testimonies, their life witness and catechetical reflections were seen in time as faith-filled expressions of hope in the risen One. Later, in the 5th century, Saint Augustine, a revered Father and Doctor of the Church, saw theology as a form of reasoning or a type of rational discourse about God and human faith. Saint Thomas Aquinas, in the 13th century, expressed the idea that theology was a study of the content of Christian faith that helps the baptized understand God's revelation. Theology was eventually defined by Christian leaders as the rational study of the content of divinely revealed truths, especially the specific doctrines, teachings, values, and practices of the Christian community as a whole.

Many thinkers today believe that human faith emerges from the experience of God and from a human "yes" to the Creator in the midst of everyday human life. Therefore deep human faith is also imaged as a firm conviction that results in a free, loving, and wholehearted response to the divine. Theology, therefore, follows upon personal and communal faith experiences. It is a form of pastoral, practical reflection and an earnest attempt to bring to limited expression a human being's own personal insights about and appreciation for the God who reveals Godself to humanity. It is possible, therefore, to say that genuine theological expressions can be crafted in many ways: through traditional spoken or written methods, or in more poetic and aesthetic forms such as music, dance, and stories.

Christian "theologians" are academic scholars, thinkers, and writers who reflect deeply upon and express 1) the meaning of Christian doctrines, 2) the real human experiences of life, and 3) the life of faith by which one attempts to live out the actual doctrines, norms, and practices of the people of God. Theologians have the right and duty, according to contemporary Catholic views, to clarify how the Spirit of God is alive and actively present within the community of the baptized and elsewhere in human cultures. Theologians are rightly expected to speak out whenever or wherever they perceive that a Christian teaching or moral norm is in error, balancing their perceptions, of course, between official church teachings and humanity's honest experiences.

Theology, however, is not only for professional, skilled theologians. All church members are called to do "theological reflection"(some call it "doing practical theology") as individuals and in small faith communities. Popular theological reflection is the natural, conscious process of identifying life experiences, reflecting on how to "find the sacred in the everyday" through these life experiences, in light of the Christian story and vision, and the naming of decisions and (new) directions for one's Christian existence as a result of one's intentional, deep reflection.

In the 20th century, church members have benefited from many great and gifted Christian theologians, including Rahner, Congar, Moltmann, Barth, Tillich, Bonhoeffer, Bultmann, Schillebeeckx, Kasper, Macquarrie, Chardin, Gutierrez, Sobrino, Boff, Cone, and many others. There are many, many branches of Christian theology: dogmatic theology, biblical theology, systematic theology, moral theology, liturgical theology, sacramental theology, historical theology, creation theology, mystical theology, ascetical theology, liberation theology (which includes branches such as feminist theology, African-American theology, and Asian Pacific theologies), ecumenical theology, political theology, existential theology, pastoral theology, process theology, and more.

"Praxis" is a term often used in liberation theology, in discussions of theological reflection, and in discussions of religious education. Praxis is a grass-roots avenue to doing practical theology and engaging in theological reflection. Christian praxis is a several-step method—a reflection process, in essence, which one can do individually or in a group setting—by which one looks at aspects of human experience, reflects on these in light of Scripture and church teachings and tradition as a whole, and moves to personal Christian action and prayer. In a sense, then, modern theological reflection, whether formal or more informal, ultimately seeks personal conversion, renewal, and the transformation of society and cultures so as to bring about human rights, liberation for all peoples, greater degrees of social justice, deeper Christian awareness among various people(s), and the dynamic realization of the reign of God.

The *Catechism of the Catholic Church* points out that the church's understanding of the realities and the terms of our common faith heritage can grow daily. In article 94, it says that through the contemplation and the study of believers who theologically ponder matters of faith in their minds and hearts, in general, and through theological research, in particular, the knowledge of God's revelation deepens in the human community.

(See also Deposit of Faith, Discipleship, Doctrine, Faith, Orthodoxy, and Witness.)

TITHING   is a practice by which a church member or a family regularly gives part of an annual income or personal possessions for charitable reasons. This generally amounts to ten percent or so of what a person or family earns. "Tithe" is a modern form of the Old English word *teotha*, "one tenth."

The payment of tithes was common among some ancient pagan peoples and the Hebrews as well (Deuteronomy 14:25). The root idea of contributing to the financial well-being of the Christian community can be found in Matthew 10:10 and 1 Corinthians 9:13–14. Among the early Christians, both Origen and St. Irenaeus spoke negatively about Christian tithing. But as the needs of the expanding church community grew more demanding, the Council of Macon in 585 instituted the practice of tithing. At first, donations were foods that came from family farms or other goods. Soon, however, money was being contributed to church officials. In the 16th century, the Council of Trent said failure to tithe would result in excommunication from the church. Mandatory church tithing came to an end not long after that. Since then the Catholic church has largely been supported by voluntary contributions of varying amounts and percentages of income from church members. To that end, the Code of Canon Law now says "the Christian faithful...freely give temporal goods to the Church" (canon 1261), and they should "support ...the church by collections...according to the norms laid down by the [local] conference of bishops" (canon 1262).

There has been a general renewal of interest in tithing in some U.S. Catholic communities in recent decades. There is, however, no church rule that anyone must give ten percent or any set amount of personal income or possessions. For some, one-fifth or one-tenth of income would be too much to contribute, yet for others it might be too little. Each Catholic is challenged to give according to his or her financial means to help build up and maintain the body of Christ locally, regionally, and worldwide.

(See also Charity; Church, Laws of; and Offertory.)

TRADITION is the rich and dynamic process by which the entire story of the people of God is handed on to diverse peoples, communities, and human cultures. The Christian tradition includes many Christian doctrines and teachings, insights from the church's great leaders, forms of worship by Christian believers, and the living and active faith witness of all the baptized through the ages, past and present. Christian tradition also encompasses, by definition, the unique customs, values, practices, moral rules, rituals, witness, and contemporary attitudes of the Catholic Christian community. The term is based on the Latin *traditio*, which means "handing down" or "giving over."

The original apostles and disciples of Jesus of Nazareth were the first catechists of the Christian community. They (and Christians since then) have handed on all that has been revealed to them by Jesus and by the Hebrew Scriptures. Through the centuries the church came to believe 1) that divine revelation had ceased at the close of the apostolic era (i.e., "with the death of the last apostle"), and 2) that which had been revealed must be preserved and faithfully handed on—or "given over"—to all generations of humanity to come.

Beginning in the 1500s, Protestant reformers began to de-emphasize the significance of Christian tradition; instead they centered almost exclusively on the Bible as humanity's ultimate source of God's revelation. In fact, many reformers took a motto: "*sola scriptura*"—by Scripture only. In response, the Council of Trent (1545–1563) maintained that there are two authentic sources of the Creator's revelation: Scripture and tradition. The Second Vatican Council (1962–1965) recently refined this Catholic Christian viewpoint, saying that there is only one divine source of revelation—God alone—a "divine wellspring" or divine river of truth of sorts, from which flow two tributaries or streams of insight (which compose one living "deposit of Christian faith"): Scripture and sacred tradition.

Many theological and pastoral leaders today say that, in a sense, revelation is not closed; rather it is developing (or evolving) even now, as the faith of the community of the baptized around the globe deepens, matures, examines, and reflects on the meaning of that which the one Source of all revelation has communicated to humanity through the ages and is communicating to us even to this day. Vatican II noted that it is the task (mission) of the church in every time to always express (and reformulate) the various teachings and spiritual values that spring from the gospel in dynamic, perhaps changing ways that can be understood and accepted by different generations of humankind.

The Catholic community today teaches that Scripture and tradition form an essential unity of God's revelation. Scripture is the inspired Word of God. Tradition is the ongoing process by which the baptized and faithful hand on their faith in God's Word to others. According to Vatican II (1960s), Catholics each must work to preserve and spread the good news of the risen Jesus, giving Scripture and Christian tradition equal honor, particularly through the contemporary ministries of evangelization and catechesis. In article 77, the *Catechism of the Catholic Church* says that the full and living gospel of Jesus should always be preserved in an unbroken succession "until the end of time."

(See also Bible, Deposit of Faith, Doctrine, Reformation, Orthodoxy, and Revelation.)

TRANSFIGURATION   is an annual church feast, the Transfiguration of the Lord Jesus, celebrated on August 6, which honors the revelation of Jesus' divine nature to several apostles. The term has Latin and French origins roughly indicating a "change in outward appearance or form."

The story of the Transfiguration of Jesus can be found in the Christian Scriptures (Mark 9:1–7, Matthew 17:1–9, Luke 9:28–36). Bible scholars have seen it as a story meant to confirm among early believers and skeptics alike that Jesus of Nazareth was and is the messiah, the anointed and true Son of God. It also points toward his second coming in all of God's glory—in the *parousia*—at the end of time to fully usher in the everlasting reign of God.

The church feast of the Transfiguration dates back at least to the 8th century. Pope Callistus III made it a universal Catholic celebration in 1457.

Some Bible commentators speculate that the origins of the transfiguration story actually lie in a primitive story about a post-Easter appearance of Jesus somehow experienced by his followers. Others dispute this though because there seem to be so many authentic echoes of the Hebrew Scriptures and other Jewish literature in the synoptics' transfiguration narratives.

Traditional church teachings on the Transfiguration of Jesus call it a decisive turning point in which the original disciples somehow saw him revealed as the long-awaited, God-sent messiah. Through the transfiguration experience, the followers of the Lord began to know deeply the essence of his redemptive work for all humanity. The Transfiguration is referred to as a prophetic and apocalyptic experience since it speaks symbolically of the conversion of all the baptized, by the grace of the Spirit, during their human journeys toward heaven's glory and the reign of God. (Note: this biblical story, therefore, also prophetically implies the ultimate glorification of all God's creation, with the Word, God's first-born Son, presiding over it.)

The feast of the Transfiguration is meant to remind all church members that Christian self-denial, sacrifice, "the cross," and death truly lead the way—as did the human and divine messiah—toward full Christian glory and hope in God.

(See also Jesus of Nazareth, Messiah, Parousia, Redemption, Reign of God.)

TRANSUBSTANTIATION   is the process of converting one substance into another. Transubstantiation is an official church doctrine which says that the substances of bread and wine truly are changed into the real presence of Jesus' body and blood during the celebration of the Eucharist.

The word is non-biblical. Yet the Christian mystery it expresses traces back to the time of the apostles (e.g., see John 6:48–66 and 1 Corinthians 11:23–25). Saints Irenaeus and Ignatius of Antioch, in the 2nd century, saw the eucharistic bread and wine as truly Jesus' flesh and blood. In the 700s, St. John of Damascus taught that church tradition had long held that bread and wine are really changed into the Lord's body and blood. The writings of Thomas Aquinas in the 1200s helped mainstream the use of the emerging term "transubstantiation" in church documents. Ecumenical councils such as the Fourth Lateran (1215), Second Lyons (1274), and Florence (1439) used it freely. As a result of challenges regarding the Eucharist by Protestant reformers, the Council of Trent, in 1551, taught about the "marvelous and extraordinary change of the whole substance" of eucharistic bread and wine into Jesus' actual body and blood "so that only the species of bread and wine remain."

Catholic doctrine strongly maintains that the presence of Jesus in the eucharistic meal is real, not just a symbolic or spiritual presence. Current theological and ecumenical discussions on this, cued by Vatican II, reflect on the mystery of Jesus' full presence in the consecrated body and blood. However, they likewise focus on how he can be truly present to Christians in other ways: 1) in and through all Christian worship assemblies (gatherings of God's people), 2) in the ministry of various Christian presbyters and other persons who call believers to prayer and who preside at worship services, and 3) in and through the Word of God (biblical texts) proclaimed in Christian Scriptures.

In contemporary theological debates, terms like "transignification" and "transfinalization" (coined by Dutch theologians just a few years ago) are sometimes used instead of transubstantiation. But these terms are often rejected by traditional teachers in the church because they seem to imply that no real transubstantiation occurs in celebrations of the Eucharist.

The *Catechism of the Catholic Church* echoes the words of Jesus of Nazareth by which the gifts of bread and wine were first converted, at the Last Supper, into his body and blood (Mark 14:22–24), then notes that the unique and real eucharistic presence of Jesus begins at the moment of consecration of the gifts within the liturgy and endures as long as the eucharistic elements are present. It notes clearly, however, that the risen One is present to the people of God in many other ways too (e.g., in assemblies of the baptized, in the Word, in the sacraments, in Christian ministries, and in the poor, the sick, and the outcasts in our midst) and so he will always be (Matthew 18:18–20).

(See Dogma, Eucharist, Jesus of Nazareth, Liturgy of the Word/ Eucharist, Option for the Poor, Sacrament, and Worship.)

TRENT, COUNCIL OF   was the nineteenth ecumenical council of the church. The Council of Trent was held from 1545 to 1563. Three successive popes—Paul III, Julius III, and Pius IV—presided over it. Trent was convened to respond to the Reformation occurring in the Christian community in Europe. The council attempted to clarify the basic teachings of the Roman Catholic tradition and to begin a complete reform and renewal of the church community as a whole.

The conciliar sessions got underway in the town of Trent, in northern Italy, on December 13, 1545. Some church leaders (ones very concerned about the effects of the Reformation process underway) had tried unsuccessfully for 25 years prior to this date to have Catholic bishops gather for an official, worldwide council meeting. It seems that only 30 or so bishops were actually present when Trent began, but by the time this council was concluded on December 4, 1563, many more Catholic episcopal leaders had traveled to Trent from around the Christian world to participate. Over 25 major sessions were held during the course of this crucial council.

Trent ranks as one of the greatest of ecumenical councils, perhaps second only to the Second Vatican Council (1962–1965) for clarifying Catholic teachings, traditions, practices, and disciplines for church members to follow. Trent's response to the widespread Protestant reform in the 1500s brought on a new era in Catholic history, one commonly called the Counter-Reformation. Some Catholic critics of Trent say that the tone and the style of the council led the Roman church community toward a centuries-long period marked by suspicions and mistaken notions about other Christian congregations and toward a spirit of anti-Protestantism, all of which have seriously delayed the realization of ecumenical ideals (i.e., a true Christian unity worldwide).

The Council of Trent defined a number of significant Catholic doctrines. For example, the church leaders at Trent noted that the Bible and tradition are the two, true sources of Catholic teachings. Conciliar sessions restated and emphasized church teachings on the Eucharist, and then formally stated the meaning and number of the Roman Catholic sacraments. Additionally, Trent authoritatively maintained that salvation is a gift from God; it proposed rules for valid Christian marriages; it led toward the foundation of seminaries for the formation of priests; and it began an index of books condemned by the Catholic community. (This index no longer exists.)

(See also Bishop; Councils, Ecumenical; Ecumenism; Reformation; Sacrament; and Tradition.)

Note of Interest: Use of the Tridentine Rite is the celebration of the Eucharist—the Mass—in accord with the pre-Vatican II Roman Missal and the official directives of the Council of Trent from 1563. (Mass in the style and format of the Tridentine Rite is sometimes still inaccurately called "the Latin Mass.") Four hundred years after the publication of the rite (in 1963), the church began an official revision of the Roman rite of worship. This was needed by Catholics to more clearly indicate the close relationship between the major parts of the Mass and to renew more active participation of those gathered for eucharistic worship. Today the Tridentine ritual is still employed, and spoken in Latin, in limited circumstances.

In 1984, Pope John Paul II authorized the use of the Tridentine Mass in certain situations by those communities that still care deeply for it. The main condition he imposed was that those who celebrate it must unequivocally, even publicly, give "evidence that the priest and people (using it) have no ties with those who impugn the lawfulness and doctrinal soundness of the Roman Missal" published anew in 1970. Six other guidelines were proposed by the pope for the proper, contemporary celebration of the Tridentine rite. These are detailed in a 1984 Vatican document issued by the Pontifical Commission, *Ecclesia dei.*

TRIDUUM can be defined as a sacred three-day period of prayer and Christian devotion. This prayer period, whether observed privately or communally, is often used to get ready for an important church feast. *Triduum* is a Latin term for three days.

Catholics today observe the Easter Triduum. It begins with the evening Mass of the Lord's Supper on Holy Thursday and concludes on Easter Sunday evening. It is the center and high point of the entire church year.

The Triduum is part of the annual Holy Week remembrance of Jesus' passage from life and death to the glory of the resurrection. In the early Christian era, there was no holy week; there was merely the celebration of the Easter Vigil and then Easter Sunday.

Holy Thursday, Good Friday, and Holy Saturday were later considered holydays. By the 1400s, a Friday–Sunday triduum within Holy Week was observed by Catholics to honor Jesus' suffering, death, burial, and resurrection in a special manner. In more recent times, the Easter triduum has been redefined as a Thursday evening to Sunday evening period, more authentically reflecting the gospel-era way of calculating days of the week (from sunset to sunset).

The sequence of Catholic religious events and observances in the current Triduum includes: Holy Thursday, on which church members remember and celebrate the institution of the sacraments of Eucharist and order in the Mass of the Lord's Supper on Thursday evening. Good Friday, on which Christians commemorate the sufferings and death of Jesus of Nazareth (church gatherings featuring Scripture reading, veneration of the cross, and a communion service occur in the early afternoon). Holy Saturday, on which the church celebrates no daytime Eucharist and prepares for the Easter vigil that night. And finally, Easter Sunday, a joyous solemnity on which Christians and others worldwide remember and prayerfully celebrate the day Jesus was raised to new life by God.

(See also Easter, Eucharist, Holy Week, Jesus of Nazareth, and Lent.)

TRINITY   is a foundational belief of the Christian community that maintains that God consists of one divine nature yet three divine "persons" or expressions: the Father, the Son, and the Holy Spirit. This belief is a great mystery (i.e., how God can be One and yet three?), a mystery that limited human beings cannot fully comprehend. Still, it nevertheless is fundamental to the Catholic Christian way. Christian theology understands that the three persons or expressions of God are eternal, equal, and yet somehow distinct, each deserving equal reverence and honor from all of humanity. The term is derived from the Latin *trinitas* and the Old English *trinitee*, which basically mean "threefold."

A primitive Christian theology of God can be found in the writings of Paul (e.g., Ephesians 5:18–20 and 2 Corinthians 13:13) in the Christian Scriptures. The Christian Scriptures also seem to suggest that Jesus of Nazareth himself adhered to a basic understanding of God as a trinity, as Father, Son, and Spirit. However, the Christian doctrine on God, as one divine nature in and through three divine persons or expressions, was only formally declared in the Nicene Creed and then by the Council of Alexandria, both of which can be dated to the 4th century c.e. The Council of Nicaea (325) said that Jesus was the truly divine and human son of God, "begotten" by the Father. A little later, a provincial church council, which met in Rome in 385, taught that the one loving and eternal God is three equal, eternal, and distinct persons.

Augustine, Anselm, and Thomas Aquinas were among those who wrote and taught about the divine Trinity. Many subsequent church councils have provided Christian teachings on the nature of the Trinity, including the Fourth Lateran Council (1215), the Second Council of Lyons (1274), the Council of Florence (1438–1445), the Council of Trent (1545–1563), the First Vatican Council (1869–1870), and the Second Vatican Council (1962–1965).

The abiding mystery of the Trinity seems too complex for many human beings to fully explain, even though it is a foundational, dogmatic matter of faith. In following Vatican II's reflections on the Trinity as divine loving community, some theologians have seen something of a parallel to the Trinity in the potential unity and harmony of all men and women and, therefore, of all human cultures around the globe. Others have seen an image of the loving, creative, and benevolent Trinity in the great love, concern, mercy, justice, and compassion that every person should offer to all others in the world.

Many theologians have speculated on the meaning of the divine Trinity and on our ongoing relationship to God in recent decades. One particular view of God says that God is transcendent, beyond, yet still somehow present to and within human beings. Through the mysterious incarnation of the Second Person (expressed in history as Jesus of Nazareth) and through the gift of the Spirit of God to the world, God remains present in history, in and through the reality of creation. Through God's grace, humans can thus enjoy an open, ongoing, ever-deepening relationship with the divine. Though God is present to all people and all of created reality, men and women remain free: God's grace does not deny human creatures the basic freedom to choose the good or to choose evil.

At best humankind can describe in a very limited way what the mystery of God is really like, by using human adjectives and phrases for the assumed spiritual characteristics of God's perfection (e.g., loving, caring, faithful, merciful, forgiving, full of compassion, joyful, humorous). Very recent images for the Trinity from various theologians say that modern people might do well to think of the divine Trinity as a "family" of sorts, whose shared love and happiness should be something for which all people strive but which is surely beyond human comprehension. Others say that a better way to speak about the Triune God might be to say that everything comes to humanity from the Creator (Parent), is made fully available in and through the Word made flesh, and that all gifts from God are fulfilled in and through the indwelling of the Spirit within the human community.

The Christian Scriptures reveal that Jesus chose to speak of God as his Father (using *abba*, "daddy") with a kind of simple but profound love that a child typically shows in addressing a caring parent. Through Vatican II, the church has re-emphasized the belief that God is the true Creator and Source of unity for the global Christian community and all of humanity. Christians trust that God existed before creation and time as we know it began and that the one God has created all that is. As loving Father or Parent, God has begotten a Son—God's eternal Word—and this Son or Word has reconciled the world to God for all time. The third expression of God, the Spirit, the creative love shared by Father and Son, has been sent to guide the people of God and the entire world.

Two favorite traditional prayers of the worldwide Catholic community that honor the eternal Trinity are called the Sign of the Cross and the Glory Be. (These traditional prayers date back at least to the time of the Council of Nicaea, in the 4th century.) The solemnity of the Holy

Trinity, which has ancient Christian roots, has been on the official church calendar since about the year 1000 and is now celebrated by the church on the Sunday after Pentecost each year.

(See also Christology, Creation, God, Monotheism, Pantheism, and Yahweh.)

Note of Interest: The *Catechism of the Catholic Church,* in a section on the human capacity for God, notes that when we speak of God we use human language which really can approach a description of God, though without being able to express God's infinite simplicity. The Catechism, quoting Thomas Aquinas, adds that "concerning God we cannot grasp what [God] is, but only what [God] is not, and how other beings stand in relation" to the Creator (see article 43).

V

VATICAN   also known as Vatican City, is a cluster of buildings and shrines within the city of Rome, the capital city of Italy. The Vatican is also the place where the pope's residence and St. Peter's Basilica are located. The official name of the Vatican is *Stato della Città del Vaticano*. It is viewed as a sovereign state, the smallest in the world. Vatican City has its own post office, radio station, offices for government bureaus, and museums.

The Vatican got its name from *Vaticanus*, which refers to one of the hills of Rome. The first official papal residence in Rome was built on the present site of the Vatican by Pope Symmacus in the year 500. The huge church building now known as St. Peter's Basilica was constructed over many years during the 16th and 17th centuries (1506–1626) and remains the world's largest Catholic church. Over centuries various popes managed to acquire the parcels of land around the papal residence and St. Peter's. In 1929 the Vatican was officially named the territorial see (diocese) of the pope of the Catholic community by the Lateran Treaty. Officially speaking, the Vatican's territory was measured at 109 acres within the city of Rome.

In modern times the Vatican has maintained diplomatic ties with many other nations in the world. It remains a politically neutral state to this day, with its worldly power being much more limited now than in some ages past. The population of the Vatican is approximately 1000 persons, which typically includes priests, religious, and a number of laypersons. The authority for officially governing Vatican City rests with the pope, yet much of the actual work of the Vatican government is done by a special pontifical commission for the State of Vatican City. Today about 3400 laypersons are employed by the Vatican's governmental and other offices. The Catholic parish church of the Vatican is called St. Ann's. Of particular note is the official Vatican Library, built by Popes Sixtus IV and Sixtus V. This library maintains over 770,000 books and some 70,000 important and rare manuscripts.

(See also Holy See, Peter, Pope, Shrine, and Vatican II.)

VATICAN COUNCIL I   also known as the First Vatican Council, was the twentieth ecumenical council of the universal church. In 1864 Pope Pius IX announced that this important council meeting would be held in Rome (at the Vatican), yet it did not actually get underway until five years later. Vatican I is perhaps most remembered as the ecumenical council that formally defined doctrines on papal primacy and infallibility.

Vatican I began on December 8, 1869. Sessions took place in St. Peter's Basilica (in Vatican City). About 750 bishops attended. Eighty-nine general conciliar meetings of bishops, coupled with four public sessions, were eventually held. Vatican I produced two major documents, *Dei filius* and *Pastor aeternus*, both published in 1870. The First Vatican Council was then concluded on October 20, 1870.

(See also Councils, Ecumenical; Infallibility; Pope; Vatican; and Vatican II.)

VATICAN COUNCIL II   also known as the Second Vatican Council, was the twenty-first and most recent ecumenical council of the church. Vatican II was called for by Pope John XXIII in 1959, yet it did not actually begin until 1962. This council was held in Rome (at the Vatican) with some 2800 church leaders plus other Catholics and non-Catholic persons in attendance. A total of sixteen major documents was produced by this most pastoral of ecumenical councils; these official church statements focused on topics such as the nature and mission of the church community, church renewal, divine revelation, Christian liturgy, the ecumenical movement, Christian education, and the roles of clergy, religious communities, and laypersons in the modern Christian church community and the world. Pope John led the first of Vatican II's four major sessions. After John's death in 1963, Pope Paul VI led the final three conciliar sessions. The council was later concluded on December 8, 1965.

Vatican II has been hailed as one of the most crucial conciliar meetings in the entire history of the global Christian community. Pope John XXIII had hoped that Vatican II, like a new Pentecost, would encourage a great movement toward Christian spirituality and a complementary spirit of renewal and enthusiasm ("a breath of fresh air") in local Catholic communities around the world. John also wanted the council to provide a much-needed sense of hope-filled expectation to contemporary church members and to bring all Christian congregations closer together through ecumenical unity. The non-voting theologians, religious order members, laypersons, and even representatives of non-Catholic religions at Vatican II proved to be of much assistance to church leaders at the council.

Vatican II was a sign of how true Christian collegiality can work among the leaders of the church community. The pope and the other bishops of the Catholic church came together as concerned pastors and shepherds in order to teach, pastorally direct, and spiritually guide the entire community of the baptized. The sixteen documents of this council are considered by many thinkers, teachers, and pastoral ministers alike as some of the finest, most pastoral, and most significant writings in recent Christian history.

(See also Collegiality; Councils, Ecumenical; John XXIII; Pope; and Spirituality.)

VENERATION   is the process of directing deep reverence and respect toward historical figures—real human beings—who lived, died, and are now believed to be in glory with God in heaven. This spiritual reverence for saints is sometimes known as the *dulia*. Prayers requesting saints' help for human causes are frequently coupled with the reverent honor given saints. "Veneration" comes from Latin words meaning "to give reverence."

Until the 400s, many saints were venerated only in or near their home towns or ministry locales. As the church community spread out, however, some local groups shared their lists of saints with others or used the stories of saints from far away. In the Middle Ages, the church in Rome produced listings of saints with great appeal to various communities (e.g., the apostles, the gospel-authors, and early martyrs). This eventually led to the publication of the Roman Martyrology, first published in 1584 and still in existence today, which lists the names of all saints traditionally honored by Catholics as well as the recently canonized. In addition, some saints have been venerated for centuries at Mass, especially through the first Eucharistic Prayer (the Roman Canon).

The church teaches that because Mary and all the saints gave witness to the gospel of Jesus, veneration of them is a way to worship the divine. They were human examples and models of how to live faithfully the Christian way of life. Saints are part of the larger human family of God. They have come from all kinds of races, lifestyles, cultures, professions, and economic roots. They can and will help those who look for their prayers, just as fair-minded Christians would do. Veneration is due all saints and angels because of the glory and heavenly honor they have been given by the Creator. Private veneration can be offered to any person whom a believer trusts is now enjoying heavenly existence. Public devotion—through communal prayer, relics, litanies, pictures, statues, icons, and other sacramentals—can be accorded to saints officially recognized by the church. Some Catholic individuals take personal patron saints (spiritual friends/guides to whom they can relate through life) due to the names they got in baptism and confirmation, a practice that took hold in Europe in the Middle Ages (see canon 855 in canon law). Some causes, professions, and communities have also taken patron saints. All saints, both patrons and non-patrons, should be venerated by the people of God according to the Catholic community, and Catholics are called to develop spiritual relationships with them.

The church adds also that saints deserve veneration because they show people today how to live the enduring paschal mystery of Jesus of Nazareth—the journey of human life through joys, sufferings, and death in order to pass over into the "raised to perfection" state of God's grace, known as heaven.

(See also All Saints Day; All Souls Day; Canonization; Heaven; and Saints, Communion of.)

VESTIBULE   is an antechamber or anteroom in a Catholic church through which people must pass in order to reach the main section of the church's worship space. One usually enters the vestibule by walking through the outer church doors. The term comes from *vestibulum*, which roughly means an "entrance hall."

The historical roots of modern-day vestibules can be found in the courtyards that were located near the entrances to private households, royal palaces, and official buildings in eras past. Catholic church vestibules in contemporary times have often become areas in which displays of books and pamphlets, parish announcement boards, and church bulletin displays can be found. Sometimes holy water containers and dispensers have also been kept in or near church vestibule spaces. In recent decades it has become quite common for the presbyter and other ministers (e.g., lectors, cross-bearers), to begin the celebration of the Eucharist by walking in procession from the vestibule area up to the main altar of the church and to return there, at the Mass's ending, to greet those who have attended the worship celebration.

VIGIL LIGHTS   also called votive candles, are wax tapers lighted by members of local Catholic communities during times of prayer and devotion. Vigil lights and candles may be found in a number of places within Catholic church buildings. Most often they are located off to the sides of the main worship space in churches or in front of statues of Mary, the saints, and other icons and holy images.

Vigil lights are Catholic sacramentals. According to Catholic traditions and custom, vigil lights are symbols of Catholics' deep hope that their prayers to God will be answered and that their special needs will be met. An ancient church tradition maintains that lighted vigil tapers are symbols of the Christian's true desire to be united with the risen Jesus continually, particularly in times of doubt, trouble, and separation from the ability to visit with the Lord readily within the church's worship space.

It is often customary for persons lighting these candles to leave a small donation to help support the local church's ministry and to cover the basic costs associated with the vigil lights.

(See also Candles, Devotions, Icon, Sacramentals, and Veneration.)

VIRTUE   is a spiritual habit or personal spiritual quality that helps individuals to choose that which is morally appropriate, to avoid sin and evil, and to live as faithful followers of the gospel of Jesus of Nazareth. The word *virtue* comes to us from the Latin *virtus*, to have strength. The three theological virtues are faith, hope, and charity (love). Religious tradition states that these virtues are given to persons by the gracious Spirit of God and animate all Christian moral choices and other behaviors. The four cardinal virtues (also known as the moral virtues), the "hinges" upon which much of daily Christian existence turns, are prudence, temperance, justice, and fortitude. The theological and moral virtues provide one with the spiritual powers and spiritual strengths necessary to recognize the good and to choose Christian goodness at all times, despite obstacles that could get in the way in the course of everyday human existence.

Virtues are sometimes described as spiritual gifts and powers, almost like power-filled daily vitamins, originating in God's divine power and grace, which can permeate one's entire life system as they are used and developed in daily life. In a sense, then, this approach also emphasizes that Christian virtues are something like living testimonies by which Christians give witness that God's life and grace are personally active in them.

Contemporary Catholic thought on the topic of virtues is outlined in articles 1810 and 1811 of the *Catechism of the Catholic Church*. It acknowledges that humanity, wounded as it is by human sinfulness, often finds it very difficult today to maintain a "moral balance." Thus every person should strive daily to develop Christian virtue. And every person should then also use the help of the Spirit and the whole Christian community regularly to forge one's virtuous character by choosing and practicing the individual virtues and by doing the work of goodness in all life situations.

(See also Charity, Discernment, Faith, Holiness, and Hope.)

Note of Interest: Asceticism is a virtue-filled way of life, a form of Christian self-discipline important for the development of an authentic Christian lifestyle. Asceticism calls one to take the gospel and the baptismal challenge seriously in one's personal journey toward perfection. Christian tradition says that authentic Christian asceticism leads one toward humble service and love for others and toward growth in patience, self-acceptance, and commitment to the building up of the reign of God within the human community. Those who embrace an ascetic way of life tend to practice radical self-denial and to be totally committed to the Christian way.

VOWS   are sacred promises by which a person promises to carry out special actions or lead a way of life centered on dedication to God, imitation of Jesus of Nazareth, and loving service for the entire people of God. Our word *vow* comes from the Latin *vovere*, meaning "to promise." Some contemporary presbyters, members of religious orders, and laypersons today choose to live the three vows known as the "evangelical counsels": poverty, chastity, and obedience. Christian tradition emphasizes that Christian vows must be made with true knowledge of the commitment (s) one is making and in a spirit of true human freedom.

Over the centuries, some Catholic Christians have chosen to make several types of vows. Some persons have professed private vows, that is, vows professed without recognition from the official church community. And some have become committed to public vows, vows acknowledged by the church community, and which are either professed perpetually (for all time) or for shorter, specific time-durations. Tradition indicates that individuals make Christian vows in an attempt to be more like Jesus of Nazareth and his earliest, deeply committed followers. They believe that a lifestyle characterized by poverty, moral chastity, and true obedience to authorities will enable them to better serve the risen Jesus, the Christian community on Earth, and all others. Perpetual vows (i.e., vows-for-life) are witnessed by a worshiping Christian assembly. The Second Vatican Council taught that Christian vows are rooted in the ministry, example, and teaching of Jesus, particularly in his love for God and all of humanity and in his deep desire to know the Creator's will for his life.

Authentic vows are gifts from God, according to church members, that lead toward an ideal in Christian witness often recommended by the great church thinkers, preachers, and teachers over the ages. Catholic tradition emphasizes that a true vow is also an act of Christian prayer and worship and as a genuine commitment to serve humanity and the reign of God to come. The *Catechism of the Catholic Church* notes that the gospel's message and values propose the evangelical counsels to every disciple of Jesus. However those who choose to profess poverty, chastity in celibacy, and obedience for the sake of the reign of God live a special way of life of consecration to God (article 915). A summary of church law on the topic of vows can be found in the Code of Canon Law, canons 1191–1198. Canon law stipulates that a vow is "a deliberate and free promise made to God concerning a possible and better good which must be fulfilled by reason of...religion."

(See also Laicization, Presbyter, Religious Orders, and Witness.)

W

WAY OF THE CROSS   sometimes called the Stations of the Cross, is a devotion and also a sacramental of the Catholic Church. Individual pictures or other symbols associated with the traditional fourteen steps or "stations" along the Way of the Cross are usually affixed to the interior walls of Catholic church buildings. These fourteen depictions or illustrations give witness to key events involved in the passion, death, and burial of Jesus of Nazareth. Praying the Way of the Cross, Catholics believe, can help one to contemplate the salvation of humanity by God and to grow in Christian spirituality.

There are some historical indications that the devotion called Stations probably got its start in the visits (or pilgrimages) that Christian pilgrims have made over the centuries to Palestine to encounter the actual sites and scenes of the life, ministry, crucifixion, and death of Jesus of Nazareth. The more formal Catholic devotion now known as the Way of the Cross actually evolved over many hundreds of years, and probably became very popular when a deep devotion to the passion of Jesus arose in European churches during the 12th and 13th centuries. By the 14th century the Franciscan religious community as a whole had begun to promote energetically the use of the stations. Saint Leonard of Port Maurice preached frequently on the devotion during the 1700s and, in 1731, Pope Clement XII established guidelines for the proper devotional use of the Way of the Cross.

Today, Catholics can pray the stations alone or in a devotion group with a prayer leader. When alone, typically a person will walk from station to station in a church, and thus meditate and pray in front of each of the fourteen pictures or symbols along the way. In recent times a fifteenth station, the resurrection of Jesus, has frequently been added. Attempts have also been made by some pastoral ministers to tie the Stations more closely to actual events recorded in Scripture.

The traditional Stations of the Cross appear on page 267.

(See also Devotion, Icon, Paschal Mystery, Pilgrimage, Prayer, and Sacramentals.)

WITNESS   is the daily Christian life example every baptized person is called to give. In other words, Christian witness is one's personal life testimony that reveals one's commitment to the risen Jesus, to the Christian way of life, and to a personal desire to seek first the reign of God through one's daily lifestyle and choices. The word has been derived from the Middle English *witan* ("know") and *witnesse*, which imply a form of knowledge and a consciousness.

The story of the Christian community over many centuries has testified to a foundational belief that Jesus of Nazareth was God's most complete self-communication, greatest revelation, and foremost witness. The original apostles and disciples of Jesus were the prime witnesses to the risen Christ—having experienced the post-Easter Jesus firsthand in some way and having been directly given a life-changing mission from him to reach out and share his gospel message of salvation to all individuals, peoples, cultures, and human communities around the world. In the present age, the members of the church try to extend and to carry on this mission from the risen Jesus by actively witnessing to belief in his good news for all and by actively serving the needs of others with the inspiration and support of his guiding Spirit.

Personal gospel witness (and communal witness too) by the baptized can take many forms: the good example of living a gospel-inspired life, works of charity and mercy, morally appropriate actions and attitudes, genuine Christian hopefulness, a lifestyle characterized by prayerfulness, celebration of the sacraments and other acts of worship, genuine Christian humility, participation in the Christian community's ministries, active participation in social justice projects and causes, and other means. One's Christian witness can be either formal or informal, or intentional or indirect. For example, one who voluntarily becomes engaged in a form of team ministry in a local faith community today can be said to be an intentional Christian witness. One who engages in a faith-filled, Christian lifestyle in the marketplace, one's family interactions and friendships, and other typical life activities can be said to be giving, in some ways, a form of indirect and informal Christian witness. Witness, when it leads another to questions about the gospel and interest in the counter-cultural way of Christianity, can be a prophetic life activity and also a form of Christian advocacy for those who suffer, are weak, or exist in conditions of injustice and oppression.

In the 1960s, Vatican II emphasized that the Christian church is a people of God and a community called and challenged to give witness to Jesus Christ. The global Christian community is thus meant to become a humble people in God's service, composed of individuals, families, and local faith communities that strive to imitate the ways of Jesus of Nazareth and the simple but fiery and committed witness of the earliest generations of his followers. The Council also stressed that every baptized person has an ongoing call (responsibility) to become a living witness and example to all individuals and groups who wish to know more about the reign of God and the life-transforming hope that Christian communities profess.

In 1990, in his encyclical *Redemptoris missio* (Mission of the Redeemer), John Paul II noted that witness is the first and most basic form of Christian evangelization. Paraphrasing earlier statements by Pope Paul VI (in 1975), John Paul said that modern men and women tend to put more trust in Christian witnesses than in preachers and teachers, in experience than in teaching, and in life and action than in words and theories, and if modern people trust teachers at all it is because they are Christian witnesses. He added that the first form of witness "is the very life of the missionary, of the Christian family, and of the ecclesial community, which reveal a new way of living." To be authentic and truly evangelical, then, witness must wordlessly stand "in marked contrast to human selfishness" causing others to raise "precise questions which lead [them toward] God and to the gospel."

(See also Baptism, Discipleship, Evangelization, Holiness, Hope, and Works of Mercy.)

WORKS OF MERCY   are virtuous human actions inspired and motivated by one's love of God and other human beings. The Christian community recognizes that the "mercy" that an individual Christian or a local Christian community offers to others is a living sign of the limitless mercy, love, and goodness that the Creator has shown and continues to show to all human beings and all human cultures over the ages.

Catholics speak of both corporal and spiritual works of mercy. The traditional Christian corporal works of mercy relate to the physical or bodily needs of human beings. The spiritual works of mercy relate more directly to the spiritual needs of the human soul. Christians have traditionally seen the various works of mercy as centered in the ministry and perfect witness of Jesus of Nazareth. Many theologians say that the traditional works of mercy can be traced to a passage in the gospel of Matthew (25:31–46), which describes the divine judgment of all peoples, and to the spirit of the beatitudes noted in Matthew 5:3–10. The Second Vatican Council taught that doing the works of Christian mercy affords the world a striking testimony of Christian life and discipleship in action. Today some Catholic Christians—individually and in groups—perform merciful deeds in pastoral care ministries, hospitals, homes for the aged, children's homes, drug-alcohol treatment centers, social service and recreation program centers, and through various charitable organizations. Catholic Relief Services is one major, missionary church agency that assists impoverished and troubled persons, communities, and cultures around the globe.

The traditional Christian "corporal and spiritual works of mercy" are listed on page 268.

(See also Discipleship, Missions, Social Justice, Virtue, and Witness.)

WORSHIP   is prayerful honor and recognition that God (the perfect Other, the Divine, the Holy, the Absolute One) has created all that is. Through religious ritual and worship, human beings seek to respond to and be in union with their God. The worship of Catholic Christians is meant to express belief that Jesus of Nazareth redeemed the world through his death and resurrection and, through his Christian community on Earth, continues to offer grace, hope, and salvation to all men and women. The word comes from the Old English *weorthscipe*, "to show reverence, honor, and dignity."

Both religion and worship (by an individual or by a community of believers) should be genuine expressions of what it means for human beings to be creatures dependent upon a loving Creator. Prayer-filled worship can be private or public. In fact, Saint Augustine emphasized in the early 5th century that all Christian worship expressed in communal (public) liturgies should originate in the religious worship of God in one's deepest (interior) heart and soul. Through Christian worship, local faith communities celebrate God's nearness through creation, recognize that they have been offered life, hope, and salvation by a loving Creator, and ask for God's help in their ongoing work for happiness, freedom, peace, hope, and justice in the world and for the unending reign of God.

The Christian Scriptures reveal that Jesus of Nazareth assured his close followers that whenever two or more are gathered in his name—in Christian prayerful, worshiping community and in other settings—he will really be present to them in a personal way (Matthew 18:20). Reflection on these matters in recent decades has underscored that Christian private and communal rituals are prayerful and symbolic actions that humbly acknowledge humanity's acceptance that the Creator has authority over all things in this world. Worship thus is a sign that Christian individuals and communities have a deep and abiding spiritual need to respond to their God in love within a living worship tradition.

Recent reforms in the liturgy and worship of the Christian community have not been proposed in order to simply do away with the prayer forms and worship traditions of past generations. Rather the recent reforms, as many comment today, have been meant to revise and improve on traditional Christian ways of worship so that the entire worshiping community will be better able to prayerfully express—through symbol, prayer, ritual actions, and self-sacrifice—their proper relationship to the divine.

Catholic communities express a deep, gospel-inspired belief that the greatest-ever act of worship was Jesus of Nazareth's total gift of his life and mission to God. Catholic tradition likewise stresses that the ultimate communal type of worship for Jesus' community of followers is the Eucharist (the Mass). The church officially recognizes today, of course, that many other public and private prayerful actions and devotions constitute true Christian worship. In the sacraments (especially the Eucharist, which Vatican II in the 1960s called a foretaste of the heavenly liturgy), Catholic communities trust that believers can honor and celebrate God's many gifts to humanity as a whole and express their faith that the Creator is present with all peoples at all times, offering them abundant and everlasting happiness.

(See also Agape, Devotions, Eucharist, God, Prayer, and Sacraments.)

Y

YAHWEH is the proper name by which the Lord God of Israel is known. When written correctly, using the English alphabet, it is spelled *yhwh*. In English it is pronounced yah-way. The word is sometimes translated "Jehovah." But a number of scholars point out that this is not a correct translation from the original Hebrew. The Catholic Christian community holds that Yahweh is the same creative, powerful, loving, one God as the God in whom it invests its faith and hope. Jewish and Christian peoples believe that the book of Exodus, in the Hebrew Scriptures, reveals that the name Yahweh was disclosed to Moses by God from a "burning bush." A popular and current translation of this holy name is "I am who am."

Some biblical scholars believe the specific and most accurate Hebrew pronunciation of the name Yahweh has probably been lost because a tradition in the ancient Hebrew community forbade people from speaking and writing God's name out of fear and awe. It was probably enough for the Hebrews to trust that they were Yahweh's chosen people and that the Mighty One, a great and divine king over all the world and above all other gods, was the Lord who had led them out of slavery in Egypt and with whom they had a loving, lasting covenant relationship (Exodus 3:14). Though the discussion goes on today over how Yahweh is to be translated most properly, some biblical exegetes and other Scripture scholars seem to have agreed in recent decades that it is likely connected with the Hebrew term *yawah*, "to be." Some have proposed that the proper name *Yahweh* could mean "I am who will be" or "The One who brings into being whatever comes into being."

The Yahweh of the Hebrew Scriptures was a protector and guide, a saving God, who helped God's chosen people through sufferings in Egypt, through their starvation-filled desert wanderings, and through many conflicts with many enemies. Christian tradition maintains that Yahweh is the one, creative, and loving Creator who has freely chosen to reveal Godself in history to great Hebrew leaders, to the prophets of Israel, to Jesus of Nazareth, and ultimately to all those who have chosen to be baptized and to follow Jesus in a spirit of Christian discipleship. Catholic tradition maintains that Yahweh was (and is) a loving and mighty Other in whom the Hebrews had faith and hope, believing Yahweh remained present to their community in a unique way.

(See also Covenant, Creation, Exegesis, God, Hebrews, Monotheism, Old Testament, and Trinity.)

YOUTH MINISTRY   is a pastoral ministry in the contemporary Christian community in the U.S. and Canada that attempts to pastorally discern, address, and respond to the particular needs and challenges faced by contemporary adolescents and their families and thus help them become maturing followers of Jesus and persons who live out their baptismal commitments to witness to a Christian way of life. Thus modern youth ministries seek to build relationships with adolescents, to foster the personal and spiritual (wholistic) growth of young persons, to attempt to serve adolescents' real-life needs and questions humbly, and to try to draw adolescents and their families more deeply into the heart of the world-transforming mission and ministry of the people of God.

Though taking many shapes and creative forms, a local faith community's youth ministry (comprehensive) model can actually involve an array of essential components: ministries of word (which includes adolescent evangelization and catechesis); prayer and worship; creating community; guidance and healing; justice and peace education coupled with service programs; enablement/training of adults and youth to minister to the needs of modern young people; family outreach; and advocacy of local adolescents' and families' particular needs.

The emerging Catholic youth ministry tradition is a ministry *to* adolescents and their families whenever a local faith community attempts to really hear and respond to youth's hopes and needs. It is a pastoral ministry *with* youth whenever local adults and youth unite their creative resources and time in order to serve the young people of the community. It is a ministry *by* adolescents whenever young people themselves are called into pastoral action and ministry to serve their peers in some way (thus it is a peer ministry). And it is a pastoral effort *for* adolescents and families when concerned members of the local faith community speak up and take action on behalf of youth-in-need who will not be heard without proper advocacy.

(See also Catechesis, Evangelization, Family Ministry, and Ministry.)

Z

ZIONISM   is a contemporary Jewish nationalist movement that originated in the late 1800s. A major goal of early Zionism was the establishment of the state of Israel; this goal was achieved in 1948. Historical evidence suggests that the terms "Zion" and "Zionism" have roots in the Hebrew *Tsiyon* and Greek *Zion* (meaning "a hill"). The original Zion (or Sion) was a hillside area captured by the Hebrew king David which eventually became a holy city, Jerusalem. After the nation of Israel was conquered by invading powers, the Jewish community lived in many countries around the world as a dispersed and scattered people. Yet the Jewish people never lost a deep desire for a return to their homeland in the Middle East.

In the 19th century the modern Zionist movement began to seek a new Zion, in other words, a permanent state of Israel. This idea was first formally proposed at the First Zionist Congress, held in Switzerland in 1897, with assistance from Great Britain and later the United Nations. The current state of Israel was officially declared on May 4, 1948. In 1952 the 23rd Zionist Congress defined modern Zionism's aims as heightening Jewish national unity, strengthening the Israeli identity, and welcoming Jews from the diaspora (scattering) around the world who wish to settle in the ancient Hebrew homeland.

(See Anti-Semitism, Catholic-Jewish Relations, Diaspora, Hebrews, Judaism, and Old Testament.)

Common Prayers, Devotions, and Practices

The Lord's Prayer
Our Father, who art in heaven hallowed be thy name; thy kingdom come; thy will be done on Earth as it is in heaven. Give us this day our daily bread; and forgive us our trespasses as we forgive those who trespass against us; and lead us not into temptation, but deliver us from evil. Amen.

Hail Mary
Hail, Mary, full of grace, the Lord is with you! Blessed are you among women, and blessed is the fruit of your womb, Jesus. Holy Mary, Mother of God, pray for us sinners, now and at the hour of our death. Amen.

Glory Be
Glory be to the Father, and to the Son, and to the Holy Spirit: As it was in the beginning, is now, and ever shall be world without end. Amen.

Apostles Creed
I believe in God, the Father almighty, creator of heaven and Earth, and in Jesus Christ, his only son, our Lord who was conceived by the Holy Spirit, born of the Virgin Mary, suffered under Pontius Pilate, was crucified, died, and was buried. He descended to the dead. On the third day he rose again. He ascended into heaven, and is seated at the right hand of the Father. He will come again to judge the living and the dead. I believe in the Holy Spirit, the holy catholic church, the communion of saints, the forgiveness of sins, the resurrection of the body, and life everlasting. Amen.

Nicene Creed
We believe in one God, the Father, the Almighty, maker of heaven and Earth, of all that is seen and unseen. We believe in one Lord, Jesus Christ, the only Son of God, eternally begotten of the Father, God from God, light from light, true God from true God, begotten, not made, one in being with the Father. Through him all things were made. For us men and for our salvation he came down from heaven: by the power of the Holy Spirit he was born of the Virgin Mary, and became man. For our sake he was crucified under Pontius Pilate; he suffered, died, and was buried. On the third day, he rose again in fulfillment of the Scriptures: he ascended into heaven and is seated at the right hand of the Father. He will come again in glory to judge the living and the dead, and his kingdom will have no end. We believe in the Holy Spirit, the Lord, the giver of life, who proceeds from the Father and the Son. With the Father and the Son

he is worshiped and glorified. He has spoken through the prophets. We believe in one holy catholic and apostolic church. We acknowledge one baptism for the forgiveness of sins. We look for the resurrection of the dead, and the life of the world to come. Amen.

Sign of the Cross
In the name of the Father, and of the Son, and of the Holy Spirit. Amen.

The Magnificat
My soul proclaims the greatness of the Lord and my spirit exults in God my savior; because he has looked upon his lowly handmaid. Yes, from this day forward all generations will call me blessed, for the Almighty has done great things for me. Holy is his name, and his mercy reaches from age to age for those who fear him. He has shown the power of his arm, he has routed the proud of heart. He has pulled down princes from their thrones and exalted the lowly. The hungry he has filled with good things, the rich he has sent away empty. He has come to the help of Israel his servant, mindful of his mercy—according to the promise he made to our ancestors—of his mercy to Abraham and to his descendants forever. Amen.

Memorare
Remember, O most gracious Virgin Mary, that never was it known that anyone who fled to your protection, implored your help, or sought your intercession, was left unaided. Inspired by this confidence I fly to you, O virgin of virgins, my mother. To you I come, before you I stand, sinful and sorrowful. O mother of the Word Incarnate, despise not my petitions, but in your mercy hear and answer me. Amen.

Come, Holy Spirit
Come, Holy Spirit, fill the hearts of your faithful and kindle in them the fire of your love. Send forth your Spirit, and they shall be re-created: and you will renew the face of Earth. Amen.

A Prayer of Joy and Contrition
O my good God, I thank you for the joys of this day—for the gift of life itself, for family and friends, for all good things which come to me from your creative hand. I am sorry for my daily sins—for selfishness and thoughtlessness, for all that is mean and miserly, for neglect of your many children whom you have called me to love. Direct tomorrow's steps in your path and give me the peace of knowing I am always with you. Amen.

Prayer of Saint Francis
Lord, make me an instrument of your peace: that where there is hatred, I may bring love; that where there is wrong, I may bring the spirit of forgiveness; that where there is discord, I may bring harmony; that where

there is error, I may bring truth; that where there is despair, l may bring hope; that where there are shadows, I may bring your light; that where there is sadness, I may bring joy. Lord, grant that I may seek rather to comfort, than to be comforted; to understand, than to be understood; to love, than to be loved. For it is by giving that one receives; it is by self-forgetting that one finds; it is by forgiving that one is forgiven; it is by dying that one awakens to eternal life. Amen.

Mysteries of the Rosary

Joyful Mysteries: 1) Annunciation, 2) Visitation, 3) Birth of Jesus, 4) Presentation of Jesus in the temple, 5) Finding the Child Jesus in the temple.

Sorrowful Mysteries: 1) Agony in the garden, 2) Scourging at the pillar, 3) Crowning with thorns, 4) Carrying of the cross, 5) Crucifixion.

Glorious Mysteries: 1) Resurrection, 2) Ascension, 3) Descent of the Holy Spirit, 4) Assumption of Mary, 5) Coronation of Mary as Queen of heaven.

Stations of the Cross

1) Jesus Is Condemned to Death; 2) Jesus Accepts His Cross; 3) Jesus Falls the First Time; 4) Jesus Meets His Mother; 5) Simon of Cyrene Helps Jesus to Carry His Cross; 6) Veronica Wipes the Face of Jesus; 7) Jesus Falls the Second Time; 8) Jesus Speaks to the Women; 9) Jesus Falls the Third Time; 10) Jesus Is Stripped of His Garments; 11) Jesus Is Nailed to the Cross; 12) Jesus Dies on the Cross; 13) Jesus Is Taken Down from the Cross; 14) Jesus Is Buried; (optional) 15) Jesus Is Raised from the Dead.

Commandments of God

1) I, the Lord, am your God; you shall have no other gods besides me. 2) You shall not take the name of the Lord, your God, in vain. 3) Remember to keep holy the sabbath day. 4) Honor your father and your mother. 5) You shall not kill. 6) You shall not commit adultery. 7) You shall not steal. 8) You shall not bear false witness against your neighbor. 9) You shall not covet your neighbor's wife. 10) You shall not covet anything that belongs to your neighbor.

The Great Commandment

You shall love the Lord your God with all your heart, with all your soul, with all your strength, and with all your mind; and your neighbor as yourself.

Jesus' Commandment

Love one another as I have loved you.

The Beatitudes

1) Blessed are the poor in spirit; the reign of God is theirs. 2) Blessed are the sorrowing; they shall be consoled. 3) Blessed are the lowly; they shall

inherit the land. 4) Blessed are they who hunger and thirst for holiness; they shall have their fill. 5) Blessed are they who show mercy; mercy shall be theirs. 6) Blessed are the single-hearted; they shall see God. 7) Blessed are the peacemakers; they shall be called sons of God. 8) Blessed are those persecuted for holiness' sake; the reign of God is theirs.

Corporal Works of Mercy
1) Feed the hungry, 2) Give drink to the thirsty, 3) Clothe the naked, 4) Visit the imprisoned, 5) Shelter the homeless, 6) Visit the sick, 7) Bury the dead.

Spiritual Works of Mercy
1) Admonish the sinner, 2) Instruct the ignorant, 3) Counsel the doubtful, 4) Comfort the sorrowful, 5) Bear wrongs patiently, 6) Forgive ail injuries, 7) Pray for the living and the dead.

Holy Days of Obligation
Christmas: December 25; Immaculate Conception of Mary: December 8; Solemnity of Mary: January 1; Ascension of our Lord: 40 days after Easter; Assumption of Mary: August 15; All Saints Day: November 1.

Days of Fasting and Abstinence In the United States
All Catholics who have reached age 14 should not eat any kind of meat (must abstain) on Ash Wednesday, Good Friday, and the other Fridays of the lenten season. For Catholics between 21 and 59 years of age, both Ash Wednesday and Good Friday are also fasting days. One full meal and two light meals may be taken on these days.

Bibliography

The following reference works are suggested for those who wish to study in more detail the topics covered in this book.

Bauer, J.B., ed. *Encyclopedia of Biblical Theology*. New York: Crossroad, 1981.

Beinert, Wolfgang, and Francis Schüssler-Fiorenza, eds. *The International Dictionary of Catholic Theology*. New York: Crossroad, 1994.

Catechism of the Catholic Church. Rome/Città del Vaticano: Libreria Editrice Vaticana, 1994. (English translation: Washington, D.C.: United States Catholic Conference, 1994).

Code of Canon Law. Washington, D.C.: Canon Law Society of America, 1983.

Dues, Greg. *Catholic Customs & Traditions: A Popular Guide*. Mystic, Conn.: Twenty-Third Publications, 1992.

Flannery, Austin O.P., ed. *Vatican Council II: The Conciliar and Post-Conciliar Documents*. Collegeville, Minn.: Liturgical Press, 1981.

Foy, Felician, O.F.M., ed. *Catholic Almanac*. Huntington, Ind.: Our Sunday Visitor, 1992, 1993.

Glazier, Michael, and Monika K. Hellwig, eds. *The Modern Catholic Encyclopedia*. Collegeville, Minn.: The Liturgical Press, 1994.

Latourelle, René, ed. *The Dictionary of Fundamental Theology*. New York: Crossroad, 1992.

McBrien, Richard P. *Catholicism* (rev. ed.). San Francisco: HarperCollins, 1994.

Metzger, Bruce M., and Michael D. Coogan, eds. *The Oxford Companion to the Bible*. New York: Oxford University Press, 1993.

National Conference of Catholic Bishops. *Sharing the Light of Faith: National Catechetical Directory*. Washington, D.C.: United States Catholic Conference, 1979.

New Catholic Encyclopedia (17 vols.). New York: McGraw-Hill, 1979.

O'Connell, Timothy E., ed. *Vatican II and Its Documents: An American Reappraisal*. Wilmington, Del.: Michael Glazier, 1986.

O'Malley, William J. *Why Be Catholic?* New York: Crossroad, 1993.

Pennington, Basil. *Vatican II: It Isn't Over Yet*. New York: Crossroad, 1994.

Rahner, Karl. *Encyclopedia of Theology: The Concise Sacramentum Mundi*. New York: Crossroad, 1975.

_____. *Foundations of Christian Faith: An Introduction to the Idea of Christianity*. New York: Crossroad, 1978.

Senior, Donald, ed. *The Catholic Study Bible*. New York: Oxford University Press, 1990.

Wilhelm, Anthony. *Christ Among Us* (5th rev. ed.). San Francisco: HarperCollins, 1990.

Index

An entry that is listed in capital letters indicates a full-length treatment of the subject, in addition to other places where the subject may be treated. The bold italicized numbers after the capitalized entry are the pages where it is found.

Of Related Interest...

The Catechism
Highlights & Commentary
Brennan Hill and William Madges
A user-friendly interpretation of the Catechism of the Catholic Church that helps readers get to the heart of the Catechism and apply its teachings to their ministries and their lives.

ISBN: 0-89622-589-5, 160 pp, $9.95

Catholic Customs & Traditions
A Popular Guide
Greg Dues
The rosary...certain colors...oils. The role of these and other practices are explained in this revised and expanded edition.

ISBN: 0-89622-515-1, 224 pp, $9.95

Faith Alive
A New Presentation of Catholic Belief and Practice
edited by Rowanne Pasco and John Redford
This is a panoramic view of the Catholic Church, its teachings, history and tradition.

ISBN: 0-89622-408-2, 320 pp, $9.95

Pilgrim Church
A Popular History of Catholic Christianity
William J. Bausch
General readers will enjoy this concise and comprehensive study of Catholicism.

ISBN: 0-89622-395-7, 480 pp, $12.95

Available at religious bookstores or from
TWENTY-THIRD PUBLICATIONS
P.O. Box 180 • Mystic, CT 06355
1-800-321-0411